WAR
ON
WAR

Lenin, the Zimmerwald Left,
and the Origins of Communist
Internationalism

by R. Craig Nation

Haymarket Books
Chicago, Illinois

First published in hardcover in 1989 by Duke University Press
© R. Craig Nation

This edition published in 2009 by Haymarket Books
P.O. Box 180165
Chicago, IL 60618
773-583-7884
info@haymarketbooks.org
www.haymarketbooks.org

Trade distribution:
In the U.S. through Consortium Book Sales, www.cbsd.com
In the UK, Turnaround Publisher Services, www.turnaround-psl.com
In Australia, Palgrave MacMillan, www.palgravemacmillan.com.au
In all other countries, Publishers Group Worldwide,
www.pgw.com/home/worldwide.aspx

This book was published with the generous support of the
Wallace Global Fund.

Cover design by Rachel Wilsey

ISBN-13: 978-1931859-82-0

Printed in Canada by union labor on recycled paper containing 100
percent post-consumer waste in accordance with the guidelines of the
Green Press Initiative, www.greenpressinitiative.org

The hardcover edition of this book was cataloged by the Library of
Congress.

10 9 8 7 6 5 4 3 2 1

To Kata, Katie, Caterina, and Kate,

with love

Contents

Preface

FROM its origins in the wake of the great French Revolution, the European social democratic labor movement embraced the causes of peace and internationalism as integral parts of the struggle for social justice. War was regarded as the clearest possible illustration of the violence and inhumanity that lay at the core of competitive capitalism. After 1848, when *The Communist Manifesto* sonorously declared that "the workers have no Fatherland," socialist internationalism was equated with the cause of the international proletariat, a class whose triumph was to open the way toward universal human emancipation. According to Marx and Engels, a new international society was not only desirable, it was necessary and inevitable. The contradictions of capitalist development were leading inevitably toward revolutionary transformations, in the course of which the nation-state would "wither" and give way to alternative forms of voluntary, communal association. The struggle of the revolutionary proletariat for a more equitable society would eventually culminate in the creation of a true world order, purged of war and enmity between peoples.

Prior to 1914 socialism was the expression of an abstract ideal. The Great War brought an end to the movement's age of innocence. Nineteenth-century social democracy, nurtured on the barricades of the class war, was originally propelled by a burning faith in socialism's millenarian promise. As the movement grew in size and influence toward the end of the century, its visionary aspirations were increasingly tempered by what seemed to be the more realistic prospect of gradual, ameliorative change. The end effect was to integrate social democracy ever more thoroughly into the fabric of the social order that it was pledged to overthrow. When, upon the outbreak of war in Europe during August 1914, the leading social democratic parties put aside their antiwar rhetoric and opted to support national defense, their action only culminated a lengthy evolution. The socialist "defensists" hoped that by engaging themselves in the war effort they would reinforce their stature within the national communities that they aspired to lead. For their critics the willful abandonment of internationalism meant a break with the very essence of socialism itself.

Socialist defensism was immediately challenged by an internationalist minority organized, after a conference held during September 1915 in the Swiss village of Zimmerwald, as the "Zimmerwald movement." The embittered debates that followed made clear that very little remained of the prewar movement's much-touted solidarity. By the end of the war the political landscape on the socialist left had been altered nearly beyond recognition. The Second International, formerly the movement's pride, was to all intents and purposes defunct, with its social democratic wing now openly embracing reformism while a dynamic new international communist current sprang up pledged to carry on the tradition of revolutionary Marxism. After the establishment of Soviet power in Russia in October 1917, socialism was no longer a beautiful dream but an occasionally grim reality, striving to fulfill its promise under immensely difficult circumstances. In the confused aftermath of the great world conflagration, the calm certitudes of the prewar movement seemed to be little more than naive illusions, products of the halcyon days of a youth that could never be recalled.

In the process of destroying the nineteenth-century social democratic tradition, the war became midwife to the communist alternative. The origins of international communism during the First World War, in the context of the "Zimmerwald Left" group organized and led by Vladimir Il'ich Lenin, constitutes the theme of the present study. While it is usually mentioned as the immediate source for the Communist International, the Zimmerwald Left has rarely been examined in its own right. Though a number of excellent studies treat the impact of the war upon the socialist labor movement in more general terms, neither the Left nor the Zimmerwald movement of which it was a part have been the primary subject of an independent scholarly investigation. Soviet historians have meticulously examined Lenin's every step and utterance during the war years, but their work, though often informative and insightful, too often suffers from self-defeating idealizations and politically motivated distortions. Almost all of Lenin's closest colleagues within the Zimmerwald Left became victims of Stalinism. Though the Communist party of the Soviet Union has recently announced the posthumous rehabilitation of the most prominent among them, including Grigorii Zinoviev, Karl Radek, and Nikolai Bukharin, unspoken taboos remain in place. The opportunity now exists for more objective evaluations to be undertaken, but a major scholarly reevaluation will require time to complete.

In contrast to the preoccupations of Soviet historians, studies of international socialism and the war produced by Western Europeans have tended to turn away from the revolutionary left in order to look more closely at the social democratic mainstream. Preconceptions based upon Lenin's blanket condemnations of "social chauvinists," it is argued with some justification, have too often obscured the continuity of a tradition pledged to the pursuit of meaningful change on a democratic foundation and within the limits of the possible. The consequence of these contrasting priorities is a curiously schizophrenic body of scholarship. Soviet and East European scholars focus almost exclusively upon Lenin and the left opposition. Their Western counterparts scorn the left as a group of isolated extremists whose importance has been exaggerated beyond measure and center their attention upon moderate alternatives. In both cases a sense of just proportion is occasionally lost.[1]

This book seeks to interpret the experience of the Zimmerwald Left in a manner that takes into account its importance without surrendering to what until recently have been the assumptions of official communist historiography. The promise of international socialism to stand for a radical vision of the future was put to the test in August 1914 and for the most part found wanting. The Zimmerwald Left was the most outspoken champion of a ruthless drawing of accounts, and it gave rise to a political alternative that has become a significant force in twentieth-century affairs. What is more, the road traveled by the Left during the war left a lasting mark

upon the communist movement's character thereafter. Lenin's theoretical contributions, still the indispensable ideological basis for the
communist left, can only be understood within the context in which
they were produced. The perceived betrayal of the social democratic
right, the Left's determined struggle against all odds for an uncom-
promised internationalism, and the inspirational triumph of the October revolution, all gave the communist movement a sense of historical legitimacy and permanently shaped its self-image. The premises
enunciated by the Zimmerwald Left also served as a source of justification for the international policies implemented by the first generation of Soviet leaders, and they remain the foundation for the Soviet
theory of international relations. Although the tenets of this theory
have been honored as often in the breach as in the observance, as the
legacy of Stalinism in the USSR is gradually dismantled, interest in
and enthusiasm for the state's authentic Leninist sources is certain
to increase. In order to trace these sources, it is necessary to look
carefully at the dialogue carried on during the war between what
were often miniscule radical factions, argued out in the columns of
little-known publications, in the back rooms of public houses, and in
the secretive conferences of an embattled minority opposition. The
dialogue was no less important for its obscurity, and its consequences
have proven to be immense.

The Zimmerwald Left is a challenging subject for historical inquiry for several reasons. Firstly, there is the problem of defining just what the Left actually was. Technically an oppositional
faction formed within the Zimmerwald movement, its lack of a
stable bureaucratic structure and formal affiliations makes the term
"organization" seem inappropriate. I choose to define the Left as a
"political tendency," a phrase intended to convey the sense of an
informally coordinated group of engaged activists, never entirely in
accord, but held together by common allegiances and enmities. The
Left was also an international tendency, with a supportive infrastructure spread throughout Europe and a relevant literature spanning a
dozen languages. Due to the conditions of wartime mobilization
within which it functioned, many of its activities were carried on in a
conspiratorial environment and are correspondingly difficult to
trace. Finally, because the Left became so important a source of
legitimization for the international communist movement, its his-

tory, whether praised or condemned, has tended to become wrapped in partisan myth that is often difficult to sort through.

In view of these complexities, and in order to develop the primary theme of internationalism as coherently as possible, I concentrate upon providing a political history of the Zimmerwald Left tendency within the context of the international socialist antiwar opposition. The popular movement of protest against the war is mentioned when appropriate, but no attempt is made to delve into the domain of social history by systematically analyzing the nature and effectiveness of revolutionary agitation at the base. Though the progress of revolutionary internationalist currents within the most significant national movements is briefly traced, emphasis remains upon the organizational and theoretical initiatives undertaken in the name of the Zimmerwald Left by its working groups and intellectuals. Lenin, as the Left's most cogent theorist and dominant personality, inevitably holds pride of place.

The text's overall organization is chronological. The first chapter summarizes Marx's ambiguous theoretical legacy as regards the problems of internationalism and war and examines the controversy to which it gave rise within the Second International, culminating with the collapse of 4 August 1914. Chapter two traces the rise of a left opposition on the national level during the war's first six months, and chapter three turns to efforts to organize the left internationally. The fourth and fifth chapters describe the activities of the Zimmerwald Left and its increasing alienation from the Zimmerwald majority through 1916. Chapter six concentrates upon the work of the Left's informal executive in Stockholm during 1917 against the background of the Russian revolution. Finally, the seventh chapter briefly describes the final phase of the Zimmerwald movement, now dominated by the Left, from the October revolution up to its merger with the Communist International during 1919.

In conclusion an attempt is made to evaluate the legacy of the Zimmerwald Left and to assess its continuing relevance. I believe that the most significant and enduring aspect of this legacy has been a sweeping reformulation of the ideal of internationalism, expressed as a synthesis of theory and practice that has not yet exhausted its potential as a motive for political action. Never posed abstractly, but always in the midst of a demanding political struggle, the Left's image of internationalism was forged against the backdrop of the collapse of socialist idealism in August 1914, the nightmarish violence of the Great War, and the era of revolution to which the war gave rise. In the long term the international communist movement that it inspired has reflected both the strengths and the limitations absorbed from these tumultuous origins.

Transliteration from the Cyrillic alphabet is rendered in a standard variant of the Library of Congress system. Until 1918 Russia utilized the Julian calendar; during the First World War; it was thirteen days behind the Gregorian calendar in use in the rest of Europe. Events in Russia prior to 1918 are dated according to the Gregorian system, with the corresponding date according to the Julian calendar given in parentheses.

Acknowledgments

IN the years during which this book was researched and written, the author has accumulated many debts. Intellectual inspiration and an appreciation for the topic's importance were provided by Warren Lerner of Duke University. The School of International Relations of the University of Southern California offered financial support for research in European archives. The manuscript was completed under ideal conditions during a stay as resident fellow with the Peace Studies Program of Cornell University. The author wishes to thank the program's director Richard Ned Lebow and his colleagues Judith Reppy, Larry Scheinmann, Charles Naef, and Kathleen Murphy for their friendship and support during a period of intensive work. Special thanks are due to Mark V. Kauppi for a careful and critical reading of the manuscript and to my wife Kate Cucugliello-Nation for assistance of all kinds. I would also like to express my gratitude to Lars Björlin, Anne-Catherine Folly-Chappuis, Antonio Franzese, Salvatore Frustace, Myron Hedlin, Max Jendly, and William Stivers. All conclusions drawn are of course my own.

List of Abbreviations

BSP	British Socialist party
CGL	*Confederazione generale del lavoro* (Italian General Confederation of Labor)
CGT	*Confédération générale du travail* (French General Confederation of Labor)
CRRI	*Comité pour la reprise des relations internationales* (Committee for the Resumption of International Relations)
ILP	Independent Labour party
ISB	International Socialist Bureau
ISC	International Socialist Commission
KPD	*Kommunistische Partei Deutschlands* (Communist party of Germany)

PCI   *Partito communista italiano* (Italian Communist party)

POB   *Parti ouvrier belge* (Belgian Labor party)

PPS   *Polska partia socjalistyczna* (Polish Socialist party)

PPS-L   *Polska partia socjalistyczna-lewica* (Polish Socialist party-Left)

PRC   People's Republic of China

PSI   *Partito socialista italiano* (Italian Socialist party)

RSDRP   *Russkaia sotsial-demokraticheskaia rabochaia partiia* (Russia Social Democratic Labor party)

RSV   *Revolutionnair socialistisch verbond (vereeniging)* (Revolutionary Socialist League [Union] in the Netherlands)

SDAP   *Sociaal-democratische arbeiders partij* (Social Democratic Labor party of the Netherlands)

SDKPiL   *Socjaldemocracja Królestwa Polskiego i Litwy* (Social Democracy of the Kingdom of Poland and Lithuania)

SDP   *Sociaal-democratische partij* (Social Democratic party of the Netherlands)

SFIO   *Section française de l'Internationale ouvrière* (French Section of the Worker's International [French Socialist party])

SLP   Socialist Labour party of Great Britain

SPD   *Sozialdemokratische Partei Deutschlands* (Social Democratic party of Germany)

SPS   *Sozialdemokratische Partei der Schweiz* (Social Democratic party of Switzerland)

SR   Socialist Revolutionary

USPD   *Unabhängige Sozialdemokratische Partei Deutschlands* (Independent Social Democratic party of Germany)

ZPTSK   *Zagranichnoe predstavitel'stvo tsentral'nogo komiteta* (Bolshevik Foreign Bureau of the Central Committee)

1

Marxism, War, and the
International

Les rois nous soûlaient de fumées,
Paix entre nous, guerre aux tyrans.
Appliquons la grève aux armées,
Crosse en l'air et rompons les rangs!
S'ils s'obstinent, ces cannibales,
A faire de nous des héros,
Ils sauront bientôt que nos balles
Sont pour nos propres généraux!

(The kings intoxicate us with
gunsmoke,
Peace amongst ourselves, war on
tyrants.
Let us strike against the armies,
Fire in the air and break ranks!
If they insist, these cannibals,
In making us into heros,
They'll soon learn that our bullets
Are for our own generals!)

—Eugène Pottiers, *L'Internationale*

ON the eve of the First World War the European social democratic labor movement could look back with satisfaction over decades of unprecedented growth. As the political voice of organized labor, European social democracy possessed a substantial popular base, and in several of the more advanced European states socialist parties had become leading contenders for governmental responsibility. No less impressive was the movement's collective strength, embodied by the Socialist International. Since the week of 14–20 July 1889, when a motley collection of radicals met in the *Salle Grenelle* in Paris on the centennial of the storming of the Bastille and federated in a "New International," social democrats had demonstrated their capacity to organize internationally and pose a challenge to the dominant bourgeois order that transcended national boundaries. Despite their diversity, the International's partisans could intone with one voice the concluding refrain of their battle hymn: *L'Internationale sera le genre humain!* (The International shall be the human race!)

International socialism achieved institutional form in 1864, when Karl Marx himself helped to create the International Workingman's Association, a federation of labor organizations intended to give substance to the contention that socialism spoke to the common aspirations of an international working class. Thereafter, the International became absolutely fundamental to the movement's identity. The "First International" collapsed in 1876 due to rivalry within its ranks between Marx's adherents and those of the Russian anarchist Mikhail Bakunin, but the precedent that it had established was soon revived. At the Paris congress in 1889 the "Second International" declared itself the successor to Marx's organization and confirmed an allegiance to its internationalist precepts. In his keynote address Marx's son-in-law Paul Lafargue emphasized that the delegates were not assembled beneath national flags, but rather "the red flag of the international proletariat," as "brothers with a single common enemy . . . private capital, whether it be Prussian, French, or Chinese."[1] Prior to 1914 the International never strayed from this profession of faith. Socialism would triumph as an international movement, it was widely presumed, or it would not triumph at all.

Despite its pretentions to universality, the International was hindered by a lack of effective central authority. Its first congresses in Paris, Brussels (1891), and Zürich (1893) were little more than rhetorical exercises. Not until 1896 was a first step toward a tighter bureaucratic regime taken by formulating conditions for membership that banned anarchists. A more decisive step came at the Paris congress of 1900, with the creation of an International Socialist Bureau (ISB) as a permanent executive organ. Based in Brussels, the ISB was mandated to manage the movement's affairs in the intervals between general congresses. Ultimately, its authority derived from the parties affiliated to it in what was essentially a voluntary confederation. Although these arrangements gave the International a reasonably well defined institutional identity, the ISB's prerogatives remained limited. Its effectiveness rested entirely upon the ability of affiliates to achieve and maintain a viable consensus.

As the International grew in size, consensus became ever more elusive. At the 1907 Stuttgart congress, over eight hundred delegates representing twenty-five nations were present. Participation on such a scale, with the inevitable problems of intercultural communication that it entailed, seriously inhibited dialogue. In an evaluation of the congress Karl Kautsky of the Social Democratic party of Germany (SPD) argued that in the future congresses should restrict themselves to "drawing up resolutions," with the task of arguing out a general line for the movement assigned to the party press.[2] Such a solution was acceptable so long as an underlying coincidence of priorities could be presumed, but it left the problem of enforcing controversial decisions unresolved. The dilemma was aggravated by the movement's dogged commitment to the principle of federalism. Opposition to any concentration of authority in the hands of the ISB was typical for most national sections, which as a rule jealously guarded their autonomy. Consequently, the International's ability to act independently was quite limited. Periodic general congresses provided colorful demonstrations of solidarity, and the ISB allowed for a modicum of coordination. But the International was not in a position to discipline its affiliates nor to take initiatives without resorting to a clumsy mechanism of consultations.

Lacking strong institutional bonds, the International's importance came to rest primarily upon its status as a living symbol of socialist internationalism. Yet even here no consensus was manifest. Internationalism was the most ambitious, but also the most abstract, of all social democratic causes, constantly invoked but seldom probingly examined. A resolution proposed by the British Independent Labour party (ILP) to the International's 1910 Copenhagen congress gave the slogan some positive content by raising the call for a European federation, but this was a minimal demand that did not come close to satisfying more visionary aspirations. For European social democrats in the age of the Second International, internationalism remained a highly romanticized notion, an important source of emotional reinforcement and legitimization, but difficult to relate to the daily struggle for political influence.

So long as the problem remained in the realm of theory, a degree of ambiguity could be tolerated. After the turn of the century, however, an increasingly unstable international situation made it imperative to define internationalism's practical as well as theoretical implications. Between 1900 and 1914 the International engaged in a wide-ranging debate concerning international policy and antiwar strategy. The debate could never be definitively resolved, and as a result the movement confronted the "July Crisis" of 1914, which heralded the outbreak of World War One, without clear guidelines for collective action. When the war arrived, rather than rallying around a common program, the leading social democratic parties opted independently to support their respective governments. In his diary entry for 3–4 August 1914, the French writer Romain Rolland spoke for all those who had placed their trust in the International by describing its effacement as "the greatest catastrophe in history . . . the ruin of our most sacred hopes for human fraternity."[3]

How could so shocking an abandonment of commitments have occurred? The most obvious explanation focuses upon the International's structural weaknesses. At the moment of truth it revealed itself to be little more than a weak federation of autonomous parties that perceived their tasks and terrain essentially in national terms. The lack of central direction could nonetheless have been overcome had the organization as a whole rested upon a more solid consensus concerning ends and means. Marx's theoretical legacy provided a point of departure for all social democrats, but it was a disputed legacy which did not lead to evident conclusions. The social democratic debacle of August 1914 in large measure reflected a failure to come to terms with the movement's real political goals and to rally around an alternative vision of world order corresponding to its highest ideals and aspirations. Much of the debate carried on within the socialist community during the long years of war that followed would be concerned with an attempt to set the failure right.

"The Workers Have No Fatherland"

European socialist thought prior to the eighteenth-century Enlightenment contained a powerful strain of universalist ethical pacifism, perhaps most eloquently expounded in the English language by the seventeenth-century "Digger" Gerrard Winstanley. For Winstanley the roots of war lay in the institution of private property, the artificial division of the earth, God's "common treasury," into tracts capable of serving as objects of power in the quest for worldly dominion. The "buying and selling" engendered by private ownership of the land "did bring in, and still doth bring in, discontents and wars, which have plagued mankind sufficiently for so doing. And the nations of the world will never learn to beat their swords into ploughshares, and their spears into pruning hooks, and leave off warring, until this cheating devise of buying and selling be cast out among the rubbish of kingly power."[4] Though his vision was millenarian, Winstanley acknowledged the futility of utopian expectations in an imperfect world. His outline of an ideal commonwealth recognized the legitimacy of defensive war, "to withstand the invasion . . . of a foreign enemy," and of revolutionary civil war, "to restore the land again and set it free."[5] Winstanley's contention that war was the product of social injustice, his attempt to define alternative institutions capable of reducing the extent of conflicts, and his utopian quest for community presaged many of the preoccupations of modern socialism concerning the problems of war and peace.

The immediate sources for the nineteenth-century socialist tradition were the secular thought of the Enlightenment and the inspiration of the French revolution, with their contradictory mélange of cosmopolitanism, patriotism, and militarism. The "Conspiracy of the Equals" led by François Noël Babeuf in 1795, often counted as the first "proto-socialist" movement of the contemporary era, claimed a primary allegiance to "the grand society of humanity," and insisted that "as peace represents the first of all blessings after that of liberty, it is neither desirable nor just to take recourse to arms except when liberty is menaced." Simultaneously, it announced that "the defense of the Motherland against an ever-possible aggression from abroad is an essential part of the wisdom of the law" and defined rigorous measures to ensure national defense.[6] Pre-Marxian socialist thought was dominated by French theorists and impregnated with the mythos of Valmy and *la patrie*. Whether expressed in the cosmopolitan Europeanism of Henri de Saint-Simon, the idiosyncratic blend of insurrectionary antimilitarism and Jacobin patriotism of Auguste Blanqui, or the nationalistic bellicism of Victor Considerent, it never succeeded in resolving the contradictory appeals of revolutionary nationalism and internationalism nor the dilemma of distinguishing between just and unjust wars. Like Winstanley before them, the "utopian" socialists were inspired by a vision of community where the sources of war had disappeared, but shared a pragmatic assessment of the need for organized coercive force to defend and preserve existing political institutions.

Marx's apparent ability to reconcile internationalism with the real-life demands of political action was a significant source of his appeal. Already in *The Communist Manifesto* of 1848, answering the charge that communists sought "to abolish countries and nationality," Marx and Engels argued in a famous passage that acceptance of the nation-state as an arena for struggle did not conflict with the goals of socialist internationalism, but rather reinforced them. "The workers have no Fatherland" they proclaimed. "One cannot take from them what they do not possess. In that the proletariat must first achieve political hegemony, must lift itself to the level of a national class, must constitute itself as the nation, it is itself still national in character, though not in the bourgeois sense of the term."[7] These brief remarks were something less than transparent. Marx and Engels repeatedly made the point that the state in class society was not a defender of the "common weal" (as in liberal or social contract theory), but the expression of specific forms of class rule. The modern nation-state was an agent of bourgeois class hegemony, the "executive committee" of the propertied. It remained true nonetheless that it was within the confines of the nation-state that the proletarian labor movement would grow to maturity. The working class must "constitute itself as the nation" as a first step toward emancipation:

"The struggle of the proletariat against the bourgeoisie is at first, in form though not in content, national in character. The proletariat must first settle accounts with its own bourgeoisie."[8] The premises of internationalism would be realized as a function of the gradual elimination of class division and social injustice. In the meantime the nation-state was neither an impartial arbiter nor the mystical distillation of *Blut und Boden* (blood and soil), but a relatively autonomous political institution that the proletariat must win over and use for its own ends.

The ambivalence of these formulations was also present in discussions of the problem of war and militarism. For Marx and Engels the coercive authority of the state, and its ability to resort to disciplined military force, were essential to its role as the guarantor of class privilege. "Dripping from head to foot, from every pore, with blood and filth," Marx wrote in the first volume of *Capital*, capital accumulation proceeded historically on a foundation of violent usurpations, culminating in "the commercial wars of the European nations, with the globe for a theater."[9] Coercive, competitive, and anarchic, the international system of developed capitalism represented an inexhaustible font of violent conflict. War was nonetheless not considered fatalistically inevitable; in any given set of circumstances a resort to arms could be avoided by conscious political action. Marx urged revolutionary socialists to "master themselves the mysteries of international politics," to seek to counteract diplomatic folly by purposeful protest actions, and to develop an alternative image of international society inspired by "the simple laws of morality and justice."[10]

Marx's optimism rested upon what he identified as underlying trends working to erode the foundations of the capitalist world order and prepare the way for socialism. In the process of overcoming feudal fragmentation capitalism had forged the centralized nation-state "as a weapon of the rising social order in its struggle for emancipation."[11] Industrial capitalism, with its insatiable appetite for markets and raw materials, was now bursting the bonds of the nation-state itself. The growth of the capitalist world market challenged the premises of nationalism by diluting national peculiarities and creating a "universal interdependence of nations."[12] It likewise gave rise to the proletariat as a social class defined within an international division of labor, a process which "alike in England as in

France, in America as in Germany, has stripped the proletariat of any and all national character."[13] Proletarian internationalism would be the very essence of the new international society toward which the socialist movement aspired, and the effort to realize the unity of the working class was therefore of fundamental importance. To the extent that workers continued to define their social identity in terms of national allegiance, they were victims of false consciousness. Nationalism, like religious affiliation, was an opiate of the peoples.

The nation-state had all the same not yet exhausted its potential. In his polemics with Bakunin Marx poured scorn upon the anarchists' demand for the unconditional "abolition of the state" precisely because they ignored its historically conditioned character. What was in question for the anarchists, Marx charged, was "not the overthrow of the Bonapartist, Prussian, or Russian state, but the abstract state, a state that exists nowhere."[14] The socialist revolution would not abolish the state "as such," but replace the mechanisms of the bourgeois state with institutions reflecting the class hegemony of the proletariat, a wrenching transformation that Marx described unrepentently as "necessarily an authoritarian act."[15] Only after a relatively lengthy transition phase, during which proletarian hegemony would be extended over the leading sectors of the world economy, would a rational organization of production and distribution on a global scale become possible, and only then would the abolition of the state in the anarchist sense begin. Engels summarized the process during 1880 in his classic *Socialism: Utopian and Scientific* with a phrase that has become a kind of synopsis of the Marxist image of internationalism: "In proportion as the anarchy of social production vanishes, the political authority of the state withers away. Humanity, at last master of its own form of social organization, becomes at the same time master over nature and its own master—that is, free."[16]

Although the internationalist inspiration of Marx's social theory was striking, its prescriptions for managing the practical dilemmas of international relations outside the "realm of freedom" remained unclear. Marx and Engels were not pacifists, and the judgments that they cast upon the armed conflicts of their own era were calculated and pragmatic.[17] The First International denounced standing armies as an incitement to militarism and championed the concept of the popular militia as an alternative but refused to negate the principle of national defense.[18] Whether the proletariat would itself need to resort to revolutionary violence in order to achieve hegemony within the nation-state was also left ambiguous. Marx always emphasized the need for a revolutionary overthrow of the bourgeois state, but in his later years Engels seemed to move away from this perspective. Near the end of his life, in a foreword to *The Civil War in France*, he questioned whether capitalism would suddenly "collapse," emphasized the need for the proletariat to achieve hegemony within as well as in opposition to civil society, and suggested that he and Marx, when writing *The Communist Manifesto* over forty years before, had been misled by the "illusion" that the nation-state was entering a stage of disintegration.[19]

Classical Marxism thus provided no patented formulas faced with the complexity of relations between states. Although Marx urged international proletarian solidarity and looked forward to "a new society . . . whose first international principle will be *peace*, because within every nation the same principle will rule—that of labor,"[20] he acknowledged the need to work within the confines of the international state system. Marxist social theory combined visionary internationalism with a healthy dose of raison d'état, contrasting elements that were not so much reconciled as uncomfortably juxtaposed. Despite its tremendous intellectual force, Marx's treatment of the problem of internationalism was filled with nuance and tortuous ambiguity.

Not One Man and Not One Penny

Anxious to assert its internationalist credentials, the Second International embraced opposition to war as a sacred trust. A unanimously approved resolution introduced by the former Blanquist and Communard Edouard Vaillant at its founding congress stated that peace was "the first and indispensable condition of any worker emancipation . . . and that war, the most tragic product of present economic relations, can only disappear when capitalist production has made way for the emancipation of labor and the international triumph of socialism."[21] The sentiments were noble, but already in its first statement on the problem the International found itself on the horns of a dilemma. According to Vaillant, peace was an "indispensable condition" for the emancipation of labor at the same time that war was fatalistically counted an inevitable product of capitalism. It was an antinomy that the International would never resolve, even though on the eve of the First World War it continued to count itself "the most energetic and decisive factor working to secure international peace."[22]

The contradictions that plagued the International reflected a larger conceptual rift concerning the primacy of revolutionary or reformist means of struggle. Most social democratic leaders took pride in their movement's insurrectionary heritage, but from the 1890s onward, in an era marked by a general, though imbalanced, rise in living standards, relative international stability, and a social climate of expansive optimism, the strength of the movement manifested itself more and more in the quest for parliamentary influence and the trade unionist campaign for improved wages and working conditions. These seemingly irresistible tendencies were given formal expression by the SPD publicist Eduard Bernstein in a series of articles published between 1896 and 1898 in Kautsky's theoretical journal *Die Neue Zeit* (The New Age) and summarized during 1899 in the seminal book *The Prerequisites for Socialism and the Tasks of Social Democracy*. Arguing the priority of the "movement" above the "goal," Bernstein suggested that classical Marxism should be revised precisely by abandoning its revolutionary pretenses. The SPD, he remarked in a phrase that effectively summarized the "revisionist" outlook, should consent "to appear what it really is today; a democratic-socialist reform party."[23]

The "revisionist controversy" that Bernstein's arguments launched was by no means purely a theoretical exercise. By the turn of the century real social movements inspired by revisionist thinking had appeared in most of Europe's advanced industrial states. These movements shared several underlying assumptions, including (1) the notion of a working class increasingly integrated into civil society rather than alienated from it and (2) the pragmatic assessment, often buttressed by references to the fate of the Commune of Paris, that in modern industrial states revolutionary seizures of power had become a thing of the past. On a theoretical plane Marxist orthodoxy prevailed, and at its 1904 Amsterdam congress the International rejected reformism as a general political orientation. Yet in practice reformism could not be so easily disposed of. Parliamentary and trade unionist activities continued to dominate the political practice of the movement's most prestigious and powerful affiliates.

As a partial consequence of the revisionist controversy's ambiguous resolution, the social democratic movement began to fracture openly after 1900. On the right an outspokenly reformist current called for gradual, evolutionary change consistent with democratic principles. On the left a "left radical" current sought to counter revisionism by reasserting the primacy of revolutionary mass struggles. A stark choice between reform and revolution was thereby posed, but neither revisionists nor left radicals were in a position to speak for the movement's mainstream. Prior to 1914 the International was dominated by a centrist consensus, committed in principle to the tenets of revolutionary Marxism but conciliatory in practice and above all concerned with maintaining consensual goals. The center pursued a policy of compromise and accommodation on behalf of unity, with ideological flexibility and tactical caution its hallmarks.[24]

The centrist consensus did not always prevail, and on a number of occasions full-scale schisms were the result. In 1903 the famous division between the Bolshevik and Menshevik wings of the Russian Social Democratic Labor party (RSDRP) came into the open. The complex differences between the two tendencies were not immediately apparent, and the Mensheviks cannot be classified as revisionists, but the Bolsheviks and their leader Vladimir Il'ich Lenin certainly represented a radical alternative. In the same year, influenced by trends in the Russian party, the Bulgarian Social Democratic Workers' party split into reformist "broad" and revolutionary "narrow" factions.[25] In 1906 the Polish Socialist party (PPS) experienced another in a series of divisions, with a PPS-Left faction pledged to revolutionary means splitting away.[26] At the end of a long controversy the Social Democratic Labor party of the Netherlands (SDAP) expelled its left wing in 1908, with the latter proceeding to constitute itself as an independent Social Democratic party (SDP) grouped around the revolutionary newspaper *De Tribune* (The Tribune).[27] Finally, in 1912 the Italian Socialist party (PSI) expelled Leonida Bissolati and its reformist right wing after they had adopted an interventionist posture during the Libyan war.[28] These various schisms were significantly diverse, but in every case a widening gap between revolutionary and reformist currents was at the root of the problem.

Though it did not result in an organizational break, the process of division set into motion by the revisionist controversy found its clearest articulation within the SPD. Propelled by Germany's unification and rapid industrialization after 1871, and inspired by success in withstanding Bismarck's antisocialist laws between 1878 and 1890, the German movement became a dominant force within the Second International, where it was usually at the center of strategic debate. The SPD right wing, led by self-confident provincial and trade union figures such as Ignaz Auer, Karl Legien, and Georg von Vollmar, dominated the party at the base and represented a virtually immovable barrier to attempts to budge it away from reformism. German revisionism was not homogenous, but it rested upon a commitment to what von Vollmar expressively described as "the path of calm, legal, parliamentary activity."[29]

The party's left wing, also well placed in a number of important regional organizations, responded with a sweeping critique that on occasion took on the aura of a factional challenge. The most talented standard bearer for the German left was Rosa Luxemburg, born in Zamość in Russian Poland, but emigrated to Berlin as a young woman, where her 1899 pamphlet *Social Reform or Revolution* became the definitive refutation of Bernstein from the left radical perspective.[30] Luxemburg rejected revisionism on the grounds that it ignored the extent to which the proletariat's recent advances resulted from a temporary economic conjuncture that could not be maintained indefinitely. The contradictions of capitalist development, she insisted, presaged an era, not of peaceful progress, but of social cataclysm that demanded an active, revolutionary role from social democracy.

The SPD center, best represented up to his death in 1913 by August Bebel, aligned with the revolutionary left during the revisionist controversy. After the Russian revolution of 1905 had infused the left with new confidence, it found itself engaged in polemics with what Kautsky called Luxemburg's "revolutionary romanticism."[31] Bebel and Kautsky defended an archly traditional variant of classical Marxism but sought to maintain a flexible posture that avoided alienating the revisionist right. Under Kautsky's skillful editorship *Die Neue Zeit* became an open forum for diverse points of view, and after 1905 Kautsky himself championed what he called a "strategy of attrition" as an alternative to revolutionary assault.[32] The center as a whole was tolerant of revisionism, increasingly hostile toward the left, and skeptical of prospects for a catastrophic crisis that would place social revolution on the agenda.[33]

When in 1912 the SPD emerged from the most successful electoral campaign in its history as the largest single party in Germany, the cautious perspective of the center seemed to have been vindicated. For left radicals such as Luxemburg, however, it was precisely the illusion that electoral politics could lead forward to socialism that needed to be exposed. Firstly, they argued, the SPD's ability to exert political influence commensurate with its popular appeal was severely limited in Germany's conservative constitutional monarchy. Secondly, the assumption that gradual progress could continue without interruption neglected the instability of the capitalist system itself. By focusing too narrowly upon proximate goals and ignoring the need to prepare for confrontation, the SPD was abdicating its responsibility as the party of the revolutionary proletariat.

By 1912, the year of the first Balkan war, the type of event most likely to interrupt the triumphant advance of European labor was clear to all. A series of colonial crises, an unprecedented arms race, and an intensification of belligerent rhetoric combined to call attention to the increasingly real threat of a general war. Though often described as an era of peace, the age of the Second International— which spanned the Spanish-American war, the Boer war, the Russo-Japanese war, Italy's campaign in Libya, and the Balkan wars—was not entirely free of armed conflicts involving the European powers. The International debated these conflicts passionately but never succeeded in arriving at an antiwar strategy acceptable to its diverse affiliates.[34]

The International's 1891 Brussels congress grounded its analysis of the problem in Marxist fundamentalism, condemning militarism as "the fatal result of the permanent state of war, actual or latent, imposed upon society by the reign of the exploitation of man by man."[35] These lofty sentiments inconveniently failed to resolve the problem of what to do about the "permanent state of war" short of accomplishing the socialist revolution. At the Brussels and Zürich (1893) congresses Domela Nieuwenhuis of the Netherlands unsuccessfully proposed resolutions infused with an anarchist-tinged antimilitarism, demanding that socialists respond to war by launching a general strike and armed uprising. Majority resolutions offered in response by Wilhelm Liebknecht of the SPD and Georgii Plekhanov of Russia rejected the general strike as impractical, and though urging "incessant agitation" against war, arrived at the fatalistic conclusion that "only the creation of a socialist order putting an end to the exploitation of man by man will put an end to militarism and ensure a lasting peace." In the terse, mechanistic formula of Plekhanov, "the roots of war are located in the essence of the capitalist order . . . When capitalism is overcome, war will disappear."[36] Such statements were entirely consistent with the assumptions of Marxism, but they brought the International no closer to a program for how to react should war actually erupt.

Not until the 1907 Stuttgart congress, the first general congress to be held in Germany and a major showpiece for the movement, was the issue confronted head on. In a carefully prepared debate on the theme "Militarism and National Conflict" no less than four contrasting resolutions were put forward. Three of them emerged from the French Socialist party (SFIO), whose national congress at Nancy several weeks earlier had failed to achieve a consensual position. The ultraleft was represented by Gustave Hervé, who repeated Nieuwenhuis' call for an insurrectionary response to a war crisis. At an opposite extreme Jules Guesde represented the dogmatic position that any and all preventive antiwar measures were futile under capitalism. The middle ground was occupied by resolutions proposed by Jean Jaurès and Vaillant for the SFIO majority and by Bebel for the SPD. Jaurès and Vaillant attempted to define practical measures capable of stemming a slide toward war ranging from petitions and demonstrations up to the general strike. Bebel agreed with the emphasis upon purposeful antiwar action but rejected attempts to fix strategy in advance. In any given conflict situation, he argued, individual circumstances would have to be evaluated and a careful distinction between aggressive and defensive intentions established. In the event that war did come, therefore, social democrats should "retain full liberty to take whatever measures they consider most effective."[37]

After acrimonious debate, the texts submitted by Jaurès/Vaillant and Bebel were sent to subcommittee for reconciliation. Bebel's text was preferred, but amended to include a lengthy passage written by Jaurès documenting the proletariat's past successes in resisting war, as well as several paragraphs submitted by Luxemburg (with the support of Lenin and Iurii Martov of the RSDRP) intended to lend the statement more consequence from the perspective of the revolutionary left. The most significant addition was the concluding paragraph. After asserting the determination to "exert every effort" to prevent war "by means they consider most effective," the resolution admonished: "Should war break out nonetheless, it is their [the socialist parties] duty to intervene in favor of its speedy termination, and to do all in their power to utilize the economic and political crisis caused by the war to rouse the people and thereby to hasten the abolition of capitalist class rule."[38] Thus refined, the Stuttgart resolution "On Militarism and National Conflict" was unanimously approved, the longest statement ever promulgated by the International and certainly one of the most contradictory. Despite the compromises accepted in subcommittee, the resolution reflected the priorities of Bebel and the SPD center. It began with the familiar pronouncement that war was inherent in the bourgeois state system but went on to urge concerted action to prevent its outbreak. A fixed strategy of resistance was deemed impractical at the same time that the seemingly more difficult task of organizing revolutionary opposition in time of war was endorsed. With its internal inconsistencies and attempt to provide something for everyone, the Stuttgart resolution perpetuated the International's conceptual dilemmas rather than overcoming them.

At Copenhagen in 1910 the International turned to the problem once again. An amendment introduced by Keir Hardie of the ILP and the indefatigable Vaillant reposed the issue of the general strike, but it was rejected in the face of strong opposition led by the SPD. In Bebel's absence Georg Ledebour argued convincingly that the general strike as a mechanism for resisting war would be prejudicial to the largest and best organized labor movements and hence to the interests of socialism as a whole. The text of the final resolution offered little that was new, asserting that war was caused by "economic competition between capitalist states on the world market," and would "not cease completely until capitalist society has disappeared."[39] The only specific antiwar tactics that could be agreed upon were mild calls for preventive measures such as the elimination of standing armies, international arbitration, the abolition of secret diplomacy, and general disarmament.

The limits of this approach were made manifest by the extraordinary congress of Basel, convened on 24–25 November 1912 to protest the possibility of escalation following the outbreak of war in the Balkans during October. Jaurès electrified the audience with a plea to make international socialism the decisive force for peace, and a parade of leaders accompanied him to the pulpit of the Basel Münster to underline the determination of the international proletariat to fight against war with all the means at its disposal. The concluding manifesto described the source of modern war as "capitalist imperialism," and boasted that "the fear of the ruling classes that a world war might be followed by a proletarian revolution" was "an essential guarantee of peace."[40] These were brave words, but without a coordinated strategy for antiwar action they rang hollow, a fact that was not lost on Europe's great powers as they went about the pursuit of their own strategic designs.

Disputes over antiwar strategy were reinforced by the International's factional subdivisions. The revisionist wing of the movement was committed to the "commonsense" assumption that progress toward socialism could only occur within the framework of the nation-state. Several of its spokespersons championed the "civilizing" role of the European nations in the colonial world and supported a variety of socialist patriotism that made allowance for an active colonial policy as well as national defense.[41] The most provocative affirmations emerging from the movement's right flank were usually repudiated by more responsible leaders, but they continued to represent a not-negligible strain of opinion. The leading figures of the center likewise conceded that under certain circumstances the resort to arms on behalf of the national community was unavoidable. In his 1907 brochure *Patriotism and Social Democracy* Kautsky stated categorically that "existing antagonisms between states cannot give rise to any war to which the patriotism of the proletariat would not be resolutely opposed" but also insisted upon the need for a "people's state" to maintain the capacity for self-defense.[42] By 1912 he was advancing the thesis that in an age where the great powers possessed a common interest in the peaceful exploitation of world markets, militarism need no longer be considered an inevitable attribute of capitalism. In this phase of "ultraimperialism" the threat of war could be neutralized by a socialist policy focusing on the arbitration of international disputes and arms control.[43] Bebel, who together with Wilhelm Liebknecht coined the slogan with which the SPD justified its refusal to support military appropriations—"For This

System, Not One Man and Not One Penny"—could also assert his party's determination "never to abandon a single piece of German soil to the foreigner."[44] Such sentiments were even more pronounced in the case of Jaurès, at one and the same time the movement's most outspoken internationalist and ardent patriot. In his *The New Army* Jaurès went so far as to reject Engels' claim that the state under socialism would "wither away," remarking that the aphorism "the workers have no Fatherland" was based upon "vain and obscure subtilties" and a "sarcastic negation of history itself."[45]

A more rigorous antiwar perspective emerged from the left radical current. Its linchpin was the concept of imperialism, defined as a phase in the development of modern capitalism characterized by the expanded reproduction of capital on a global scale and the appearance of an ever more unified world market dominated by a handful of leading industrial states. In direct contrast to Kautsky left radicals argued that the intensified competition for control of the non-European world that imperialism brought in its train pointed inexorably toward an era of crisis and war. By provoking an increasingly bitter struggle for economic and political supremacy, Luxemburg wrote in *The Accumulation of Capital*, "imperialism grows in lawlessness and violence, both in aggression against the non-capitalist world and in ever more serious conflicts among the competing capitalist countries. The mere tendency toward imperialism by itself takes forms that make the final phase of capitalism a period of catastrophy."[46] Confronted by such prospects, the development of a realistic antiwar strategy assumed heightened, even central importance.

Left radicals argued that imperialism exposed the impending exhaustion of the national form as a vehicle for social progress. In a review of Jaurès' *The New Army* Luxemburg mocked the attempt to establish legalistic criteria for differentiating between wars of aggression and defense. "The only viable means for struggling against the crimes of war and colonial policy," she wrote, was the will of the working class "to transform a world war provoked by the infamous interests of capital into a rebellion of the exploited and dominated for the creation of world peace and a socialist reconciliation of peoples."[47] In an article written during 1908 Lenin likewise rejected the concept of "defending the Fatherland" and insisted that only the interests of the international proletariat provided a valid foundation for revolutionary politics.[48] Karl Radek, writing on behalf of the

Bremen left radical group in the spring of 1912, went further by suggesting that in the long-term imperialism would tear away even that facade of civility with which the bourgeois state sought to secure its own legitimacy. Only proletarian revolution and the transition to socialism provided an alternative to the gradual disintegration of the international system, marked by war and the triumph of ever more brutal and unmitigated forms of class rule.[49] To act in the spirit of Luxemburg's addendum to the Stuttgart resolution and prepare to exploit an impending crisis for revolutionary ends—here was the conclusion toward which left radical analysis pressed.

The warnings issued by theorists like Luxemburg were dramatic, but they never took the form of a comprehensive political challenge. Left radicalism in the prewar International was an intellectual tendency concentrated in large measure within the SPD. No attempt was made to move beyond criticism to a programmatic alternative. The left radicals' main fire was directed toward revisionism, and their analysis was often imprecisely delineated from that of the center. As confirmed Marxists, they also rejected the moralistic absolutism of the anarcho-syndicalist perspective and granted the need for a minimum program aimed at asserting popular control over the military function rather than insisting upon total and complete disarmament. Despite the priority attached to internationalism, left radicals also assumed that the fight for political power must first be waged and won within the national arena. Though supportive of reforms designed to tighten discipline, they shared a broad consensus in favor of the International's federative structure. The International itself was considered sacrosanct, a challenge to its unity unthinkable.

Soviet historiography has emphasized Lenin's efforts to extend the left radical critique by creating a politically organized faction within the Second International. Though a few hesitant steps in such a direction were indeed undertaken, their intention is by no means clear, and no special importance need be attached to them.[50] At Stuttgart in 1907 Lenin attempted unsuccessfully to convene a caucus of left radicals. Three years later at Copenhagen the effort was renewed, and a brief session bringing together left-oriented delegates did take place, but the deliberations were informal and produced no results of lasting significance.[51] The fact that no follow-up was attempted seems to indicate that the caucus was primarily a sounding board for opinion rather than an organizational initiative. The Bolshevik faction was aligned only peripherally with the left radical critique, and it did not exert influence outside of the Russian milieu. What was distinctive about Leninism prior to the world war amounted to little more than the postulates developed in the 1902 tract *What Is To Be Done?*, with its call for a disciplined party of "professional" revolutionaries to serve as the vanguard of a proletariat judged incapable of achieving political consciousness without sophisticated leadership. These were challenging proposals, but Lenin did not try to defend their relevance outside the autocratic czarist empire. Luxemburg, among other left radicals, rejected them as overly authoritarian and inapplicable to Western Europe.[52] Georges Haupt has concluded that at least up until 1912 (when the ISB moved to judicate the Bolshevik/Menshevik rift) "Lenin maintained a total optimism and absolute confidence in the International."[53]

The Second International was fundamentally divided over the issues of war and militarism, but up to the First World War its differences were patched over by vague pronouncements that assumed a common ground of internationalism based upon the premises of classical Marxism. The resolutions accepted unanimously by its Stuttgart, Copenhagen, and Basel congresses were most notable for their failure to specify effective means of resistance to a danger that all acknowledged to be clear and present. What were the implications of the assumption that war was inevitable within the bourgeois state system? How could the contradictory pressures of national affiliation and international commitment be balanced in the event that war did come? Could modern war become a catalyst for social revolution, and should social democrats orient their work in this direction? The events of the summer of 1914 would make clear just how serious the failure to resolve such issues was to be.

The Policy of 4 August

European socialists proved no more prescient than others in divining the consequences of the assassination of the Austrian Archduke Francis Ferdinand in the Bosnian capital of Sarajevo on 28 June 1914. During the July Crisis that followed, the International organized antiwar demonstrations and arranged consultations but refrained from any decisive action. Though Austria's ultimatum to Serbia on 23 July greatly increased the possibility of a fight, hope remained that

it could be localized in the Balkans. An extraordinary session of the
ISB's executive committee was held on 29–30 July as the specter of
general war began to loom larger, but at this point the International
was being overtaken by events. The Brussels sessions were remarkable only for the evident futility of efforts to define a strategy for joint
action. In a memoir Angelica Balabanov commented upon the terrible realization that effective antiwar action would not be forthcoming. "Never," she lamented, "had the powerlessness of the International come so clearly and tragically to the fore."[54]

On 28 July Austria declared war on Serbia, and within days Europe's great powers had launched themselves into the cataclysm. On
1 August, with mobilizations already underway, Herman Muller of
the SPD traveled to Paris to consult with SFIO leaders. Discussions
focused upon the symbolic gesture of opposing war appropriations.
Muller expressed his personal conviction that the SPD Reichstag
fraction would never agree to vote for war credits, but communication remained exploratory, and no definite commitments were made
by either side. On the very eve of the war Europe's two leading
socialist parties demonstrated a complete incapacity to coordinate
policy. Could more purposeful action by the International have made
a difference? With over three million members affiliated to twenty-
seven parties worldwide, three million socialist voters in Germany, a
million each in France and Austria-Hungary, a half-million in Great
Britain, and a wide-ranging network of supportive social organizations, the International was a real political force. It remained a minority opposition all the same, politically exposed, tactically unprepared, and confronted by populations systematically conditioned
to accept the coming of war as a part of the nature of things. It was not
the failure to prevent war, but the inability to muster resistance, that
signaled the International's *faillite*.

On 4 August, while Russian troops mobilized for a push into East
Prussia, German armies violated Belgian neutrality and swept toward France with the goal of eliminating their enemy to the west
with a single blow. Also on 4 August, confronting the war as a fait ac-
compli, the parliamentary representatives of the SPD and SFIO voted
unanimously in the Reichstag and Chamber of Deputies to support
emergency war appropriations. The SFIO's decision was made informally and without debate. In a caucus of the SPD Reichstag fraction
fourteen of ninety-two members declined support but bowed to party

tradition dictating bloc votes. The existence of dissent within the fraction was not made public, and the apparent unanimity of the decision made a strong impression. "In the hour of danger," intoned Hugo Haase before the Reichstag in a phrase that seemed to contradict decades of socialist antimilitarism, "we will not leave our own Fatherland in the lurch."[55] Within a week the SPD had rallied behind a policy of *Burgfrieden* (civil truce), while its French counterpart enunciated a more flamboyant *union sacrée*. Europe-wide, most other social democratic parties whose countries were engaged as belligerents followed suit, proclaiming a "defensist" program that legitimized socialist support for the war effort and "suspended" class struggle for its duration.

Immediately, 4 August 1914 was recognized as a seminal moment in the history of socialism. The "policy of 4 August"—a policy of acquiescence in the pursuit of the war and acceptance of the consequences of such acquiescence—became an emotionally charged symbol that made unbridgeable divisions that had been widening for over a generation. Socialist defensism was firmly grounded in the ethic of raison d'état, positing a distinction between aggressive and defensive wars and invoking the need to defend the national sanctuary against unprovoked assault. Particularly during the war's first phase, when expectations were widespread that the conflict would be brief and relatively painless, defensism was justified on narrowly pragmatic grounds as well. Many activists were impressed by the near unanimity with which the working class appeared to heed the call to arms and feared isolating themselves from the masses. Others pointed to the threat to party organizations posed by repression; in the absence of a predetermined strategy opposition seemed a risky gamble not commensurate with attendant costs and risks. No less impressive was the spirit of unity that emerged so dramatically during August, providing a psychological environment conducive to reconciliation with a national community from which many social democrats had long felt estranged. "One could," wrote the repentant left radical Konrad Hänisch, "for the first time in almost a quarter century, join with a full heart, a clear conscience, and without a sense of treason in the sweeping, stormy song, '*Deutschland, Deutschland, über alles!*' "[56]

In individual instances the war entirely shattered former affiliations. Particularly striking was the conversion of leftists such as

Hervé and Guesde of the sFIO, Hänisch and Paul Lensch of the sPD, Plekhanov of the rSDRP, and Henry Hyndman of the British Socialist party (BSP), who performed amazing transformations to emerge as partisans of "war to complete victory." In its larger contours, however, the shock caused by the policy of 4 August reproduced the familiar tripartite division of the Second International. Defensist majorities closely identified with their respective governments' declared war aims and committed themselves to the pursuit of military victory. Their more uninhibited partisans unambiguously linked defensism to a *plaidoyer* for reformist priorities. For Wilhelm Kolb of the sPD the war represented a watershed; henceforward social democrats would be required to acknowledge that "the Fatherland is not an imaginary phantom for the proletariat but a *living reality*," to adopt in consequence "a policy of political and social *reform* within a democratically ruled *people's state*," and to abandon "lunatic" hopes for social revolution.[57] In the first months of the war the most prominent leaders of the center sided, albeit uncomfortably, with defensism. As the nature and extent of the conflict became more clear, a significant number gravitated toward an oppositional stance that rejected socialist participation in a war waged for annexationist ends. The wartime center sought to restore social democracy as a force for peace by forwarding a negotiated settlement "without victors or vanquished." Finally, a small left wing announced that the war had conclusively proven the validity of the left radical critique. The task of revolutionary Marxists would now be to reject any compromise with nationalism and encourage a revolutionary response to what appeared to be an open-ended crisis. These broadly defined tendencies structured the wartime debate over socialist strategy; a debate that would conclude in the postwar years with the permanent division of the labor movement.

The great schism of European socialism was without question rooted in the increasingly incompatible political outlooks that found in Marxism a common source and had come to coexist within the Second International. "The war gave rise to a schism within the party," wrote Phillip Scheidemann of the sPD in 1921, "but I believe it would eventually have come to pass even without the war."[58] Direct parallels between debates within the prewar International and the much more intense controversies of 1914–1918 should not, however, be drawn too literally. As David Kirby has remarked, attempts to apply rigidly the right/center/left schema after 4 August 1914 tend to oversimplify the complexity of socialist responses to what was, after all, a completely unprecedented situation.[59] In an atmosphere laden with suffering and death, civilized political discourse became nearly impossible. The resentments engendered by the excesses of defensism, the disruption of party organizations occasioned by mobilization, and the socioeconomic changes wrought by the experience of total war combined to transform the political environment. A primary victim was the Second International's centrist consensus. With the world around it aflame the verities that had held the movement together for a generation seemed to lose all relevance. It was the war itself that became the crucible within which the conceptual paradigms and underlying assumptions that would come to dominate twentieth century socialist and communist thought were forged.

Perhaps the most fundamental of these paradigms was socialist internationalism. In embracing the cause of national defense and maintaining it through four years of grotesque carnage, the social-democratic right wing stepped beyond the bounds of constraint that allowed a meaningful commitment to internationalism to survive. During August 1914 Emile Vandervelde of Belgium, the executive secretary of the ISB, as well as Guesde and Marcel Sembat (later joined by Albert Thomas) of the SFIO entered war cabinets as ministers of state. Mainstays of the International such as the SFIO and the Belgian Labor party (POB) refused any discourse with socialist representatives of hostile powers. The defensists' condemnations of the "enemy," propagation of atrocity rumors and other excesses of military agitation, as well as bellicose posturing and general intolerance created a climate unconducive to joint work. Within individual parties right-wing attacks upon the antiwar opposition reached levels of vituperation once reserved for representatives of the bourgeois state. On 18 August the Belgian socialist daily Le Peuple saw fit to editorialize on the necessity in the "hour of final victory . . . without superfluous compassion . . . to cast out the teutonic race from the family of humanity."[60] Such extremism was not atypical. It indicated how fast and how far the policy of 4 August had turned the movement away from its former commitments. The priorities of defensism were incompatible with internationalism, and it was the policy of 4 August that triumphed at the outset of the war. In the words of Jules Humbert-Droz, written fifty years after the event: "The International died on 4 August 1914, killed not by the war, but by the renunciation of the socialists themselves."[61]

In a September 1914 entry in his diary the Italian writer Zino Zini sought to capture the tragedy of the International's failure by comparing it to the failure of another institution with tarnished claims to universality—the Catholic Church:

> The war has seen the collapse of two universalisms: The ancient universalism of Christianity, and the much more recent one of socialism. Both profess international peace and fraternity, but practice war and the egotism of people and races ... Socialism, like the village church, subordinates itself within each country to the communal interest, and threatens to become an instrument at the service of the nation ... This is the greatest danger threatening the complex of doctrines and institutions that we call the philosophy and practice of the proletariat as a class.[62]

These were severe, but not unfair judgments. The policy of 4 August made it necessary to confront the question of whether the visionary internationalism based upon proletarian class consciousness to which Marxism laid claim could ever be more than a chimera. Above all, it was in attempting to reject the implications of defensism, to defy the impression that socialism was incapable of transcending the nation-state, and to define a new image of internationalism closer to Marx's original intent that the embattled wartime left, and beyond it the international communist movement, groped its way toward an independent political identity.

2

Against the Current

"And yet, look! There is one person who has lifted himself above this war, whose name will live on for the beauty and the greatness of his courage. . . ." I listened, leaning on a stick, bent toward him, absorbing this voice that emerged, in the dusky stillness, from a mouth that remained almost always silent. He cried out in a clear voice: "Liebknecht!"

—Henri Barbusse, *Le Feu*

THE Reichstag vote of 4 August shocked the entire international community and provoked widespread disbelief. As late as 20 August the Romanian social democratic press referred to published accounts of Haase's speech as "an incredible lie," claiming that "the censor has changed the text in accordance with the desires of the government."[1] In fact, the lie that was being exposed was the revolutionary pretense of the Second International. With the European proletariat mustered behind national flags and defensism apparently triumphant, socialists hoping to muster opposition found themselves isolated, intimidated, and impotent. Frustration was heightened by the psychological disorientation produced by the wartime environment. As the Menshevik leader Martov wrote from Paris on 19 August: "Gradually you become used to living in an atmosphere of worldwide catastrophe, but in the first weeks of the offensive it completely dejected me; it seemed I was losing my mind."[2]

Viewed from the left, the political balance sheet for the war's first months appeared bleak indeed. Although the socialist parties of the major neutral nations spoke out against a continuation of hostilities, among the belligerent powers opposition was virtually invisible. European workers passively obeyed the call to arms, a disillusioning result but one that should have come as no surprise. Constant invocations of proletarian unity could not alter the fact that in 1914 the European working class was often intensely nationalistic. The social democratic movement was dominated by the representatives of a minority of organized workers in the advanced industrial states. Beyond its class-conscious core stretched millions of unorganized, poorly educated, and politically malleable laborers, migrants, and peasants. Any kind of resistance was dependent upon determined leadership, a prospect that was precluded by the policy of 4 August. Working class militancy was also dampened by the short-term benefits derived from the military emergency. The war temporarily put an end to mass unemployment (over two million in France alone during the first seven months of 1914), and workers whose efforts were considered important to the war effort achieved significantly higher salaries. At the same time, the surveillance and harassment of labor leaders was intensified. Lack of direction, fatalism, vested self-interest, and fear of reprisals all combined to discourage dissent.

The morale of the opposition was further undermined by the fact that the International seemed utterly to have abandoned its mandate. War brought an abrupt halt to preparations for the long-planned general congress about to convene in Vienna. Although the ISB restructured its executive and transferred its headquarters from Brussels to The Hague in order to preserve an appearance of neutrality, it remained paralyzed by the categoric refusal of the SFIO and POB to work together with the representatives of hostile powers.[3] By clinging to the principle of consensus the ISB condemned itself to inactivity and the International to irrelevance.

The impression that the left had been completely eclipsed by events was nonetheless deceiving. The left radical wing of the movement had always been a militant minority. Intensified repression, censorship, and restrictions upon movement and communication after August 1914 were significant barriers to coordinated action, but they were barriers that could be overcome. Moreover, embattled isolation could bring advantages if it led toward greater coherence and discipline. What was remarkable, under the circumstances, was the pace at which a socialist left committed to an internationalist alternative reappeared.

The greatest boost to the fortunes of the left was provided by the generals and strategists, whose ruinous misconceptions rapidly created a military debacle of unprecedented proportions. At the end of August, following the early successes of his offensives in Belgium and Lorraine, the German commander-in-chief von Moltke bravely remarked that "in six weeks this will all be over."[4] Immediately thereafter the high-risk logic of Germany's "Schlieffen Plan" began to unravel. In response to an unexpectedly rapid Russian thrust into East Prussia, von Moltke diverted two corps from the west, thereby weakening his drive on Paris. During the second week of September French and British armies stopped the German advance on the Marne, forcing a general retreat and bringing an end to hopes to win the war with a sudden thrust. French commander-in-chief Joffre's counteroffensive, carried forward by soldiers anachronistically attired in red trousers and featuring the *charge à la baïonette*, proved even more murderously misconceived. With attacks by both sides blunted, a "race to the sea" ensued, in fact a series of flanking maneuvers that had the effect of pushing the front northward into Flanders. By the onset of winter, in place of the war of movement originally envisioned, a static confrontation had developed, waged along an immobile front consisting of reinforced lines defined in depth, stretched across a broad swath of Belgium and France from the Channel to the Jura. Subsequent efforts to break through these formidable positions, whether via mass assault, artillery barrage, or poison gas attack, proved futile. The western front had been born, and the costly stalemate waged around it would continue for four long years.

The Russian offensive in East Prussia was also quickly turned around. During the August campaigning Russian forces led by the ill-fated General Samsonov became badly overextended; in the first weeks of September, simultaneous to the Battle of the Marne, the Germans isolated and routed them at Tannenberg and the Masurian Lakes. In an offensive launched into Galicia on behalf of beleaguered Serbia the Russians did better, defeating Austrian forces near L'vov and pressing forward to the Carpathians, but their successes could not be exploited after the disaster in East Prussia. The "Russian steam roller" of allied fantasy proved to be a chimera. In the course of 1915 Russian armies bore the brunt of a series of Austro-German attacks. The Imperial Army suffered terrible casualties and was forced to abandon the czar's Baltic, Polish, and Galician provinces, but it remained in the field. Despite their exploits in the east, the Germans were being forced to wage a protracted two-front war.

In May 1915, attracted by secret treaties promising territorial booty, Italy joined the Entente, launching an ill-conceived attack against Austrian positions in the Trentino and giving rise to yet another stalemated front. Meanwhile, in the Balkans Austria's "punishment" of Serbia degenerated into a travesty. After initially capturing Belgrade, the Austrians were overwhelmed by a Serbian counterattack and expelled beyond the Sava. Soon the entire peninsula was engulfed by war. In February and March 1915 a British/French expedition launched against Turkey's Gallipoli peninsula proved to be an embarrassing failure. Its demoralized survivors were eventually evacuated to Saloniki, where a neutral but politically divided Greece was pressured to accept them. Simultaneously, Turkish offensives into the Caucasus and toward Suez came to naught. A vast tragedy followed as the Turkish authorities elected to expel the entire Armenian population from their exposed Caucasian frontier zone, an "expulsion" that in practice became a campaign of extermination leaving over a million victims in its wake.

Encouraged by the British humiliation at Gallipoli, Bulgaria sided with the Central Powers during October. The intervention was the final straw for a Serbian army already exhausted by the price of its victories in 1914 and ravaged by a typhus epidemic, which now broke down completely under combined pressure from north and south. Its disorganized remnants, accompanied by the Serbian King Peter traveling in an oxcart, withdrew across the Albanian mountains to the sea in a forced march during which over 10,000 perished from hunger and cold. Serbia's collapse gave Germany a direct rail link to its allies in the Near East, but a final decision in the Balkans was not in sight. A force of 40,000 Serbian survivors was evacuated to the French-controlled island of Corfu and eventually retransferred to a new Saloniki front. Turkish and Russian forces continued to clash in the Caucasus, and the Near East remained a bed of intrigue. Years of fighting, with immensely destabilizing consequences, still lay ahead.

Within months the war bore little resemblance to what had been envisioned in the euphoria of its first days. The intervention of Turkey, Italy, and other secondary powers considerably extended its scope. The stabilization of the fronts and new technologies of warfare created a grinding war of attrition that produced terrible casualties without commensurate strategic results. The voracious appetites of the fronts were fed by the engagement of entire populations in the war effort, inflationary fiscal policies, and the institution of centralized economic controls. The twentieth century's first total war, complete with genocidal atrocities, resort to weapons of mass annihilation, starvation blockades, and terroristic strikes against civilian populations, had begun.

The conviction that the cumulative burden imposed by the war would inevitably lead to a popular reaction became the foundation for revolutionary politics after August 1914. At first that meant a politics of small gestures. Simple political agitation had suddenly become a capital offense, punishable by lengthy incarceration or even death. The workers were mobilized and dispersed, their organizations voided and ineffective. Public attitudes, primed by sacrifices and a steady diet of official propaganda, were predominantly patriotic. Lenin and Zinoviev later titled a collection of their wartime writings "Against the Current," a fair description of the course that the opposition was compelled to pursue as the war's first campaigns played out.[5] The process of reflection and debate from which the left opposition was to emerge went forward against a difficult background of repression and intolerance.

The Age of Bayonets

Proponents of revolutionary alternatives to the policy of 4 August appeared in every social democratic organization, but with hindsight it is clear that their most influential partisans were Lenin and his comrades within the Bolshevik wing of the RSDRP. Though still a relatively unknown figure in 1914, Lenin quickly became one of the most forceful critics of the International's "betrayal." In so doing he extended his own horizons. Prior to the war Lenin wrote very little about international affairs; subsequently, a theory of world politics would become essential to his political analysis. Lenin's attack upon the policy of 4 August was uniquely severe. Its vigorous radicalism established a foundation for his later accomplishments as a revolutionary leader.

Though not entirely immune to the inroads of nationalism, the Bolshevik party network inside Russia and abroad was more successful in weathering the storms unleashed by the war than most other socialist organizations. The party represented the militant left wing of a divided movement, and the low degree of social and political integration achieved by its industrial working-class constituency ensured a base of support for radical alternatives. Working-class disaffection was demonstrated on the very eve of the war as a series of strike actions, including pitched battles around barricades, swept through the czarist capital Saint Petersburg. A police crackdown left the Bolshevik organization in chaos at the moment that war was declared, but a core of activists remained intact and rallied around an antiwar position.[6] On 8 August (26 July) the Bolshevik and Menshevik Duma fractions read a joint declaration refusing support for military appropriations and walked from the assembly prior to the vote. By September the Petersburg party organization (the capital was renamed Petrograd during the war, but the Bolsheviks retained the former designation as a protest against chauvinism) had distributed several antiwar broadsheets.[7]

Bolshevik sections abroad were more visibly affected by the patriotic swell. In a first flush of enthusiasm several members of the Committee of Organizations Abroad located in Paris joined the "volunteer movement" among Russian émigrés and enlisted in the French army, while at a general meeting of Bolshevik sections in Paris eleven of ninety-four delegates voted in support of defensism.[8] The extent of defection was small compared with other parties, but it revealed a degree of pro-Entente sympathy that was no doubt echoed within Russia. Mobilization found Bolshevik institutional coordination in disarray. The party's agitational journal *Sotsial-Demokrat* (Social Democrat) had been out of print for almost a year, directive organs had not yet recovered from revelations of infiltration by police agents, and procedures for consultation had disintegrated. Nonetheless, the party in its majority demonstrated a spirit of militant opposition. No prominent leaders dissented publically from an oppositional posture, the parliamentary fraction refused to support war credits, and the indigenous organization agitated against the war from the underground. In September 1914 Lenin was in the almost unique position of being able to speak for a mass-based labor party with a firm record of resistance to its government's pursuit of the war.

At the beginning of August Lenin and his wife, Nadezhda Krupskaia, were vacationing in the Polish village of Poronin, in the Tatra mountains south of Kraków. Upon the war's outbreak Lenin was arrested by overzealous local officials as a "suspicious alien," but with the support of associates, including Victor Adler in Vienna, he was granted permission to leave the country.[9] On 5 September Lenin arrived in Bern, the "small, dull little village," as he chose to describe the Swiss capital, that would serve as a temporary refuge.[10] Shortly after Lenin's arrival Bern also became the residence of Zinoviev, at age thirty-one a party leader and member of the Central Committee's Foreign Bureau. On 28 October Karl Radek made Bern his home as well, not yet a Bolshevik but a capable agitator whose outspoken opposition to defensism could not have failed to attract Lenin's attention.[11] Pressed together by chance rather than design in the relatively open environment of neutral Switzerland, Lenin and his associates set out to confront the consequences of the policy of 4 August upon the International.

Lenin's evaluation of the war crisis was well developed even prior to his arrival in Bern. As early as 31 July, with Austria and Serbia at arms and the threat of general war acute, he prepared the draft of an article entitled "War and Revolution" that included frequent references to underground resistance and the pointed phrase "the best war against war is revolution."[12] On 6 September, his first full day in Switzerland, Lenin gathered the small group of Bolshevik émigrés on hand and presented a document, known as his "Theses on the War," in which a programmatic response to the crisis was outlined.[13]

Lenin's seven theses may be summarized in four points: (1) the war is described as "bourgeois, imperialist, and dynastic in character," a contest for global hegemony waged by the ruling classes; (2) the defensist postures of the leading social democratic organizations are said to represent "a direct betrayal of socialism" and to signal "the ideological collapse of the International"; (3) the primary task of Russian social democrats, in war as in peace, is defined as the unrelenting pursuit of a struggle against czarism; and (4) social democratic leaders are urged to break with the "petty bourgeois opportunism" of the Second International, now declared defunct, and to agitate among the masses to end the war by means of revolution. Socialist organizations are therefore enjoined to reject the *Burgfrieden*, support fraternization at the fronts and protest actions in the rear, and summon the proletariat to struggle against its own governments regardless of the military consequences. Under the prevailing circumstances these were ferociously radical propositions, the means for whose realization appeared to be nowhere in sight.

Arguments based upon short-term expediency were not calculated to impress Lenin, for whom it was precisely a lack of vision and daring that had brought the International to its present sorry plight. The Bolshevik leader had never placed much confidence in preventive antiwar measures, which he once described as "simple stupidity," and he agreed that the outset of a war was the worst possible moment to launch effective mass actions.[14] The essence of his position in the Theses on the War was that socialists must hold fast to the long-term necessity of revolutionary solutions and prepare for the crisis that would follow in the war's wake, a position summarized by the slogan "to transform the imperialist war into a civil war for socialism." That meant that socialist parties must at a minimum disassociate themselves from the pursuit of the war, if need be in defiance of popular patriotic fervor. Equally important, the collapse of the International had to be admitted openly and the goal of a new International "purged of opportunism" placed on the agenda. The Bolshevik section in Bern was quickly converted to these precepts, and on 6 September it approved the Theses on the War unanimously. In the following week Lenin elaborated upon them in an article entitled "The War and Russian Social Democracy," intended to serve as a party program. Both texts were circulated among party sections in an effort to rally the organization around a common line.[15]

The most controversial of Lenin's theses was the sixth, which postulated that "from the point of view of the laboring class and the toiling masses of all the Russian people the lesser evil would be a defeat for the czarist monarchy." In "The War and Russian Social Democracy" the notion of defeat as "lesser evil" was broadened to a principle with universal relevance. Labeled "defeatism," Lenin's logically severe conclusion called forth misgivings both within and without Bolshevik ranks. Although most party sections accepted the spirit of the Theses on the War enthusiastically, the invocation of defeat generated considerable dissent. Prominent Bolshevik leaders or sympathizers such as Lev Kamenev, Nikolai Bukharin, Aleksandr Shliapnikov, Aleksandra Kollontai, and Radek questioned whether such provocative terminology made political sense.[16] Lenin's rivals within the Russian labor movement were more openly critical. The Menshevik defensist Plekhanov countered with the deterministic argument that defeat would retard economic development and hence put off the coming of socialism, while the Socialist Revolutionary (SR) Viktor Chernov preferred the slogan "neither victory nor defeat."[17] More pointed objections were posed by Martov, who noted that encouraging defeat simply played into the hands of rival imperialist powers. As an alternative he offered the slogan "peace," defined as "the quickest possible end to the war and the most radical possible steps toward disarmament." In a series of articles written during October Martov predicted that as the war dragged on the call for peace would become a compelling appeal that "in the ears of the proletariat will assume a profoundly revolutionary character." As a result of the war, an awareness that capitalism could not secure a lasting peace would be reinforced and the masses primed for radical alternatives.[18] In opposition to Lenin's insurrectionary appeals, Martov proposed a "peace strategy" which sought to use popular yearning for peace as the foundation for a program whose priority was to reinforce the movement at the base.

On a tactical level Lenin gave some ground, and the slogan "defeatism" was never prominently featured in Bolshevik agitational literature during the war. As a matter of principle, however, the concept remained sacrosanct. Defeatism was impolitic, but it was the clearest possible expression of the uncompromising internationalism that informed Lenin's reaction to the policy of 4 August, of what Neil Harding has called his "Marxist fundamentalism."[19] According to the Theses on the War, Marx's aphorism "the workers have no Fatherland" was "a basic truth of socialism"; indeed, as Lenin explained to Inessa Armand, it expressed four related truths: "(a) that the workers' economic situation as wage laborers is not national, but international; (b) that their class enemy is international; (c) the conditions for their liberation as well; and (d) that international unity of the proletariat is *more important* than national unity."[20] For socialists to support national defense by voting for military appropriations and to urge the proletariat into fratricidal slaughter meant an abandonment of the very principles that defined their movement's historical individuality. Socialist internationalism would be furthered not by the victory of one or another imperialist bloc, but by the solidarity of the international proletariat expressed in mass actions in defiance of the bourgeois state.

In a series of speaking engagements during the autumn Lenin defended his revolutionary priorities uncompromisingly. "We cannot allow," he wrote to Shliapnikov on 14 November, "that we be thrown together with the petty bourgeoisie, sentimental liberals, etc. The age of *bayonets* is upon us. This is a fact, and in consequence we must fight *with similar weapons*." Scornful of attempts to promote a democratic peace, he returned time and again to the leitmotivs of mass action and civil war. "The slogan of peace is in my mind incorrect," he wrote, "a proletarian solution must demand civil war."

Our slogan is civil war. All arguments to the effect that this slogan is unworkable, etc., etc., are pure sophism. We cannot "make" it, but we propagate for it and work in this direction. In every country one must struggle first of all against *one's own* proper chauvinism, awaken hatred for *one's own* regime, call (repeatedly, persistently, ever again, tirelessly) for solidarity among the workers of the warring nations. No one is proposing to *guarantee* when and to what degree this work will prove practicable or justified: *This is not what is at issue*. At issue is the *line* of work. *Only* such work is socialist and not chauvinist. And it *alone* will bear socialist fruit, revolutionary fruit.[21]

Lenin did not gloat over the coming of the war, which he never described as less than a monumental tragedy.[22] His arguments were primarily concerned with elevating principle above expediency by achieving a theoretically consistent response to the European crisis. Above all, they were animated by a desire to repudiate the failure of the Second International. By perpetuating the illusion of peaceful progress, revisionism (or "opportunism" as Lenin preferred to phrase it) had left the labor movement unprepared to confront a critical conjuncture. Defeatism and the invocation of revolutionary civil war were the symbols of a radical alternative.

During the winter of 1914–15, Lenin succeeded in carrying the Bolshevik party apparatus behind him. His influence becomes particularly clear when examining the evolution of the Petrograd-based Russian Bureau of the Central Committee. During September the Petersburg section managed to draft an open letter to the socialists of Austria-Hungary that criticized their support for the *Burgfrieden*, an answer to a well-publicized appeal by Vandervelde urging Russian socialists to support the Entente, and a number of other agitational documents.[23] The pronouncements reflected the influence of the Russian Bureau led by Kamenev and were primarily anticzarist in spirit, with the call to end the war, attacks upon absolutism, and the demand for a democratic republic as featured themes. Following Fedor Samoilov's arrival as an emissary from Bern on or around 20 September with copies of Lenin's Theses on the War, the emphasis began to change. The "Answer to Vandervelde" was redrafted to encompass Lenin's views and in general the anticzarist tone of earlier statements was broadened to an anti-imperialist line with more universal implications. Accommodation to the priorities of the Foreign Bureau did not occur overnight or without resistance. The term "imperialist" does not begin to appear in Bolshevik agitational literature until November and the term "civil war" not until February

1915.[24] Eventually, however, Lenin was able to impose his larger vision upon the party's general line.

On 13–14 October (30 September–1 October), in Kamenev's country home near the junction of Mustamiaki, Finland, the Russian Bureau affirmed its support for the Theses on the War. On 15–17 November (2–4 November) an "All-Russian" party conference was convened in Petrograd (representatives from party sections in Ivanovo-Voznesensk, Khar'kov, Petrograd, and Riga were present) with the goal of coordinating policy on a national scale. The sessions opened in controversy as Kamenev led an attack against Lenin's defeatist thesis, but on the second day the conference was brought to an abrupt halt by a police raid, resulting in the arrest and eventual internal exile of Kamenev and the entire Duma fraction.[25] Significant issues remained unresolved, but at this point the party's antiwar orientation was well established. A tenuous link had been created between the Foreign Bureau, the Russian Bureau, and a number of regional sections, and a political line corresponding to that developed by Lenin had been approved. In Switzerland Lenin was able to use the "Answer to Vandervelde" as an expression of support for his position, and in Petrograd agitation in the spirit of the Theses on the War went forward. By February 1915 the Petersburg section had begun to issue a full-scale newsletter entitled *Proletarskii Golos* (Proletarian Voice) that in its first number ran the entire text of Lenin's "The War and Russian Social Democracy."[26]

The Bolsheviks simultaneously sought to place their viewpoint before an international audience. Accounts of Lenin's public presentations appeared in the socialist press, and through the collaboration of supporters, such as Shliapnikov in Sweden, Kollontai in Norway, Maksim Litvinov in London, and Liudmilla Stal' in Paris, the distribution of Bolshevik literature began to be coordinated on a European scale. Copies of "The War and Russian Social Democracy" were sent to the ISB, the Copenhagen conference of neutral socialists, and a number of social democratic newspapers. Shliapnikov spoke at the Swedish social democratic party congress on 24 November in Stockholm, and in February 1915, at the Conference of Socialists of the Allied Countries in London, Litvinov attempted to read a statement of protest before being interrupted and expelled.[27]

The degree of unity displayed by the Bolsheviks contrasted sharply with the remainder of the Russian labor movement, which after 4 August 1914 shattered into a welter of conflicting tendencies. The SRS, always extremely decentralized, split in two over the issue of national defense. At a meeting of foreign sections in Baugy-en-Clarens (a Russian émigré colony near Montreux) on 22 August 1914, confrontation between a defensist majority and an internationalist minority made consensus impossible.[28] Chernov and Mark Natanson led the left opposition, refusing support for either warring bloc and appealing to a "third force" of workers and peasants as the foundation for a democratic peace. The SR émigré journals *Mysl'* (Reflection) and *Zhizn'* (Life) also condemned the war, but limited their positive recommendations to preventive measures such as disarmament and arbitration.[29] The SR majority, which had supported the Vaillant/ Hardie general strike amendment at Copenhagen in 1910, turned its back on the past and opted for "defense of the Fatherland" in 1914.

The Menshevik organization, one of the mainstays of the Second International, fractured even more severely. On the right Plekhanov led a pro-Entente current that in the spring of 1915 briefly united with SR defensists in the *Prizyv* (Appeal) group.[30] A more nuanced variant of defensist opinion represented by the journals *Nashe Zaria* (Our Dawn) and *Delo* (The Cause) adopted a "neutral" posture but refused to undertake any actions likely to hinder the war effort.[31] The party's directive organs, the Organization Committee abroad and the Duma fraction headed by N. S. Chkheidze, evolved toward the opposition. Chkheidze and Pavel Aksel'rod called for popular protest and emphasized the demand for peace.[32] The party's left flank, represented by the Paris-based journals *Golos* (The Voice) and *Nashe Slovo* (Our Word) and the Menshevik Central Initiative Group in Petrograd, sought to give the slogan peace more revolutionary content.[33] Conflict between these various tendencies ensured that a coherent political initiative would not be forthcoming from the Mensheviks. Bolshevik unity was far from absolute, but it was much more impressive than that achieved by the party's leading rivals.

The coincidence of priorities between Bolsheviks and left Mensheviks led to a brief effort to create a common oppositional front. On 6 February 1915 the *Nashe Slovo* group sent letters to the Bolshevik Central Committee and the Menshevik Organization Committee, seeking to generate a joint statement for the upcoming London conference of Entente socialists. Lenin replied in a guardedly positive manner on 9 February but insisted that the Bolshevik platform serve as the basis for cooperation. Aksel'rod, on behalf of the Organization Committee, also seems to have responded openmindedly.[34] Encouraged, the *Nashe Slovo* group prepared a declaration of common principles containing elements drawn from both Bolshevik and Menshevik platforms.[35] The attempt at compromise seems to have pleased no one, however. No joint action at the London conference was forthcoming, and hopes to convene a unity conference quickly faded.

Rather than encouraging Lenin to look beyond the history of factional struggle within the RSDRP on the basis of a common commitment to internationalism, the collapse of 4 August seems to have confirmed him in the determination to remain uncompromising. Nor were Menshevik reactions to the prospect of cooperation entirely sanguine. "I have no desire to work with him [Lenin]," wrote Martov on 14 October 1914, "and I prefer that we [the Organization Committee] declare ourselves in this manner," and on 27 October "Lenin and company will compromise us more than they will prove useful." By 17 December Martov was denouncing Lenin's views as "demagoguery and stupidity."[36] On 5 February 1915, in a communiqué sent on behalf of the Organization Committee to the ISB, Aksel'rod referred sympathetically to some aspects of the political line represented in *Sotsial-Demokrat*, but criticized Lenin's "unconditional" insistence upon creating splinter organizations. By May Aksel'rod too was attacking Lenin as a "disorganizer . . . striving to carry over his beloved methods of sectarian struggle into the International."[37]

Bolshevik/Menshevik rivalry had come to express in microcosm larger differences building up within the antiwar opposition. Both groups shared a determination to combat defensism. However, as Lenin broadened his platform to include demands for organizational schisms, the creation of a new International, and the slogans "civil war" and "defeatism", collaboration became all but impossible. In October, speaking in rebuttal to Plekhanov in a public forum in Lausanne, Lenin hailed *Golos* as "the best social democratic newspaper in Europe" and emphasized the common ground that he shared with the left Mensheviks.[38] On 25 February 1915 Radek wrote to Aksel'rod and Martov urging them, as the leading internationalists within the Organization Committee, to resist more forcefully the chauvinist line defended by other Menshevik leaders in order "to save the party from disintegration."[39] But simultaneously Lenin be-

gan to rage over the "turnabout" of Martov and others. Aksel'rod became a particular target for abuse. On the same day on which he received the proposal for joint action from *Nashe Slovo*, Lenin wrote:
"Hope for agreement with them is small, for Aksel'rod, they say, is in
Paris, and Aksel'rod is a social chauvinist . . . we will see what is
dearer for *Nashe Slovo*—antichauvinism or accommodation with
Aksel'rod."[40]

In the end attempts to further Bolshevik/Menshevik cooperation
only served to reveal more clearly the chasm that divided the two factions. At issue were vital questions of orientation, and when forced
to choose, both sides preferred to reject concessions. Aksel'rod's
charge that Lenin sought to carry "sectarian" tactics into the International was partly correct, but it is important to note that in distinction to his opponents, Lenin's "sectarianism" was anchored upon a
unified party organization. The miserable fate of the Second International was a salutary lesson in the value of unity purchased at the
price of principle. Revolutionary politics demanded different kinds of
priorities, and these Lenin was determined to enforce even at the cost
of temporary isolation.

The culmination of efforts to unify the Bolsheviks behind a revolutionary program came on 27 February–5 March 1915 at a general
conference of Bolshevik sections abroad in Bern. Since the first wartime number of *Sotsial-Demokrat* had appeared on 1 November with
a statement of the leadership's position, a number of internal disputes had surfaced that threatened to decrease the effectiveness of
the party's agitation.[41] Theoretical quibbles moved the Paris and
Baugy-en-Clarens sections to request approval to publish independent journals. Organizational procedures were confused due to the
dislocations produced by the war. An attempt by Lenin to relocate
the Committee of Organizations Abroad from Paris to Bern was being
resisted by the Paris section, and essential bureaucratic tasks remained poorly delegated. The Bern conference was called in order to
resolve these problems and to reinforce the party's commitment to a
general line.[42]

The delegates who assembled at Bern were a representative sam-
pling of Bolshevik émigrés, in the main supportive of Lenin's program.[43] Organizational matters were managed without difficulty,
with the leadership imposing its will in all cases. The Committee of
Organizations Abroad was moved to Switzerland and restructured to

ensure fealty. Requests for permission to issue independent publications were turned down in favor of concentrating all available resources upon *Sotsial-Demokrat*. In general, the party abroad was placed firmly under the control of Lenin and his associates in Bern. Theoretical issues, on the other hand, generated heated debate and revealed significant divergences in outlook.

Lenin's keynote address included a strong plea for the concepts of defeatism and civil war. He restated the goal of a "United States of Europe" and the demand for a new, third International. His remarks also included a controversial thesis on the colonial question, arguing that in the age of imperialism social democrats must support revolutionary struggles for national self-determination waged by colonialized peoples even when the immediate goals of such struggles were bourgeois-democratic rather than socialist. The demand for militant opposition to the war was likewise reiterated, including a rejection of support for military appropriations and participation in bourgeois governments, condemnation of the *Burgfrieden*, the creation of underground organizations capable of pursuing an illegal struggle, encouragement of fraternization, and support for any and all popular antiwar actions.[44]

Criticisms issued from the sections of Toulouse, Montpellier, and Baugy-en-Clarens, each of which submitted its own project resolution.[45] All three dissenting resolutions took issue with the use of the term defeat and echoed Martov by posing a peace strategy as an alternative. The call for a United States of Europe, already a bone of contention prior to the war, was opposed on the grounds that it would merely encourage the emergence of a new and more powerful imperialist bloc. Speaking for the Baugy-en-Clarens section, Bukharin also objected to Lenin's references to a "democratic-republican" phase in a future Russian revolution. The issue, inherited from the postmortem appraisal of the revolution of 1905 that the Bolsheviks had never entirely resolved, seemed irrelevant in the context of 1915, but its implications were significant. In the spirit of the left radical critique Bukharin insisted that the struggle for socialism must be led by the organized proletariat of the advanced industrial states, with a socialist order as its goal. Lenin's image of the revolutionary process, which reached out to include tactical alliances with the peasantry on behalf of a democratic-republican minimum program in Russia and common cause with anticolonial movements worldwide, was in comparison quite iconoclastic and controversial. Though only touched upon at Bern, the issue would become an important focus of debate within the socialist left during the First World War.

Theoretical differences were not allowed to deflect the quest for a common program. Bukharin was appointed to the committee charged with drafting resolutions, and Lenin tempered several of his own more disputed contentions. In concluding resolutions the theme of defeatism was played down. The call for a United States of Europe was eliminated pending "further study" and eventually dropped altogether.[46] In other cases controversy was simply glossed over. The debate conducted at Bern was often intense, but in contrast to the Bolshevik/Menshevik rivalry it was argued out within a larger consensus that made unity achievable. Indeed, the Bern conference provides an excellent example of the principle of democratic centralism at work within the pre-1917 Bolshevik organization. Although Armand would write to Lenin shortly afterward that she feared an opposition emerging from the Baugy-en-Clarens group, no such development occurred.[47] The issues that had been swept under the rug at Bern would emerge again in other forums, but the Bolsheviks departed as a reasonably united party with a militant antiwar orientation. Willi Gautschi notes correctly that the results provided "a platform for the Bolsheviks in their subsequent conduct of the Zimmerwald Left, and . . . a point of departure for the founding of the Third International."[48]

As the first campaigns of the war ground to a close during the spring of 1915, the Bolsheviks found themselves uniquely placed to raise the banner of protest. The party remained what it had always been, the radical wing of a divided movement, repressed at home and suspect internationally. But the shock of 4 August had shattered traditional affiliations, and the party's strong stance on the war issue attracted attention. Russia was the largest and most populous country in Europe as well as a major belligerent, and the Bolsheviks possessed a significant mass base. The Bern conference bestowed legitimacy upon Lenin's program, and he was well aware that the war offered special opportunities. Within living memory both the Franco-Prussian war of 1870–71 and the Russo-Japanese war of 1904–05 had provided the spark for social revolution. That the present conflict, so vastly wider in scope, would lead in the same direction was the uncomplicated foundation upon which Lenin's convictions rested. With unshakable confidence he set out to engage his party in a struggle, not only against the war, but for the larger revolutionary promise that it contained.

J. P. Nettl has described Lenin's confrontation with the socialist collapse of 1914 as his "single most remarkable achievement."[49] Lenin was not alone, but his analysis stood out for the passionate force with which it condemned the corrupt opportunism of a movement upon whose banner was inscribed "Workers of the World, Unite!" but which in practice had lowered itself to acquiescence in a war whose coming it had foreseen and condemned. With unconcealed contempt the Bolshevik leader poured scorn upon open and disguised "social chauvinists" and leaped to the conclusion that 4 August 1914 represented a point of no return. Henceforward, the politics of revolutionary Marxism could not be pursued within the centrist consensus that had dominated the Second International. A new orientation was required, not yet clearly defined, but embodied in the goal of a third International. Lenin's indictment was unconditional, and the ability to speak for a unified party lent his views weight. For the first time in its history Bolshevism could aspire to become a force in the international arena. Lenin relished the prospect. On 17 October, responding to Shliapnikov's trepidations concerning the slogan of defeatism, he wrote: "Our task is now an absolute and open struggle with international opportunism. . . . This is an international task. It rests upon us, for there is no one else. We cannot put it aside."[50]

The Left Opposition

The Bolsheviks were not quite so alone as Lenin's remarks implied. During the war's first six months, despite demoralization and intimidation, a left opposition began to assert itself Europe-wide. The political forces which combined to constitute the opposition were extremely diverse, including intact parties, dissenting factions, and isolated individuals. Its program was at first inchoate, and even the best represented groups could not claim to speak for a substantial mass movement. As hopes for a quick end to hostilities faded, however, the extent of dissent increased. Within a groundswell of dissatisfaction and protest, revolutionary conceptions comparable to those developed by Lenin came to constitute a distinct current of analysis on the movement's left flank.

As had been the case during the Balkan wars of 1912, a standard for principled resistance was established by the small socialist parties of southeast Europe. Dragiša Lapčević and Triša Kaclerović of the Serbian Socialist party set the tone on 4 August by voting against war credits in their national parliament, arguing that Serbia was merely being used as a pawn in the imperial rivalries of the Great Powers.[51] Though for the time being they were considerably less exposed, most other Balkan socialist organizations reciprocated the gesture. Prior to Romania's entry into the war in August 1916, its social democratic party united behind a demand for neutrality.[52] Afterwards, the party split into defensist and internationalist factions, but the left wing, represented by Christian Rakovski, remained a voice for radical priorities within international forums. In Greece, where a united socialist party did not exist, the autonomous Socialist Workers Federation of Saloniki, headed by Abraham Benaroya and Aristotle Sideris, led an oppositionist current and dominated a Panhellenic socialist conference held in Athens during April 1915.[53]

Most radical among the Balkan groups and closest to Lenin was the "Narrow" wing of the Bulgarian movement. On 29 August the Narrows issued a ringing antiwar manifesto, and their agitational literature raised the demands for a new International, revolutionary mass actions, and the creation of a Balkan federation (a goal not dissimilar to Lenin's call for a United States of Europe). Party leader Dmitur Blagoev justified the intransigent rhetoric by arguing in October 1914 that the culmination of the war in social revolution had become an "inescapable necessity."[54] The revolutionary line was given an official imprimatur at an extraordinary party congress in Sofia during August 1915 and reiterated after Bulgaria's entry into the war in October.[55]

A high point for antiwar activism in the Balkans came in July 1915, when a second Inter-Balkan Socialist Conference was convened in Bucharest. Representatives of the Bulgarian, Greek, Romanian, and Serbian movements called for a revival of the International and a Balkan socialist federation and created a permanent executive with its seat in Bucharest. "If the International Bureau [ISB] refuses to assume its role," threatened Vasil Kolarov of the Narrows, "we will support any initiative that seeks to revive the International in the name of revolutionary socialism."[56] The Balkan parties were small, urban-based organizations, struggling to establish roots in traditional agricultural societies. They would be severely struck by repression in the course of the war. Their militant response to the war crisis was therefore all the more impressive, and the Narrows in particular provided an organizational base for the revolutionary left in an important European region.

Outside the Balkans the socialist parties of neutral states usually limited the extent of their opposition to passive gestures. Only on the extreme left, among youth groups or splinter organizations, did revolutionary alternatives appear. The Social Democratic party of Switzerland (SPS) voted on 3 August to support an extension of extraordinary power to the government during the crisis, in effect a neutralist variant of the *Burgfrieden*. More radical responses were confined to youth leagues, a small group of left radicals based in Zürich around the informal *Eintracht* (Concord) league, and radical pacifist organizations in the Jura *Neuchâtelois*. Geneva, Lausanne, and La Chaux-de-Fonds (home of the revolutionary newspaper *La Sentinelle*) also became centers for the publication of oppositionist tracts.[57] The Socialist party of America opted for a bland neutrality, though a left wing led by Eugene Debs pushed for stronger antiwar engagement. Only small, sectarian organizations such as the Socialist Propaganda League, founded early in 1915 as a vehicle for antiwar agitation, the Socialist Labor party of North America under the idiosyncratic leadership of Daniel DeLeon, the anarcho-syndicalist Industrial Workers of the World, and émigré leagues led by Louis Boudin and Ludwig Lore aligned with the revolutionary left.[58] The Socialist party of Spain initially supported strict neutrality but shifted ground under the influence of predominantly pro-Entente elite opinion. In reaction a so-called "minoritarian" opposition current took hold within several party sections and the Young Socialists of Madrid youth league. Much closer to Lenin in spirit were the Spanish anarcho-syndicalists, strongly rooted in the mass movement and uncompromisingly antimilitarist.[59]

A more significant bloc of neutralist opinion emerged from the Dutch and Scandinavian parties. Led by domineering personalities such as Hjalmar Branting of Sweden, Thorvald Stauning of Denmark, and Pieter Troelstra of the Netherlands, the "northern neutrals"

remained skeptical of popular activism and backed their governments in the effort to remain outside the conflict (Stauning joined
the Danish government in October 1916). Though pledged to a negotiated peace, the Scandinavian socialist majorities shied away from
ideological controversy and preferred to approach the crisis, in the
words of Martin Grass, as "less a theoretical than a practical problem."[60]

These were on balance extremely cautious policies, and as a result
the revolutionary wing of the movement received considerable impetus. In Sweden the leftist Social Democratic Youth League had
crossed swords with its parent party on several occasions prior to
1914 and could claim the allegiance of thirteen parliamentary deputies, three daily newspapers, and a number of charismatic leaders,
including the poet Carl Zeth Höglund and the mayor of Stockholm
Carl Lindhagen. A national congress of the socialist party in November 1914 gave rise to a public confrontation, as Höglund attacked
Branting for refusing to criticize the defensist orientation of the SPD
majority. At its own conference on 29–30 December, the Youth
League threatened to run separate candidates for public office should
the party fail to speak out more forcefully against the war. Subsequently, twenty-two parliamentary deputies voted against military
appropriations.[61] Höglund's outspokenness attracted Lenin's attention, and though the thrust of the Swedish youth leader's politics
remained an idealistic antimilitarism that Lenin scorned, the two
men would become allies of convenience in international forums
during and after the war.[62] In Denmark and Norway socialist youth
leagues also became focal points for dissent. On 23 February 1915 a
successful antiwar rally was staged in Christiania (Oslo). Kollontai
praised the ambiance within Norwegian working-class circles, which
she interpreted as hostile to the official socialist leadership, and noted
sympathy for the slogan "civil war."[63]

The most outspoken opposition to Troelstra and the SDAP majority
emerged from the SDP "Tribunists." Already on 1 August an SDP agitational leaflet made use of the phrase "war on war," and in the following weeks the party joined with pacifist and anarcho-syndicalist
groups in a "United Labor Organization" with a radical antimilitarist
line. The SDP functioned as a conduit for antiwar agitation in Flanders and northern Germany, and beginning in March chairperson
David Wijnkoop maintained a regular correspondence with Lenin.[64]

The Tribunist publicist and poet Herman Gorter also produced a major theoretical investigation of the International's collapse that in its uncompromising radicalism stood comparison with Lenin's work. Though written entirely by Gorter, the text of *Imperialism, the World War, and Social Democracy* was edited and approved by a committee of Tribunist leaders, including Wijnkoop, Anton Pannekoek, and Willem van Ravestejn, at a session in Bussum (near Amsterdam) on 30 October 1914. The finished product may therefore be said to reflect the party's collective effort to come to terms with the policy of 4 August. Gorter treats the problem historically, tracing the International's evolution over several decades and identifying a shift from an "heroic period" of struggle and real accomplishment to a phase of bureaucratic stagnation after 1900. In this prism the theory of revisionism is dismissed as little more than a shallow rationalization for the alienation of social democratic bureaucrats from the masses and their loss of will to confrontation (*strijdlust*). The failure of the center (whose leaders Gorter calls "radicals") to maintain the primacy of extraparliamentary mass actions, to reject the principle of national defense, and to make a clean break with reformism is described as a disguised capitulation leaving the movement disarmed at the decisive moment. In anguished passages reflecting deep disillusionment Gorter attacks the "cowardice" and "servility" of reformers and radicals alike, whose comportment he compares to that of the German liberals of 1848. The threat of united action by labor, he insists, might still have prevented a decision for war. Failing that, principle and a concern for the movement's long-term viability demanded protest and resistance regardless of the consequences.[65]

Gorter's hopes for a revival are placed upon a third group of "revolutionary Marxists" concentrated on the left wing of the SPD (in addition to Luxemburg, to whom his book is dedicated, he names Liebknecht, Franz Mehring, Pannekoek, and Clara Zetkin). His six-point "program of struggle" may profitably be compared with Lenin's Theses on the War as a blueprint for a revolutionary antiwar program. In the age of imperialism, Gorter proposes, capitalism had become a world system that could only perpetuate itself through intensified international aggression. The war represented a contest for hegemony between opposing imperialist blocs whose outcome was of no interest whatsoever to the proletariat. Revolutionary Marxists should therefore reject class collaboration, oppose war credits, sponsor popu-

lar protest actions, and work toward the creation of a new, revolutionary International. Only by looking beyond the "outdated national
mentality" that had produced the *Burgfrieden* to "mass actions by the
international proletariat" could a strategy commensurate with the
exigencies of imperialism be crafted. Though acknowledging the
weakness of the left, Gorter holds fast to his premises; revolutionary
mass actions inspired by proletarian internationalism were the sole
means by which the war could effectively be combated and the
conscience of socialism redeemed.[66]

Lenin received a copy of Gorter's *Imperialism, the World War, and
Social Democracy* shortly after the appearance of the first Dutch
edition in March 1915. He immediately wrote to both Gorter and
Wijnkoop with congratulations and praise.[67] Gorter's analysis corre-
sponded to Lenin's in most essentials, but for a number of reasons the
Tribunists would not play the role within the international movement assumed by the Bolsheviks. Gorter was not a political leader of
Lenin's stature. His work lacked a tactical dimension and was predominantly pessimistic, a jeremiad directed against the SPD majority.
After its publication Gorter withdrew from active political work for
two full years in order to devote himself to literary composition. The
SDP, like the Bolsheviks and the Bulgarian Narrows, was an independent party with a consistently revolutionary outlook, but it did not
offer a solid base for politics in the international arena. During the
war the Tribunist leadership would repeatedly find itself paralyzed
by internal differences, and the group lacked a significant popular
following. Not least, the Netherlands was a small neutral country.
Really effective oppositional activity, as Gorter himself acknowledged, could only emerge from within the major belligerent powers.

The socialists of the Entente and Central Powers were subjected to
intense pressures to rally behind a civil truce. The patriotic press
portrayed the consequences of defeat in lurid terms, the example of
the workers' sacrifices at the fronts was held up in admonition, and
reprisals were threatened against resisters. Threats soon passed over
to outright repression, but the growth of the left was not prevented.
Within months defensist majorities found themselves challenged by
a variety of oppositional tendencies, including a revolutionary current on the extreme left.

Already divided on the eve of the war, the British labor movement
split even more complexly after 4 August. During August the British

trade unions accepted an industrial truce for the duration of hostilities, and the National Executive of the Labour party agreed to a policy of national reconciliation, including Labour participation in military recruitment campaigns. The powerful umbrella organizations of the British left thus opted four square for defensism. The most significant exception was the Independent Labour party. As ILP members of the National Executive, Keir Hardie and W. C. Anderson spoke out against support for recruitment, and on 7 August the ILP's Ramsay MacDonald resigned as chairperson of the Parliamentary Labour party in protest. On 6 August the party's central organ *The Labour Leader* carried a double headline reading "Down With the War," and on 11 August the national council published a manifesto decrying the abandonment of internationalism.[68] But the ILP also asserted the legitimacy of national defense and turned its back on revolutionary rhetoric. The party's intention was to reject the war's barbarity but not to oppose Britain's role unilaterally. During August 1914 a number of prominent intellectuals close to the ILP, including Norman Angell, MacDonald, and Bertrand Russell, formed a "Union of Democratic Control" as a vehicle for antiwar agitation, with a platform calling for a negotiated peace based upon democratic principles. Membership grew rapidly, reaching over 300,000 by the autumn of 1915, but the Union remained a liberal pressure group only marginally linked to the socialist left.[69]

The Marxist British Socialist party also fractured, as its founder and leader Henry Hyndman moved to embrace defensism, while an "Internationalist" faction led by Albert Inkpin, Edwin Fairchild, and Joe Fineberg carried opposition into the party rank and file. In February 1915 the BSP's London section condemned the leadership, bringing the party to the verge of a schism.[70] Further to the left the DeLeonist Socialist Labour party (SLP) and Socialist party of Great Britain adopted strong antiwar appeals, but these were sectarian splinter groups without real influence. It was a poor but predictable showing from the perspective of the revolutionary left. Litvinov wrote to Lenin from London in January 1915 that "in England a left tendency does not exist."[71] A revival of strike activity during 1915 in the Clyde river valley near Glasgow, where David Kirkwood, John Maclean, and Tom Gallacher, respectively of the ILP, BSP, and SLP, led workers in a series of actions in defiance of the established unions, was the exception that proved the rule. Though the Clydeside events attracted considerable attention, they were isolated and untypical.[72] The real news through 1915 was the degree of support for the civil truce evinced by British labor.

In France, with ten departments occupied and Paris threatened, the left remained virtually invisible during the war's first months. After Jaurès' assassination on 31 July, the SFIO swung immediately toward the *union sacrée*. The antimilitarist traditions of the anarcho-syndicalist General Confederation of Labor (CGT), which had culminated during 1912 with a bitter campaign against the extension of military service to three years, also melted away. Convening on 2 August in special session, the CGT's national council voted unanimously to support national defense. In the years to come, torn by dissension, the organization would decline precipitously, with sharp drops in membership and revenues.[73]

The first significant public protest was raised by Romain Rolland (to be awarded the Nobel Peace Prize for 1916) in an essay entitled *"Au-dessus de la mêlée"* published in the *Journal de Genève* on 22 September 1914, an emotional outpouring infused with a spirit of pacifist humanism. Rolland's essay served as a catalyst, and thereafter opposition among socialist party sections and trade union federations became more visible.

During October resistance took on more coordinated forms, as a small group of militants began to meet informally in the Paris office of the syndicalist journal *La Vie Ouvrière*. In December its editor Pierre Monatte demonstrably resigned from the CGT National Executive, declaring in an open letter that the government's war aims were "illusions" and decrying socialist acquiescence.[74] The Federation of Metal Workers and its secretary Alphonse Merrheim stepped forward to lead dissent, and on 1 May 1915 its newsletter *L'Union des Métaux* ran a special edition urging international cooperation in the cause of peace.[75] At the CGT national conference on 15 August 1915, a resolution sponsored by Merrheim and Albert Bourderon entitled *"Cette guerre n'est pas notre guerre"* received twenty-seven votes against seventy-nine for chairperson Lèon Jouhaux's defensist motion.[76] Opposition within the SFIO also gathered momentum slowly, spearheaded by the Federation of Haute-Vienne (Limoges) and by a substantial minority in the Federation of the Seine led by Jean Longuet. In May 1915 the Federation of Haute-Vienne circulated an open letter among party sections that criticized defensism. At a session of the SFIO national council on 14 July, Adrien Pressemanne, Paul Mistral, and Paul Faure overcame heckling to read out denunciations of the leadership.[77] The left within the CGT and SFIO was not overtly revolutionary; Merrheim described its caution as a "stab in the back" to Liebknecht and the more outspoken Germans.[78] Organizations calling for a revolutionary alternative, including the *Nashe Slovo* and *La Vie Ouvrière* groups and a "Women's Action Committee for Peace and Against Chauvinism" founded by SFIO member Louise Saumoneau, were small and isolated. But contestation in France was rooted in the mass organizations of the left and reflected a growing malaise with the *union sacrée*.

A partial exception to the trend toward defensism was provided by Italy. Having already confronted the problem of war during the Libyan campaign of 1911, both the PSI and the Italian Labor Confederation (CGL) opposed entry into the European conflict under any circumstances.[79] The PSI's resolution was reinforced during the autumn, when a "revolutionary interventionist" faction calling for Italian participation in the war sprang up around the volatile personality of Benito Mussolini.[80] On 21 October Mussolini was dismissed from his position as editor of the party's central organ *Avanti!* (Forward!) and on 24 November was expelled from the party. Beginning in December, under the editorship of Giancinto Serrati, *Avanti!* became a clarion for the antiwar left.

Though the elimination of the interventionist wing united the PSI behind an antiwar position, friction remained concerning the degree of resistance that was realistic. A debate between moderates and radicals surfaced at a session of the PSI directorate (*direzione*) on 16 January 1915 in Florence. After a series of acrimonious exchanges a commitment to neutrality was reasserted, but proposals by the left to prepare for active resistance in the event that war was declared were voted down. One week prior to Italy's decision to join the Entente, on 15–16 May, at a joint session of the PSI directorate, parliamentary fraction, and CGL national council in Bologna, these priorities were reiterated as the slogan *né aderire né sabotare* (neither support nor sabotage) was approved over the protest of Serrati and the left.[81] The phrase summarized a cautious strategy of passive dissent that did not always correspond to the militant spirit of the rank and file. Still, the Italian movement had withstood the test of war more impressively than most of its counterparts. It had expelled its interventionist minority, rallied as an organization behind a position critical of the government, and refused actively to endorse the war effort. The revolutionary left, albeit in the minority, retained access to party forums where it could agitate for its own priorities.

Within Italy's Austro-Hungarian rival, the status of the opposition was considerably more complex. The labor movement of the multi-national Habsburg empire had been reorganized along ethnic lines, and the extent of opposition differed considerably from one region to another. The Austrian German party, led by Victor Adler, opted over-whelmingly for defensism. What resistance could be mustered was confined to a small circle around Friedrich Adler in Vienna. Among non-Germanic minorities enthusiasm for the war was less evident. In September the Bohemian and Slovakian party groups criticized the Vienna leadership for its "chauvinism," and the Italian section based in the Trentino protested loudly against the *Burgfrieden*.[82]

Radical opposition was more visible in the Polish provinces of the three central European empires.[83] On 2–3 August the Social Democracy of the Kingdom of Poland and Lithuania (SDKPiL)-Main Presidium, the PPS-L, and the Polish Jewish Workers' Bund called for a general strike to resist mobilization and attempted to organize an interparty council in Warsaw as a forum for antiwar action. The SDKPiL-Regional Presidium defended a revolutionary program close to that of Lenin in its journal *Gazeta Robotnitsa* (The Worker's Gazette), two numbers of which were issued in Zürich during the war. On 1 May 1915 the SDKPiL-Regional Presidium circulated a broadsheet in Warsaw including the slogan "civil war" and at a rump party congress convened in June approved a strong antiwar resolution.[84] Elsewhere within the vast czarist empire, the Lettish Social Democratic party, the United Jewish Workers' Bund, and a Geneva-based Ukranian group known as *Borotba* (Struggle) adopted revolutionary platforms.[85]

These various manifestations of dissent offered dramatic alternatives to defensism, but they emerged from small radical factions and, if anything, served to call attention to the weakness of the left within the more established mass parties. For contemporaries it was here, and above all within the SPD, the bastion of left radicalism and undisputed leader of the Second International, that the policy of 4 August needed to be addressed. Zinoviev provided a representative evaluation in May 1915 when he described the German left as "the only hope for the internationalist elements of all lands."[86]

In a memoir Kollontai spoke dramatically of the "loneliness and isolation" of oppositionists in Berlin after the shock of 4 August.[87] The left was clearly caught unprepared, but it was not intimidated into inactivity. On the evening of 4 August a group of militants gathered in Luxemburg's Berlin apartment, agreed to work together to oppose the *Burgfrieden*, and sent telegrams to over three hundred party members requesting their support. Suddenly deprived of its institutional prerogatives, the German left confronted the primordial tasks of developing programmatic guidelines relevant to the present crisis and rebuilding organizational ties. The former task was accomplished almost single-handedly by Liebknecht, who by launching a one-man campaign against the policy of 4 August turned himself into the leading symbol of socialist resistance Europe-wide, "the most popular man in the trenches" according to the begrudging appraisal of Kautsky.[88] In August and September Liebknecht bombarded the SPD executive with letters of protest, spoke out publicly against the *Burgfrieden* during a visit to Belgium, and on 2 December shattered the SPD's artificially imposed unity by casting a lone dissenting vote against the government's second war credits bill.[89]

Liebknecht's opposition was emotional and sometimes histrionic, more often expressed in rhetoric than in measured analysis. The absence of theoretical pretensions probably only served to reinforce the impact of his selfless crusading, capsulized in powerful slogans such as "war on war," "the main enemy is at home," and "civil war, not civil truce." Liebknecht was the heart of the German left. Its intellectual focus was Berlin, where by December a core of activists had begun to meet regularly as an opposition forum. Significant centers of contestation grew up around several regional centers as well.[90] In Stuttgart the SPD organization had already split by the autumn of 1914 in a battle for control of the local party organ, and in Hamburg and Bremen autonomous left radical groups attacked the center with a renewed sense of purpose.

The transition from the left radical critique of the prewar period to an oppositional posture following 4 August 1914 was best illustrated by the Hamburg left radicals Heinrich Laufenberg and Fritz Wolffheim in an important brochure published in November 1914 with the title *Imperialism and Democracy*. Much of their argument consists of ex post facto justification and is concerned with countering the premises of defensism in light of the left radical position during the revisionist controversy. The war is therefore characterized as a "natural product of imperialist development," and the motives of the belligerents castigated as uniformly aggressive and hegemonic. Capitalist imperialism, Laufenberg and Wolffheim propose, destroyed the foundations of reformism by making an enlargement of democracy impossible and prepared the ground for an era of international crisis that would see a "scrics" of world wars before reaching its denouement. Under these circumstances the goal of socialism could only be pursued in the context of a new International committed to transcending the bourgeois state and building a "global community of struggle."[91] Like Lenin and Gorter, the Hamburg left radicals assigned primary blame for the collapse of 4 August to the revisionist distortion of Marxism and called for a settling of accounts.

The SPD majority reacted to such dissent with an intolerance that only served to aggravate tensions. When in February 1915 the opposition managed to achieve a majority within the SPD fraction in the Prussian regional parliament (*Landtag*) and used its position to criticize the conduct of the war, a furor erupted that revealed nearly absolute polarization.[92] Political rivalry assumed a popular dimension on 1 May when demonstrations were organized in defiance of the leadership's request for a moratorium on such actions and on 28 May when a small protest demonstration before the Reichstag in Berlin was dispersed by armed force. In a climate of growing unrest repression against the left was intensified, often to the tacit satisfaction of the SPD majority. In February Luxemburg was incarcerated on the basis of a prewar conviction and Liebknecht, despite his legal immunity as a Reichstag deputy, was conscripted into the army. More arrests of radical leaders, including Zetkin and Wilhelm Pieck, followed in the course of the year.

An important step toward autonomy for the German left was taken on 15 April when the Berlin opposition published the first number of a theoretical journal entitled *Die Internationale* (The International). In the lead article Luxemburg declared the demise of the Second International, ridiculed the leaders of the SPD center as "obliging maidens" lacking the courage to act in accordance with their convictions, and posed the choice between a party of class struggle or class collaboration.[93] Dubbing itself the International Group (*Gruppe Internationale*), the Berlin opposition henceforward would function as an organized center of factional resistance.

The appearance of *Die Internationale* encouraged clearer demarcation within the movement as a whole. On 19 June the SPD center attempted to distance itself from defensism by publishing an article entitled "The Task at Hand" (*Das Gebot der Stunde*) in the *Leipziger Volkszeitung* over the signatures of Bernstein, Haase, and Kautsky. The article questioned the government's claim to purely defensive motives, asserted that annexationist war aims would not be supported, and urged the party to work for a negotiated peace. The SPD executive responded four days later with a vague peace program of its own.[94] Nothing came of either initiative, but the exchange was revealing. Under pressure from a reviving left the center had been moved away from the assumptions of the *Burgfrieden* and the defensist right had been forced to guard its flank with a gesture toward negotiations.

Organized opposition appeared to the left of the International Group as well, notably within a group of Berlin intellectuals led by Julian Borchardt and rather grandly designated as the International Socialists of Germany. During 1914 and 1915 Borchardt's theoretical journal *Lichtstrahlen* (Rays of Light) became, so far as the censor would allow, a forum for revolutionary analysis. Borchardt himself insistently argued that the policy of 4 August made ongoing collaboration with the SPD majority both undesirable and impossible. "The Task at Hand," he proposed, represented an attempt to resurrect the prewar centrist consensus where what was required was a ruthless drawing of accounts. An autonomous left would grow out of the fight against defensism, but "a struggle against the right cannot be carried on without a simultaneous struggle against the conceptions of comrade Kautsky . . . a struggle for the unification of all left elements within the party."[95]

An even more sweeping critique emerged from the pen of Radek, closely linked to the Bremen left radical group and, as a regular contributor to the *Berner Tagwacht* (Bern Reveille) and other left journals, an intellectual force behind the German left radical tendency. More than any other revolutionary theorist, Radek emphasized the degree to which the policy of 4 August was the triumph and logical conclusion of revisionism. What reformists sought to build, he suggested, was the "bourgeois-national labor party," a party that would necessarily be compromised and corrupted by its search for concessions within the parameters of the bourgeois state and the imperialist world order. However well-intentioned, reformism could not build a foundation for fundamental social change nor deflect capitalism away from its inherent tendency toward crisis and decline. For Radek the war itself provided the clearest possible refutation of such conceptions. It displayed the vulnerability of the capitalist world order, the futility of hopes for a peaceful transition to socialism, and the inability of bourgeois-democratic norms to perpetuate themselves under the aegis of imperialism. Radek too raised the specter of revolution as the war's most probable outcome, led by a proletariat that had been conditioned by suffering "to hear the call of revolutionary socialism with a transformed consciousness."[96]

Arguments such as these grew out of a raging controversy that by the summer of 1915 was pushing European social democracy toward schism. Rivalry within the SPD had come to reflect, in a somewhat more developed form, fissures opening up within the entire international movement. Lenin's call "to transform the imperialist war into a civil war for socialism" was not that of a voice crying in the wilderness. It was reciprocated by revolutionary Marxists throughout Europe, expressed in varying forums and with different intonations, but pointing in a common direction. The left opposition was still small, but as the preceding survey has attempted to demonstrate, it was very much alive, with broad international representation and the fundaments of a political analysis. The miniscule left groups that sprang up independently during the period of disorientation that followed the triumph of the policy of 4 August would eventually serve as the building blocks for a significant internationalist alternative.

Si pacem vis para bellum

During the first year of the world war, encouraged by the stalemate at the fronts and the intolerance of defensist majorities, a social democratic opposition gradually established itself. The extent of active resistance was quite modest, and the echo that it managed to call forth on the popular level was virtually inaudible. As a tendency within the social democratic movement, however, the growth of an opposition was very significant indeed. In attempting to challenge the policy of 4 August, the left was forced to address fundamental issues that the Second International's centrist consensus had obscured. The open-ended debate that resulted revealed deep and enduring divisions and prepared the way for a challenge to the movement's unity.

Recent Western historiography, often reacting against exaggerated or hagiographic Soviet accounts, has tended to emphasize the wartime left's weakness and marginality. Its leaders are characterized as isolated intellectuals, blind to the real aspirations of those they claimed to represent, engaged in "sterile squabbling in theoretical disputes."[97] Such conclusions may provide a certain corrective, but they verge on caricature and exaggeration in their own right. Although the revolutionary left found itself momentarily pushed aside by the wave of nationalism that swept through Europe in August 1914, to describe attempts at redressment as "sterile" seems unwarranted. Suddenly reduced to a core of dedicated activists and with many illusions shattered, the socialist left was forced to confront more realistically its own prospects and limitations. The result was one of the most intense and creative debates in the entire history of socialist thought, a debate about alternative visions of revolutionary transformation in the circumstances of the twentieth century.

The opposition's common denominators were a rejection of the *Burgfrieden* and a desire to resurrect socialist internationalism by engaging in positive work for peace. Beyond these fundaments contrasting strategic perspectives emerged. Moderate leaders such as Kautsky, Longuet, MacDonald, and Stauning proposed a "curative" program designed to rebuild the International by forwarding a negotiated peace without victors or vanquished. In contrast, revolutionaries such as Gorter, Lenin, Luxemburg, and Radek urged a tactic of confrontation that could transform the war into a struggle for socialism. For theorists such as the Mensheviks Aksel'rod and Martov the goals of "peace" and "revolution" were not necessarily mutually exclusive. They recommended a long-term peace strategy that sought to use work for peace in order to strengthen and radicalize the socialist mass movement. It was in the give-and-take between these contrasting conceptions, vividly argued out within the socialist left press and in public forums of the opposition, that revolutionary analysis became sharpened and refined.

Contemporaries perceived 4 August 1914 as the end of an era. With the workers displaying a firm allegiance to the institutions of the bourgeois state, it was observed, the age of barricades and romantic internationalism could safely be put to rest. Henceforward, social democracy would remain national in scale and reformist in inspiration. Within months of the war's outbreak the growth of the left opposition exposed such conclusions as premature. The revolutionary left was no more marginal after 4 August than before. In the course of the war it would become considerably more clear-sighted. Wartime controls had much more effect upon legal political action than they did upon revolutionary means, and the cumulative burden of the fighting greatly increased popular disaffection. As Lenin and others confidently predicted, the war would indeed eventually culminate in social revolution. By shattering Europe's political stability, destroying the International, discrediting revisionism, and forcing a reconsideration of inherited assumptions, the war gave revolutionary currents within the labor movement a tremendous boost.

In the first attempts to come to terms with the crisis by Lenin, Gorter, Luxemburg, and other revolutionary theorists, the beginning of a major reassessment may be discerned. Though neither systematic nor coordinated, a core of analysis was being established around which the left could be assembled. Several premises set this analysis apart. The war's origins were perceived to lie in the contradictions of advanced capitalism. What was unfolding was not a contest for culture or democracy, but a predatory war of imperialism. The International's surrender to nationalism was considered to be a direct consequence of revisionism; at issue was not merely a tactical choice, but the long-term orientation of the socialist labor movement. Internationalism was essential to the meaning of socialism, and its premises demanded that the war be opposed by rejecting the *Burgfrieden* and supporting popular protest actions. Most important, the struggle against the war must be linked to the restoration of an authentically revolutionary Marxism, inspired by the maximalist goals of visionary internationalism and human emancipation.

Spokespersons for the left opposition consciously identified with their movement's insurrectionary tradition. Marx's observation that no ruling class in history had ever surrendered privileges voluntarily was taken seriously, and the prospects for achieving meaningful change without revolutionary violence evaluated pessimistically. All the same, the issue of insurrectionary tactics did not lie at the center of the radical critique of the policy of 4 August. Most oppositionists rejected a Blanquist fixation upon frontal assault and concurred that for the moment a revolutionary situation did not exist. The point was not blindly to instigate violence but to achieve what Lenin called a "line of work" based upon a radical alternative. What the war crisis had made clear was that revolutionary politics did not rest upon piecemeal reform, but rather a commitment to structural transformation. Even as embattled minorities the left could keep that commitment alive, expose betrayals, and prepare for a day of reckoning. Nor was there any need for undue pessimism. The twin convulsions of war and revolution had been linked throughout history. Tactical flexibility was deemed to be essential, but in contrast to the revisionists frontal assaults were not ruled out a priori.

Within the gestating left opposition Lenin and the Bolsheviks occupied a special place, not only after the October revolution, but from the first day of the war. Lenin's response to the crisis stood out for its forcefulness and consistency. The Bolsheviks were not a sect, and with a unified organization, émigré cadres dispersed throughout the European continent, and a foreign bureau in neutral Switzerland at the nerve center of what would become the socialist antiwar movement, they were well placed to serve as a goad to radical elements elsewhere. As the question of antiwar action moved beyond isolated protest and into international socialist forums, Lenin was appropriately positioned to lead a revolutionary alternative.

3

The Zimmerwald
Movement

Workers, fight on till the last drop of
blood!
The earth, a mountain of scrap iron
Mixed with the rags and tatters of
humanity.
In the midst of the madness,
Sober and alone, appeared Zimmer-
wald.

—Vladimir Maiakovskii, *Vladimir
Il'ich Lenin*

EVEN against the background of the war international cooperation remained a goal that social democrats felt loath to abandon. Though the paralysis of the ISB made consultations organized through the mechanisms of the Second International unlikely, to the point where Kautsky could argue that the International was in essence an "instrument of peace" that should not be expected to function during wartime, efforts to renew contacts independently sprang up from a variety of sources.[1] Soon a proliferation of conference initiatives became another reflection of the disarray into which war had thrown the movement.

The first joint actions were undertaken by representatives of the neutral states. An offer to sponsor an international conference made by the Socialist party of America on 19 September went nowhere, but on 27 September, after hurried consultations, delegations from the PSI and SPS came together in Lugano in the Swiss Ticino. The Lugano conference's first purpose was to underline socialist support for Swiss and Italian neutrality. Mario Ferri of the SPS, seconded by Filippo Turati and Giuseppe Modigliani of the PSI, countered more radical voices by insisting upon Switzerland's right to self-defense should its sovereignty be threatened. A final declaration nonetheless condemned the war as "the result of the imperialist policy of the great powers," and urged work for peace. Lugano also posed the more ambitious goal of reconciliation within the movement, with SPS veteran Hermann Greulich sponsoring a well-received motion to convene an international conference of socialists from the neutral states in Switzerland.[2]

While Greulich's proposal percolated within the SPS, international initiatives passed into the hands of the northern neutrals group, which conducted regional conferences of the Scandinavian and Dutch parties in Stockholm on 11 October and Copenhagen on 17–18 January 1915. At Copenhagen the preventive antiwar strategy of the prewar International was revived, including demands for international arbitration, disarmament, and the abolition of secret diplomacy. The war was deplored, but action for peace outside the purview of the ISB rejected as inappropriate. Copenhagen also created friction between the northern neutrals and the Swiss and Italian parties, both of which sought to broaden participation to include all neutral states, and ultimately refused invitations.[3] The initiatives of the autumn and winter, and the disputes to which they gave rise, revealed that neutral opinion was far from uniform. Divided by contrasting pro-German or pro-Entente sympathies, the issue of national defense, and varying degrees of commitment to the integrity of the prewar movement, the socialist representatives of neutral states did not constitute an effective bloc.

The defensist wing of the movement also sought to guard its internationalist credentials. Conferences of the Socialists of the Allied Countries in London on 14 February 1915 and Socialists of the Central Powers in Vienna on 12–13 April affirmed contrasting variants of the policy of 4 August and attempted to justify the quest for military victory in the name of universal values. These painfully divisive sessions underlined how far the movement had fallen from its former ideals, and encouraged the attempt to build an alternative. The continued inactivity of the ISB, the inadequacy of neutral initiatives, and the spectacle of defensist socialism's uncritical support for the war combined to create a political vacuum that only the left opposition was in a position to fill.

Despite some doubts about the propriety of independent action, efforts to stimulate international socialist action for peace gained ground steadily, culminating with the conference at Zimmerwald, Switzerland, on 5–8 September 1915. Zimmerwald was the first important assembly of oppositionists during the war to unite representatives of hostile powers and a major landmark in the modern history of socialism. The conference was an extraordinary session, undertaken in spite of resistance on the part of the ISB. It launched a movement of protest against the war to which the disparate elements that comprised the socialist left could rally and thereby reproduced on the international level the divisions already gaping within national parties. Perhaps most importantly, Zimmerwald provided a context within which contrasting conceptions of the role of the opposition could be articulated and defended.

The original source of the Zimmerwald project was the special relationship between the PSI and SPS born at Lugano. The organizers' intention was to reclaim the international movement as a force for peace, not to challenge its unity, and from the outset the Zimmerwald alternative contained an important strain of restorationism. Its first principle was that of Martov's peace strategy—the presumption that by rallying around the common denominator of peace, the movement could be recalled to a state of grace and the stain of defensism erased. An equally cogent, though usually unstated goal was to neutralize the extreme left, widely considered to be dangerously volatile and inveterately sectarian. The results provided a classic example of unintended consequences. A left bloc laboriously assembled by Lenin appeared at the conference as a distinct minority, but it made a considerable impact. Instead of contributing to a new basis for social democratic unity, Lenin and his supporters were outspoken in demanding a clean break with the compromised past. For the first time an independently organized international tendency enunciated its disdain for the premises of the prewar movement. Rather than encouraging a return to the fold, the Zimmerwald conference became the springboard for a challenge that would permanently divide the left.

"The International is Dead! Long Live the International!"

During the spring of 1915 Zimmerwald was foreshadowed by small conferences organized within the International's semiautonomous women's and youth sections. Convened independently of the ISB, these sessions brought together socialist representatives of warring states, condemned the *Burgfrieden*, and established patterns of interaction that would become characteristic for the socialist left thereafter. Unencumbered by the weighty responsibility to speak for the entire movement, and with their own traditions of resistance to militarism, the women's and youth sections were logical rallying points for the left opposition.

The Second International was ground-breaking in its support for women's rights. A serious effort was made to integrate women's issues into political analysis, women's conferences were convened in association with the International's general congresses in 1907 and 1910, and a special administrative apparatus was put in place headed by an International Women's Bureau. In its 1910 Copenhagen resolution, the "Women's International" declared the "special duty" of women to resist war, located the underlying cause of conflict between nations in "the social contradictions called into being by the capitalist mode of production," and argued that a lasting peace could only be achieved through the victory of socialism.[4] With the coming of war, efforts to generate some kind of women's action for peace were launched immediately.

One such effort was undertaken by Inessa Armand on behalf of the Bolshevik women's journal *Rabotnitsa* (Working Woman), who during November drafted a proposal for an unofficial assembly of women representing the revolutionary left.[5] Armand's suggestion was taken up by the International Women's Bureau and its secretary Clara Zetkin. In late November Zetkin prepared an appeal "To the Socialist Women of all Nations," which was published in the *Berner Tagwacht* on 10 December and distributed as a leaflet in Germany, calling for coordinated action by women to oppose the war.[6] Zetkin did not share Armand's fixation upon the "revolutionary" left. As secretary of the international bureau her first concern was to provide a common ground for a challenge to defensism. "It would be rather difficult to draw a line between right and left among women," she wrote to Armand during January: "Many of them do not know what side they are on; others will waver; and others will absolutely refuse to participate in a conference of 'radical' women only."[7] Zetkin quickly took charge of preparations for a conference, leaving the Bolsheviks no choice but to acquiesce to her more pragmatic approach. The thirty-odd delegates that eventually assembled in the Bern *Volkshaus* (People's House) on 26 March included a substantial German representation, Bolshevik and Menshevik members of the RSDRP, a British delegation representing the ILP and the British International Women's Council, and individuals from the SDKPiL-Regional Presidium, France, the Netherlands, Switzerland, and Italy. Among them, only Anna Kamenska of the SDKPiL supported the Bolsheviks, while a clear majority aligned with Zetkin and her emphasis upon moderation.[8]

The delegations were nonetheless far from united in their conceptions of the opposition's role. In their opening statements the British and Swiss delegates spoke against an overly harsh condemnation of the policy of 4 August, noting the special circumstances that had brought it about and appealing for reconciliation. Louise Saumoneau of the French Women's Action Committee pointed to the gap between the timidity of socialist leaders and the antiwar sentiments of the masses but did not offer a positive program. Beside the Bolsheviks a revolutionary perspective was defended by Käthe Duncker of the German International Group, who urged support for a new International "that will not only declaim red words, but teach solidarity by deeds." In her own brief remarks Armand raised the call for an immediate break with the defensists and revolutionary civil war. Under her leadership the Bolshevik delegation adopted a tactic that would come to characterize the party's comportment in international forums throughout the war, challenging the dominant moderate consensus but striving to avoid an open break. The Bolshevik goal was to use the conference as a platform to air an alternative viewpoint, to recruit supporters, and to exert some influence upon final resolutions.

On the second day of deliberations, during a discussion of the theme "International Solidarity on Behalf of Peace," the conference divided into three currents. The British delegation, on the right, identified "war in general" as the root problem and urged that opposition be conducted in a spirit of radical pacifism. A centrist position backed by the majority expressed allegiance to the principle of international class struggle but argued that in the present situation the slogan peace should be emphasized without ideological encumbrances to confuse the masses. Isolated on the left, Armand demanded that the imperialist essence of the war be acknowledged and that "pacifist phrases about peace" be replaced with an exhortation to revolution. She absolutely refused any sort of conciliatory gesture toward the defensists, who had "replaced socialism with nationalism." "Of course," Armand noted in a phrase that echoed Lenin, "we do not claim that civil war will come about immediately, but we must guide our activity in this direction."[9]

Conflicting perspectives surfaced once again in the debate over final resolutions. The project manifesto and resolution prepared by Zetkin identified the source of war as "capitalist imperialism" and opposed defensism as irreconcilably contrary to the interests of the working classes but emphasized the demand for peace and made no reference to the issue of organizational division.[10] A resolution introduced by Saumoneau was considerably more cautious, opposing open criticism of defensist majorities and seeking to limit demands to a general plea for peace.[11] Armand presented a resolution that had been drafted by Lenin, characterizing the war as imperialist and exhorting that: "If the working woman wants to shorten the period of suffering produced by the imperialist war, her striving for peace must be combined with *insurrectionary activity, with the struggle for socialism.*"[12] These general principles were accompanied by a list of specific demands, including rejection of the *Burgfrieden* and war credits, support for fraternization and mass protest actions, and the creation of underground organizations.

In the first test of the Bolshevik program in an international assembly, Armand's resolution was unanimously rejected. The Mensheviks criticized its failure to cite peace as an aspiration valid in its own right, the Dutch delegate rejected attacks upon entire party organizations, and Zetkin, though not unsympathetic, declared that its implications extended beyond the competence of a women's conference. In a final tally Zetkin's resolution was approved by a count of twenty-one to six. Armand immediately announced that the Bolsheviks would not vote for the majority resolution "because from a principled point of view it is insufficient and incomplete." In a memoir Balabanov notes that the declaration created "panic," but in fact it represented little more than a trial balloon.[13] After a private meeting with Zetkin the Bolsheviks agreed to join the majority on the condition that their own documents be included in the official protocol.

The women's conference adjourned on 29 March with real achievements to its credit. For the first time during the war socialist representatives of belligerent powers had come together and, in Zetkin's words, set "a purposeful and powerful united peace action . . . in the works."[14] According to the conference manifesto, only mass actions led "resolutely, and with a clear sense of purpose," by the social democratic movement could force an end to the war.[15] That was precisely what the major social democratic organizations were refusing to do, and the implied condemnation was sufficiently clear. The Bolsheviks recognized as much in their own evaluations, noting that despite its "timidity" the conference had exposed "two worldviews" in conflict.[16] Although accounts of the conference were normally censored, brief descriptions in the socialist press (including *The Labour Leader* and *L'Humanité*, the central organ of the SFIO) and informal communication through personal channels assured that the results would be perceived. In conjunction with a public demonstration against war-induced inflation before the Reichstag in Berlin on 18 March, it seemed to signal a reviving will to resist. *Nashe Slovo* greeted the two events together on 13 April and noted their "not coincidental" relatedness. The successful outcome of the conference gave a stimulus to oppositional activity. Balabanov's later assertion that "it laid a foundation for the future Zimmerwald movement" was substantially correct.[17]

One week later, in the identical Bern auditorium, another assembly of the opposition brought together representatives of socialist youth leagues. The Socialist Youth International, created like the Women's International in 1907 and organized around an International Youth Bureau, had a proud record of radical antimilitarism. Calls for an antiwar gesture on the part of socialist youth followed on the heels of mobilization, but the Youth Bureau's secretary Robert Danneberg in Vienna balked at the prospect of independent action. As a result, initiatives passed into the hands of the young German Willi Münzenberg, working through the SPS Zürich section and with the backing of the Scandinavian and Italian youth leagues. In January 1915 Münzenberg launched the project by drafting a circular letter calling for an international meeting independent of the Vienna Bureau.[18]

On 5 April the youth conference opened with at least fourteen delegates representing ten nations present.[19] The complexion of the gathering was more radical than that of the women's conference, but once again the Bolsheviks found themselves nearly alone on the extreme left. Debate erupted immediately during the discussion of the theme "The War and the Tasks of the Socialist Youth Organizations," as a project resolution drafted by Robert Grimm and Balabanov ran into strong criticism from the Bolshevik and SDKPiL delegations.[20] Frustrated by their isolation, the Russians and Poles surprised the assembly by walking from the hall to protest the allocation of voting mandates. In their absence the Grimm/Balabanov resolution was unanimously approved. Münzenberg, Bernd Luteraan, and Ernst Christiansen argued for sharper tactical formulations, but they were countered by Grimm, who insisted, in terms that recalled those of Bebel at Stuttgart in 1907, that condition varied too widely from country to country to legitimize general guidelines.

The Bolsheviks returned to the floor after their procedural demands had been accommodated, bringing with them a project resolution and numerous amendments to the majority resolution.[21] All of their initiatives were voted down, but sparring was renewed as discussion moved on to the theme of disarmament. General disarmament had long been a cause célèbre for the youth movement, but it was opposed by the Bolsheviks as utopian and misleading. When a motion from the Scandinavian and Swiss delegations calling for general and complete disarmament was approved by a count of nine to five, the Bolsheviks clung to principle and voted with the minority, thereby distancing themselves from potential supporters.[22] Despite their repeated frustrations, however, the Bolsheviks' maneuvering was not in vain. Upon Armand's demand a sentence was added to the final resolution committing young socialists to oppose the *Burgfrieden*, and the Bolshevik resolution was included in the official protocol. Consistent agitation from the left, it seemed, was capable of exerting some influence. Aksel'rod wrote to Balabanov after the conference asking how the delegates could have allowed themselves to be "terrorized" by the Bolshevik "uninvited guests."[23]

The youth conference's most dramatic initiatives were administrative in nature. In its final session the assembly declared unanimously that Danneberg and the Vienna bureau had forfeited their functions and appointed a Zürich-based secretariat with Münzenberg, Christiansen, Ansgar Olaussen, Friedrich Notz, and Amadeo Catanesi as permanent members in its place. An "International Youth Day" was proclaimed as a festival of peace, a "Karl Liebknecht Fund" was created to finance antiwar activities, and plans were made to publish an international journal entitled *Jugend-Internationale* (Youth International). Modest as it may have been, a first step toward schism within the international movement had been taken. An article by Edwin Hörnle in the first number of *Jugend-Internationale* entitled "The International is Dead! Long Live the International!" underlined the gesture's larger implications.[24]

During both Bern conferences the Bolshevik delegation played a provocative role, insisting upon a maximalist orientation with civil war as its watchword. The approach left the party without significant allies, but Lenin did not soften his determination to pursue an intransigent revolutionary line. If anything, the debates strengthened his conviction that a peace strategy seeking to rally a broad-based antiwar movement behind the social democratic banner was unacceptable. In their first formal interactions with the international left, the Bolsheviks displayed their hand. As efforts to convene a general opposition conference gathered momentum, Lenin's campaign to build an alternative to the Second International would increasingly be linked to a struggle against what he disparagingly called the "pacifist" orientation of the moderate opposition.

The Road to Zimmerwald

The women's and youth conferences blazed a trail for those within the PSI and SPS working to sponsor a more significant peace action. By the spring and summer of 1915 these efforts had come to be embodied in the working relationship between Grimm and Oddino Morgari. Both men were incongruous candidates for the role of radical internationalist. Morgari was a moderate by temperament, more closely aligned with the PSI center behind Turati and Constantino Lazzari than with Serrati and the left, and a proponent since 1906 of an "integralist" line that sought to downplay theoretical disputes in favor of a vaguely defined socialist unity. His role as organizer derived less from personal conviction than from his party's engagement with the international opposition.[25] Grimm, thirty-three years old in 1914, was moved by the war to set his compromising political instincts aside. On 3 August he voted with the SPS parliamentary fraction in favor of a national union, but the carnage at the fronts soon caused his views to evolve. By September Grimm was criticizing the terms of Swiss neutrality. At Lugano he urged sponsorship of an international conference as a "base of operations" for the left, and during the autumn he conducted a wide-ranging correspondence with leaders of the German left including Liebknecht, Luxemburg, and Zetkin.[26] In January 1915 Grimm visited Paris and Berlin. Upon his return he became intimately involved in planning for the women's and youth conferences. By the spring of 1915, in his newly founded theoretical journal *Neues Leben* (New Life), he was developing the ideas that would serve as a foundation for his role as the leader of the socialist antiwar movement.[27]

Grimm's explanation for social democracy's sudden turnabout in August 1914 emphasized the corrosive effects of nationalism. Encouraged by revisionism, the labor movement had linked its fate to that of the ruling classes within the nation-state, thereby sacrificing autonomy and abandoning its real long-term interests. As the "house servant of imperialism," he wrote, the proletariat could not pursue its historical destiny. Socialism was "international in its innermost essence" and could only be forwarded by reviving the principle of class struggle as an alternative to the national ideology embodied in the *Burgfrieden*. Grimm's slogan "class struggle, not civil truce" seemed to echo Liebknecht, but his political conclusions were not identical to those of the revolutionary left. For the Swiss leader class struggle referred primarily to the need for labor to ensure that its goals remained distinct from those of the possessing classes. Under the present circumstances, he argued, international class struggle and the struggle for a just peace were synonymous, a conclusion that betrayed the influence of Martov's peace strategy. Grimm rejected "premature" mass actions and opposed organizational schisms. Adherence to the principle of class struggle did not require splitting existing organizations or the establishment of a rival International. The point was to restore the integrity of the prewar movement by resurrecting its political and ethical standards. These postulates would become broadly influential, though Christian Voight's characterization of them as "the essential principles of the Zimmerwald movement" is only partially accurate.[28] Grimm defended one image of what the opposition should become, an image that contrasted sharply with that enunciated by Lenin.

Friction between moderates and the revolutionary left was constantly present in the background of the efforts to coordinate the opposition which grew from the SPS/PSI partnership. On 2 October and 13 November sessions of the SPS managing committee (*Geschäftsleitung*) launched these efforts by committing the party to carry on the work of Lugano. Though the goal was ambitious enough, the immediate tasks that were defined—attempts to stimulate action by the ISB and to organize a conference of socialists representing the neutral states—were cautious and exploratory. A motion by Fritz Platten on 2 October "to invite at least some comrades from the belligerent states" was overwhelmingly rejected.[29] On 22 January a proposal by Johann Sigg and Platten mandating the SPS to sponsor a general conference of the opposition was turned down on the grounds that such a conference would be subject to manipulation by the ultraleft. Emil Walter spoke plainly of the concern that "irresponsible elements" and "intransigent extremists that have already been discredited in their own countries" would "place their stamp upon the proceedings . . . and create an entirely false picture of the social democracy." Sigg, himself by no means a leftist, countered scaldingly that "thirty or forty" social democratic deputies tried for high treason would be a small sacrifice in the cause of peace.[30] For the time being, however, the moderate wing of the SPS leadership blocked attempts by radicals to convene a general conference.

Attempts to sponsor a neutrals' conference went forward in spite of resistance, spurred on by the commitments made at Lugano, the disappointing results of the Copenhagen conference, the increasingly open hostility of the ISB, and a dawning awareness that the war would be long. On 18 and 22 February, in the midst of an informational journey sponsored by the PSI with the aim of "rebuilding relations between proletarian movements," Morgari attended sessions of the SPS managing committee in Bern. The Italian described his purpose as the "rebuilding of the International" and requested that an SPS representative accompany him in his travels in order to strengthen the cooperative character of their effort. When he moved on to the need to convene a neutrals' conference, however, Morgari encountered resistance from both right and left. Paul Pflüger, SPS president, spoke against a "special" conference of any sort, while Platten described consultations limited to neutrals as "useless." In the end the managing committee voted by a narrow margin to support Morgari's mission, but revealed its own hesitancies by providing only a letter of endorsement in lieu of an envoy.[31] The SPS leadership's support for the neutrals' conference project was apparently begrudging at best. On 6 March, in a letter addressed to ISB secretary Camille Huysmans, the party requested that the ISB take up the project on its own behalf and characterized a general conference uniting representatives of belligerent powers as an "utopia."[32]

In April Morgari resumed his consultations, visiting Switzerland, France, the Netherlands, and Great Britain. Prior to setting out he once again made clear that his intentions did not extend beyond the attempt to encourage a plenary session of the ISB and to build the foundation for a neutrals' conference.[33] By now, however, the women's and youth conferences were about to provide examples of more decisive international actions. On 28 March the SPS executive committee (*Parteivorstand*) voted in favor of a motion by Sigg to convene a neutrals' conference.[34] Grimm exerted an important influence upon the outcome, arguing that, if it wished to remain true to the spirit of Lugano, the party was obligated to act where the ISB would not. After one more futile attempt to shake the ISB executive from its lethargy, the managing committee announced on 22 April that a neutrals' conference would be convened on 30 May in Zürich. A project manifesto drawn up by Greulich carefully specified his party's moderate intentions, noting that its purpose was to align the movement with popular yearning for peace, but not to divide or disrupt it.[35]

These elaborate deliberations were more important for the interactions which they set to work than for their practical results, for during April and May plans to convene a conference of neutrals collapsed. After a stormy confrontation with Vandervelde in Paris on 19 April, Morgari was forced to abandon any hope of involving the ISB in efforts to rebuild international contacts. In a sharp exchange that revealed the moralistic inflexibility that was motivating the ISB executive, Morgari accused Vandervelde of holding the bureau "hostage," to which the Belgian replied: "Yes, but a hostage for freedom and justice."[36] In letters to the SFIO dated 6 May and to the SPS dated 11 June Huysmans reiterated that without the unanimous acquiescence of all affiliates neither an ISB plenum nor a conference of neutrals could be considered.[37] After Italy's entry into the war on 24 May the concept lost much of its appeal at any rate. What is more, responses to the SPS invitation were disappointing. By mid-May only the socialist parties of Bulgaria, Italy, and Romania had accepted—too narrow a foundation for a significant international initiative.[38] With the project in abeyance the door leading toward the more significant goal of a general conference began to swing open.

During his discussions in Paris, importantly influenced by conversations with Martov, Morgari was won over to the view that the ISB's inactivity made an independently organized conference of the opposition essential. The political logic of the conclusion was provided by Martov's peace strategy. "It is only a concerted action for peace by the organized proletariat of all nations," the Menshevik leader wrote during March, "that will be capable of reforming the broken ties between the sections of the workers' International and reviving the revolutionary spirit of the proletariat."[39] Continuing on to London, Morgari found support for the idea of a general conference within the ILP and BSP as well.[40] Convening in special session to discuss his report on 15–16 May in Bologna, the PSI directorate approved the recommendation to sponsor a general conference and went a step further by urging the participation of all "socialist parties or party groups" that opposed the *Burgfrieden*, thus sanctioning a role for minority factions. On 18 June the directorate issued a declaration announcing its intention "to continue work with those parties, or fragments of parties, which have remained faithful to the ideals of socialism, to relaunch international activity as soon as possible, and to initiate an extraordinary international conference, an energetic movement to secure peace in Europe."[41] Though posed as an "extraordinary" action, the PSI's gesture constituted a major challenge to the ISB.

The PSI's Swiss partner was not ready to reciprocate the gesture. After consultations with Morgari Grimm carried the proposal for a general conference to the SPS executive committee on 22 May. With the ISB "a hostage in the hands of the French," he insisted, international activity would have to be sponsored independently. Class struggle could not be put off until after the war, and it fell to the SPS "to call together opposition groups in the individual belligerent nations to a conference in Switzerland." No doubt somewhat surprised at how far its own audacity had taken it, the executive committee rejected the proposal out of hand.[42] But Grimm was not to be so easily deterred. He argued for and obtained his party's approval for "individual" action on behalf of peace and used it to justify ongoing organizational efforts. Operating within a broadening network of international contacts, unconstrained by the need to seek approval from party forums, and with the backing of the PSI, Grimm now became the driving force behind the coordination of a general conference. As a first step, he announced the scheduling of an unofficial preliminary meeting (*Vorbesprechung*) among interested parties for 5 July in Bern.[43]

Up until June Lenin was completely uninvolved in the effort to convene a conference of the opposition. The road to Zimmerwald was paved by moderates, often acting with scarcely disguised animosity toward the ultraleft. Grimm insisted that an extraordinary conference did not imply an organizational rupture or challenge the premises of social democracy. Rather, it would reaffirm these premises in the face of the distortions caused by the war. "Nothing can be achieved through the official parties," he wrote to Aksel'rod on 8 May, but a "conference of opposition elements naturally does not mean a split. In my opinion it should concern itself only with the establishment of a tactical line for the struggle against the war."[44] For Martov socialist action for peace was necessary in order to counter "sectarian" tendencies, and in his consultations with Morgari he recommended avoiding contact with Lenin, who "can only throw a stick into the wheels of our project."[45] In view of its origins a conflict between moderates and radicals was "built into" the Zimmerwald movement from the outset.

Lenin was isolated from the planning for a general conference physically as well as politically. From June through October 1915 he resided in the village of Sörenberg, at the foot of the Brienzer Rothorn in the Swiss canton of Luzern, where Krupskaia recovered from a bout with illness. Informed by Radek of Grimm's project, Lenin was immediately convinced of its potential as a vehicle for mobilizing the left.[46] Significantly, Grimm's first invitations to the preliminary meeting did not include the Bolsheviks. When Radek explained to Lenin that in his opinion the snub was the result of an "oversight," the Bolshevik leader responded with a stormy letter, composed in a pithy combination of Russian and German, committing the Bolsheviks to attend and outlining a tactic for participation that demanded action independent of the moderate elements assembling around Grimm. According to Lenin, the Bolsheviks must prepare: "(1) To attend, as soon as we are invited; (2) to call together the proponents of *revolutionary action* against *their own* governments; (3) to put before the Kautskyite shitheads [*Kautskianskim govniakam*] *our* project resolution (the Dutch + ourselves + the left Germans + 0, but no matter, for *later* it will not be zero, but all!); (4) to put forward two or three speakers at the conference." Urging Radek to represent the left at Bern, Lenin concluded "write and tell me what you think about this program. Its essence is opposition to the obtuse and traitorous slogan of peace."[47] With this approximation of a strategy Lenin prepared to do battle with the moderate opposition, which he was coming to despise even more roundly than socialist defensism.

Despite the best efforts of Grimm and Morgari, only seven delegates were able to attend the preliminary meeting when it convened in Bern on 11 July. The Italian delegation was the only one to arrive from abroad, and as a result the meeting was disproportionally weighted toward the Russian and Polish parties, with their émigré bases in Switzerland. Even so, the delegates stood firmly behind Grimm. As a spokesperson for the Bolsheviks, Zinoviev was completely isolated on the left flank.[48]

Grimm opened the sessions by outlining his intention to organize an international conference. To that end a list of participants and working agenda had to be determined. The way in which these matters were resolved would go a long way toward fixing the socialist antiwar movement's political complexion, and they sparked heated debate. Grimm spoke for the majority in formulating criteria legitimizing the participation of all "parties or factions" that "support the renewal or continuation of the class struggle, oppose the *Burgfrieden*, and are ready to take up the struggle for peace." Zinoviev, alone in dissent, demanded a commitment to revolutionary action and a "clear demarcation of principles," insisting that "theoretical clarity is more important than the question of peace." An agreement was achieved to limit attendance to groups with an explicit antiwar orientation, but rivalry flared up over the issue of relating to the German centrist opposition emerging behind Kautsky, Haase, and Bernstein. Aksel'rod described invitations for the Kautsky group as "profoundly to be desired," while Zinoviev labeled them more dangerous than the defensists. In the end the issue was left unresolved, though a consensus in favor of some kind of rapprochement had been demonstrated. Kautsky was Lenin's particular bête noire, and the majority's willingness to accommodate to the German center did not augur well for continuing collaboration.

Zinoviev stood alone once again in presenting a list of left groups, including the Tribunists, the Serbian Socialist party, the International Socialists of Germany, the Lettish Social Democratic party, the SDKPiL-Regional Presidium, and the Scandinavian youth leagues, whom he argued should be invited to attend a second preliminary meeting. Together these groups constituted an amorphous left wing within the international socialist community that Lenin hoped to rally as a supportive faction. Zinoviev's proposal was rejected by five to one with one abstention on the grounds that ISB affiliation should be maintained as a criterion for participation. Breaking with the standard meant stepping outside the structures of the Second International, a step that most delegates were reluctant to take.

Perhaps due to his isolation, Zinoviev's bearing was more flexible than those of the Bolshevik delegations at the women's and youth conferences. He himself sponsored a unanimously approved motion citing the PSI manifestos of 16 May and 18 June, which emphasized the goal of peace as a basis for a common program and acquiesced in a working agenda that highlighted moderate themes. Grimm was able to close the session by reiterating the intention "to begin a practical proletarian movement for peace and against the *Burgfrieden*." Immediately after the meeting, however, Zinoviev composed a circular letter in which the results were criticized. "Where," he asked "were the *truly lefts* of the International?"[49] The tone of the letter revealed Lenin's influence and indicated that the Bolsheviks would not passively allow their position to be marginalized.

In the weeks between 11 July and 5 September, when the Zimmerwald conference convened, Grimm undertook a concerted effort to ensure substantial participation that would reflect his own moderate priorities. Working through contacts in Paris, he was able to obtain a commitment to delegate representatives from both the SFIO and the CGT. During a second visit to London in August, Morgari extracted a commitment to participate from the ILP and BSP "Internationalists." Invitations to the German opposition were smuggled across the border, and a substantial representation secured.[50] Despite such efforts, some of the most significant representatives of the moderate opposition were not present at Zimmerwald. The British delegation was unable to obtain exit visas, an Austrian contingent including Friedrich Adler failed to arrive on time, and in the end the leaders associated with Kautsky in Germany chose not to attend. Still, the work of Grimm, Morgari, and their collaborators insured that the conference would possess a predominantly moderate orientation.

Lenin and Zinoviev were similarly occupied. During the spring the Bolsheviks moved to assuage tension within their own ranks by allowing Bukharin, Georgii Piatakov, and Evgeniia Bosh to assume the editorship of a new party journal entitled *Kommunist* (Communist), two numbers of which appeared in a combined edition during July. Lenin contributed a substantial article which drew the conclusion that political action outside the bounds of the "former" International was a vital necessity. Together with Zinoviev he also prepared an updated statement of the party platform, the pamphlet *Socialism and War*, which was translated into German and distributed at the Zimmerwald conference.[51] The obvious intention was to close ranks around a theoretical position that could serve as a rallying point for the revolutionary left.

Though it is an uneven work, marred by simplistic and self-serving attacks upon Menshevism, *Socialism and War* remains one of Le-

nin's most significant statements on the problem of war and peace.
The text begins with an attack upon the slogan of peace, rejecting
"bourgeois pacifism" and all related attempts to consider the phenomenon of war apart from its social origins. As an alternative, a
typology of just and unjust wars is presented. Just wars are cate-
gorized as *wars of national liberation,* deemed capable of playing a
progressive role in the historical transition away from feudalism, and
revolutionary civil wars waged "by the oppressed classes against
their oppressors." Unjust wars in the contemporary epoch are described generically as *wars of imperialism.*

Like any other complex sociopolitical event, war possessed a class
character. Socialist strategy in regard to any given armed conflict
could therefore only be determined by carefully evaluating the larger
historical context. For Lenin war was an eminently political act, "the
continuation of politics by other, namely violent, means." This statement paraphrased the Prussian military theorist Carl von Clausewitz, whose classic *On War* Lenin had read attentively earlier in the
year.[52] It has often been cited as an example of Bolshevik ruthless-
ness, but in 1915 the implications were rather more straightforward.
The imperialist war, defined in Clausewitzian terms, was a struggle
for supremacy between the leading world powers. The victory of one
or another imperialist bloc might well lead to the temporary establishment of a new global hegemon. It could not resolve the contradictions of advanced capitalism or create a lasting peace. That was the
political task which the war posed for revolutionaries: to make use
of the resultant sufferings and destabilization to promote radical
change and begin the construction of an internationalist alternative
to the capitalist world order. The point was "to make use of the
struggle between the bandits in order to overthrow them" by exploit-
ing the revolutionary attitude that the war would inevitably create
among the masses:

Our duty is to assist in creating this attitude, to deepen and help
form it. This problem can be properly addressed only by the
slogan transformation of the imperialist war into a civil war, and
all consistent class struggle in time of war, all serious use of the
tactic of "mass actions," inevitably leads to this. It is impossible
to know whether a powerful revolutionary movement will flare

up in reaction to the first or the second imperialist war, during the war or afterwards, but in any case our indisputable duty is to work systematically and unbendingly precisely in this direction.[53]

Lenin's analysis revealed the lingering influence of the Guesdist tradition. Wars are presumed to have their roots in the injustices of class society, and their elimination "without the elimination of classes and the creation of socialism" is considered to be impossible. His conclusions are nonetheless far from being fatalistic. For the first time in history, Lenin suggests, socialist revolution had become more than an utopian fancy. Capitalism had forged a level of economic development sufficient to provide a basis for socialist construction; an "objectively revolutionary situation" was in place, and the imperialist war offered a conjuncture capable of placing radical change on the political agenda. The slogan "civil war" was not a rhetorical exaggeration, but the summation of a strategic outlook, for it was only through the struggle for socialism that the cycle of inter-state conflict could be broken. These harsh realities were too often ignored by all those who shrank from insurrection in the name of peace, mass struggle, or some other convenient euphemism. "The struggle for a rapid end to the war is necessary," Lenin remarks, "but only through the call to *revolutionary* struggle does the demand for 'peace' receive a proletarian content." "Marxism is not pacifism," and "without a series of revolutions a so-called democratic peace remains a petty-bourgeois utopia."[54]

For Lenin, the question of a break with the defensists was "irrevocably decided." The real danger lay not in the evident apostasy of the social chauvinists, but in the misleading tactics of the moderate opposition. A negative attitude toward "neoKautskyism" was described as the "touchstone" of authentic internationalism; only parties committed to a consequential break with opportunism in all its forms belonged in the ranks of the Marxist left. The vital question was not whether the creation of a revolutionary International was possible, but only the pace at which it could be achieved. In July the editors of *Kommunist* listed the International Socialists of Germany, the International Group, the French opposition behind Merrheim, Pierre Monatte, and René Nicod, the ILP, the BSP "Internationalists," the Swedish Youth League, the Bulgarian Narrows, the Dutch SDP, and left factions within the PSI and SPS as the basis for an international left tendency. "To rally together these Marxist elements," Lenin concludes, "no matter how small they might be at first . . . here is the task at hand."[55]

Rallying the left meant undertaking an organizational effort to secure as many voting mandates as possible for the approaching general conference and the theoretical work of uniting sympathizers around a common platform. To these ends Lenin conducted a flurry of correspondence with potential allies, battled with Grimm to extend the left's representation, and strove to develop a coherent revolutionary program.[56] By mid-August the decision had been made to dispense with a second preliminary meeting and proceed with the general conference on the basis of the 11 July guidelines. The Bolsheviks responded with a note to Grimm protesting against using ISB affiliation as a criterion for participation.[57] Lenin also harangued his own closest associates concerning the need for ideological rigor. In July he wrote to Kollontai that "in our opinion, the left must make a common *ideological* declaration . . . an ideological declaration of the 'lefts' from several countries would have *gigantic* meaning"; to Radek in August, "for us . . . the most important thing of all is a clear, precise statement of principles (*Prinzipienerklärung*)"; and again to Kollontai, "a common ideological declaration of *left* Marxists would now be devilishly important."[58]

The search for supporters proved frustrating. Left groups close to the Bolsheviks within the Russian and Polish labor movements expressed a readiness for joint work, but others remained noncommital. The Bulgarian Narrows claimed sympathy for Lenin's orientation but rejected a factional role within the opposition.[59] Lenin's exaggerated solicitude for Borchardt's tiny *Lichtstrahlen* group only served to alienate more substantial components of the German left. Perhaps most disappointing, the Dutch Tribunists refused to take part in a conference organized by the "centrist" Grimm.[60] In the entreaties which he addressed to potential allies Lenin reduced his conditions for affiliation with the left to three: (1) unconditional condemnation of opportunism and social chauvinism; (2) a revolutionary action program (with the concession that whether one preferred the slogan "mass action" or "civil war" was of secondary importance); and (3) refutation of defense of the Fatherland.[61] Obviously crafted to appeal to a broad stratum of opinion, the conditions were in fact somewhat disingenuous. They ignored what were becoming the most controversial aspects of Lenin's program—the demand for the creation of independent left radical parties and a third International.

It was clear that a viable international left would have to be built upon a more substantial foundation than that provided by the Bolshevik party and its satellites. A logical person through whom to work in order to broaden the left's appeal was Radek, who enjoyed excellent contacts with German left radicals and the SDP. During the summer of 1915, however, Lenin and Radek experienced the beginning of a personal falling-out. Both men shared the opinion that the German left held the key to a new International, but in his urgent haste to locate sympathizers Lenin exaggerated the importance of the Borchardt group beyond proportion. Radek responded cynically and emphasized that to be effective the left needed a mass base. His pointed remark that "the opposition in Germany is a product of unrest among the masses, while Bolshevism is the orientation of a small group of revolutionaries" struck at the heart of Lenin's politics and elicited a strong rejoinder. "This is not Marxism," Lenin scolded:

> This is Kautskyism—pure deceit . . . Is there not 'unrest among the masses' in Russia? The left in Germany will make an historic mistake, if on the pretext that 'they are the product of unrest among the masses' . . . they refuse to come forward with a statement of principles. *For* the development of 'unrest among the masses' a left declaration is necessary. *In view of* such unrest it is necessary. *For* the transformation of 'unrest' into a 'movement' it is necessary. *For* the development of 'unrest' in the rotton International *it is necessary*. And *immediately*!! You are 1000 times wrong![62]

Radek was not deterred and took up the challenge by submitting his own project resolution to compete with that being prepared by Lenin as the basis for a left platform. Lenin reacted with some bile, attacking the "academic" quality of the writing and demanding revisions.[63] The charge of academic formality was rather peculiar when addressed to Radek, a polemical journalist of the first order. More to the point was Radek's desire to introduce an element of flexibility into Lenin's analysis in order to give the left a wider appeal. Radek was also more sympathetic toward Grimm, with whom he kept in close touch in Bern, assuring Lenin that "he will side with us."[64] The differences in perspective between the two men were subtle but significant and would become a real hindrance to the left in its effort to emerge as a valid international alternative.

Final preparations for the general conference were carried out behind a veil of secrecy. Grimm arranged for the delegates to assemble in Bern, but for the actual venue reserved facilities for an "ornithological society" in the village of Zimmerwald, located some ten kilometers to the south amidst a splendid prealpine landscape. The participants, handpicked by Grimm, consisted of thirty-eight individuals representing eleven countries.[65] On the morning of 5 September the group crowded into carriages at Bern's Eigerplatz and departed for the mountains. Trotsky later remarked in bitter jest that "half a century after the formation of the First International it was still possible to fit all the internationalists in Europe into four coaches."[66] Certainly there was some incongruity between the task which the group was about to undertake and its isolation, perched high above the ravaged plains of central Europe where whole nations tore at one another across boundaries of trench and barbed wire. The rest home *Beau Séjour* was the ironic locale for their efforts. As one delegate described the proceedings: "In the course of an entire week, in a small hotel, where in 'happy' years reserved Englishmen drank marvelous Swiss coffee or milk, looking out through the windows onto the snow white peak of the Jungfrau, we conducted a passionate and historic discussion."[67]

The Zimmerwald Conference

Much of the passion generated at Zimmerwald emerged from the clash between the moderate bloc assembled around Grimm and Lenin's left faction. On the eve of the conference, aware that every vote would carry weight, Lenin lobbied intensively to gain support. He traveled to Bern from Sörenberg several days prior to the delegates' scheduled arrivals, met potential sympathizers at the train station, and twisted arms to win them over.[68] On either 2 or 3 September a caucus was held between the Russian and Polish delegations that constituted the core of Lenin's backing, where by a majority vote Radek's project resolution was chosen over Lenin's to be presented to the conference.[69] Lenin also sponsored an open meeting in Zinoviev's Bern residence on 4 September in order to coordinate tactics and encourage last-minute recruitment. Trotsky was present along with a large part of the German delegation, Merrheim and Albert Bourderon, Jan Berzin, Borchardt, Platten, Radek, Höglund, and Ture Nerman.[70] Discussion seems to have lingered on general principles. Radek's project resolution was once again preferred but subjected to a number of revisions that betrayed Lenin's influence. The meeting also gave birth to a project manifesto and formalized an agreement among some of the participants to function as a left bloc during the conference sessions. Thus armed with the collective support that he had worked so persistently to muster, Lenin boarded the carriage bound for Zimmerwald on 5 September.

The debates conducted at Zimmerwald involved three issue areas. The first concerned procedures and the troublesome matter of voting mandates, technical questions but critical to fixing a balance between moderates and radicals. More substantial friction emerged during the attempt to specify the opposition's political goals, with disagreements focused upon the wording of resolutions and appeals. Finally, the antiwar movement's institutional relationship with the Second International proved to be a source of disaccord. In every case debate was dominated by a confrontation between Grimm's moderate posture and the Leninist left, whose persistent interventions left an indelible imprint upon the proceedings.

The first two days of the conference were taken up with opening statements and procedural bickering.[71] Grimm brought the sessions to order on the afternoon of 5 September, condemning the "illusory existence" of the ISB but disavowing any intention to construct a new International and stressing the goal of "calling the proletariat to a common action for peace." His priorities were shared by a clear majority of delegates, though an emotional moment during the first session arrived when a fiery letter from Liebknecht, written in a German military prison, was read aloud. Liebknecht raised the leftist slogan "civil war, not civil peace" and called for a new International "to rise from the ruins of the old," but it was his stature as a symbol of the opposition rather than radical exhortations that earned stormy and unanimous applause.

The strongest of the opening statements was that presented by the youth leagues of Sweden and Norway. Their project resolution demanded support for antiwar mass actions and described peace without revolution as an "utopia." Most other delegations, led by the Mensheviks, the PSI majority, and the German majority behind Georg Ledebour, stressed the need for more pragmatic tactics. Friction within the German contingent was revealed as Ledebour raised veiled criticisms of Liebknecht's comportment in the Reichstag, to which Bertha Thalheimer of the International Group replied by describing her own organization as a "minority within the minority" and disavowing Ledebour's right to speak for a united German left. Zinoviev represented the Bolsheviks, offering a slightly toned-down exposition of the party line and denying any intention to represent a "special Russian tactic." Preliminary statements revealed wide-ranging disagreements and made clear that the search for consensus would not be easy or automatic.

Skirmishing between moderates and radicals erupted during the discussion over procedures. An executive bureau composed of Grimm, Lazzari, and Rakovski, with Balabanov and Henrietta Roland-Holst as secretaries, was appointed to monitor problems. It was immediately drawn into a confrontation with the left by accepting a challenge to Borchardt's right to carry a mandate on behalf of a representative organization and changing his status from that of accredited delegate to observer without voting privileges. Though probably justifiable, the decision was a slap in the face to the radical wing. In response the Bolsheviks requested that independent voting mandates be granted to each of the factional subdivisions within the Russian and Polish movements. The decision to allocate five mandates to each national delegation, to be distributed among factions by "consensual" agreement, also effectively disadvantaged the left. The politicized essence of "procedural" issues and the dominant position of Grimm's moderate bloc were made clear from the opening bell.

Only on 7 September did the conference turn to its first substantial agenda item, entitled "Peace Action by the Proletariat." Radek opened the debate by reading the left's project resolution and attacking the social democratic center, described as "a more dangerous enemy than the bourgeois apostles of imperialism." Revolution, not peace, was the goal, for without social revolution a lasting peace could never be achieved. With these brief remarks the left had thrown down the gauntlet, and the moderate leaders speaking for the majority immediately found themselves forced onto the defensive.

Grimm was the first to pick up the challenge, characterizing

Radek's statement as "unsuitable." "Do we want a manifesto for party comrades," he asked, "or for the broad masses of the workers?" Ledebour responded with a project resolution of his own, arguing that "we have come together here to fulfill the duty that the ISB has failed to fulfill, and not in order to found a third International." Ledebour also attacked Lenin's right to speak for a legitimate international tendency and suggested rather meanly that his extravagant statements could only be made by émigrés; within the warring states the bearer of a document such as the left resolution could be summarily shot. It was not an argument calculated to move an experienced conspirator such as Lenin, who replied with references to the Bolsheviks' underground campaigns in Russia and a denunciation of the "passive revolutionism" of the SPD center. At the end of the day, in an attempt to bridge the gap between moderates and radicals, Trotsky and Roland-Holst hastily composed a third project resolution that endorsed revolutionary goals but preferred a tactical emphasis upon peace in order to attract the war-weary masses.

The debate of 7 September, which filled three complete sessions and stretched well into the night, called attention to the isolation of Lenin's left faction. According to Ledebour, Zimmerwald's sole purpose was "to restore the International and to work for peace." Lazzari noted that as "a minority in parties that are a minority within their nations" the Zimmerwaldists could not afford Radek's "pretentious" tone. Bourderon pleaded for an end to abstract theorizing, and Roland-Holst regretted the "sectarian" impression left by Radek's motion. Many delegates oriented toward the left were also critical. Serrati opposed what he perceived as a failure to allow for the special difficulties imposed by the wartime environment. "If the war were not a fact," he explained, "I would vote for Lenin's resolution. Today it comes either too early or too late." Bertha Thalheimer and Ernst Meyer rejected the left resolution for its tendency to "dictate" tactics to national sections. Faced by this wave of criticism, Radek remained uncompromising. The opposition must avoid the purely rhetorical radicalism that had been the undoing of the Second International, he insisted. A restoration of the prewar movement was impossible, and the slogan "peace" only perpetuated illusions. Though constantly in the minority, the left's stubborn logic succeeded to a considerable degree in structuring debate and blocking the emergence of a moderate consensus.

During the evening session of 7 September Merrheim attempted yet another refutation. We want peace action by the proletariat, he pleaded, not "narrow formulas" that could not be implemented. "A revolutionary movement can only grow from a striving for peace. You, comrade Lenin, are not motivated by this striving for peace, but by the desire to set up a new International. This is what divides us." Merrheim's appeal for unity behind the premises of a peace strategy received lively applause and served to rally the majority. By a vote of nineteen to eleven the issue of drafting a resolution including specific tactical recommendations was shelved, and a drafting commission (made up of Ledebour, Lenin, Trotsky, Grimm, Merrheim, Modigliani, and Rakovski) was charged with composing a more generally phrased manifesto. No underlying issues had been resolved, however, and within the commission a confrontation quickly developed as Lenin demanded the inclusion of an injunction against support for war credits. Ledebour responded with the ultimatum that if any such commitment was made the German delegation would withdraw, and the matter was set aside. In the end it was Trotsky, who stood on the left but was not associated with Lenin's faction, who was appointed to draw up a final text.

On the morning of 8 September, in open session, the debate over war credits surfaced once again, as Roland-Holst and Trotsky joined with Lenin's left faction (Lenin, Zinoviev, Radek, Borchardt, Berzin, Platten, Höglund, and Nerman) to repose the demand that support for military appropriations be rejected under all circumstances. Ledebour repeated his ultimatum of the night before, and the motion was abandoned for a second time, though with some ill will. Other proposed amendments broke against the resistance of Grimm, who argued that at this point what mattered was the spirit of the appeal, not fine points of interpretation. At the last moment Morgari surprised all present by reverting to his past caution in the face of the highly ideological arguments of the left and opposing the manifesto altogether as "simplistic and incorrect."[72] After some purposeful elbow twisting, however, the Italian came around and the Zimmerwald manifesto was unanimously approved.

Though Trotsky borrowed some phrases from Radek, his text was primarily an emotional appeal aimed at the masses, not the statement of principles that Lenin originally desired. The war was said to "unveil the naked form of modern capitalism," the social democratic movement condemned for a "failure of responsibility," and the goal of the opposition defined as "to join anew the broken ties of international relations and to summon the working class to reorganize and begin the struggle for peace." The manifesto differed from the left's project resolution primarily in what it left unsaid. A commitment to oppose war credits, open condemnations of revisionism, and the invocation of revolutionary civil war were all lacking. "You must make use of all your organization and publications," the left resolution declaimed by way of contrast, "in order to call forth a revolt against the war among the broad masses which groan under its burden. You must go *into the streets*."[73]

Lenin and his followers approved Trotsky's text but also submitted a brief statement that noted its "insufficiencies." The manifesto was criticized for the absence of tactical guidelines and for the failure to disassociate the movement from "either open opportunism or opportunism covered up by radical phrases." At the same time, support was offered for a "call to struggle" in which "we are anxious to march side by side with other sections of the International."[74] The statement constituted a declaration of ideological independence by an internationally organized revolutionary faction. Though it remained to be seen how well the new tendency would fare, its existence and general orientation had been established. Lenin had accomplished his primary goal at Zimmerwald and succeeded in opening a gap between the moderate opposition and the revolutionary left.

With a manifesto in hand the conference went on to create an International Socialist Commission (ISC) as a standing executive committee. The need for some kind of agency to coordinate antiwar activity was apparent to all. Defining the prerogatives of the ISC proved to be considerably more problematic. The left insisted in regarding the creation of the ISC as a step toward a new International. Ledebour spoke for the moderate majority in demanding that its responsibilities be limited to overseeing an "exchange of correspondence" in order to avoid any appearance of competing with the ISB. Once again, moderate priorities prevailed. Grimm, Charles Naine, Morgari, and Balabanov were appointed to the commission as permanent members, a group that did not include a single representative of the left. Grimm immediately announced that the ISC would restrict its activities to coordinating international work for peace and the publication of an international bulletin. His definition of tasks was nearly minimal. It remained true nevertheless that by creating the ISC the Zimmerwald conference gave birth to a movement that could not help but be perceived as an institutional challenge to the Second International.[75]

After a brief discussion of finances, during which most delegations pledged contributions to stock an ISC treasury, Grimm officially closed the conference at 2:30 A.M. on the morning of 9 September. Balabanov has left an evocative description of the concluding moments. "The surroundings where the voting took place reflected the mood that had reigned among socialists since the coming of the war . . . A small, dark, enclosed, smoke-filled room, on a dreary, cloudy autumn night. Most of the delegates were exhausted, scraps of paper lay about on the tables—the work was completed, but the weariness was so great that almost no joy could be taken in its realization. Still, the most important things had been done."[76] Direct, intense, and more often than not unresolved, the debates at Zimmerwald also reflected the ferment at work within the opposition after more than a year of war. Something had certainly "been done." The antiwar left had rallied in defiance of socialist defensism, initiated an international action for peace, and created alternative institutions to coordinate an ongoing movement. In the process, however, important divisions were revealed within the ranks of the opposition itself. In the long term these divisions would prove more enduring than those provoked by the policy of 4 August. Lenin's modest left faction was the seed from which a major challenge to the legacy of the Second International would grow. Conceived in order to create a new foundation for socialist unity, the Zimmerwald conference had instead opened the door to a schism whose consequences would dominate the political landscape of the twentieth century.

Zimmerwald and the International

News of the Zimmerwald conference only gradually made its way through Europe, where information of all kinds was increasingly subject to military censorship. The patriotic mass media essentially ignored the event, but brief accounts filtered into the socialist press, and the manifesto was widely distributed as a leaflet.[77] In at least one case legal publication was accomplished via guile. In Italy Serrati was able to place the manifesto in a special edition of *Avanti!* on 14

October after submitting a doctored version to deceive the censor.[78] Slowly but surely the results of the conference became public knowledge, and the name Zimmerwald a source of inspiration for antiwar activists. "The conference of Zimmerwald has saved the honor of Europe," editorialized *Nashe Slovo* on 19 October, "and the ideals of the conference will save Europe itself."[79]

What were the ideals of Zimmerwald? On 20 September, writing in the *Berner Tagwacht*, Grimm described the conference as "the beginning of a new epoch" which demonstrated that "the International lives and has stood up again on the basis of revolutionary class struggle."[80] Such optimism was not entirely unjustified, for against the dismal background of the First World War Zimmerwald's symbolic impact was very great. Its "primordial effect," in the words of Humbert-Droz, was to galvanize the dispersed elements of the opposition and to lend them legitimacy by providing a demonstration of will to resist.[81] Weighed in the scales of history, the conference's achievements appear considerably more modest. The domination of the moderate line represented by Grimm assured that Zimmerwald would remain limited to an extraordinary action for peace. The conference's initiatives were repeatedly described as provisional, care was taken not to burn bridges to the ISB, and the door was held open to an eventual reconciliation. Grimm's intent was to rescue the premises of social democracy from the distortions of defensism rather than to move beyond them. Under his direction the Zimmerwald movement's goal was restoration rather than transformation; in Agnes Blänsdorf's summation, "to revive the Second International upon the old principles of prewar Marxian socialism."[82]

Lenin was unwilling to accept such limits. It was precisely the theory and practice of the Second International, he felt, that had led it to default in an hour of world historical significance. Zimmerwald represented an opportunity to begin anew by exposing the sources of the *Burgfrieden* and creating the foundations for a third International that would defend revolutionary principles "not in words but in deeds." During the women's and youth conferences and the 11 July preliminary meeting these goals were defended by the Bolsheviks more or less alone. At Zimmerwald Lenin succeeded in assembling a small supportive faction and stepped forward as the leader of an international alternative.

On the grounds that Lenin's "bid for domination" and hopes to stage "a founding conference for the third International" fell short, some historians have described his efforts at Zimmerwald as a "failure."[83] The judgment is unfair, for Lenin harbored no such unrealistic expectations. His intention, clearly outlined in letters to Radek and in *Socialism and War*, was not to "dominate" the movement, but to rally together an independent left and challenge the assumptions of a peace strategy. In the end Lenin's left faction remained small and unrepresentative. Lenin, Zinoviev, Radek, and Berzin all emerged from the political milieu of the czarist empire. Borchardt's status within the German left was questionable at best, and Platten was isolated on the left fringe of the sps. Höglund and Nerman consistently stood with the left, but they were not in accord with Lenin on every particular.[84] Nonetheless, the left did succeed in functioning as a bloc, and its impact upon the proceedings was disproportionately large. Lenin's reticence at the conference (he spoke rarely and never at great length) should be understood, not as a sign of impotence, but as a conscious effort to downplay his personal role and emphasize the left's international character. Despite the intentions of its organizers the Zimmerwald conference split the International and made its eventual demise more likely. Lenin was the only leader to step forward as a claimant for the mantle of internationalism that he believed had been abandoned on 4 August 1914. What he prescribed was similar to the concept of the vanguard party as described in *What Is To Be Done?*, an International "of a new type" corresponding to the demands of the age of imperialism. In many ways Zimmerwald was Lenin's triumph, the moment at which his challenge to the failed International and invocation of a radical alternative took on political form.

The goal of a third International was not unique to Lenin. Blagoev, Gorter, Liebknecht, Trotsky, Pannekoek, and a number of other theorists had raised the demand early in the war.[85] Many felt that despite its claims to provisional status the isc would inevitably become the source for a new international socialist organization. Similar sentiments were expressed by militants at the base. When Modigliani, a moderate member of the Italian delegation, described the results of Zimmerwald to the psi's Bologna section on 27 November, they were greeted in an unanimous motion as "a vote for the new International."[86] It was Lenin's conception of the way that a third International would emerge that set him apart. Lenin's aggressive tactical postulates, including the concept of defeatism, were widely considered unnecessarily provocative. His insistence upon organizational schisms was not calculated to appeal to left factions struggling to guard their positions against attacks from the defensist right. At a time when the international opposition was just beginning to draw together, Lenin's splitting tactics seemed to provide a recipe for sectarianism. As a result important segments of the revolutionary left, including the Bulgarian Narrows, the International Group, the left Mensheviks and SRs, and the Serrati wing of the PSI, refused to support Lenin's left faction at Zimmerwald. Its isolation was to a degree self-imposed.

The precariousness of Lenin's position was illustrated by his relations with the International Group, still widely considered to be the key to a viable international left. Though reduced to communicating via correspondence from her prison in Berlin, Luxemburg remained the group's most influential theorist. Her first reactions to Zimmerwald seemed to echo Lenin. In November Bertha Thalheimer wrote to Grimm that Luxemburg was "storming in her cell" and "of the opinion that not enough has emerged from the Z[immerwald] C[onference]."[87] In December Luxemburg expressed to Leo Jogiches her fear that the opposition had been set on a "false track" by the conference due to its lack of "sharpness and consequence." "Our tactic," she proposed, "should not be to try and bring the entire opposition under one roof, but on the contrary to separate from this porridge the small, determined, action-prone core that can group itself around our program."[88]

Lenin could not have put it better, but when it came to translating their respective strategic assumptions into a political program he and Luxemburg moved apart. The thrust of Lenin's recommendations was organizational; left radical parties and a third International were counted as prerequisites for effective mass actions. Luxemburg's emphasis was agitational; systematic propaganda and proletarian mass actions would have to precede and prepare the way for organizational initiatives. In a "Resolution on the Character of a New International" written by Luxemburg and unanimously approved by the International Group at its first "national conference" on 16 March 1916, she made her position crystal clear:

The new International that must revive after the collapse of the former on 4 August 1914 can only be born as the result of the revolutionary class struggle of the proletarian masses in the most important capitalist countries. The existence and viability of the International is not an organizational issue, not a question of understandings within a small circle of individuals who come forward as representatives of the oppositionally-inclined strata of the working population, but rather a question of the mass movement of the proletariat of all lands. . . . The first word of this struggle must be systematic mass action to force the achievement of peace.[89]

Luxemburg argued that only the revolutionary mass movement could provide the impetus necessary for the formation of a new International, that work for peace was the best way to encourage such a movement, and that organizational initiatives in the absence of a proletarian revival were premature. Her views were widely shared. Writing on 24–25 November in *Nashe Slovo*, Trotsky denounced the Leninists as "extremists and sectarians," seeking "to substitute the question of organizational boundaries for that of political action." What was needed, he suggested, was a "Marxist center" positioned between the "passive internationalism" of Grimm and the disorganizing tendencies of the ultraleft.[90] During his dispute with Lenin prior to Zimmerwald, Radek seemed to be moving in the same direction. What were the parameters of revolutionary Marxism? Lenin offered one set of assumptions, but they were not universally shared.

Neither criticisms nor isolation affected Lenin's determination to go on with the effort to build a new movement around whatever cadre could be assembled. His unabashed voluntarism, conviction that radical intellectuals must not tail the mass movement but rather foresee and lead, and insistence upon the critical importance of the organizational factor were qualities that Trotsky, among others, would later come greatly to prize. Socialist politics in the age of imperialism, he insisted again and again, demanded a new International inspired by an unshakable revolutionary vision. At Zimmerwald the effort to construct this International became the self-proclaimed raison d'être of Lenin's left faction.

4

The Zimmerwald Left

Non piú nemici, non piú frontiere
Sono i confini rosse bandiere
O proletari, alla riscossa
Bandiera rossa trionferà!

(No longer enemies, no longer borders
Red flags are our horizons
Proletarians, to arms
The red flag will triumph!)

—Italian Communist Anthem

ON the morning following the adjournment of the Zimmerwald conference, Lenin caucused with the handful of delegates who had supported his platform (Zinoviev, Radek, Berzin, Borchardt, Platten, Höglund, and Nerman). The group christened itself "The Zimmerwald Left," adopted Radek's project resolution as a working program, and designated Lenin, Zinoviev, and Radek as a coordinating bureau.[1] At the moment of its creation the Left was a highly informal organization, without an affiliated membership or significant institutional resources. Lenin was clearly its driving force, but Willi Gautschi's suggestion that the designation was merely a "synonym for the Bolsheviks" seems exaggerated.[2] The Left emerged from Zimmerwald as a thinly represented but legitimately international political tendency.

According to Krupskaia, Lenin returned to Sörenberg after the conference in a state of exhaustion.[3] Fatigued or not, he immediately threw himself into the effort to carry on the work that Zimmerwald had begun. The Bolshevik Central Committee issued a summary of the conference that emphasized the contributions made by the Left, and a special edition of *Sotsial-Demokrat* appeared on 11 October including the Left's resolution and manifesto. An article by Lenin entitled "The First Step" acknowledged Zimmerwald's importance but regretted the majority's "timidity." The Left would support what was positive in the movement, he suggested, but also intended to present itself as a radical alternative.[4] Radek spoke for the Left in the German language press, and though his evaluations were often more nuanced than Lenin's, they arrived at an identical conclusion. Writing in *Neues Leben* he praised the Zimmerwald manifesto as a "brave and historic" document which despite "imperfections" represented a call to struggle. The Left would contribute to the struggle by providing an "axis for the crystallization of all proletarian revolutionary elements." An article appearing in *Lichtstrahlen*, also entitled "The First Step," sounded a more critical theme. "We stand now at the beginning of a process of reorientation," Radek posited, where "half measures" would not suffice. "The conference produced many such half measures and much lack of clarity. The Marxist left struggles against this."[5]

The struggle against "half measures" required that the Left's perspective be clearly differentiated from that of the Zimmerwald majority. The urgent need to assert his own tendency's independence helps to explain the severity of Lenin's attacks upon Grimm in his new role as chairperson of the ISC. During September Lenin repeatedly objected to Grimm's accounts of Zimmerwald for their failure to acknowledge the role played by the Left.[6] The summary of the conference appearing in the first *ISC Bulletin* on 21 September provoked particular ire due to Grimm's understated description of the ISC and its responsibilities. According to the Zimmerwald chairperson, the commission was strictly provisional and would function only until "the ISB can once again take up its normal duties."[7] Lenin underlined the latter passage in his personal copy of the *ISC Bulletin*, added the marginal notation "no decision about this," and protested to Radek concerning Grimm's "disloyalty."[8] In fact the issue had been debated at Zimmerwald, and Grimm's definitions were entirely consistent with the conditions imposed there by the majority. It was the conditions themselves that Lenin now sought to contest. Was Zimmerwald a "first step" toward a fundamental reorientation of the international socialist movement or an extraordinary antiwar conference whose goal was to restore the Second International?

The Left announced itself to the international community by initiating the publication of a newsletter. On 9 November Lenin wrote to Kollontai: "In a few days we are publishing here (in German, then later *we hope* in French, and if we can turn up the money, in Italian) a small pamphlet on behalf of the *Zimmerwald Left*. Under this name we should like to launch into international circulation, as widely as possible, our left group at Zimmerwald."[9] One week later the first of an intended series of brochures entitled *Internationale Flugblätter* (International Broadsheets) was issued on behalf of the Left by the Bolshevik section in Zürich. The first (and only) number of the *Internationale Flugblätter* carried the subtitle "The Zimmerwald Left on the Tasks of the Working Class" and included the Left's resolution and manifesto. An introduction written by Radek once again greeted Zimmerwald as a "first step" but placed greater emphasis upon the need for a radical alternative. The Left announced its determination to serve as a clarion for the revolutionary confrontations that the war would inevitably provoke. "We do not wish to create the illusion that we are already a large, collective power," Radek cautioned. "We are representatives of the first, gradually awakening part of the international working class . . . [but] with every day our circle will grow, until we are a great, militant army."[10]

Nashe Slovo mocked the appearance of *Internationale Flugblätter* as a gesture "by which the 'eight' decisively constitute themselves as a separate faction."[11] Contemporaries commonly perceived the creation of the Left as an exercise in sectarianism, and yet Radek's hopeful prognosis was not entirely unfounded. The history of international communism begins with the Zimmerwald Left, and the "militant army" to which Radek referred would eventually appear in the ranks. The Left had launched an extremely ambitious political challenge. No effort was made to disguise the fact that the rudimentary organization that emerged from Zimmerwald was far from being in a position to realize its goals. Rather, hopes were placed upon the transformations being wrought by the war. The immediate task of revolutionary Marxists was not to throw up barricades but to assume a correct strategic line, rally support, and prepare for gathering storms.

To this end the Left's supporters set out to refine a critical analysis that exposed the inadequacy of the moderate opposition. Splitting tactics were forwarded within national movements, aimed at fracturing the artificial consensus imposed by defensism and encouraging the creation of independent left factions. Within Zimmerwaldist forums a challenge to Grimm and the moderate majority was mounted relentlessly. These single-minded efforts were alienating to some, but they bore fruit. The Left did not flourish as an organization, but it guarded its political identity. Though the Zimmerwald movement was not won over, pressure from the Left combined with the catastrophic international situation worked to radicalize it. Social democratic organizations continued to fragment, with revolutionary factions taking form on the left flank. Radek's "process of reorientation" was clearly at work.

The Precursor

One of the Zimmerwald Left's most ambitious undertakings was the effort to found an international theoretical journal. Since the turn of the century, when he set out to provide direction for czarist Russia's emerging labor movement through the publication of the journal *Iskra* (Spark), Lenin had attached special importance to the "central organ" as a tool of mobilization.[12] *Internationale Flugblätter* was too limited a format to serve that end and was abandoned after the first number. To replace it plans were made to initiate a more substantial, German-language theoretical journal as the central organ of the Zimmerwald Left.

The Zimmerwald Left possessed no independent resources, and a prerequisite for the initiation of any sort of publication was the securing of funds. Radek took the initiative on 12 October, addressing a long letter to Henrietta Roland-Holst in the Netherlands to solicit her support for a publishing venture on behalf of the "international left." Radek praised Roland-Holst's work in Holland but suggested that she might more fruitfully make use of her time and resources by founding an international journal than by "manipulating" among Dutch sects. "If you could found an international review, in the German language, as an organ for discussion among the lefts," he wrote, "you would perform a truly great service ... We, that is, I, Lenin, J[ulian] B[orchardt], Anton [Pannekoek] will regularly support the journal. I have spoken with Lenin. He agrees. I fear only that he might refuse if Trotsky were to become a collaborator."[13]

Radek's proposal arrived in the midst of a major organizational reshuffling within the Dutch left. At an extraordinary party congress in Arnhem during January 1915 the SDAP majority, led by Pieter Troelstra and aligned with the northern neutrals, found its cautious neutrality challenged by approximately a third of the delegates present. Frustrated in their efforts to move the organization toward a stronger antiwar posture, groups of militants proceeded to organize a network of "Revolutionary Socialist Clubs," which in May 1915 amalgamated to form a Revolutionary Socialist League (*Revolutionnair Socialistisch Verbond*—RSV). After September 1915 the severe criticisms directed toward Zimmerwald by Troelstra and the SDAP majority served to precipitate a split that had long been in the making. Led by Roland-Holst, the RSV threw itself wholeheartedly behind Zimmerwald and became the movement's leading representative in the Netherlands.[14]

The RSV's confrontation with the SDAP majority raised the issue of its attitude toward the SDP Tribunists. The RSV's charter declared the intention "to create a bridge between the SDP and the 'opposition' in the SDAP," while Roland-Holst described her organization as an internationalist alternative between two extremes, "one opportunistic and nationalistic, the other dogmatic and impossibilist."[15] "Impossibilist" was not too strong a term for the Tribunists, who distinguished themselves as the only significant left faction in Europe to deny even critical support to the Zimmerwald action. *De Tribune's* editor Wijnkoop rejected the "compromised" results of the conference, which he reviled as an "historical farce." Wijnkoop took care to note that his objections were not meant to apply to the "so-called Zimmerwald Left," but the Tribunists had refused Lenin's plea to send a delegation to Zimmerwald, and their platform differed from that of the Bolsheviks in several particulars, including the disarmament and national questions.[16] At the same time, a faction within the SDP led by Pannekoek and the youth leader Bernd Luteraan urged support for Zimmerwald and affiliation with the Left, described by Pannekoek as "a small group of revolutionaries who have not for an instant abandoned the standpoint of class struggle and internationalism, and have not made a single concession to the national point of view." "In this pitch black night," he wrote, "even so small a light as Zimmerwald can do service."[17]

Dutch social democracy had divided into no less than four currents: the SDAP's neutralist majority; the RSV, aligned with the peace strategy of the Zimmerwald majority; the Pannekoek group in the SDP associated with the Zimmerwald Left; and the Tribunist maximalists behind Wijnkoop. Under the circumstances Radek's proposed publishing venture provided a convenient rallying point for internationalists. Roland-Holst, a highly emotional poet who would later turn away from Marxism to Christian socialism, was being thoroughly radicalized by the horrors of the war. She received Radek's proposal enthusiastically and sought to rally support among her associates. During the final months of 1915 the RSV moved steadily to the left, allying with radical trade unionists in a renamed Revolutionary Socialist Union (*Revolutionnair Socialistisch Vereeniging*). On 2 January 1916, at a conference in Amsterdam, the "new" RSV voted to sever all ties with the SDAP and announced its affiliation to the Zimmerwald Left. The RSV also made overtures to the SDP, and a process of conciliation was set in the works that would result in a merger of the two organizations during May.[18] The Dutch left, positioned within an important neutral state and with solid institutional resources, seemed to be swinging behind Lenin's priorities.

Only Wijnkoop's maximalists remained apart from the movement toward unity on the left and refused to cooperate with Radek's project. A tendency to favor pro-Entente positions colored the Tribunist leader's judgments, and he absolutely refused to countenance joint work with Roland-Holst, accusing her of "political stupidity and moral cowardice."[19] The verdict was categorical, but Pannekoek was able to isolate Wijnkoop by rallying most other prominent Tribunists behind the publishing venture. On 22 and 24 October he wrote long letters to Wijnkoop supporter Willem van Ravestejn, soliciting his collaboration and describing the proposed journal in some detail. Six editors would be appointed, Pannekoek explained. He and Roland-Holst would serve as editors-in-chief, with Lenin, van Ravestejn, Radek, and Trotsky as coeditors. Potential contributors, "in order to make the journal truly international," included Mehring, Borchardt, Merrheim, Grimm, Zetkin, Louis Fraina (a member of the U.S. Socialist Labor party), and "an Englishman and a Swede." In question was "an organ of the left-wing of the internationally inclined remnants of the social democratic parties" whose first goal would be "to reach an understanding over the correct theoretical line for the new International."[20]

On 26 October Roland-Holst also wrote to van Ravestejn, endorsing Pannekoek's outline and stressing the provisional character of the entire undertaking, "while certain individuals who must belong to the editorial board . . . i.e. Rosa Luxemburg . . . for the moment cannot take part." Van Ravestejn bowed to the entreaties, and over Wijnkoop's objections to association with "a new international mishmash à la Zimmerwald," he agreed to function as an editor.[21] For Radek, who monitored the quarrel within the SDP from Switzerland, the priority now became to get the project off the ground at once, before factional disputes scuttled it altogether. On 23 November he advised Roland-Holst "not to wait until a full understanding has been reached. That could take months. Let us get out the *first number*, then things will develop on their own."[22]

As outlined by Radek, Pannekoek, and Roland-Holst, the proposed journal was intended to speak for the "international left." The gap between their standards for participation and the tighter criteria preferred by Lenin was made clear by the inclusion of Grimm, Merrheim, and Trotsky as potential collaborators. Trotsky, in agreeing to function as a coeditor, emphasized the project's moderate orientation: "Around Roland-Holst, who represented my own point of view, there gathered a group of more or less like-minded coworkers; the *Nashe Slovo* group, Germans from *Die Internationale*, a Frenchman, Rakovski, and others. The established relations guaranteed a coalition journal, in which the extremists would be represented by Pannekoek."[23]

Roland-Holst's shift to the left blurred Trotsky's balance of forces, and in December the editorial board described the journal, now dubbed *Der Vorbote* (The Precursor), as "representing the point of view of the Zimmerwald Left." The Left's coordinating bureau was granted special editorial privileges, and the place of publication was designated as Switzerland. For Trotsky these steps signaled Lenin's ascendancy, and in January he withdrew from the project, complaining to Roland-Holst: "You wrote about a coalition journal. . . . Meanwhile, *Vorbote* has become an organ of the so-called Zimmerwald Left, that is, Lenin's group . . . I don't believe that such a journal is capable of gathering around itself real support in the sphere of the German and French labor movements . . . Russian and Dutch extremists together cannot found an International."[24] Other moderate oppositionists contacted as potential contributors expressed similar reservations. Grimm inquired whether the SDP was not being "captured" by Lenin; Zetkin rebuked the Left for sectarianism, and David Riazanov of the *Nashe Slovo* group ridiculed the isolation of *Vorbote*'s combative "*enragés.*"[25]

The confusion over *Vorbote*'s political complexion reflected different perspectives within the editorial board itself. Radek was the project's prime mover, and in contrast to Lenin's rigid insistence upon maintaining principle at all costs, he urged a flexible orientation capable of appealing to a wider spectrum of left opinion. At issue, after Roland-Holst's conversion in November, was not whether the journal would stand "for the point of view" of the Zimmerwald Left, but how much diversity that point of view should encompass.

Lenin and Radek had already crossed swords on several occasions over the type of approach necessary to build the Left. The issue around which their differences crystallized during 1916 became the "national question," a rather abstract point of discord, but one which contained important implications. The long-standing controversy within the socialist camp over justifications for nationalism and national self-determination was reposed with particular force by the war, itself a terrifying demonstration of the power and danger of the national idea. These were problems that touched upon the very essence of the Left's aspiration to represent an alternative image of world order. *Vorbote* was intended to become the "precursor" of a new, authentically internationalist world socialist movement. Who were its constituents, and where did its political horizons lie? The debate over the national question which erupted in the background of the *Vorbote* venture revealed that a common understanding of the Left's priorities was not yet in place among its own leaders.

The National Question

The national question within the Second International was first of all concerned with whether socialists should consider national self-determination to be a legitimate aspiration. The International's 1896 London congress approved a motion by the pacifist George Lansbury endorsing self-determination as a "right," but the decision was contested and did not reflect a consensus. In effect the problem was never resolved, and on the eve of the war three contending positions on the national question continued to clash.[26]

The most widely supported position followed Lansbury in endorsing self-determination more or less unconditionally. Among the more outspoken proponents of the demand were the Bolsheviks, who perceived it as a means of struggle against the czarist "prisonhouse of peoples." At its second congress in 1903 the RSDRP wrote self-determination into its program, defined as the right to territorial autonomy and national independence subject to approval by a popular referendum. While asserting that the right to self-determination did not necessarily imply its desirability, the party insisted that the principle be incorporated in its minimum program. Iosif Stalin's 1913 pamphlet *Marxism and the National Question* provided the definition upon which claims to independence were legitimized: "The nation is an historically developed, ordered collectivity of individuals, arising on the basis of a common language, territory, economic life, and psychological orientation, defined within a common culture."[27] The criteria were demanding, but with all conditions in place the claim to national status was conceded to be justified. The

Bolshevik position was further distinguished by Lenin's argument that a struggle against "great power chauvinism" demanded support for national liberation struggles against colonialism and the application of the principle of self-determination in the non-European world as well.[28]

A contrasting position emerged from the "Austro-Marxist" school of Otto Bauer and Karl Renner. Bauer's ideal of "cultural-national autonomy" for ethnic minorities within a unitary federal state corresponded to the exigencies of Austria-Hungary's national dilemma and was adopted as the basis for the Austrian party's nationalities program at its Brünn congress in 1899. In Bauer's rather arcane terminology the nation was "the totality of individuals bound together through a community of fate into a community of character," or for Renner "a cultural community." Bauer and Renner emphasized the diversity of the social democratic movement and argued against universal formulas that ignored its multinational context. Self-determination, they suggested, was too simplistic a notion to solve what was in essence a complex sociocultural dilemma.[29] Lenin denounced such arguments as obscurantist, and Stalin's *Marxism and the National Question* was in significant measure intended as a polemic against Bauer.

A third position, associated with the left wing of the Polish movement led by Luxemburg, rejected the entire issue as a distraction from the real essence of social democratic politics—class struggle and social revolution. The SDKPiL split from the RSDRP in 1903 to protest against support for self-determination and remained an outspoken opponent of the Polish national movement. Luxemburg also challenged Lenin by refusing to accord weight to revolutionary nationalism in the colonial world. Colonial oppression was a particularly brutal form of class oppression, she felt, but its roots lay in the imperialist world economy and could not be eliminated by encouraging parochial nationalism. The battle for social democracy would be waged within the advanced industrial states, with its base in the organized proletariat. Evaluated objectively, self-determination was an illusion, a bourgeois panacea that worked to divide and weaken the international labor movement.[30]

Luxemburg spoke for the entire left radical wing of the Second International, and her views were shared by a number of prominent Bolsheviks. The national question surfaced briefly during the clash between Lenin and Bukharin at the Bolsheviks' Bern conference in March 1915. Subsequently Lenin attempted to assuage ill will by turning over editorship of the journal *Kommunist* to Bukharin and his allies, but the issue was not put to rest. Relocated in Stockholm during the summer of 1915, Bukharin and his fellow editors Georgii Piatakov and Evgeniia Bosh became even more outspoken. When the first number of *Kommunist* appeared in September 1915, Lenin was extremely put off by its independent orientation and reacted by withdrawing party support. The Stockholm editors protested in vain. In November they responded by issuing a set of theses that made their differences with Lenin clear, including direct attacks on the principle of self-determination and "national" liberation.[31] The issue pushed under the rug at Bern had burst into the open, with Bukharin aligning with the Luxemburgist wing of the international left in opposition to the Bolshevik majority.

The *Kommunist* controversy was resolved by administrative fiat on the part of the Central Committee, but the problem which lay at its core soon moved into the international arena. At the Zimmerwald conference the SDKPiL-Regional Presidium presented a set of theses on the national question which reiterated its opposition to all forms of self-determination.[32] During October Radek summarized the theses in a series of articles for the *Berner Tagwacht*, provoking a sharp though discreet response from Lenin.[33] Undeterred, Radek continued to defend his position publicly. In December he published a more polished article in *Lichtstrahlen* that compared his views with those of Luxemburg and cited her repudiation of self-determination as a "petty-bourgeois formula that has nothing in common with Marxism." "The fact is," Radek polemicized, "that within a capitalist state the right of self-determination for nations does not exist, never has existed, and also never shall."[34]

Luxemburg herself now entered the fray. On 1 January 1916, in a conspiratorial gathering in Liebknecht's Berlin apartment, the leaders of the International Group renamed their organization the Spartacus League, and approved a set of "guidelines" (*Leitsätze*) based upon a text written by Luxemburg as a preliminary program.[35] The fifth of the guidelines restated Luxemburg's position on the national question, arguing that in the age of imperialism "national wars can no longer exist." In her most developed analysis of the war crisis, the pamphlet *The Crisis of Social Democracy*, written in prison during

1915 and published under the pseudonym "Junius" during 1916, Luxemburg took the point further. Really autonomous national communities, she posited, could only result from a socialist restructuring of the imperialist world system: "So long as capitalist states exist, that is so long as the global policy of imperialism continues to define and determine the internal and external existence of states, the right of national self-determination has nothing to do with their activities either in peace or war." "National" liberation in the colonial world would not lead toward socialism or the defeat of imperialism. "Only from Europe, only from the most modern capitalist states, can the signal for social revolution and the liberation of humanity emerge. Only the English, French, Belgian, German, Russian, and Italian workers can collectively lead the army of exploited and enserfed peoples of the seven continents."[36]

Lenin responded in a series of articles published at intervals in the course of 1916.[37] Repeating the contention that self-determination formed an integral part of a minimum program embracing general democratic goals, he rejected the counter that such a program was unrealizable under capitalism. All general democratic goals were unrealizable under capitalism in an absolute sense, but in relative terms they provided a focus for protest action and broadened the context of class struggle. Though the Bolshevik maximum program aspired to the "convergence" (*sliianie*) of nations in a universal socialist federation, that was a point of orientation, not a concrete demand. For Lenin under certain circumstances self-determination was a narrow but necessary objective. It referred "exclusively to the right of independence in a political sense" and to a "resolution of the question of determination by means of a referendum." In arguing that the global hegemony of imperialism negated national struggles, Bukharin and Luxemburg confused a trend with consummated reality. Uneven and unequal development remained the most prominent attribute of the international system of developed capitalism, and for that reason the national form and national self-determination retained some relevance.

Lenin distinguished three types of situation where the principle of self-determination could be applied even in a world system characterized by the hegemony of imperialism: (1) within the leading imperial powers, where "bourgeois-progressive" national movements had long since been completed, but which retained exploited internal colonies such as Ireland; (2) within the multinational states of Central and Eastern Europe, where bourgeois-democratic revolutions remained incomplete and self-determination was a prerequisite for their culmination; and (3) within colonized regions or semicolonized nations such as China, Iran, or Turkey, where only limited progress toward bourgeois democracy had been accomplished and where outright colonial exploitation still held sway. In ways corresponding to each of these categories, Lenin insisted, revolutionary socialists must support self-determination "unconditionally" if proletarian internationalism was not to become an empty phrase. In the first instance, national ideology had lost its progressive content, but the existence of exploited internal colonies placed fetters upon the labor movement. In the second instance, national movements represented positive alternatives to remnants of feudalism. In the third instance, a direct link was posited between the extent of exploitation in the colonial world and the viability of the imperialist world system. Far from contradicting international solidarity, support for self-determination was a prerequisite for its realization.

As the champion of revolutionary defeatism, Lenin was the first to agree that claims by the belligerent powers to represent "national" values were hypocritical. He nonetheless refused to accept Luxemburg's categorical conclusion that in the age of imperialism national wars were no longer possible. National liberation struggles against colonialism were inevitable, bourgeois-national conflicts might still lead to positive ends, and revolutionary civil wars, which could also be waged as interstate conflicts, were an unavoidable aspect of social revolution. These realities imposed three unambiguous tactical conclusions: (1) the proletariat must demand the "uninhibited right of political self-determination" for nations and colonies oppressed by the imperial powers; (2) socialists within the oppressed nations must strive to realize a "full and unconditional" unity with the workers of the oppressor nations; and (3) socialists must support "the more revolutionary elements within the bourgeois-democratic, national-liberation movements" in the oppressed nations and aid them in pursuing an armed struggle against imperialism.[38]

In making such assertions Lenin moved beyond his contemporaries and displayed considerable foresight. Marx and Engels strove to craft a universal social theory based upon scientific premises, but their personal horizons were Eurocentric. The internationalism of the Second International reflected the narrow priorities of the European mass parties that dominated it. Even the left radical critique, with its fixation upon the leading role of the proletariat, envisioned the fate of socialism being decided within the advanced industrial states. Lenin shared these priorities to some extent. After the Irish Easter Rebellion of 1916 he commented that a blow struck against imperialism in Europe was "a hundred times" more important than a similar blow struck in Africa or Asia.[39] More than any other socialist theorist of his generation, however, Lenin was also filled with a sense of the promise held out by the rise of revolutionary nationalism in the colonial world, regions containing, as he repeatedly noted, well more than half of the world's population.

In the 1916 debate over the national question within the Marxist left, Luxemburg, Radek, Bukharin, and their allies represented an orthodox position anchored within the terms of reference of the Second International. Their image of revolutionary change rested upon a kind of left-wing economism that harked back to Kautsky's *The Road to Power*. Proletarian revolution was considered immanent within modern industrial society, a direct function of the contradictions of advanced capitalism. Imperialism voided the national form of any progressive content and made the national question irrelevant to the "revolution of the producers." Lenin's response was radically innovative. Imperialism had not altered the need for proletarian revolution, but it imposed a redefinition of the relationship between revolutionary nationalism and proletarian class struggle. For Lenin these were complementary aspects of an emerging global confrontation between the forces of movement and a hegemonic imperialism. Revolutionary transformation would occur "in the course of an epoch," uniting "civil war waged by the proletariat against the bourgeoisie in the leading nations with an *entire sequence* of democratic and revolutionary, to include national-liberation, movements in the underdeveloped, backward, and oppressed nations."[40] The transition from capitalism to socialism would be, in a phrase that soon became a summary for Lenin's entire strategic outlook, a world revolution.

These conclusions moved Lenin away from the positivistic determinism of Kautsky and toward a reconceptualization of the fundaments of Marxist theory. The scholastic debate over the national question was leading to the clarification of an essential point of departure between the Second and Third Internationals. Lenin argued for a larger, more comprehensive, and more nuanced image of revolutionary change, conceived not as an isolated event, but as a process that would unfold on the scale of history. The eventual triumph of his theses would go a long way toward fixing the character of revolutionary Marxism in the decades to come.

The Demise of Vorbote

Theoretical implications aside, the immediate consequences of the debate over the national question were highly unpalatable for the Zimmerwald Left. The issue drew Lenin and Radek into a direct confrontation, undermined the cohesion of the Left's coordinating bureau, and became the undoing of the entire *Vorbote* venture. The controversy gave rise to a struggle for control of *Vorbote*'s editorial line where Radek's influence with the Dutch left proved decisive. On 15 January 1916, with the first number of *Vorbote* nearly complete, the Left's coordinating bureau met formally in Bern. Conflict immediately arose between Lenin, who sought to emphasize *Vorbote*'s character as a "party" journal subject to tight editorial control, and Radek, who reiterated his broader conception of the publication as a voice for the international left. Several days later Lenin was informed by Pannekoek that *Vorbote*'s editorial board was being reformed. Pannekoek and Roland-Holst remained editors-in-chief, but the co-editor designation was dropped, with Lenin, Zinoviev, Radek, and van Ravestejn reduced to the status of contributors.[41] *Vorbote* still represented the Zimmerwald Left, but it was clear that Lenin would be prevented from imposing a personal stamp upon editorial policy.

The Zimmerwald Left's coordinating bureau met again on 25 January. The first number of *Vorbote* was now ready for press, with an editorial comment committing the journal to the program of the Zimmerwald Left, but also an article by Radek that attacked Lenin's position on the national question.[42] Lenin reacted by presenting the Left bureau with a letter addressed to Pannekoek and Roland-Holst protesting the elimination of coeditors, demanding that *Vorbote* speak "as an organ of" the Left, and offering a set of contrasting theses on the national question.[43] Both the letter and the theses were approved by Lenin and Zinoviev over Radek's objections and forwarded in the name of the Zimmerwald Left to the Netherlands.

Roland-Holst's reply was conciliatory, reaffirming that she and

Pannekoek would continue to function as the exclusive editors but promising that *Vorbote*'s pages would remain open to Lenin and his allies. For the Bolshevik leader the arrangement was far from ideal, but he determined to live with it. In early March he wrote to Roland-Holst and expressed the desire to continue joint work.[44] In April the second number of *Vorbote* was issued, with contrasting statements on the national question from the Bolshevik Central Committee (the text of Lenin's "Socialist Revolution and the Right of Nations to Self-Determination"), the SDKPiL-Regional Presidium (the theses originally presented at Zimmerwald), and Radek. The format represented a triumph for Radek's broader conception of the journal as an open forum for the international left and a defeat for Lenin.

The second number of *Vorbote* was also the last to appear. In April and May the merger between the RSV and SDP presented the Dutch left with new responsibilities. A revamped *De Tribune* began to be issued as a weekly during April (it had previously appeared as a biweekly), and on 24 April the two organizations cosponsored an antiwar congress. An increasingly tense domestic political environment punctuated by a brief war scare created opportunities for direct action that culminated with a mass demonstration against hunger and war on 21 June in Amsterdam. Under the circumstances, and given the unresolved controversy over editorial policy, Roland-Holst elected to withdraw her support, and *Vorbote* languished. During the summer the Bolsheviks initiated a new Russian-language journal entitled *Sbornik Sotsial-Demokrata* (A Social Democrat's Notebook) to replace the defunct *Kommunist* and to provide an alternative outlet for the Zimmerwald Left. But *Sbornik Sotsial-Demokrata* was a party journal, hardly a substitute for an international, German-language publication.[45]

In conjunction with the demise of *Vorbote*, Lenin's relationship with Radek disintegrated. Certainly neither man was an entirely congenial associate. Lenin was notorious for his aggressive political demeanor, and Radek had made a career of alienating associates in one organization after another. Their differences derived in part from personality and style of work, but they were essentially political.[46] Radek remained attached to the left radical tradition and hoped to rebuild the revolutionary left upon the solid foundation of the German opposition. His disputes with Lenin—over the slogan of defeatism, Borchardt's group, and self-determination—all reflected a concern to broaden the Zimmerwald Left's appeal. Lenin, in contrast, was determined to achieve theoretical consistency no matter what the cost. By disrupting *Vorbote*, publicly disputing the Left's program, and plotting behind the back of the coordinating bureau, Radek was making the emergence of an international left "purged of opportunism" more difficult. The final straw came in January 1916 when the SDKPiL-Regional Presidium central organ *Gazeta Robotnicza* suggested that Lenin no longer attached to the slogan of defeatism "the same revolutionary significance as in the first months of the war." Describing the reference as a symptom of larger differences, Lenin sent Radek a brief note in which he melodramatically announced that "our common struggle in Russian and Polish affairs is *finished*."[47]

In the face of such petulance some of Lenin's closest associates began to question his judgments. Shliapnikov remarked upon Lenin's "uncompromising" stance; Zinoviev criticized a step away from the German left as inexpedient, and Armand interpreted the break with Radek as an abandonment of the Zimmerwald Left itself. Lenin sought to defend himself, pointing rather unconvincingly to *Sbornik Sotsial-Demokrata* as a forum "which gives us the opportunity to *lead* the party (and the international left) and not to follow behind." Later in the year he wrote to Armand that "because of the insolence and huckstering meanness of one person [Radek] the Zimmerwald Left does not cease to be the left."[48] All the same, the *Vorbote* episode was a setback for Lenin in his efforts to build an international left faction. The journal's failure left the Zimmerwald Left without an international forum to develop its views; Lenin's hope to use the central organ as a tool of mobilization had come to naught. Rather than encouraging unity, the theoretical disputes that erupted around the project revealed new sources of discord. Nor did the rift between Lenin and Radek, the Left's most talented leaders, contribute to the dynamism of the coordinating bureau. The setback was certainly not insurmountable, but it was profound.

Stratification Within the Opposition

If the Zimmerwald Left failed for the moment to develop as an organization, the revolutionary internationalist current that it represented made discernible progress. The Zimmerwald conference lent impetus to the process of stratification within the European social democratic movement set off by the policy of 4 August and stimulated the emergence of an autonomous left. Lenin and his associates encouraged the process to the extent that they could by supporting splitting tactics that urged a clean break with defensist majorities.

It was within the SPD, tormented by Germany's ambiguous role in the war, that division was most pronounced. During 1916 antiwar demonstrations and strike actions became recurrent events. Sensitive to the barometer of public opinion, on 21 December 1915 twenty-one social democratic deputies joined Liebknecht in voting against the government's fifth war credits bill and an additional twenty-two symbolically abstained by leaving the hall prior to the vote. The SPD Reichstag fraction was irremediably divided, and on 24 March 1916, provoked by a violent debate during which Haase made amends for his presentation of 4 August 1914 by denouncing the war, a split was consummated. Following his interventions, Haase was expelled from the fraction by the defensist majority and followed out in solidarity by a group of supporters including Kautsky, Bernstein, Wilhelm Dittmann, and the Zimmerwaldists Ledebour, Jozef Herzfeld, and Ewald Vogtherr. The opposition declared itself an independent Reichstag fraction with the name Social Democratic Working Group (*Sozialdemokratische Arbeitsgemeinschaft*), a title of convenience created in order to guard parliamentary status. The SPD center had achieved autonomy, not by choice but in defiance of the intolerant extremism of the defensist right.[49]

The revolutionary left reacted to the creation of the Working Group circumspectly. Liebknecht mocked its leaders as "windblown sand" (*politische Flugsand*) and looked for an alternative to the "determined revolutionary minority," a veiled reference to the newly created Spartacus League. Speaking for the Zimmerwald Left in *Lichtstrahlen* on 8 January, Borchardt downplayed the significance of the impending split and urged the Spartacus League to distance itself from the centrist opposition.[50] For the time being, however, a schism was not on the Spartacists' agenda. Though it possessed a national base, the league was small (its active membership numbered in the thousands) and poorly coordinated. For an illegal organization without a significant mass following, a break from the mainstream of the opposition was not considered a realistic option.

Though cautious about immediate prospects, the Spartacus

League made no secret of its attachment to the revolutionary left. The 1 January guidelines which served as a working program for the organization began with a diatribe against the betrayal of 4 August, said to have "eliminated the results of forty years of work on the part of European socialism," undermined the movement's "moral prestige," and destroyed the International. The war was described as a product of "imperialist rivalry between the capitalist classes of various nations for world hegemony," and diplomatic solutions were rejected as futile. Imperialism was the source of interstate conflict, and it could only be challenged by revolutionary mass actions. The guidelines emphasized the need for a new International to coordinate these actions and went beyond anything ventured on the German left in the past in appealing for discipline and centralization. The new International, it was specified, must become the "focal point of the class organization of the proletariat," with national sections obliged to follow directives upon pain of expulsion.

The guidelines were considerably more radical than the more general formulas of *Die Internationale* published eight months earlier. The moderate opposition took note of the trend, and Ledebour and Hoffmann reacted with a highly critical circular letter.[51] The Spartacists' revolutionary credentials were impeccable, but their position conflicted in several particulars with that of the Zimmerwald Left. The guidelines' outspoken critique of self-determination and rejection of a splitting tactic were direct challenges to Lenin. The League placed its focus upon mass actions, not political disorganization. According to the manifesto issued by its second national conference during March, "not division or unity, not old party or new party is the concern, but the winning back of the party from below, through the rebellion of the masses, who must take the organization and means into their own hands, not with words, but with the fact of revolt."[52]

Perhaps the clearest expression of the priorities motivating the Spartacists was Luxemburg's *The Crisis of Social Democracy*. A passionate and intellectually vital examination of the policy of 4 August and its consequences, the "Junius Pamphlet" was without question one of the most refined works of political analysis produced during the war. Luxemburg described the world conflagration as a direct consequence of imperialism, defined as "the competitive struggle of a capitalism now fully blossomed for world domination,

for the exploitation of the last remnants of non-capitalist regions."
She condemned the policy of 4 August as the product of revisionism,
rejected the means of "bourgeois diplomacy" as a road to peace, and
insisted upon a popular alternative. Lenin hailed her pamphlet as a
"splendid Marxist work" that "has played and will play an immense
role" in the struggle against defensism."[53]

Despite Lenin's praise, the conclusions drawn in *The Crisis of
Social Democracy* paralleled those of the guidelines and thus conflicted in important ways with his own analysis. The national question remained a point of contention, and Luxemburg once again
rejected attempts to substitute "technical recipes and organizational
initiatives" for the proletarian mass movement. "The international
proletariat," she noted pointedly, "does not lack postulates, programs, or solutions. Rather, it lacks deeds, effective resistance, readiness to attack imperialism at the decisive moment, precisely in time
of war." Luxemburg did not shrink from a harshly pessimistic view of
the consequences of the European crisis. The war marked a turning
point in the history of modern capitalism, she argued, but it was not
necessarily the prelude to social revolution. Unchecked by the revolutionary intervention of the proletariat, and regardless of its military outcome, it meant the beginning of "an era characterized by the
undiluted hegemony of militarism and reaction in all of Europe . . .
with a new world war for its final result." Luxemburg accepted Lenin's proposed antidote to this ominous vision; the creation of a
revolutionary International to lead the fight for an alternative. Her
perception of how the new International would emerge remained
distinct. Under her tutelage the Spartacists clung to the role of an
inner-party opposition and concentrated their limited means upon
systematic antiwar agitation.

The leading proponents of a splitting tactic in Germany were not
the Spartacists, but rather Borchardt and the Bremen Left Radicals. In
June 1916 the Bremen section's left wing led by Johann Knief broke
from the center and founded an independent left radical organization.[54] The group's central organ, the *Bremer Arbeiterpolitik* (Bremen Workers' Program), immediately endorsed the Zimmerwald Left
and became its most important organized affiliate in Germany. For
the duration of the war the *Arbeiterpolitik* was published legally, a
lonely public voice for the extreme left. Its success in avoiding suppression was perhaps due to the fact that its main attacks were

directed against the centrist opposition rather than the government. The leader of the Bremen section's moderate wing, the former left radical Alfred Henke, was a member of the Working Group. The split in Bremen thus seemed to presage an emerging schism between the moderate opposition and the revolutionary left nationwide. For the time being the Bremen phenomenon remained isolated, but by the summer of 1916 the German labor movement had fractionalized into four distinct currents: the unrepentant defensist majority, now heir to the official SPD; the Working Group, aligned with the moderate opposition; the Spartacus League; and the Bremen Left Radicals and International Socialists of Germany, identified with the Zimmerwald Left.

A comparable process of stratification went forward elsewhere. In Vienna, the Friedrich Adler group rallied behind the Zimmerwald action, and at the national conference of the German Socialist party of Austria during March 1916 the moderate opposition publicly challenged the defensist majority for the first time.[55] Stimulated by the creation of the Working Group in Germany, during March Friedrich Adler and his supporters founded an informal Karl Marx Association (Verein Karl Marx) as a forum for the left.[56] Within the association a small revolutionary current also coalesced, with Fritz Koritschoner (a nephew of Rudolf Hilferding) as its leading personality. Koritschoner's faction adopted the name "Left Radical Action Committee" and gradually drew closer to the Zimmerwald Left.[57] Compared with its counterpart in Germany, the Austrian opposition was relatively weak, but by the spring of 1916 a familiar left/center/right trichotomy had appeared.

In France a parliamentary opposition appeared during 1916, but the socialist "minoritaires" led by Jean Longuet took pains to distinguish themselves from the Zimmerwald movement. At a public debate conducted in Paris on 7 November 1915, at which Pierre Renaudel represented the SFIO right, Longuet the emerging centrist opposition, and Merrheim and Bourderon the left, Longuet absolutely rejected action outside the structures of the Second International. Longuet assigned Germany primary responsibility for the war, promised that the defense of French territory would remain a priority, and limited his demands to a revival of international action for a negotiated peace through the intermediary of the ISB.[58] At a general conference of the SFIO on 25–30 December the federations aligned with the opposition established a tenuous unity but shrank from launching a public challenge.[59] At the SFIO National Council session of April 1916, however, Longuet and Pressemanne introduced a motion calling on the ISB to act in the service of peace, and following the session the minoritaires inaugurated an independent press outlet entitled *Le Populaire*. Alfred Rosmer later described the initiatives as "the first affirmation of the minority and its will to organize for the struggle."[60]

Zimmerwaldist opposition in France came together on 7 November around a *Comité d'action internationale*, which in January 1916 broadened its base by uniting socialists and syndicalists in a rechristened *Comité pour la reprise des relations internationales* (CRRI). The CRRI described its goals as consonant with those of the Zimmerwald majority, rejecting any intention to rival the SFIO or CGT and claiming that it would "exist only for so long as the Zimmerwald commission [ISC] exists."[61] It was itself divided between a moderate majority led by Merrheim and a radical wing following Rosmer, Monatte, and Trotsky. The CRRI lacked significant representation on the part of the Zimmerwald Left, which remained without an organized base in France.[62] A small Bolshevik party section in Saint-Nazaire led by Georgii Safarov maintained "cordial and mutually supportive" relations with the CRRI according to Rosmer, but in January 1916 Safarov was deported. Liudmilla Stal' propagated the Left's line within the Women's Action Committee for Peace, but the arrest of its leader Saumoneau on 2 October isolated the organization from the mainstream of the opposition.[63] Late in 1915 Lenin wrote almost desperately to Gregorii Belen'kii in Paris, asking "if there exists some kind of French group standing *for the position* of the Zimmerwald Left, *definitely* and *immediately* send us even a short article (or declaration) from this group for the journal [*Vorbote*]. Hurry!"[64] Armand traveled to Paris during January 1916 to seek out support but returned to Switzerland empty-handed. Of the CRRI she commented unenthusiastically that "it is unlikely that we will be able to obtain any serious results from the committee."[65]

The situation within the British movement appeared even less promising. The ILP published the Zimmerwald manifesto in *The Labour Leader* and expressed support for the action, but the journal (whose circulation leaped upward during the war due to the energetic editorship of Fenner Brockway) had moved substantially to the left of

the party leadership. Though drawn into an anticonscription movement by a militant rank and file, the ILP concentrated its energies
upon defining the terms of a democratic peace. MacDonald refuted
any intention to build a "stop the war" movement, and the party
declined to appoint a representative to the ISC. Membership in the ILP
grew steadily, no doubt an expression of latent popular antiwar sentiment, but the leadership was successful in imposing its cautious
priorities. At its Newcastle conference on 23–25 April 1916 the ILP
handily turned back demands from the left to sever ties with the
Labour party.[66]

The real struggle on the left occurred within the overtly Marxist
but considerably smaller BSP (it listed membership as 6435 in 1917),
where the confrontation between Henry Hyndman and the "Internationalists" climaxed in the spring of 1916. In September 1915 John
Maclean's Glasgow based BSP section inaugurated the publication of
The Vanguard as a voice for the revolutionary left, endorsed Zimmerwald, and demanded a repudiation of the Hyndman-controlled BSP
central organ *Justice*.[67] Maclean represented an extremist position,
but the balance between right and left within the party's direction
was shifting to Hyndman's disadvantage. On 30 September *Justice*
was constrained to publish the Zimmerwald manifesto, and at its
September session the BSP executive committee voted five to three
with one abstention to approve the Zimmerwald action.

The Internationalists' progress was impressive, but it did not
equate to progress for the Zimmerwald Left. For the moment the BSP
Internationalist current was most closely aligned with the more
cautious right Zimmerwaldists such as Ledebour and Oddino Morgari. Its leader Edwin Fairchild, in a motion drawn up during October
1915, denied any desire to "endanger national defence," and limited
his goals to encouraging a "united demand of the international working class for the conclusion of peace" and "the immediate reestab-
lishment of the International." In December the BSP affiliated with
the ISC but simultaneously voiced its opposition to "any move to
form a new international organization apart from or in opposition to
the International Socialist Bureau."[68]

Even these limited gestures were too much for the Hyndmanite defensists. The arrest of Maclean and other Clydeside leaders in December, to the barely disguised satisfaction of the BSP right, brought
the issue to the boiling point. With the Glasgow section decimated

by arrests, *The Vanguard* was forced to cease publication. Its place was immediately taken by a London-based publication edited by Fairchild entitled *The Call*. The BSP had split in all but name, and at a general party congress in Salford on 23–24 April, faced with a hostile majority, Hyndman and his supporters walked out in a bloc. The Internationalists had captured the party from within. The BSP proceeded to salute the "magnificent" Zimmerwald manifesto, but the Zimmerwald Left could only muster a handful of supporters on the party's extreme left wing. As late as September 1916 Maksim Litvinov could write to Lenin from London that: "Things are even worse than I had expected. Of Zimmerwald one finds not a trace."[69]

In Bulgaria, Greece, Portugal, Romania, Spain, the United States, and as far afield as Argentina and South Africa, the organized socialist opposition rallied behind the Zimmerwald majority.[70] During November 1915, at a general congress in Aarau, the SPS voted by a large margin to adhere to the movement it had contributed so much to launching, while motions proposed by the Zimmerwald Left were weakly supported.[71] When the PSI directorate formally endorsed the Zimmerwald action on 12 October 1915 in Turin, the party's important left wing declined to acknowledge an affiliation with the Left.[72] Even members of the Left such as Höglund and Nerman downplayed its significance in the accounts of Zimmerwald which they composed for the Swedish left press.[73] The Swedes' commitment to militant antiwar action was nonetheless impressive. A "Workers' Antiwar Congress" sponsored by the Youth League in Stockholm on 18–19 March 1916 attracted national representation and issued a manifesto calling for extraparliamentary resistance.[74] In its wake, in a harsh gesture intended to intimidate radicalism, Höglund, Erik Heden, and L. N. Ivan Oljelund were arraigned by the government for high treason.

In sum, as political stratification within national movements continued during the winter and spring of 1915–1916, the Zimmerwald movement made steady gains while the left tendency struggled to find a foothold. One of the greatest drawbacks that the Left confronted was its lack of a clear institutional identity, a problem that the *Vorbote* failure certainly compounded. Some trends nonetheless worked to the Left's advantage. An important component of the international movement was lining up behind the banner of Zimmerwald. If in the main this represented support for the peace strategy of the moderate opposition, it also meant a step away from the premises of defensism and toward permanent division. The continuation of the war encouraged radicalism, and the incidence of popular antiwar actions was steadily increasing. The Left's ability to penetrate national movements and extend its presence was being demonstrated even if the results were still modest. With the political situation entirely in flux, its prospects remained wide open.

"Who Says A Must Come to Say B"

An additional arena within which the Left aspired to enlarge its presence was the Zimmerwald movement itself. Lenin made no secret of his hope that a significant portion of the socialist antiwar movement could eventually be won over to revolutionary priorities and transformed into the kernal of a third International. As Grimm and the ISC moved to capitalize upon the momentum established at Zimmerwald, partisans of the Left prepared to pursue more actively their role as an "opposition within the opposition."

At its first formal session on 10 September 1915 in Bern the ISC arranged for the distribution of the Zimmerwald manifesto, delegated Grimm and Balabanov authority over administration and finance, and agreed to begin the preparations for a second general conference.[75] In a circular letter dated 27 September the commission made public its intentions, describing the Zimmerwald conference as "the first step in a common action" based upon the principles of "struggle against the Burgfrieden, recommencement of the class struggle, and struggle against the war." The circular letter took note of the ISC's imperfectly representative character and proposed the creation of an "Enlarged Committee" consisting of delegates from all affiliated organizations as a consultative organ.[76] Despite its self-proclaimed "provisional" status, the ISC's actions signaled an intention to turn Zimmerwald into a dynamic movement with the potential to grow.

Toward that end Grimm took considerable pains to attract affiliates and establish a viable administration. His efforts were crowned with some success. The ISC's second circular letter, dated 22 November, listed a respectable number of members. Grimm collected dues, solicited contributions, and managed to keep the movement comfortably in the black.[77] He also sought to broaden Zimmerwald's base by attracting participation from the centrist opposition grouped around Kautsky in Germany, Friedrich Adler in Austria, and Longuet in France.[78] The opening to the center conflicted with Lenin's priorities, but for the moment it led nowhere. Moderates such as Kautsky continued to cling to the hope that the ISB might yet offer a less divisive path to a renewal of the International. The ISB's secretary Huysmans kept such hopes alive with an address delivered on 9 January 1916 in Arnhem. While directing a veiled critique toward Zimmerwald by scolding "impatient comrades" for attempting to go beyond the limits of the possible, he also bowed to pressures by announcing that the ISB would begin a series of consultations with its affiliates in order to gather information concerning acceptable terms for a negotiated peace.[79] If anything, these belated and minimal initiatives only strengthened Grimm's resolve to build the Zimmerwald movement as an alternative.

The ISC also pursued new directions. At its session of 18 December Morgari proposed the convention of a conference of socialist parliamentary fractions to spearhead a campaign against war credits.[80] As Grimm outlined the project in a letter to Liebknecht on 26 December, the intention was to prepare a common declaration demanding a ceasefire, to be read simultaneously in all European parliamentary assemblies. Grimm seems to have taken the idea seriously, but coordination presented nearly insurmountable problems, and by January it had been indefinitely postponed.[81] The suggestion to call together an enlarged committee to reinforce the work of the ISC proved more viable. The ISC's 22 November circular letter announced that the concept had been unanimously approved. At its December session the ISC scheduled an enlarged committee session for 6 February and adopted a tentative agenda.

The ISC's activities entangled Grimm in a running feud with Lenin. According to the Bolshevik leader, the parliamentary focus of Morgari's proposal was misplaced and the enlarged committee nothing more than a device for isolating the Left. During October the Bolshevik Central Committee sent Grimm an activities report for the second *ISC Bulletin*, written by Zinoviev and highly polemical in tone.[82] Grimm objected to its length and requested revisions. He also informed Aksel'rod of its contents and suggested that the Mensheviks prepare a response.[83] Lenin was infuriated by what he perceived as a cabal directed against his party, demanded that Zinoviev present all proposed deletions to him personally "underlined in red pencil," and even toyed with the idea of breaking with the ISC altogether.[84] Meanwhile, the Mensheviks too jumped upon Grimm for abetting the Bolsheviks' "sectarian" tactics and agreeing to publish "inaccuracies." Aksel'rod accused Grimm of allowing the *ISC Bulletin* to become "a channel for the discrediting of our faction" on behalf of the "Lenin-Radek clique" and reviled the inspiration of Radek's articles in the *Berner Tagwacht* as "Nechaev à la Lenin."[85] Grimm struggled to retain a degree of impartiality and published reports from both the Bolsheviks and the Mensheviks in the *ISC Bulletin*'s second number. His effort was to little avail, and exposure to the bitterness of factional rivalry within the RSDRP did nothing to improve an already strained relationship with the Zimmerwald Left.

The Left approached the enlarged committee session with the same aggressive distancing tactics that it had employed in the past. Once again an attempt was made to extend the Left's representation by accumulating additional voting mandates. The procedure for allocating mandates outlined in the ISC's circular letter of 27 September specified that each national delegation would receive two or three votes, "based upon a consideration by each country of the special conditions of organization *in that country itself*." Affiliation with the ISB was no longer used as a criterion, and groups such as the Bulgarian Narrows, the SDKPiL-Regional Presidium, the Scandinavian Youth Leagues, and the Lettish Social Democratic party were accepted as participating members. Lenin pressed the point by requesting that fractional mandates (one-half vote) be granted to smaller left factions and renewed the demand that the *Lichtstrahlen* group be recognized as the representative of a legitimate tendency. On 15 November Borchardt wrote directly to Grimm requesting a voting mandate for his organization, to be assigned to Lenin, Radek, or Zinoviev in the event that he could not be present in Bern.[86] The request for fractional mandates was refused summarily, though when the ISC convened on 2 February to complete preparations for the enlarged committee, the composition of the German delegation was still up in the air. Grimm was at any rate no partisan of Borchardt, and he made clear his moderate preferences by opposing Balabanov's suggestion that the ISC draft a "statement of principles" such as Lenin had sought at Zimmerwald.[87]

The enlarged committee session was the first major follow-up to the Zimmerwald conference, and Grimm was anxious to reinforce a commitment to action for peace by steering clear of divisive theoretical disputations. The twenty-three delegates that gathered in Bern on 5 February in the main shared his priorities.[88] Given the absence of representatives from Great Britain and France, Grimm announced in his opening remarks that the sessions would possess an advisory character only. Lenin and Radek worked cooperatively despite their personal estrangement, but with its efforts to win additional mandates come to naught, the Left was even weaker in relation to the majority than at Zimmerwald. Though Platten and Kolarov provided occasional support, only Lenin, Zinoviev, and Radek consistently voted for the Left's motions.

During the opening session Radek made one further attempt to expand the Left's voting strength by requesting a mandate for Münzenberg on behalf of the new Youth International. Grimm rejected the proposal on the grounds that in its abbreviated form the enlarged committee did not have the authority to make such a decision—a convenient pretext for once again reducing the Left's relative weight. On 6 February Lenin and Radek presented mandates on their behalf signed by Roland-Holst and Borchardt, which were invalidated on the same grounds. The issue of Borchardt's status also set off a renewed debate within the German delegation. Gustav Laukant, a future revolutionary shop steward, denounced the International Socialists of Germany as a facade "with no organization behind it" and insisted that in Germany "there is only one opposition." Bertha Thalheimer was quick to respond for the Spartacus League, emphasizing the fundamental differences that divided the German left, but also refuting Borchardt. Lenin rallied to his protégé's support, insisting that only partisans of the Zimmerwald Left represented an authentic revolutionary alternative.

Feuding over the allocation of voting mandates led into a discussion of the larger goals of the antiwar movement during which the contrasting priorities motivating moderates and radicals were once again made clear. Modigliani, for the PSI majority, emphasized the primacy of the struggle against the war and rejected attempts to create splinter organizations. Zinoviev responded for the Left, claiming that objective realities were forcing the question of division to the fore whether delegates like Modigliani liked it or not. Clearly, the search for consensus would be no easier than it had been at Zimmerwald. Summarizing the day's proceedings, Grimm welcomed the "healthy discussion" but drew moderate conclusions that seemed to be addressed directly to Lenin. "Our struggle must be to bring the masses together," he insisted. "It is not our task to stand up upon a mountain and call to the masses, come join us!"

Only on the morning of 7 February did the committee turn to the substantive part of its agenda, the drafting of a response to the criticisms leveled against Zimmerwald by Huysmans. Grimm took the initiative, presenting a project manifesto that sought to clarify the Zimmerwald movement's goals and proposing that a circular letter be drafted as a direct reply to the ISB. Lenin strongly opposed any communication with the ISB's "social patriots" but was not able to have his way. The majority of delegates opposed the drafting of a manifesto as overambitious but were anxious to clarify their intentions to the ISB executive. Martov summarized their views by recommending that a letter be composed to respond to Huysmans, with Grimm's proposal for a manifesto put off until a second general conference. In an abbreviated session on 8 February Radek raised a stir by characterizing opposition to a manifesto as "opportunistic," but his protests were in vain. The idea was interred, and a drafting commission (Balabanov, Grimm, Laukant, Martov, Rakovski, Serrati, and Zinoviev) was appointed to compose a circular letter addressed to Huysmans.

In its concluding session on 9 February the committee hurried through a number of significant decisions. First, the question of delegate selection for a second general conference was considered. Grimm asked for more formal criteria than had been applied in the past, and after some debate organizational autonomy and ISC affiliation were approved as standards for representation. A working agenda was also discussed and a five-point program approved emphasizing action for peace. Lenin presented a project agenda for the Zimmerwald Left, including such controversial themes as "The Tactics of the International Proletariat in Opposition to Imperialism," and "The Self-Determination of Nations," but it was overwhelmingly rejected. Finally, Grimm suggested that consideration be given to inviting the Kautsky group. Zinoviev was quick to go on record in opposition, and by the evening Lenin had prepared a written protest, but the proposal was never brought to a vote.

The enlarged committee completed its work by approving a

strongly worded circular letter based upon an original draft submitted by Grimm.[89] In what had become a patented response the Left supported the text while simultaneously issuing a separate statement, signed by Lenin, Zinoviev, and Radek, that made its support conditional. The distancing tactic was almost unnecessary, for the circular letter was by some distance the most radical document produced by the Zimmerwald movement to date. In defiant language the rise of popular protest against the war was greeted, the ISB's inaction condemned, and the "revolutionary intervention of the international proletariat" invoked as a necessary foundation for a lasting peace. Socialist deputies were enjoined to vote against war credits "regardless of the strategic situation," to agitate for antiwar actions, and to refuse participation in institutions "which serve the cause of national defense." These were conditions for which the Left had agitated in vain at Zimmerwald. Lenin's tireless agitation, it seemed, was not entirely without effect.

The Left sought to evaluate the results of the enlarged committee in as favorable a light as possible. Krupskaia conveyed optimism in describing its work to Kollontai a few days after adjournment. "From the left," she wrote, "beside those from Bern . . . there was no one, but the manifesto [circular letter] ended up decidedly leftist. Everything has its logic, and who says A must come to say B."[90] Zinoviev prepared a report on the session and described it as a "considerable step forward" for the Zimmerwald Left.[91]

Evaluations from the Left also contained a familiar critical dimension. Zinoviev regretted the continuing dominance of the peace strategy and explained the circular letter's militancy as a result of the "logic of the situation" produced "in spite of" the committee's composition. Only pressure from the Left could guarantee that a process of radicalization would continue. "The right center of Zimmerwald is mobilizing its forces," he warned, "we should mobilize ours."[92] The confrontational tone was revealing. The outcome of the enlarged committee session had revealed the possibilities, but also the limitations, inherent in a distancing strategy. How far could it be pursued without posing the question whether the movement was amenable to being won over from within? Was there a potential majority to the left of Grimm? If not, at what point would the Left possess sufficient strength to assert its independence, and how could such strength be mustered? In tentatively raising these issues Zinoviev could only refer to the decisive importance of the struggle within the German left. How Zimmerwald would evolve, he brooded, was "impossible to predict."

Toward the World Revolution

In the months following the Zimmerwald conference the Zimmerwald Left failed to cohere as an organization. The *Vorbote* controversy split the Left's coordinating bureau and left it without that sine qua non of revolutionary politics, an independent central organ. Within individual national movements factions associated with the Left made halting progress at best. As a left bloc within the Zimmerwald movement its impact was greater, but the Zimmerwald majority remained committed to a moderate peace strategy.

Despite setbacks, Lenin and his allies evaluated the Left's progress hopefully. Though it had not built a stable institutional base, the Left's identity as a political tendency had been reinforced. Nuances of opinion divided its leading theorists, but they were able to defend a consistent general line in international forums. Under the pressures of the war the social democratic movement was breaking apart. Zimmerwald had driven a wedge into the International, and the resultant gap showed no signs of closing. Though revolutionary exhortations had as yet made little impact on the popular level, there was no reason to presume that the masses would remain passive indefinitely. The young machinist Karl Retzlaw, drawn into agitational work for the Spartacus League in Berlin, observed that the German authorities perceived the antiwar movement as a whole as "a phenomenon within the organized labor movement, but not as an opposition among the people."[93] His graphic descriptions make clear the difficulties with which antiwar activists were required to grapple. Organization was of necessity conspiratorial and inaccessible to more than a committed minority. As a result popular protests were often spontaneous and ineffective, provoked by disintegrating living standards as much as by convictions concerning war aims. The status of laborer was a privileged one compared with the lot of the frontline soldier, and the possible consequences for participation in strikes or demonstrations were severe. Nonetheless, as the war dragged on the incidence of such actions increased. The potential for a popular mobilization was always latent, not least in the wake of military defeat.

Lenin emphasized that the real problem was not an absence of popular discontent, but rather a failure of leadership. The special conditions imposed by the war did not negate the realities of class society. "We, the Zimmerwald Left," he wrote in June 1916, "are certain . . . that a socialist revolution is completely possible in the very near future, 'from one day to the next,' as Kautsky once expressed it."[94] Though often mocked by his detractors for "learning of the February revolution from Swiss newspapers,"[95] Lenin never suggested that revolutionary situations developed mechanically and predictably. Political organizations could not conjure revolution from the blue, but they must be ready to step forward when the time was ripe. Confidence in the program of the Zimmerwald Left rested upon a conviction that a call to struggle would not remain unanswered indefinitely. By extending state control over industry and encouraging the concentration of production, the war was accelerating the evolution of the capitalist mode of production and aggravating its imbalances. The fiscal burden imposed by the conflict, and the sacrifice of millions of lives at the fronts, shattered the legitimacy of Europe's institutions, called its world leadership into question, and eroded capitalism's political facade. That a revolutionary challenge would erupt during or after the war was deemed nearly certain.

Confronted with these heady prospects, the Second International had ignominiously collapsed. Lenin's fundamentally hostile attitude toward the Zimmerwald majority expressed a belief that its restorationist program failed to measure the magnitude of the failure. The Zimmerwald Left was conceived as the foundation for a new movement, capable of applying the precepts of revolutionary Marxism to a conjuncture where socialist revolution had become a real historical possibility. Its justification rested upon the assumption that the capitalist world system, with roots in the sweeping socioeconomic transformations of the fifteenth and sixteenth centuries, now confronted a crisis that heralded its eventual demise.

Lenin's interventions in the debate over self-determination indicated the direction in which his thought was tending. What he encouraged was not only an alternative strategy, but a new Marxism, liberated from the encrusted determinism of the Second International and aware that an epoch of struggle for socialism on a global scale had dawned. In his theoretical work during 1916 and 1917 Lenin would take these illuminations much further. His arguments occasioned dissent and contributed to the Zimmerwald Left's organizational dilemmas. They also defined a series of premises that made long-term coexistence between Lenin's Left and the Zimmerwald majority impossible. At stake was much more than a campaign to end the war. The red flags that lined the Left's horizons beckoned toward the vision of a world turned upside down, where the roots of war had been burned away. Viewed from these rarified heights, the Zimmerwald Left's birth pangs were not preoccupying. As the precursor of the world revolution, it had not yet begun to fight.

5

Zimmerwald Left and Zimmerwald Center

Shamed, dishonored, wading in blood, stinking of filth; thus does bourgeois society appear before us, as it is. Not when, well-groomed and proper, it mimes culture, philosophy and ethics, order, peace and the rule of law—as a raging beast, as a witches' sabbath of anarchy, as a pestilential miasma for culture and humanity, thus does it reveal its true, naked visage.

—Rosa Luxemburg, *Die Krise der Sozialdemokratie*

IN February 1916 German forces began a major offensive along the heights above the fortress city of Verdun. Frustrated by the stalemates of 1915 and confronted with the likelihood of allied offensives in the spring, commander-in-chief Erich von Falkenhayn had conceived a strategy intended to pin down the French by attacking at a strategically vital point and "bleeding them white" through superior fire power. The first assault achieved impressive successes, crowned by the fall of the foreboding Fort Douaumont, but a defensive perimeter was quickly reestablished. Soon the great battle had degenerated into an almost formless sequence of punishing attacks and counterattacks. For six months, at a cost of more than a million casualties, hideous combat raged within a tightly constricted area in the hills along the Meuse, amidst piles of putrifying corpses and the ruin of nature.

The allies responded by setting new offensives into motion. On 4 June Russia again took to the field in Galicia. The "Brusilov offensive" (named for its most successful commander) achieved a breakthrough at the fortress of Lutsk, before overextending and crashing to a halt. Pressure on the Isonzo and Saloniki fronts was relieved, and on 27 August, lured by promises of territorial aggrandizement and reassured by Russian victories, Romania joined the Entente. The gesture proved to be premature, and in December a German army led by the "Death's Head" general, August von Mackensen, marched into Bucharest. A British/French offensive on the Somme in Flanders, begun on 1 July with a catastrophic assault that saw over 60,000 soldiers perish in the space of a single day, likewise ground into a standoff, claiming more victims than Verdun before being broken off in late September. On 6 August the Italians attacked along the Isonzo, recapturing Gorizia, but failing to accomplish any significant change in the strategic balance.

Although the vastness of the campaigns was unprecedented, they moved the war no closer to an end. With their resources strained to the limit all belligerents were constrained to impose ever greater sacrifices upon their populations. Implacably, dissatisfaction grew together with the worsening material situation. After the "Kovel massacres" that concluded the Brusilov offensive, both Russia and Austria-Hungary were exhausted, their imperial structures discredited and revolution at the door. Germany shed quite as much blood at Verdun as did the French; Britain was maimed by its losses, and in France the grim pride taken in the defense of Verdun was partially dissipated by the pointless expenditure of lives in the latter stages of the Somme offensives. In these savage battles, marked by the calculated sacrifice of millions of lives, the true face of modern war was being revealed. To meet the accompanying fiscal burden all of Europe passed into the shadow of America's growing economic power. Atop the hecatombs at the fronts came inflation, declining real wages, rationing, and assaults upon basic freedoms. The "*Götterdämmerung of the bourgeois order*" that Bebel once heralded in the Reichstag seemed almost to have arrived. European governments had drawn upon large reserves of popular trust in opting for war. After more than two years of inconclusive fighting little credit remained, and in Trotsky's words "the notes were coming due."[1]

The social tensions generated by military stalemate gave hope to the Left and widened the cracks within the Zimmerwald bloc. In its third international bulletin, published on 29 February 1916, the ISC announced the scheduling of a second general conference for April.[2] According to an official report issued by the ISC to clarify its intentions, the conference was to be conducted "within the framework of the Zimmerwald decisions" and would not attempt "to separate the workers from their present organizations, but rather *to bring about a spiritual renewal of the proletariat within these organizations and groups*."[3] These were cautious, curative priorities that did not seem to take account of the disintegrating political environment. In the third *ISC Bulletin* statements by the *Nashe Slovo* and *La Vie Ouvrière* groups, the Dutch RSV and SDP, and the Spartacus League challenged them by calling for more aggressive antiwar actions.[4] Lenin was considerably more critical. In February he and Krupskaia moved to Zürich, a larger and more cosmopolitan city than Bern and the center of the SPS left. In a series of public lectures he emphasized once again that it was only by breaking irrevocably with the legacy of the Second International that revolutionary socialism could continue to advance. He and Zinoviev also wrote articles attacking the effort to construct a socialist "peace program" and calling the hope of achieving a democratic peace without "a number of revolutions" a "bourgeois deception."[5] The contrasting outlooks dividing currents within the Zimmerwald union had become open and undisguised. During 1916 the history of the movement became a history of rivalry and particularly of confrontation between the moderate center and Leninist Left.

Controversy bedeviled Grimm as he threw himself into work for the second general conference. Lenin briefly toyed with the idea of boycotting, on the grounds that the "Kautskyite" elements would inevitably dominate. In the end, however, he elected to continue working to build the Left as an internal opposition. "Things stand as they did prior to Zimmerwald," he wrote to Zinoviev on the eve of the second conference, "we have our 'resolution' and must not renounce *a bloc of the left*."[6] Once planning had commenced, the battle of voting mandates erupted with renewed force.[7] Grimm sought to resist claims to representation by marginal factions, which he associated with the disruptive tactics of the Left. On 24 February he revealed his priorities by writing to Riazanov that "it is not possible for us to assemble simply a discussion club, behind which there is no support. In order to be effective we need the workers and their organizations, else any mass action is simply unthinkable."[8] The standards were indisputable, but the conditions of organization imposed by the war made them difficult to maintain. National labor movements were hopelessly divided, and in attempting to win back "the workers and their organizations" Zimmerwald confronted starkly contrasting strategic options.

The second Zimmerwald conference marked both a high point for the movement and the beginning of its disintegration. By the spring of 1916 the ISC seemed to be excellently placed to draw upon the momentum of popular unrest. Simultaneously, however, the growth of a centrist opposition standing apart from the Zimmerwald movement (with Longuet's minoritaires and the northern neutrals as prototypes), and a renewal of activity on the part of the ISB, opened channels for antiwar action without the taint of a "special conference." At the second general conference the Zimmerwald Left made a strong plea for a new International, while the movement's right wing pressed for a turn back to cooperation with the ISB. Between these two poles the Zimmerwald "center", grouped around Grimm, Balabanov, and Martov, was unable to assert a convincing alternative.[9] After a series of confrontations the conference con-

cluded by reaffirming a peace strategy emphasizing the primacy of
the struggle against the war. The limits of the approach appeared
precisely at the point where work for peace within the structures of
the prewar movement once again became possible. Should Zimmerwald commit itself to constructing an alternative to a "bankrupt"
movement or accept the legitimacy of the Second International and
work toward its revival? The failure of the second general conference
to resolve the issue signaled the Zimmerwald alternative's eventual
polarization and decline.

Kiental

The delegates to the second Zimmerwald conference assembled in
Bern on 24 April 1916. On the following morning they embarked for
Kiental, a modest village in the heart of the Berner Oberland. Once
again the fate of international socialism would be argued out in a
rustic alpine inn, spiritually distant from the murderous rivalries
that were transforming Europe into a charnel house. Forty-three
delegates representing seven nations managed to avoid restrictions
upon international travel in order to attend.[10] Edmondo Peluso of
Portugal later described the setting for discussions: in "the spacious
dining room of the Hotel Bären," with tables arranged on either side
of a presidium into "right and left, exactly as in parliaments."[11] The
physical layout, which accentuated division, was reflected in the
composition of the delegations. Resolutions submitted on behalf of
the Zimmerwald Left were supported (though not always consistently) by Lenin, Armand, and Zinoviev for the Bolsheviks; Radek,
Bronislaw Stein, and Mieczyslaw Bronski for the SDKPiL-Regional
Presidium; Paul Frölich for the Bremen Left Radicals; Fritz Platten,
Ernst Nobs, and Agnes Robmann for the SPS-left; Serrati for the PSI-
left; and Kaclerović of Serbia. The tally indicates an increase in
strength when compared with Zimmerwald, but the Left remained
dominated by its Russia/Polish component and often lacked cohesion. Kaclerović, Serrati, Nobs, and Platten offered only conditional
support, and the Bolsheviks and SDKPiL-Regional Presidium were at
odds over the national question. On the right the Working Group
majority, the three French parliamentarians, and the PSI-right demonstrated greater unity in their effort to keep the movement within
the confines of the Second International. A vaguely outlined center,

including Grimm and Balabanov for the ISC, the Mensheviks, and SRS; the Spartacists; Adolf Warszawski of the SDKPiL-Main Presidium; and Stanislaw Lapinski of the PPS-L, found itself caught between conflicting extremes. Rivalry between these three currents dominated the Kiental debates.

In his opening remarks Grimm outlined the conference's tasks in long-term perspective. "We know that an entire world has collapsed," he began, "and that it is a question not only of the collapse of socialist organizations, but of the need to create a new ideological orientation." The search for "new directions" would inevitably create "misunderstandings and frictions," but these must not be allowed to obscure Zimmerwald's achievements and potential. Though the Zimmerwald chairperson's tone was optimistic, the intensity of the friction that he mentioned would soon become all too obvious.

The entire day of 25 April was taken up with activities reports from the German and French delegations. Typically, the Germans provided the clearest expression of the divisions opening up within the opposition. Speaking for the Working Group, Adolf Hoffmann posed the goal of a democratic peace "without victors or vanquished" and appealed for a "return to old principles." The Spartacist Ernst Meyer repeated his organization's emphasis upon mass actions. Paul Frölich of the Bremen Left Radicals went further, dismissing the call for a negotiated peace as unrealistic and urging the Spartacus League to declare organizational independence. The reports offered by the French delegation were less rigorous, but even more contentious. Pierre Brizon disavowed the goal of a third International and stressed the need to pressure the ISB to act for peace, while Alexandre Blanc offended all present by making provocative references to the atrocities attributed to German occupation forces in Belgium. The theme was a favorite among belligerent French nationalists, and Grimm felt obliged to intervene and request that Blanc read over Ledebour's speeches at Zimmerwald before proceeding in such a vein. Henri Guilbeaux, editor of the recently founded journal *Demain* in Geneva and oriented toward the Zimmerwald Left, responded by suggesting that the French parliamentarians themselves come forward more demonstrably against the war. Guilbeaux's remarks were accompanied by a motion on behalf of the Left, taking up where it left off at Zimmerwald by demanding that the movement's affiliates be obliged to vote against war credits.[12]

With confrontation rather than cooperation already established as the watchword of deliberations, the conference turned to the theme "The Attitude of the Proletariat to the Question of Peace" on the morning of 26 April. This central point of discord generated no less than seven distinct project resolutions, submitted respectively by Grimm, the Spartacus League, the Zimmerwald Left, Martov, the PPS-L, Ernst Graber, and Guilbeaux. Grimm sought to pave the way toward a compromise, noting the "utopian" character of the search for peace under capitalism and emphasizing class struggle as the essence of the social democratic program, while also citing the positive goal of a negotiated ceasefire as the prelude to a socialist peace initiative. In response the resolution submitted in the name of the Zimmerwald Left by the Bolsheviks, the SDKPiL-Regional Presidium, and the Bremen Left Radicals warned against the "mirage of a 'democratic' peace" that would "represent nothing more than an agreement between imperialist bandits . . . and increase the menace of new wars." "To summon the proletariat to struggle and organize it for a resolute attack upon capitalism," the Left concluded defiantly, "this is the only peace program of social democracy."

During the evening session it remained for Brizon to scandalize the assembly by launching into a long-winded panegyric to the Gallic virtues that ultimately threatened to provoke a brawl. After a rather inappropriate paean to France's contributions to socialism, Brizon at last announced his willingness to vote against war credits in the Chamber of Deputies. The enthusiastic response with which the declaration was greeted soon turned to indignation, however, when Brizon added "but only if the military situation allows it." The Zimmerwaldist alternative was premised upon the assumption that the socialist commitment to peace was independent of the military-strategic situation, and a number of voices, led by Radek, were raised to demand Brizon's expulsion. For Lenin, who chose not to comment during the performance, the episode must have reinforced a conviction that the moderate opposition was not to be relied upon.

Debate broke off on 26 April without a consensus in place. In order to head off a deadlock, two drafting commissions were appointed to allow work on the wording of resolutions to proceed in a less confrontational atmosphere. The first was charged with drawing up a compromise statement on the peace question and the second with facilitating the next agenda item, a discussion of the relationship between the Zimmerwald movement and the ISB.[13] The central issue motivating the debate of 26 April—whether international conflict within capitalist class society could be contained by diplomatic means without revolutionary upheaval forcing structural change—was left entirely unresolved.

After a pause to allow the drafting commissions to pursue their work, the conference turned to the problem of the ISB on 28 April. It was a highly divisive issue, but critical to the movement's future. Zimmerwald's claim to autonomous status as a protest movement hinged upon whether it chose to fully endorse, critically support, or absolutely reject an ISB initiative for peace. With the Left loudly enunciating its unconditional opposition to any restoration of the prewar movement, relations with the ISB became an essential point of contention between rival wings of the Zimmerwald bloc.

Lazzari opened the discussion by reading the project resolution that had been endorsed by the drafting commission majority. The text urged action upon the ISB and listed five conditions as prerequisites for Zimmerwaldist support for such action. The members of the ISB executive, accused of actions detrimental to socialism, were asked to resign. The ISB was abjured to oppose war credits, to expel members serving as ministers in the ruling coalitions of bourgeois states, to renounce the *Burgfrieden*, and to endorse the goal of a negotiated peace. Though these conditions amounted to the demand for an unambiguous break with defensism, they were not phrased inflexibly. The resolution also expressed hope to "win over" errant comrades and confined Zimmerwald's raison d'être to that of a pressure group seeking to push the ISB toward the left. In contrast, the project resolution endorsed by the drafting commission minority (signed by Lenin, Thalheimer, and Warszawski) labeled cooperation with the ISB of any sort as "completely offensive and shameful" and "against the logic of the Zimmerwald decisions."

The vivid debate that followed revealed the impasse at which Zimmerwald had arrived. Lenin objected to Lazzari's attempt to rebuild the movement with people who were "politically lifeless." Thalheimer attempted to distinguish between the Spartacists' "legitimate" decision to struggle within the SPD on the national level as a means of retaining access to the masses and the "worthlessness" of the ISB as an international forum. Hoffmann and Aksel'rod spoke in rebuttal, arguing that the Zimmerwald movement itself provided an effective basis for joint work with the ISB if the drafting commission majority's conditions were accepted. Martov and Grimm rejected the notion of "pressuring" the ISB, but supported Zimmerwaldist participation in the event that some kind of peace action was undertaken under ISB auspices. At one point the debate became so intense that an exasperated Grimm lost his temper, reacting to an interpolation from Lenin and Radek with the retort: "Are these people really interested in this business or not!" In response the Zimmerwald Left group walked from the hall in a gesture of solidarity and protest.[14] It was a revealing episode that laid bare the confrontational attitude informing the relationship between the Left and the moderate majority.

Eventually four project resolutions were put forward in addition to the majority and minority resolutions presented by the drafting commission. Texts by Hoffmann and Serrati described action by the ISB as highly to be desired and demanded that Zimmerwald affiliates participate "unconditionally." "We are not a third International," Hoffmann intoned in a gesture of defiance toward the Left, "we are merely a rump parliament." Serrati broke with the Left on the issue and, like Ledebour at Zimmerwald, threatened to leave the conference should cooperation with the ISB be rejected. Lapinski and Zinoviev presented slightly amended versions of the drafting commission majority's report which condemned the ISB's passivity, but temporized by suggesting that a decision to support or reject a new peace initiative be left to the ISC enlarged committee. Neither for the first nor the last time, Zinoviev displayed a penchant for accommodation that left him at odds with his closest allies. Both Lenin and Radek spoke against his project resolution and repeated their rejection of the ISB's "social chauvinists."

After a sense of the assembly poll indicated a plurality supportive of the compromise embodied by Zinoviev's amendments, a new drafting commission (Lapinski, Zinoviev, Serrati, and Nobs) was appointed to compose a final text.[15] The final document combined criticisms of the ISB's inaction with the concession to consider joint work "in principle." It was further specified that should a concrete ISB initiative be forthcoming, the problem of how to react would be turned over to the enlarged committee. Given the importance of the issues, this was a remarkably noncommittal statement. Once again the essential question, in this case the movement's attitude toward the heritage of the Second International, was left hanging.

On 29 April, Modigliani, Meyer, and Radek (representing respectively the right, center, and left) were appointed to a new drafting commission charged with preparing the text of a manifesto. Their work proceeded smoothly, and by the next morning they had produced a document which was approved unanimously by acclamation—a rare show of unity in a conference dominated by contentious wrangling. The reworked resolution on "The Attitude of the Proletariat Toward the Question of Peace" was also approved, although the wording elicited a number of criticisms. The most pointed critique was a formal statement from the Zimmerwald Left (signed by Radek, Stein, Frölich, Zinoviev, Armand, Lenin, Platten, Kaclerović, and Bronski), which voiced a scornful dismissal of "bourgeois diplomacy" as a means to peace but followed tried and true tactics by according the resolution conditional support "as a step toward the rejection of the social pacifist utopia." Another resolution from the Left hailed the imprisoned Höglund and the Swedish left radicals for their sacrifices in the cause of revolutionary socialism.

To conclude an agenda that left many loose ends, Grimm announced that a second meeting of the enlarged committee would be held on 2 May in Bern in order to take advantage of the presence of foreign delegations in Switzerland. The conference ended in the early hours of 1 May, its adjournment extended at the suggestion of Balabanov in order "to await the sunrise of International Labor Day . . . the symbol of working class unity."[16] The unity to which Balabanov referred, always elusive, was certainly not dramatically manifest at Kiental. The Zimmerwald movement had managed to reaffirm its original commitment to work against the war, but the failure to resolve issues of long-term orientation did not augur well for its future.

The Kiental manifesto, entitled "To the People Driven to Ruin and Death," surpassed even the enlarged committee's circular letter in the extent of its radicalism.[17] "There is but one effective means of preventing future wars," it declared with a nod to the Left's position on the peace question, "the seizure of political power and the abolition of capitalist property by the working class." By characterizing the war as imperialist, criticizing the ISB, and condemning war credits, the manifesto brought the movement closer to the Zimmerwald Left on a number of points. It nonetheless remained within the parameters of a peace strategy, concluding with the demand for an immediate ceasefire and peace negotiations. At Kiental the Zimmerwald Left group was somewhat larger than in the past, but it remained a distinct minority even as its relationship with the moderate majority became openly adversarial. The Left's ability to expand also appeared to be limited, due first of all to its lack of progress in encouraging accommodation with the Spartacus League. Though Thalheimer occasionally supported the Left's interventions at Kiental, in their evaluation of the conference published as a "Political Letter" during May the Spartacists maintained a characteristic emphasis upon mass actions as the necessary prelude to organizational initiatives. "International socialism does not consist of conferences, resolutions, or manifestos," insisted Spartacus, "but of deeds, of struggle, of mass action."[18]

Writing to Shliapnikov during May, Lenin evaluated the results of Kiental more positively: "In general, the acceptance of a manifesto represented a step forward . . . a resolution critical of pacifism was accepted and also a resolution sharply critical of the International Socialist Bureau. In general this is *more or less*, and despite the mass of defects, a step toward a break with the social patriots."[19] Zinoviev also called the results a "step forward" for the Zimmerwald Left but added the caution that it was not yet possible to assert "that the die has been cast, that the Zimmerwaldists have entirely entered upon the road toward a break with the 'official' socialists, that Zimmerwald *has become* the embryo of the third International."[20] These reactions signaled a willingness to continue to take "steps forward" with Zimmerwald, but only for so long as the movement continued to move away from the remnants of the Second International. The Left's perception of Zimmerwald was instrumental, and its frustration with the moderate majority was growing.

The issue of relating to the ISB was posed again, and with new immediacy, when the enlarged committee convened on 2 May in Bern.[21] In the twenty-four hour interval since Kiental's adjournment, the text of the ISB's May Day proclamation announcing its intention to convene a conference of neutrals on 26 July in The Hague had been received. Rather than being a hypothetical possibility, an ISB initiative for peace was now a reality to which Zimmerwald would have to react. In attempting to determine whether or not to recommend participation to its neutral affiliates, the enlarged committee predictably deadlocked. In lieu of a decision, ISC circular letters of 3 and 15 May urged individual parties to make their own choice, inspired by the "spirit" of the Zimmerwald action.[22] The abdication of responsibility only added to the Left's malaise. Despite the optimism of Lenin and Zinoviev, the Kiental conference marked a turning point in their evaluation of Zimmerwald's usefulness. The movement's inability to resolve the debate over the ISB exposed the limits of its capacity to evolve toward the "embryo of the third International" that the Left aspired for it to become. In the wake of Kiental, the Left's comportment would be correspondingly hostile and disillusioned. Any attempt to revive the Second International was considered unacceptable, and in order to build an alternative, it now appeared, it might well be necessary to look beyond the confines of the Zimmerwald bloc.

Imperialism the Highest Stage of Capitalism

Lenin's most significant work in the months surrounding Kiental was scholarly rather than organizational. During the conference he was already at work on what would become one of his most influential statements, the book *Imperialism the Highest Stage of Capitalism*.[23] The implications of this seminal study have been much discussed and may be briefly summarized. What deserves special attention, because it is so often neglected, is the context in which it was written. *Imperialism the Highest Stage of Capitalism* was intended to provide a foundation for the political line defended by the Zimmerwald Left. The bankruptcy of reformism; the existence of an objectively revolutionary situation; the nature of the war as a crisis of imperialism; the link between national liberation struggles and the battle for socialism; and the need for a revolutionary International to coordinate the socialist labor movement worldwide—all of these assertions found their justification in Lenin's tightly written text. *Imperialism the Highest Stage of Capitalism* may be considered as the theoretical bedrock both of the Zimmerwald Left and of the international communist movement to which it gave rise.

Lenin had wanted to compose a study of imperialism at least since the beginning of the war, and in a Lausanne referendum during October 1914 he was already referring to imperialism as capitalism's "highest stage."[24] Relocated in Zürich by February 1916 and able to draw on considerably richer library facilities than those available in Bern, he threw himself into research with an enthusiasm that is reflected by the meticulously organized notebooks compiled during his work.[25] Lenin's subtitle, "A Popular Outline," accurately described his intentions on one level, not necessarily to break new ground, but to extract from an extant literature a series of conclusions relevant to the contemporary political environment. In his introduction Lenin doffs his hat to the liberal British economist John Hobson, whose 1902 text *Imperialism: A Study* is praised as "a very fine and thorough description of the basic economic and political features of imperialism." The implied intellectual debt is real, but it may easily be exaggerated. Lenin rejects Hobson's liberal premises and what he calls his "bourgeois social reformism and pacifism." His own conclusions emerge from the tradition of Rudolf Hilferding's *Finance Capital*, Luxemburg's *The Accumulation of Capital*, and Bukharin's *Imperialism and the World Economy*, a tradition whose basic tenets were articles of faith on the social democratic left well before 1914.[26] Lenin's "Popular Outline" seeks to interpret the war crisis in the context of the Marxist theory of capitalist imperialism and arrives at conclusions that defy the entire spectrum of liberal economics.

Marx's study of capitalist development identified a tendency for an unrestrained competitive market to produce a concentration of capital in fewer and fewer hands as firms that were larger, more capital intensive, and better organized devoured their less efficient rivals. The direction was toward monopoly control, but Marx did not pursue the implications of his theory beyond an identification of trends. For Marx the concentration of capital also meant the ongoing disenfranchisement and "proletarianization" of the labor force. The intervention of the proletariat as a revolutionary class and the "expropriation of the expropriators," it was hopefully posited, would interrupt the process long before it could reach its "natural" limits.[27]

Lenin's theory of imperialism rests upon the premise that in the twentieth century, as a necessary extension of capitalist development, concentration was progressing to the point where the very nature of the capitalist mode of production had been altered. Lenin makes the point in the first two sections of his text, which document the rise of cartels and monopolies able to dominate whole areas of production and the merger of industrial capital with the fluid financial resources managed by the modern banking system. What Hilferding dubbed "finance capital," and the export of capital that it facilitated, brought an end to the laissez-faire ethic of the classical economists. In place of the ambitious entrepreneur appeared the vast, impersonal corporation, perfectly capable of manipulating the "free" market to its own advantage.

Lenin argues that monopolization contained both progressive and reactionary traits. On one hand, the concentration of capital meant the socialization of production, the introduction of planning mechanisms into the most advanced industrial branches, greater efficiency, and the organization of markets on an unprecedented scale. Imperialism was capitalism's "highest" stage and contained within itself new patterns of productive relations "in embryo." On the other hand, concentration served as a brake on innovation. In the context of private ownership it contained a tendency toward what Lenin described as "stagnation and decline." Most significantly, concentration proceeded unevenly, creating and exacerbating imbalances between sectors and increasing the structural instability of the capitalist system as a whole. Given the "anarchy of production" that all Marxists considered to be a basic trait of capitalism, concentration allowed stronger sectors to fix prices and extract "tribute" from weaker sectors. The resultant disparity between city and country, heavy and light industry, and individual productive branches would inevitably grow larger. The achievements of the capitalist world economy and the residual benefits that it generated were apparent, but they had to be measured against accumulating contradictions leading toward crisis and breakdown.

Kautsky had already supplied a counter to Lenin's arguments with his theory of "ultraimperialism," asserting that to the degree that monopolistic concerns shared a common interest in a stable international economic environment, imperialism might eventually become the foundation for an era of general peace.[28] Lenin attempted to refute these arguments in turn, pointing out that "cooperation" between monopolies could not be permanent in a competitive and anarchic international environment. Rather, the widening gap between sectors to which concentration gave rise made rivalry more intense and increased the incidence of violent confrontations. "The elimination of crisis by means of cartels," he writes, "is a fairy tale spread by bourgeois economists who seek to portray capitalism positively no matter what. On the contrary, monopolies, created in *certain* branches of industry, strengthen and intensify the chaos and anarchy inherent in capitalist production *as a whole*." At issue were structural imbalances. At issue was "the whole," and in the age of imperialism that could only refer to the international system. In the concluding sections of his text Lenin attempts to demonstrate that a competitive struggle for markets and raw materials, under conditions of semimonopoly control, was leading to a full-scale crisis of the capitalist world system, a crisis for which the First World War was the harbinger. Driven by the tendency of the rate of profit to fall and fed by the export of capital, imperialism created a division of the world into a handful of "advanced" countries juxtaposed with a mass of mercilessly impoverished colonies and semicolonies. Competition for supremacy between the imperialist powers on a global scale and the ever-widening gap between the rich and poor sectors of the world economy were the most explosive contradictions to which the capitalist mode of production had yet given rise.

One reflection of the crisis was a shift in patterns of hegemony within the bourgeois state. Britain, the model of capitalist industrialization, had become a parasitic "rentier" state by the turn of the century, its creative forces drained, prolonging its existence by preying off the colonial domains. Within the metropolitan centers of world capitalism, the superprofits extracted from the colonies permitted the creation of a relatively privileged "workers' aristocracy" (the phrase was borrowed from Engels) that provided a foundation for opportunist tendencies within the labor movement. In the end, however, it was nothing less than shameless exploitation that made possible a "softening" of class hegemony through the forms of bourgeois democracy. The fatal error of the bourgeoisie's revisionist epigones was to mistake the temporary advantages generated by imperialism for a sustainable trend and model. Colonialism had become essential to the survival of competing "national" imperialisms, and with most of the world already partitioned the struggle for influence could only become more intense. Herein lay the underlying cause of the present war, and a source for more terrible wars in the future. Democratic forms would be hard pressed to survive the strains to which a declining imperialism would give rise. Nor would the subjugated colonies eternally suffer humiliating exploitation or the deteriorating status within the world economy to which they had been condemned. Drawn into the web of capitalist productive relations, for which they were in most cases historically unprepared, their inevitable revolt would take the form of national liberation struggles, threatening capitalism's lifeline and undermining its ability to maintain equilibrium.

Lenin paints with broad strokes, and there is no doubt that certain technical aspects of his analysis are wide open to challenge. His arguments are sometimes criticized for their tendency to reduce the dynamics of world politics to a simple function of economic interaction, but it is the larger political vision that inspires them that is most significant. In accord with Luxemburg and Bukharin, and quite unlike Hobson, *Imperialism the Highest Stage of Capitalism* defines modern capitalism as an interdependent world system, whose structural contradictions provided a foundation for socialist revolution on a global scale. It was the *reality* of imperialism that legitimized the programmatic demands of the Zimmerwald Left. The war exposed the vacuity of the revisionist faith in peaceful progress by unleashing the full fury of unrestrained imperialist rivalry. It destroyed the "vain, hypocritical, and cowardly" dream of a reformist path to socialism. A reckoning with imperialism demanded structural transformations that could only result from "an epoch of wars and revolutions." In order to coordinate the process and maintain a coherent image of its goal a third International was required. Its necessity is the conclusion to which Lenin's analysis is designed to lead.

The historical task of the Zimmerwald Left was to announce the coming of the world revolution and to prepare the way for its vanguard. *Imperialism the Highest Stage of Capitalism* was written to provide the new International with a conceptual foundation. In accomplishing that task Lenin also managed to compose one of the most important political texts of the twentieth century, a work which, despite its imperfections, continues to inspire passion. Lenin insists that capitalist imperialism is condemned to decline, that world revolution is both possible and necessary, and that an era of revolutionary transformation has dawned. It is the magnitude of this vision, rather than any technical aspect of the analysis, that gives his work its enduring power.

"Down With the War! Down With the Government!"

By the summer of 1916 the intractability of the issues dividing European social democracy was apparent. The ISB's belated appearance held forth the promise of a reinvigorated Second International, but when the long-awaited Hague conference finally convened on 31 July–2 August 1916, discussions never progressed beyond the exploratory stage. Within the socialist community a standoff had developed comparable to the stalemate at the fronts. Following Kiental, Grimm argued that the time was no longer ripe for major international initiatives and that further jousting over the ISB was futile. The ISB could only express the will of its affiliated parties, and it was on the national level, in confrontation with defensist majorities, that the Zimmerwaldists' battles would have to be waged.[29]

Within the belligerent powers the frustrations generated by the war gradually began to assume threatening dimensions. On 1 May 1916 large demonstrations organized in defiance of socialist majorities in a number of European cities featured the demand for peace. Over 10,000 gathered in Berlin's Potsdamer Platz in response to appeals distributed by the Spartacus League. When police attempted to disperse the crowd, Liebknecht, in uniform, was arrested while shouting "down with the war, down with the government!" During the summer hunger strikes and demonstrations, including confrontations around barricades and a declaration of martial law in Leipzig, swept through German industrial centers. Whether such manifestations of discontent possessed revolutionary potential is a moot point. For contemporaries they were expressions of outrage at the course of the war; Francis Carsten speaks of the "overwhelming longing for peace" described in all official reports.[30]

Lenin considered the rise of mass protest to be an affirmation of his political line and drew conclusions which reinforced the work of the Zimmerwald Left. "In the entire world," he wrote in the spring of 1916, "two parties have come to exist in fact. In fact there already exist two Internationals."[31] If the Zimmerwald majority refused to acknowledge the need for schism, he warned, it would be left behind by a rising tide of popular unrest. In the months between Kiental and the first Russian revolution of March (February) 1917, the Zimmerwald Left doggedly pursued its splitting tactics with the aim of encouraging the creation of independent left radical factions. Its efforts were reinforced by the growth of popular dissatisfaction. Left groups oriented toward Lenin's position sprang up and expanded, and even as radical minorities their relative influence increased.

As always, it was Germany that led the way. Like most other social democratic parties, the SPD had fallen on hard times by 1916. Its membership had declined by 63 percent since August 1914, and subscriptions to the party press were reduced by half.[32] The Working Group was mounting a real challenge to the official Reichstag fraction, and on the left both the Spartacus League and the Bremen Left Radicals launched scathing attacks against the leadership. Increasingly under siege, the SPD executive committee elected to schedule a national conference for 21 September in Berlin in order to reassert its authority. The allocation of voting mandates was manipulated to favor the right, but the opposition nonetheless managed to demonstrate considerable grass-roots support. The Spartacus League was represented by Käthe Duncker, who participated in debates but refused to cast votes, arguing that their outcome had been determined beforehand. Haase, for the Working Group, accused the government of primary responsibility for the continuation of the war. Although the defensist majority eventually approved a series of motions condemning the opposition, the impression that remained was one of widespread dissent rather than disciplined unity.[33]

The Zimmerwald Left's reaction to the SPD national conference focused on the need to create an independent German left. Though committed to the establishment of a left radical party, the Bremen Left Radicals hesitated to move without the Spartacus League. In a series of articles written for the *Arbeiterpolitik* Radek reluctantly supported their position. With the left radical current confined to "nothing more than a small staff of ideologues reaching their hands toward the masses," he wrote, a break was impossible. The creation of an independent left was vitally important, but the Spartacists were necessary to its viability. "We will direct friendly criticism toward them," Radek noted, "but we recognize that they are the core of German left radicalism."[34] Early in 1917 Radek prepared a blueprint for constructing a left radical alternative that emphasized agitation from the base: "Central and local gatherings of left radicals with the aim of launching a general struggle for left radical ideas . . . creation of a left radical organization . . . participation in opposition conferences with the aim of expressing the contradiction between the left radicals and the party center . . . that is the path toward the building of a left radical party."[35] Radek's scenario was quite optimistic, and it left the problem of attracting the prestigious leaders attached to the Spartacus League to the international alternative represented by the Zimmerwald Left completely unresolved.

The September conference had at any rate revealed that the SPD was no longer a coherent organization, and in its wake the party sped toward a schism. During October the executive committee removed control of the central organ *Vorwärts* from the hands of the opposition and tightened disciplinary pressures intended to inhibit the expression of dissent. On 19 November members of the opposition gathered secretly in Berlin to discuss their response and placed an all-German conference of the left on the agenda. One hundred fifty-seven delegates representing seventy-two party sections (approximately a fifth of the total) gathered in Berlin on 7 January 1917 and approved a resolution offered by Kautsky demanding a negotiated peace.[36] The conference witnessed numerous clashes between partisans of the Working Group and the Spartacus League, but the two wings of the opposition managed to contain their differences and maintain a united front.

On 8 January the SPD executive announced that the Berlin conference meant a schism and declared all participants to be expelled from the party. After some soul-searching, on 6 April in Gotha, where in 1875 the SPD was created by a "Unity Conference" joining the Lassallean and Eisenacher wings of the German socialist movement, the opposition reassembled to announce the creation of a new Independent Social Democratic party of Germany (USPD). The party's strength was unevenly distributed, but it constituted a significant challenge to its parent organization. In a statement of principles the "Independents" attacked the majority's betrayal and dedicated themselves to the ideals of Zimmerwald and Kiental.[37]

At Gotha, representatives from the Bremen and Hamburg left radical groups refused to join the USPD and called once again for a revolutionary alternative.[38] Loyal to the priority of retaining access to the masses, the Spartacus League agreed to join on a "temporary" and "tactical" basis. Leo Jogiches, a dominant force in the league after the arrests of Luxemburg and Liebknecht, justified the decision on the grounds of expediency. Spartacus would back the centrist opposition where areas of agreement existed, he explained, while simultaneously striving to expose its "cowardly, wavering, and often unprincipled policy." The Bremen Left Radicals countered that the decision would lead to "political impotence."[39] For the moment, however, the left radical movement's weakness blocked progress toward an independent revolutionary left.

Developments in Austria were a pale reflection of those in Germany. After Kiental the Karl Marx Association announced its attachment to the Zimmerwald movement, while Koritschoner's Left Radical Action Committee moved closer to the Left.[40] The national question originally constituted a point of contention between Austrian left radicals and Lenin. Koritschoner aligned with Luxemburg on the issue and was delegated by the Action Committee to support Radek's theses on the national question at Kiental. During the course of 1916, however, the Action Committee's majority was won over to Lenin's position. Division within the Austrian opposition was accentuated when on 21 October Friedrich Adler, despairing of his party's passivity and determined to force the issue by personal demonstration, drew a pistol at point blank range and assassinated the Austrian War Minister Karl Graf Stürgkh. The Karl Marx Association rallied to its founder's support and on 26 October found itself dissolved by government decree. The elimination of a common opposition forum placed left radicals in a better position to act on their own behalf. At the Austrian party's national conference in November 1916 both the centrist opposition and the left radical current, though weakly represented, attempted to present contrasting resolutions.[41]

In common with most of the Marxist left Lenin condemned the Stürgkh assassination as immature and counterproductive. On 25 October he wrote to Koritschoner that "as concerns a political evaluation of the act, we stand, of course, upon our old, tried experience derived from decades of work, that individual terrorist methods are an *unproductive* means of political struggle. . . . Adler might have been much more useful to the revolutionary movement if, not fearing a schism, he had systematically engaged in propaganda and agitation."[42] It was to systematic agitation that Austrian left radicals now turned, with some measurable success. By early 1917 an "Action

Committee of Left Radical Working Youth" was established with a program—the so-called Biel Program—that reflected the priorities of the Zimmerwald Left. On 22 April the Biel program was approved by the Vienna Young Workers' League. In an environment characterized by explosive social tensions the left radical movement had begun to expand.[43]

In France, by way of contrast, the success of the centrist opposition led by Longuet and Pressemanne served to discourage the emergence of a dynamic Zimmerwaldist alternative. After Kiental, Blanc, Raffin-Dugens, and Brizon were censored by the SFIO for their association with the movement, but in a tumultuous session of the Chamber of Deputies on 24 June the three so-called pilgrims of Kiental voted against war credits in the face of considerable abuse.[44] Fearing that its defenses were being breached, the majority reacted by scheduling a National Council for August, with the intention of forcing the Longuetist minoritaires to commit themselves for or against Zimmerwald, and thereby to split the left. The tactic succeeded only in part. The minoritaires maintained the support they had mustered during the National Council of 9 April, and Brizon scandalized the right by throwing back their imprecations with the words: "You drag us before the socialist tribunal; but the socialist party isn't here, it's in the trenches, and its heart is at Zimmerwald and Kiental."[45] The centrist bloc remained intact and continued to chip away at the defensists' majority. Further to the left, the CRRI failed to establish roots within mass organizations and concentrated its limited energies upon agitation for peace. After the National Council its unity began to crack, with the more radical members looking askance at the willingness of some of their colleagues (including Brizon, Jean-Pierre Raffin-Dugens, and Bourderon) to support the moderate resolutions offered by Longuet.[46]

Within the CRRI a dilemma similar to that confronted by the Zimmerwald movement now developed, as moderates sought to move back toward Longuet and the center while the left pressed for greater autonomy. The creation of a short-lived *Comité de défense du socialisme internationale* in October, uniting some minoritaires with CRRI moderates, indicated the direction in which alignments were tending. As the SFIO's National Congress approached in December a line of separation between the Longuet group and the moderate Zimmerwaldists attached to the CRRI became more and more difficult to maintain.

The December congress was marked by new progress for the minoritaires, whose motions were defeated by the narrowest of margins. It also saw a dilution of the Zimmerwaldist alternative, as a number of CRRI members broke ranks to support Longuet.[47] Woodrow Wilson's December 1916 offer of mediation, endorsed by the SFIO on 4 March 1917, represented another lure away from leftist intransigence. The CRRI left, dominated after Trotsky's expulsion from France in December by Fernand Loriot and the Russian émigré and former SR Charles Rappoport, absolutely rejected any compromise with the minoritaires and the "illusions" of Wilsonianism. By April the CRRI had split, with the right wing joining the Longuet group, leaving Loriot, Rappoport, Saumoneau, and others to rebuild its remnant into a force for radical change.[48] The CRRI, "purged of opportunism," had at last become the type of organization for which Lenin had been searching, an "action-prone core" capable of serving as a fulcrum for revolutionary politics.

A more significant schism occurred within the Swedish movement. After the prosecution of Höglund, Heden, and Oljelund during May 1916, polarization within the party passed the point of no return. In January 1917 the recently founded journal *Politiken* (Politics) declared itself to be the voice of a "Left Socialist" alternative. One month later, a majority at the Swedish party's tenth congress backed Branting in demanding the youth movement's "complete submission." In reaction the radical leaders, Fredrik Ström, Ivar Vennerström, and Karl Månsson, resigned from the party's directive organs. Finally, on 13–16 May in Stockholm a congress of the left founded an independent left Socialist party of Sweden.[49] Though the Swedish left socialists were not convinced Leninists, the Zimmerwald Left greeted the split as an important step toward the emergence of an autonomous international left. In a note to Ström written after her return from a second North American tour in February, Kollontai urged on the "great schism" as a contribution toward the creation of a third International. Lenin was similarly positive and wrote to Kollontai asking her to steer the Swedish left socialists closer to the Zimmerwald Left.[50]

Movement toward the left was also manifest in Britain. Following

Hyndman's withdrawal from the BSP, the moderate bloc behind Edwin Fairchild was challenged by an emerging revolutionary faction, including Theodore Rothstein, the imprisoned Maclean, the Russian émigré Petr Petrov, and the future Bolshevik and Soviet foreign minister Grigorii Chicherin (still a Menshevik during the war and a member of the BSP's Kent section.) At the Labour party's national conference in January 1917 the BSP platform reflected Fairchild's priorities, urging a negotiated peace and revival of the Second International. The BSP's 1917 Easter conference saw these goals openly criticized from the left. In August 1916 the ILP and BSP reactivated a United Socialist Council to encourage antiwar agitation, and as British losses mounted the movement as a whole gathered momentum.[51]

Though the PSI clung to the slogan "neither support nor sabotage," its left wing also became more vocal as the burden of the war grew heavier. The party remained a bastion of the Zimmerwald alternative, and a joint session of the directorate and parliamentary fraction in Bologna on 16–17 September 1916 restated an unambiguous commitment to the movement.[52] By 1917, however, Italian society was moving toward a crisis for which the PSI's essentially cautious posture would no longer suffice. A vacuum was growing on the left, which began to be filled during 1916 by "revolutionary intransigent" factions drawn together within industrial centers such as Milan, Turin, and Florence. The leading intellectual force behind the revolutionary intransigent current was the young Neapolitan engineer Amadeo Bordiga, an outspoken critic of the PSI directorate from the first days of the war. At the PSI's Rome conference in February 1917 Bordiga led a challenge to the center that was defeated by a surprisingly narrow margin. On 24–27 July representatives of the revolutionary intransigent tendency met in Florence to create an autonomous party group and issued a manifesto that attacked the PSI for its willingness to compromise with the *"patria borghese"* (bourgeois Motherland).[53]

Altogether, a common picture emerged on the European left during the months between the Kiental conference and the first Russian revolution. Defensist majorities maintained a precarious hold on party machines, but everywhere both the centrist and the revolutionary opposition gained ground. A popular consensus for war *"jusqu'au bout"* could no longer be assumed, and the premises of the policy of 4

August were visibly crumbling. The revolutionary left, though still an isolated minority, was infused with new confidence. In a number of cases (the SPD, SDAP, BSP, and Swedish Socialist party) pressures led to outright schisms and the creation of independent Zimmerwaldist or left radical parties. In France the minoritaires were on the verge of winning control of the party from within. The Zimmerwald Left seldom entered directly into the disintegration of traditional organizations, but its arguments were influential. In every significant national movement a left radical faction aligned with Lenin's position had come into being well prior to the fall of the czar. The Zimmerwald Left tendency was on the way to becoming a movement, not because of an emulative desire to "do as they've done in Russia" (later a slogan of the Italian left), but due to the process of division set into motion by the policy of 4 August.[54] The specter of revolution began to loom larger, and as the prophet of revolt, in the third year of the Great War, the Zimmerwald Left stood upon firm ground.

The Zimmerwald Left in Switzerland

The Zimmerwald Left's most direct involvement with an individual national movement occurred in Switzerland. As a Swiss resident, Lenin was a member in good standing of the SPS, and during his months in Zürich he became actively involved in the party's internal debates. Lenin's attention was captured by a developing confrontation between right and left factions within the Swiss socialist movement, which by 1916 was badly divided, with a worsening economic situation encouraging militance. In addition he was motivated by what had become a personal vendetta with Grimm. In a memoir Krupskaia comments upon the "tragic" quality of the period, with Lenin reduced to raging against petty Swiss provincialism, "without an outlet for his colossal energies."[55] Swiss provincialism could be a real source of annoyance, but Lenin's engagement in the affairs of the SPS was also highly revealing of the Zimmerwald Left's situation and priorities on the eve of revolution.

While still in Bern, Lenin established contacts with Platten, Münzenberg, and other left-oriented leaders in Zürich through the intermediary of the Bolshevik Moses Kharitonov. By the time of his relocation Zürich left radicals were conducting weekly meetings in a variety of locales within the old city along the Limmat. This was political interaction on its most primitive level, but Lenin became an active member of the group, which in moments of optimism was referred to as the "Workers' Education League of the Zimmerwald Left."[56] With work on *Imperialism the Highest Stage of Capitalism* behind him, and after a brief alpine holiday during July, Lenin concentrated his attention upon the SPS just as it was about to enter a major internal debate.

At a session of the SPS executive committee on 7 April Grimm made the point that as a Zimmerwald affiliate, the party's position on the issue of national defense—since the 1906 Olten congress an endorsement of armed neutrality—required review.[57] The question was not a new one, but with the European war raging on all sides it became particularly controversial. Public sentiment undoubtedly supported the Swiss militia system, but since 1903 the SPS contained an outspoken Antimilitarist League (of which Grimm had briefly been a member). Since the war's outbreak several widely publicized abuses of military justice, and an active youth movement demanding the right of conscientious objection, kept the issue alive. A young socialists' conference in Aarau on 23–24 April 1916 precipitated matters by raising the demand for complete Swiss disarmament and demobilization.[58] Suddenly placed under pressure, the SPS managing committee reacted by appointing a special commission charged with drawing up a report as a basis for further discussion.

The party's commission on the military question immediately divided between partisans of "minority" theses offered by Gustav Müller that called for support of armed neutrality and "majority" theses composed by Grimm rejecting the "principle" of national defense. Grimm's radical conclusion represented a considerable evolution in his own views. At the SPS October 1914 Bern congress he had labeled Charles Naine and Graber's critique of Swiss national defense policy "naive." The intervening years of state-sanctioned massacres left him less confident in a position that was moreover incompatible with the role of Zimmerwald chairperson. In his theses, an article, and a pamphlet published during the summer and autumn of 1916, Grimm shifted his stance toward the left.[59] Militarism, he now posited, was an integral aspect of capitalism that had to be consistently combated. As a minority party, the SPS could afford to set an example by making a refusal to support the national defense part of its "general orientation." The distinction between aggressive and defensive wars must be rejected, "defense of the Fatherland" excluded, and the movement oriented toward the goal of replacing the national state with a voluntary socialist federation.

Though Grimm's views were more than sufficient to horrify the SPS right wing, they were conditioned and accompanied by sharp attacks against the left. In the *Berner Tagwacht* Grimm railed against the "opportunistic radicalism" of Platten and Münzenberg. He ridiculed demands for immediate demobilization and exhortations to armed uprising as "word games." Increasingly, his criticisms were aimed directly at the Zimmerwald Left. The positions espoused by the left at Aarau, he remarked, revealed the influence of the "grey eminence" Lenin.[60] By taking the initiative on the issue Grimm evidently hoped to retain his hold on the SPS left, but his elaborate arguments produced an impression of irresolution. The military question in the tiny Helvetic Confederation was bringing into the open suppressed tensions that lay at the core of political rivalry within the Zimmerwald movement as a whole.

Despite Grimm's criticisms, the Swiss left radicals led by Platten and Ernst Nobs chose to support his majority theses in order to keep the party's antiwar elements united.[61] The SPS was polarized on the military question, and it was by no means clear on which side the balance lay. At sessions of the managing and executive committees on 14 July and 5 August, Grimm was scolded for going public with his views before the issue had been resolved within the party itself. In view of the controversy that had resulted, it was decided to bypass the question at the annual party congress scheduled for November in Zürich and take it up separately at an extraordinary conference tentatively set for February 1917.[62]

Lenin now added his voice to the debate. The Bolshevik leader perceived three related issues to be at stake, all of which touched upon the fortunes of the Zimmerwald Left. The first was theoretical in nature and concerned the implications of the slogan "disarmament". The second related to the status of the left within the SPS, which Lenin was encouraging to move toward independence. Finally, the military question provided an opportunity to expose and damage Grimm in his role as Zimmerwald chairperson. At Lenin's initiative on the eve of the November congress a consultative meeting among Swiss left radicals approved a resolution demanding that the party orient its work according to the principles of the Kiental manifesto.[63]

When the congress convened on 4 November, Nobs and Platten read the left resolution and attacked both the right wing led by Greulich and the center behind Grimm.[64] Lenin, it seemed, had won over a portion of the Swiss left to a splitting tactic and forced Grimm toward the right.

Lenin simultaneously sought to refine a theoretical alternative to Grimm's theses on the military question. Though many of the groups associated with the Zimmerwald Left—including the Dutch Tribunists, the Swedish Left Socialists, the BSP, and the Youth International—were proponents of general disarmament, Lenin consistently opposed the slogan as an expression of bourgeois pacifism rather than revolutionary Marxism.[65] In a series of articles written during the winter of 1916–17, he addressed the problem by returning to the themes that he had introduced more than a year before in *Socialism and War*.[66] Rejecting the demand for immediate and total disarmament as an abstraction that ignored the sources of conflict built into class society, Lenin repeated the assertion that revolutionary civil wars and wars of national liberation were necessary to ensure the defeat of imperialism. His catalog of "just" wars was also extended to include a third category—wars in defense of socialism once established in one or several countries. In "The Military Program of the Proletarian Revolution" the category was defined in a manner that presaged the appearance of a Soviet national security policy after 1917:

> The development of capitalism increases to the highest degree inequalities among various nations. . . . From this fact an unchallengeable conclusion emerges; socialism cannot triumph simultaneously *in all* countries. It will triumph first of all in one or several countries, while the remainder, for some time, will remain bourgeois or pre-bourgeois in character. This will create not only conflict, but direct attempts on the part of the bourgeoisie of other countries to destroy the victorious proletarian socialist state. In these circumstances, war will be necessary and just from our perspective. This will be a war for socialism, for the liberation of other peoples from bourgeois hegemony.[67]

According to Lenin, capitalism could be nothing less than violent and destructive, the source of "horrors without end." Viewed objectively, the call for disarmament was at best the articulation of a beautiful dream, realizable only after the universal triumph of socialism. Partisans of the demand, he insists, conveniently ignored the fact that organized violence was necessary to achieve and defend the socialist revolution. A victorious revolution, surrounded by rivals, could only take the form of a "dictatorship of the proletariat," and "dictatorship means government by force, directly dependent upon *violence*. Violence in the epoch of the twentieth century . . . does not mean fists or clubs, but *organized military power* [*voisko*]." The refusal to acknowledge these harsh truths was a veiled form of opportunism, a refusal to accept the imperatives of revolutionary struggle. It was "one of the main insufficiencies of Zimmerwald and Kiental, one of the basic reasons for the possible fiasco (failure, collapse) of these embryos of the IIIrd International."[68]

Some Soviet historians have attempted to detect in Lenin's insistence upon the legitimacy of the armed defense of the revolution a preliminary justification for what is called the "Leninist theory of socialism in one country."[69] In fact, what Lenin defended was something diametrically opposed, an internationalist vision that portrayed progress toward socialism as being possible only on a global scale. It was obvious, he argued, that effective resistance to capitalist militarism did not equate to pacifism. The real danger of slogans such as disarmament was not the fact that they posed an utopian ideal. The problem was that they tended to obscure the most important point—the need to accomplish a revolutionary transformation of the capitalist world system if maximalist demands were ever really to be achieved. Disarmament as a goal "in itself" could never be brought about, neither by proclamation nor by gradual reform. Swords would become plowshares only after the hegemony of imperialism was broken by the force of the world revolution.

Lenin's position on the military question clashed with the prevailing temper on the socialist left and probably hindered his campaign to build an autonomous Swiss left radical faction. The results of the November congress, which Radek described as "a portrait of complete confusion," convinced him that a schism was necessary.[70] Unity on the left broke down, however, as the Zürich left radical group turned to the task of drafting a resolution on the military question for the extraordinary conference set for February.[71] Lenin hoped to use the conference to engineer a confrontation. His plans were scuttled by the Swiss left's reticence to strike out independently and by the caution of the sps executive. On 26 December the managing committee heard a plea from the chairperson of its military commission Emil Klöti, who suggested that the conference be postponed until the necessary preparations had been more thoroughly accomplished. Klöti's request reflected the commission's puzzlement. It was irremediably divided and concerned about plans to provoke a split. The call for rescheduling also divided the managing committee, with Grimm breaking from the left to support postponement "for an indefinite period." A meeting of the executive committee on 7 January, after acrimonious debate and by a narrow margin, opted for postponement.[72]

In attempting to justify the decision to put off a discussion that he himself had initiated, Grimm expressed concern that the issue provided fodder for left schismatics. Preparations indicated "too little understanding," allowed "too little time for discussion," and aroused emotions "which could lead to a division of the party." In response to the rhetorical question whether the party should refuse military service under all circumstances, Grimm answered with an unambiguous "no!" "If war should break out tomorrow," he continued, "should the party proclaim an uprising, the revolution? . . . In this case we would be beaten down, like the Commune." Such interventions conflicted with Grimm's published arguments and raised questions about where he really stood. The left discerned in them an unwillingness to act in accordance with principle when the stakes were high: the same fatal flaw that had paralyzed the International on 4 August 1914. Platten accused Grimm of "shrinking back from the consequences of his own theory" and called his position "a disavowal of Zimmerwald." Indeed, Grimm had placed himself in a compromising situation, tactically allied with the right wing of the Swiss party, whose representatives ridiculed the left as "Radikalinski" and "terrorists."

Lenin reacted to word of the extraordinary conference's postponement with a series of slashing attacks.[73] Dismissing references to the need for more preparation as "hypocritical," he located the real source of the about-face in Grimm's disguised opportunism. Grimm's failure to carry the struggle against nationalism into his own party, his willingness to accommodate with the right, revealed the reformist essence of his politics—the politics of a "social democratic careerist," not a revolutionary Marxist. Grimm refused to allow the party to resolve the military question, Lenin suggested, because he feared the possible consequences. The champion of Liebknecht, Höglund, and other revolutionary fighters imprisoned in distant gaols shrank back from confrontation in his own backyard. "The chairman of the Zimmerwald movement," Lenin remarked to Inessa Armand, "and such a political scoundrel."[74]

Lenin did not give up the fight. On 15 January, at a meeting conducted in Münzenberg's Zürich apartment, he once again urged partisans of the Zimmerwald Left to declare themselves an independent faction.[75] Nobs and Platten led the opposition to his proposals, arguing that channels of communication to Grimm should be held open. They likewise sabotaged an effort by Lenin's supporters to have Bronski elected to the SPS Zürich section's executive committee by withdrawing their support at the last moment. Lenin responded with personal attacks. "Nobs and Platten are completely characterless people (if not worse)," he wrote, "and they 'fear' Grimm like fire."[76] He encouraged the Swiss Left group to sponsor a referendum to reverse the postponement of the extraordinary conference and continued to agitate to win converts. In late January the Zürich left radicals issued a pamphlet endorsing Lenin's views on the military question on behalf of a formally titled "Swiss Zimmerwald Left Group," and at the SPS party conference for the canton of Zürich on 11–12 February the Zimmerwald Left Group presented an independent resolution.[77] Lenin greeted these modest initiatives enthusiastically, but his larger goal of engineering a schism was far from being accomplished.

The reluctance of oppositionists like Nobs and Platten to accept the need for an organizational break rested upon concerns common to revolutionary internationalists throughout Europe. Fear that independent factions would be reduced to insignificant sects without influence and lingering loyalties to the principle of unity inhibited the emergence of an autonomous left. The debate over the military question made clear that Lenin's patience with Grimm and the moderate opposition was exhausted, but an alternative to Zimmerwald as a forum for the revolutionary left was not on hand. Though the dilemma was real, it would prove to be short-lived. Far from Lenin's Swiss retreat events were brewing that would open up new and unexpected horizons.

Zimmerwald in Retreat

Antagonism between left and center within the Zimmerwald movement only grew stronger as the ISC scaled down its activities after Kiental. Six months passed between the issuance of the fifth *ISC Bulletin* on 10 July 1916 and the sixth (and final) number on 6 January 1917. In the interim the ISC attempted to revive Morgari's plan for a conference of socialist parliamentary fractions. Although a small group of parliamentarians was assembled on 22 August in Bern, nothing substantial resulted. Delegates from the most important belligerent powers (including Britain, France, and Germany) were unable to attend, and the session adjourned without issuing an official statement.[78] Unable to generate a unifying consensus, the ISC adopted Grimm's dictum that it was within individual national movements that the fight against defensism needed to be concentrated and retreated to its original role as a "coordinating center" for the international opposition. Lenin considered the resulting loss of dynamism to be one more indication of Zimmerwald's declining relevance.

The question of relating to the ISB also continued to brake the movement's momentum. Following the Hague conference of neutrals, the ISB made its presence felt once again by agreeing to cosponsor with the SFIO a second conference of socialists representing the allied powers. The ISC discussed the proposal on 12 December 1916, after the PSI had already requested permission to attend.[79] Naine sought to resolve the issue of dealing with the ISB once and for all by endorsing participation carte blanche, but he was overridden by Grimm and Balabanov, who referred back to Zimmerwald's principled opposition to any division of the socialist community into blocs representing rival military alliances. Once again the Zimmerwaldists found themselves hopelessly divided.

The ISC was able to reassert its radical credentials by drafting a circular letter, published in the sixth *ISC Bulletin*, which criticized the "pacifist idealism" underlying Woodrow Wilson's November peace program. The only force capable of achieving a lasting peace, the letter claimed, was "the awakening power of the international proletariat, the determined will to turn the weapons, not against their own brothers, but against the enemy at home."[80] This was a decidedly leftist text that in effect endorsed the Leninist slogan "civil war." It would require more than revolutionary rhetoric, however, to alter the fact that by the winter of 1916–17 the Zimmerwald movement was in the doldrums. In his interventions at the 12 December ISC session Grimm spoke at length about the commission's growing isolation and the difficulties it was encountering in attempting to maintain a coordinating function.

The Zimmerwald Left used the ISC's relative quiescence as a pretext for renewing attacks upon Grimm and the center. On 15 November the Zimmerwald chairperson replied to Radek's demands for a revitalization of the movement by claiming that almost all ties with members had been broken. "In my opinion," Grimm reiterated, "the time is not ripe for proclamations, but for work within the individual nations, and, so far as our reports indicate, such work is in general moving forward."[81] Radek responded by carefully formulating the motives that were pushing the Left toward a break. It was essential, he insisted, that the ISC disassociate itself once and for all from the ISB and that the Zimmerwaldists strive to become more than a "tea society gathering once a year." Lacking a more convincing demonstration of leadership, Radek warned that action by the Zimmerwald Left independent of the ISC was inevitable: "Should the bureau [ISC] refuse to demonstrate an immediate intention to act, the Left has the *duty* to do this itself."[82] Coupled with Grimm's antagonistic comportment during the debate over the military question within the SPS, the ISC's passivity worked to convince the Left's leaders that Zimmerwald's usefulness as a political vehicle was exhausted.

Lenin's inclinations were reinforced by the outcome of a rump session of the ISC enlarged committee, convened in Olten on 1 February 1917 in order to discuss yet again the issue of participation in a conference of allied socialists. The near total absence of visiting delegations gave the assembly a very radical cast. A promising start was made when a proposal from the ISC to schedule a third general conference was unanimously approved. Consensus collapsed, however, when a hostile Zimmerwald Left contingent (Radek, Münzenberg, Zinoviev, and Paul Levi) renewed an assault upon Grimm's role in the Swiss military debate and demanded nothing less than his expulsion from the movement. Dialogue degenerated into name calling, and no final decisions could be reached. Rivalry between center and left had brought the movement to the point of paralysis.[83] On 17 February and 5 March Lenin wrote to Kollontai to express his frustration, venting his spleen against the moderate opposition and speaking bitterly of the "bankruptcy" and "death" of Zimmerwald. These outbursts were accompanied by untypical manifestations of weariness and pessimism, as well as bouts with severe and protracted headaches. On 18 December Lenin lamented to Armand: "There it is, my fate. One fighting campaign after another . . . against political stupidity, opportunism, philistinism, etc.," and on 12 February he consoled a downhearted comrade by confiding, "you are not alone, to tell the truth, in having bouts with pessimism." On 9 January Lenin lectured to a conference of Swiss socialist youth and remarked almost wistfully that "we elders, perhaps, may not live to see the decisive battles . . . of the approaching proletarian revolution."[84]

Lenin's ill-humor was misplaced. On 3 March (18 February) a strike action began in the huge Putilov arms factory in the imperial capital Petrograd. By 10 March (25 February), against the background of years of war, political scandal, and economic disintegration, the action had become a citywide general strike. After being ordered in to quell demonstrations, units of the Imperial Guard mutinied on 11 March (26 February), opening arsenals and joining the side of the people in what had become, with shocking suddenness, a revolution. Four days later Nikolai II Romanov, czar of all the Russians, abdicated his throne. A provisional government built upon an unstable coalition of liberal Duma representatives picked up the reins of power only to find its authority challenged by the Soviet movement with its base in the industrial working class. In the pale light of the northern winter the masses, so often invoked as an abstraction by the Marxist left, stepped forward as a living, revolutionary force. The army mutinied, the people armed, the czar deposed, the proletariat in the vanguard—it was a vindication for the line that Lenin defended almost alone during the first days of the war.

The Zimmerwald Left Group in Zürich performed a last service by helping Lenin to negotiate right of passage across Germany and on to Petrograd in the famous "sealed train."[85] Events in Russia were developing with breathtaking rapidity, and yet on the eve of his departure Lenin did not neglect to interpret the revolution as a justification for the Zimmerwald Left. In his "Letters From Afar" and "Farewell Letter to Swiss Workers" Lenin called upon his European comrades to make real the international struggle for socialism:

> When in November 1914 our party put forward the slogan "Turn the imperialist war into a civil war of the oppressed against the oppressors for the attainment of socialism," the social patriots met this slogan with hatred and malicious ridicule, and the social democratic "center" with incredulous, skeptical, meek, and exceptional silence. Now, after March 1917, only the blind can fail to see that it is a correct slogan. Transformation of the imperialist war into a civil war is *becoming* a fact. Long live the proletarian revolution that is *beginning* in Europe.[86]

It was a conclusion of tremendous power. The despised "extremist and sectarian" had indeed to be credited with a certain foresight. Henceforward Lenin's stature as a revolutionary leader was assured. Regardless of how the revolutionary process played out in Russia, his internationalist alternative had received an impetus that would insure its longevity.

The Left On the Eve: An Assessment

By placing Lenin and the Bolsheviks at the head of a revolutionary government the Russian revolutions of 1917 contributed so much to establishing the viability of international communism that they are often regarded as "day one" of the movement. An unfortunate result is the tendency to perceive the aim of communism as first and last a struggle for power, rather than principles and ideals. In the dark winter of 1916–17 Lenin and his supporters were not calculating opportunists, but embattled revolutionaries working against all probable odds for a radical vision of the future. That vision, still inchoate prior to 1914, had grown in the course of the war into an integrated theory, embodied by the Zimmerwald Left and its challenge to the Second International. On the eve of the February revolution the challenge was fully matured. Though the explosion in Russia gave Lenin's cause a huge push forward, the elements that would combine to create an autonomous communist left between 1917 and 1921 were already in place prior to the czar's abdication. International communism did not spring from the "accident" of revolution, nor was it ever a simple extension of the Bolsheviks' fight to seize and maintain state power. Its roots lay in the left opposition's reaction to the socialist collapse of 1914 and the international movement of protest against the world war that followed.

The ideological foundations of the international communist movement are summarized by Lenin's wartime writings. Though they consist in the main of polemical tracts, cumulatively their intellectual force is considerable. Imperialism, Lenin argued, made the international system "as a whole" (v obshchem i tselom) ripe for a transition to socialism. The war was the direct result of imperialist rivalry and was bound to be followed by a crisis of hegemony that would make socialist revolution an imminent possibility. Because the source of the crisis lay in the structural contradictions of the capitalist world system, its flash points could not be predicted mechanically. More important than where a breakdown might occur was the nature of the transformations that it would initiate. Lenin believed that the battle against imperialism would unfold as a world revolution, encompassing struggle on a variety of levels and spanning "an epoch." It was the responsibility of the third International to oversee the process and insure its allegiance to the principles of revolutionary Marxism. The goal which inspired the struggle, resurrected from the purgatory to which the revisionists had sought to consign it, was a world without exploitation or war, organized as a cooperative socialist federation. It was a grandiose vision. "Lenin was much greater than his socialist contemporaries," Pannekoek wrote many years later, "because he defined tasks and objectives that were greater."[87]

As the self-declared precursor of the third International, the Zimmerwald Left accomplished several meaningful steps forward. Though constantly battling from the minority, it established a political identity and made itself a part of the landscape on the international left. Within every important European region left radical factions or parties aligned in whole or in part with the Left's program had come into being. Occasional ideological disputes among the Left's theorists, unavoidable under the best of circumstances, did not affect its ability to defend a general line. By 1917 Lenin could claim to speak for a small but dynamic tendency with the capacity to grow.

These modest accomplishments did not obscure the fact that the Left possessed only the most rudimentary of organizations, that it lacked organic ties to the labor movement, and that its affiliations, in addition to being informal, were extremely imbalanced. Radek's characterization of "a small staff of ideologues reaching their hands toward the masses" was only too accurate. The Left remained overly dependent upon the Russian and Polish components of the international left. Much of its backing derived from constituencies that were at odds with Lenin over one issue or another. Within the Zimmerwald movement the Left's distancing tactic led it into an open conflict with Grimm and the center. Though by 1917 Lenin's declared intention had become to split the movement, there could be little doubt that the Left was not yet sufficiently representative to serve as the foundation for a viable international organization. Like the movement of which it was a part, the Zimmerwald Left confronted an impasse. Its commitment to the creation of an independent left was not supported by a sufficient organizational infrastructure, range of affiliates, or mass base.

In an article written for *Neues Leben* in the summer of 1916 Radek took the bull by the horns, suggesting that principled isolation might be preferable to continued compromise with the Zimmerwald "swamp."[88] In response to charges of "sectarianism" leveled by Gustav Müller of the SPS, he pointed out that the real source of division within European social democracy was not the Zimmerwald Left. The movement was split due to the unrepentant revisionism and vulgar nationalism of the defensist majorities. Two conflicting conceptions of socialism now confronted one another, between which no compromise was possible. If the Zimmerwald majority refused to acknowledge the need to strike out independently then it too would have to be jettisoned. The "hue and cry" over sectarianism, Radek insisted, "leaves us cold." Even if the exhausted and disillusioned masses should remain passive for "decades," the Left's task would be to continue to hold up the banner of revolutionary Marxism, to "seek to gather about itself . . . a radical core capable of serving as a backbone for the movement during the struggles to come."

Radek was quick to add that pessimistic assumptions were not necessarily the most probable. The Left was not a sect, but "a broad workers' movement." The First World War was shaking the bourgeois world order to its foundations, and in its wake no turning backward would be possible. "The transformations created by the war are moving in a common direction in all countries. After the war it will not be possible to beat back the triumph of reaction with exclusively legal means. Everywhere, the masses will have to be set into motion. *Thus does imperialism, for the first time, create the preconditions for a unified international revolutionary movement."*[89] This was a recipe for radical intransigence. Radek predicted that the war would lead to political polarization and an era of struggle in which there would be no place for comfortable turn-of-the-century revisionism. In order to wage the struggle a unified left rallied around a revolutionary International was indispensable. With the Left's leaders thinking along these lines its space for maneuver within the confines of Zimmerwald was reduced to nil.

A profound ambiguity characterized the Zimmerwald Left's situation prior to the February revolution. Despite obvious shortcomings, it did not shy away from presenting itself as an alternative to the corrupt Second International, as the bearer of a new revolutionary paradigm, and as the heir to the legacy of socialist internationalism cast aside on 4 August 1914. The theses had been nailed to the church door, the legates defied, and the stage set for a confrontation. The Left's viability now remained to be tested on the field of battle of the class war, a war whose first shots had begun to echo along the boulevards of the Russian capital.

6

Petrograd and Stockholm

At the will of tyrants
The peoples tore at one another
You rose up, Petrograd toilers
And were the first to begin the war
Of all oppressed
Against all oppressors, thus to destroy
The very seed of war itself

—Anatoli Lunacharskii

ALTHOUGH the collapse of czarism riveted the world's attention upon revolutionary Russia, the February revolution was only the most dramatic of numerous popular protests that erupted Europe-wide in the course of 1917. In every case the war was a direct causal factor. The ignominious failure of the "Nivelle offensive" on the Chemin des Dames in April 1917 became the prelude to a series of paralyzing mutinies within the French army.[1] British offensives at Passchendaele during the summer and autumn fared no better, degenerating into pointless butchery in a sea of mud. In both France and Britain the incidence of strikes and protest actions increased dramatically. Italian workers in Turin erupted in a virtual urban insurrection during August, provoking a military intervention that left scores dead.[2] Coupled with the effects of the Russian revolution, these varied manifestations of discontent seemed to call the entire Allied war effort into question.

Germany's military campaigning appeared to proceed more successfully. In the east the war had to all intents and purposes been won, and on the western front the army carried out an efficient strategic withdrawal to the imposing "Hindenburg Line." The impression that victory was within reach was nonetheless deceptive. Economically, Germany was at the end of its tether, and a desperate attempt to break the allied naval blockade by declaring unrestricted submarine warfare bore bitter fruit. In April 1917 the United States entered the war, and although the Americans were not capable of making a decisive military contribution in the near future, there was no doubt that the staying power of Germany's rivals had increased. Austria-Hungary directed a devastating blow against Caporetto on 24 October, totally destroying the Italian Second Army, but the crumbling Habsburg empire lacked the means to exploit its own success. On the home fronts shortages and accumulating hardships created fertile ground for revolutionary agitation. During August 1917 a mutiny traumatized the German North Sea Fleet. In Germany and Austria-Hungary protests culminated in January 1918 with general strikes in Berlin and Vienna. Nor was unrest limited to the belligerent powers. In 1917 and 1918 general strikes erupted in Spain and

Switzerland, and Sweden was swept by labor unrest.³ The burden of the war threatened to destabilize Europe as a whole.

Though encouraged by the rise of militant protest, the revolutionary left was too weak to transform it into a real challenge to the established order. In Britain the United Socialist Council took the lead in organizing a demonstration of solidarity with revolutionary Russia in Leeds during June 1917. The Leeds Convention was a high point for antiwar agitation, and ILP Member of Parliament W. C. Anderson raised a stir with the demagogic call for "Soviets in Britain." Anderson's Soviets never appeared, however, and very little of consequence ever emerged from the Leeds rhetoric.⁴ The French army mutinies were contained after a series of executions, and in November the *jusqu'au-boutiste* Georges Clemenceau became president of the Council of Ministers. If anything, the Caporetto disaster only strengthened Italy's determination to fight on. Effective power in Germany gravitated into the hands of the high command, which pursued its overambitious plans for military victory oblivious to declining popular morale. When necessary, protests were intimidated by armed force or drowned in blood. In December 1917 Max Weber wrote that the war would go on so long as a majority remained inwardly prepared "to defend the state as *their* state."⁵ Despite the terrible weight of suffering and loss, the threshold of alienation was not crossed. The crisis of 1917 was real, but in Western and Central Europe it was not "politically decisive."⁶

Russia was the exception. Here, the war had brought a three-hundred-year-old dynasty to the ground, and the consequences could not be ignored. While the entire gamut of social democratic tendencies were forced to come to terms with the revolution, they attempted to do so in ways that suited their individual priorities. For the socialist defensists of the allied countries, the creation of a Russian republic removed the embarrassment of alliance with the most reactionary power in Europe and permitted the proclamation of a "war for democracy." Germany perceived the revolution primarily as a means to weaken its opponents. Acting through social democratic intermediaries, it attempted to encourage instability by channeling funds to the "antiwar" Bolsheviks.⁷ According to the centrist opposition, the revolution was first of all a force for peace. The results of a failure to bring a timely end to the fighting were now clear, and important elements within the new Russian government stepped forward to champion peace negotiations. For the revolutionary left it was the vision of socialism itself that suddenly took on flesh. From her prison cell Luxemburg looked forward to the Russian proletariat storming the barricades left unconquered in 1905 and opening the door to a people's peace. Partisans of the Zimmerwald Left such as Anton Pannekoek and Johann Knief located the key to the revolu- tion's future in its ability to expand beyond the Russian frontier, and particularly to impact upon Germany.[8] Differences over the nature of the revolution and its implications became yet another expression of the contrasting images of socialism that had hardened during the war.

For Lenin there was no doubt that the revolution was the result of a crisis of imperialism and that the dilemmas which it posed could only be resolved on the international level. The campaign for pro- letarian hegemony in Russia, the fight against the war, and the inter- national struggle against imperialism were now one and the same. Between March and November 1917 the Bolsheviks were swept up into a complex struggle for power in revolutionary Petrograd. They nonetheless made time to pursue a commitment to the Zimmerwald Left, whose prospects Lenin consistently described as critical to the future of revolutionary socialism. With an unofficial executive relo- cated in Stockholm, the Left retained its character as a loosely struc- tured international tendency. Its spokespersons continued to inter- vene in international forums on behalf of revolutionary causes, pursued splitting tactics on the national level, and sought to hold the Left aloft as an international faction capable of becoming the founda- tion for a third International. The entire rationale of the political alternative that Lenin sought to build during the war was uncom- promising internationalism, and it was in this light that the events in Petrograd were interpreted.

During the months between the February and October revolutions the Left remained attached to the Zimmerwald bloc, even as Lenin raged against its "uselessness." In the course of 1917, however, the Zimmerwald alternative, understood as a curative program designed to revive the socialist commitment to internationalism through an independent movement for peace, effectively collapsed. While im- portant components of the Zimmerwald majority such as the ILP, the French minoritaires, the PSI, and the USPD gravitated back toward the centrist opposition in hopes to work for a negotiated peace under the auspices of the ISB, the Bolsheviks prepared to break with the movement and launch an armed insurrection. The Zimmerwald "center," and the peace strategy with which it was associated, disintegrated between two conflicting extremes. In the end the contest between branches of the antiwar opposition was decided as a battle for the Winter Palace in Petrograd. The Bolsheviks' victory seemed to vindicate the program of the Zimmerwald Left all along the line and made the creation of a Leninist third International ineluctable.

To the Finland Station

Immediately following the czar's abdication, the first Russian Provisional Government, formally headed by Prince G. E. L'vov but effectively dominated by foreign minister Pavel Miliukov, confirmed Russia's commitment to pursue the war in concert with its allies.[9] In contrast, the Petrograd Soviet, at this point controlled by a coalition of Mensheviks and SRs, demanded a more concerted effort to achieve a negotiated peace. On 27(14) March the Soviet approved an appeal for peace, which in its emotional tone revealed a distinct Zimmerwaldist influence.[10] The famous "dual power" created by the revolution was illustrated with particular clarity by the problem of foreign policy priorities.

The Soviet's stance was modified, and also softened, upon the return from Siberian exile of the Menshevik leader Irakli Tsereteli. During the war Tsereteli and a small group of Menshevik associates in exile assumed a moderate antiwar orientation that earned them the designation the "Siberian Zimmerwaldists." In outlining his position before the Soviet's executive committee on 3 April (21 March), however, Tsereteli revealed priorities at odds with those of the Zimmerwald movement. The new, democratic Russia, he argued, could claim a legitimate right to defend its territorial integrity and institutions. The imperatives of defense required pursuing the war effort at a level commensurate with alliance commitments, while simultaneously engaging in a vigorous search for a negotiated alternative. Tsereteli became a dominant force within the Soviet during April and May, and his program of "revolutionary defensism" became the foundation for its foreign policy.[11] On 9 April (27 March), after acrimonious negotiations between the government and the Soviet, a joint statement was issued that renounced territorial acquisitions and called for a democratic peace, while also committing the regime to "the defense of our inheritance by every means, and the liberation of our country from the invading enemy."[12] By endorsing its defense policy Tsereteli had secured the government's begrudging support for peace negotiations. He now turned to the All-Russian Conference of Soldiers' and Workers' Deputies on 11 April (29 March) with a plea to Russia's allies to abandon aggressive war aims and join in defining the terms of a cease-fire.[13]

In the wake of the February revolution the Bolshevik position on the war issue took some time to clarify. On 12 March (27 February), prior to the czar's abdication, the three-member Bolshevik Central Committee in Petrograd, led by Aleksandr Shliapnikov, issued several pronouncements coinciding with the line of the Zimmerwald Left, including the call to "transform the imperialist war into a civil war for socialism."[14] The return of Kamenev, Stalin, and other exiled leaders from Siberia in late March caused the leadership in Petrograd to shift its stance closer to that of Tsereteli. "When army stands against army," wrote Kamenev in the Bolsheviks' resurrected central organ *Pravda* (Truth) on 28(15) March, "it would be the blindest of all policies which called upon one of them to lay down its arms and go home. . . . A free people will staunchly remain at its post, answering bullet for bullet."[15]

Kamenev's position contradicted both the letter and the spirit of the party's wartime resolutions, and Lenin did not delay to challenge it upon his return from Switzerland on 16(3) April. The very first of the programmatic demands read by Lenin in Petrograd to gatherings of Bolshevik leaders, known to posterity as the "April Theses," directly attacked the premises of revolutionary defensism:

> In our attitude toward the war, which as concerns Russia and also the new government of L'vov and Co. remains a predatory imperialist war in light of the capitalistic character of the government, not the slightest concession to "revolutionary defensism" may be allowed. The politically conscious proletariat can give its support to a revolutionary war, truly warranting a policy of revolutionary defensism, only under the conditions: (a) of a transfer of power into the hands of the proletariat and the poorest segment of the peasantry which has joined with it; (b) of a refusal of all annexations in fact, and not just in words; (c) of a complete

rupture with all the interests of capital. . . . To end the war with a fully democratic peace, as opposed to a peace imposed by force, is *impossible* without the overthrow of capital.[16]

These arguments called to mind Lenin's contributions to the debate on the military question in Switzerland. For the outspoken opponent of "bourgeois pacifism" it was not the principle of revolutionary defensism that was at issue, but rather the revolutionary credentials of the Provisional Government. According to Lenin, this remained a bourgeois government. Only its overthrow, accompanied by a transfer of power to the working class, would legitimize a "war in defense of socialism." The call for the Bolsheviks to prepare for a new revolution that would create the dictatorship of the proletariat in Russia was the controversial essence of the program outlined in the April Theses, a program that many Bolsheviks found difficult to accept. *Pravda* printed Lenin's April Theses on 21(8) April accompanied by an editorial comment from Kamenev noting that the views expressed were "personal opinions" and not those of the editors or the party.[17] Not for the first time, Lenin was required to "sell" a disputed policy to his closest comrades.

The effort to win over the Bolsheviks to a line of confrontation, though neither easy nor automatic, was greatly assisted by the abject failure of the international initiatives undertaken by the Soviet and the Provisional Government. Revolutionary defensism represented a coherent policy, but the government's endemic divisions and weakness prevented it from being consistently pursued. On 1 May (18 April), as required by its agreement with the Soviet, the Provisional Government sent a diplomatic note to the allies defining its war aims.[18] Drafted by Miliukov, the note was phrased ambiguously and in spite of disclaimers seemed to hold out the possibility of territorial acquisitions in the event of victory. A hue and cry immediately erupted amidst a public no longer willing to "die for the Straits," culminating with Miliukov's resignation and the reshuffling of the government on 15–18 (2–5) May. The new cabinet, though still headed by L'vov, embodied an opening to the moderate left and contained six socialist ministers (Mensheviks and SRs) including minister of war Aleksandr Kerenskii and Tsereteli. Nonetheless, the government emerged from the incident with its reputation damaged. Miliukov's fall triggered a period of chronic instability that would result in two more cabinet restructurings prior to the October revolution. At the All-Russian Soviet Congress in June, though the revolutionary defensist line still carried by a large majority, it encountered fierce opposition from the Bolsheviks, Menshevik-Internationalists, and left SRs. The government's attempt to balance a reinvigorated defense effort with progress toward a negotiated peace was failing on both counts. Internally divided, neither the Soviet nor the Provisional Government ever achieved sufficient authority to permit a reconsideration of their commitments once they had begun to flounder.[19]

Attempts to draw upon the momentum of the revolution in order to stimulate peace negotiations were launched with great enthusiasm. On 15 April the Dutch members of the ISB executive decided to set up a headquarters in Stockholm in order to undertake "consultations" with ISB affiliates regarding the terms of a peace platform. One week later, on behalf of his parent organization the SDAP, Huysmans invited all ISB affiliates and the Petrograd Soviet to convene in Stockholm on 28 May. In the Swedish capital a combined "Dutch-Scandinavian Committee" was set up on 3 May, representing the northern neutrals bloc, which followed up on Huysmans' initiative by calling for an international peace conference for mid-June. The Dutch-Scandinavian Committee, despite its formal neutrality, was a thinly veiled reincarnation of the ISB. Shaken from its torpor by the czar's fall, the Second International at last seemed to be moving purposefully toward an international peace action.[20]

The ISB's initiatives were paralleled by action on the part of the Petrograd Soviet. At the Soviet conference on 12 April (30 March) the Menshevik Mikhail Goldman (Liber) sponsored a call for an international peace conference to be convened under Soviet auspices. The Soviet executive committee received the suggestion enthusiastically and instructed its newly formed Department of International Relations to undertake the necessary preparations.[21] When Fredrik Borgbjerg arrived in Petrograd as a delegated representative of the Dutch-Scandinavian committee and the ISB executive on 27 (14) April, an initiative for peace had already been launched by the Soviet itself.

One day after Borgbjerg's arrival his proposal to sponsor an international peace conference in Stockholm was debated within the Soviet executive. A fundamental difference of opinion was revealed reflecting the line of demarcation between the moderate opposition and the Zimmerwald Left, with the Menshevik/SR majority supportive and the Bolsheviks, the Petrograd Group of the SDKPiL-Regional Presidium, and the Lettish Social Democratic party strongly opposed. In the end, however, joint work was overwhelmingly approved.[22] A Soviet delegation joined the Dutch-Scandinavian committee in Stockholm on 11 July. Within days the two groups issued an invitation to a peace conference to all ISB affiliates, the ISC, and the Trade Union International. During the following months complex and frustrating negotiations were pursued in an attempt to bridge the gap between belligerents and make an international conference possible. Confronted by intransigence on the part of the socialist defensists, and an unrelinquished quest for military victory by the belligerent powers, the efforts came to naught. The proposed Stockholm peace conference was never held. With its demise an essential component of the policy of revolutionary defensism lay in ruins.[23]

The Provisional Government's attempt to demonstrate its resolve by reinvigorating Russia's military effort proved no more successful. Following Miliukov's resignation, and against the council of senior commanders, minister of war Kerenskii prepared the ravaged Imperial Army for what he described bombastically as a "final offensive." On 1 July (18 June) the "Kerenskii offensive" was launched in Galicia, smashing through Austrian lines in the area of Galich before breaking down, in a depressingly familiar pattern, as it overextended in an attempt to exploit early successes. In a matter of days the offensive degenerated into a rout, accompanied by massive desertions. With war-weariness universal and a social revolution in full gallop, the army found itself in a state of near collapse. The defeat was followed by armed demonstrations against the Provisional Government in the streets of Petrograd, which culminated in the rioting of the "July Days" on 16–19 (3–6) July and provoked the outlawing of Bolshevism as well as the replacement of prime minister L'vov by Kerenskii. By early September German forces were in Riga, within striking distance of Petrograd. Revolutionary defensism without a capacity to defend was no policy at all. With its peace initiatives stillborn and its military program in ruins, the Provisional Government had all but exhausted its options.

The travail of the February revolution was mirrored by that of the Zimmerwald movement. Lenin minced no words concerning the Stockholm conference project; it was a "comedy" intended to perpetuate the Zimmerwaldist illusion of a democratic peace achieved through negotiations conducted according to the canons of bourgeois statecraft. Hopes for a "democratic" settlement were in fact chimeric, and the only way to avoid a peace "imposed by force" that would carry within itself the seeds of new wars was to extend the revolution by encouraging mass struggle for socialism.[24] It was this option that Lenin enunciated upon his arrival from Switzerland at Petrograd's Finland Station in April. Edmund Wilson would later interpret the moment as an historical watershed. By announcing the intention to prepare for a new revolution, Lenin heralded the day when socialism would cease to be an utopian dream and become incarnate as a "really existing" alternative.[25] The long-term consequences of Lenin's defiance were for the moment not apparent, but it already served to make continued cooperation with the moderate wing of the Zimmerwald bloc impossible. The failure of the Provisional Government's foreign policy bolstered Lenin's stature, transformed his party into a real claimant to state power, and made it possible to realize the revolutionary challenge that the Zimmerwald Left had never ceased to enunciate.

The ISC in Stockholm

The leaders of the Zimmerwald movement perceived immediately that the fate of the Russian revolution was critical to their work for peace. An extraordinary session of the ISC in Bern on 20 March voted to relocate the commission in Stockholm in order to maintain proximity to events, delegated Grimm and Balabanov to Stockholm and Petrograd as emissaries, designated a committee tasked with facilitating the repatriation of Russian political exiles, and issued a fiery manifesto including the leftist slogan "either the revolution will kill the war or the war will kill the revolution."[26] In Stockholm by late April, Grimm and Balabanov sought to rally Zimmerwald affiliates and rebuild the ISC, distributed the final number (no. 6) of the *ISC Bulletin*, and on 5 May initiated the publication of a new ISC press organ entitled *ISK Nachrichtendienst* (ISC News Service) under the editorship of Fredrik Ström. In a 10 May circular letter the ISC described the overtures of the Dutch-Scandinavian committee and recommended that Zimmerwald affiliates meet in order to discuss a common response.[27]

The issue of participation in a peace conference sponsored by the social democratic center, which conjured up the unresolved dilemma of relations with the ISB, was bound to be controversial. Groups aligned with the Left remained absolutely opposed to cooperation, but for a substantial number of Zimmerwald affiliates the project had definite appeal. En route to Stockholm in the spring of 1917 Morgari wrote to Huysmans that he was coming "in a spirit of reconciliation. The Bureau has convened the International: there is nothing more to say."[28] An Austrian delegation with strong left-wing representation legitimized its willingness to participate by describing the project as an "emergency action, not a festival of reconciliation with the traitorous social patriots."[29] For the moderate opposition attached to Zimmerwald the prospect of a reconciled socialist community reentering the international scene as a significant actor was too enticing to resist.

A priority for Grimm and the ISC in Stockholm was to coordinate their work to the extent possible with that of the Petrograd Soviet. Since his arrival Grimm's hopes to visit Petrograd had been frustrated by the repeated refusals of the Provisional Government to grant him an entrance visa. On 14(1) May he set out to accompany a large group of Russian political exiles returning to Petrograd via Stockholm as far as the border in order to provide time for consultations. Under way it was announced that the first L'vov government had fallen. At the personal invitation of the new socialist minister and Zimmerwaldist Viktor Chernov, Grimm was now permitted to pass the frontier. In the last half of May both he and Balabanov became extremely active in and around Petrograd, consulting with Russian Zimmerwaldists and addressing enthusiastic public gatherings.[30]

In Petrograd on 28–29 (15–16) May Grimm and Balabanov represented the ISC in an important session bringing together representatives of the various Russian Zimmerwald affiliates.[31] The discussion, which Grimm was careful to designate as an "exchange of opinion" only, was dominated by two issues: (1) the Zimmerwald movement's attitude toward the proposed Stockholm peace conference and (2) the propriety of socialist participation in the reconstructed Provisional Government. Lenin, Zinoviev, and Kamenev demanded that the ISC formally censure the Russian socialist ministers, arguing that they had placed themselves in the compromised position of serving a bourgeois government, one that was moreover fully engaged in the imperialist war. Opposition to "ministerialism" found nearly unanimous approval (only Martov and Natanson dissented), though in the end it was decided that as a non-Russian body the ISC was not in a position to intervene. Discussion of the Stockholm conference project was considerably more acrimonious. A left resolution, submitted by Trotsky, Kamenev, Riasanov, and Balabanov, recommended an outright boycott. An alternative proposal from Grimm, Aleksandr Martynov, Rakovski, and Natanson argued that participation was desirable in order to ensure that the Zimmerwaldist perspective would be represented and could be rationalized on the grounds that the conference was being sponsored, not by the ISB, but by the revolutionary Soviet. The debate made clear that under the impact of the revolution the balance between left and center within the Zimmerwald bloc was shifting to the former's advantage. True to form, however, no final decision was achieved. An ISC circular letter of 10 June announced that the question would be taken up again at a third general conference, to be scheduled no less than three days prior to the Stockholm peace conference, if and when the project finally matured.[32]

In the midst of these consultations the Zimmerwald movement was forced to undergo a wrenching change of leadership. Once established in Petrograd, Grimm assumed the familiar role of the movement's leader and sought to use his influence in order to further moderate priorities. Zealous but also calculating, his conviction that a negotiated peace was vital to the revolution's future led him to commit a fatal diplomatic blunder. On 9 June (28 May) news accounts began to circulate labeling Grimm a foreign agent charged with carrying a peace proposal from Berlin to the Soviet, conveyed through the intermediary of Hermann Hoffmann, the Swiss federal councillor charged with foreign affairs in Bern. After initially denying all allegations, Grimm was eventually forced to admit to having exchanged coded telegrams with Hoffmann in an attempt to obtain information about German reactions to the Soviet peace program. Though certainly free of ulterior motives, Grimm's hubris had not served him well. The incident conjured up the image of the Swiss German Grimm intervening on behalf of a Russo-German separate peace and contradicted the oft-expressed opposition of the Zimmerwald movement to secret diplomatic exchanges. Over the protest of his Menshevik comrades Tsereteli decided to react by expelling Grimm from Russia, thereby encouraging suspicions of guilt. Politically damaged, Grimm was required to withdraw from the ISC in disgrace.[33]

In a letter to Morgari, the Italian representative to the Youth International Isacco Schweide described the fall of the man who had created Zimmerwald almost single-handedly as "a truly Shakespearean tragedy."[34] On a personal level Grimm's embarrassment marked the end of his prominence within the international movement, though it did not prevent him from playing an important role in the Swiss general strike of 1918 nor as a social democratic labor leader in Bern for decades to come. In political terms the elimination of its undisputed leader meant the virtual collapse of Zimmerwald as a unified movement capable of containing the contrasting branches of the antiwar left. After Grimm's resignation the ISC was restructured to include the Swedish left socialists Höglund, Carl Carleson, and Nerman in addition to Balabanov. All three Swedes were members of the newly constituted Left Socialist party; Höglund and Nerman, recently emerged from prison, had signed the Left manifesto at Zimmerwald, and Balabanov was shifting toward the Bolsheviks. In effect, the ISC had been "won over" by the Zimmerwald Left.[35]

Balabanov's comportment as leader of the ISC in Stockholm revealed the commission's more radical orientation. On 3–4 July she met with representatives of the Soviet and delegates from various Zimmerwald affiliates assembled in the city in order to consult with the Dutch-Scandinavian committee. The decision to convene a third Zimmerwaldist conference immediately prior to a Stockholm peace conference was reconfirmed, but Balabanov went further, insisting that if the project fell through, an increasingly likely eventuality as the summer progressed, a Zimmerwaldist conference should be scheduled in its stead. Radek was present at the meeting, and he openly attacked the Soviet delegation, announcing that under no circumstances would the Zimmerwald Left participate in a conference conducted even in part under ISB auspices.[36] On 11 July, without consulting its affiliates, the ISC issued a circular letter that bluntly rejected any collaboration with the Dutch-Scandinavian committee, claiming that its work "conflicted with furthering the class struggle."[37] In subsequent meetings between the ISC and Zimmerwald affiliates on 13 July and 1 August Balabanov continued to reject cooperation with the Stockholm conference project. At the latter session a third Zimmerwaldist conference was tentatively scheduled for 5 September.[38] By forcing the issue of a break with the Dutch-Scandinavian committee without consultations, the ISC was acting with a casual disregard for delegated authority that would have been unimaginable during Grimm's tenure.

The ISC's assertiveness was in good measure the product of fresh winds blowing from Petrograd. After the failure of the Kerenskii offensive and the July Days, the issue of political power could no longer be ignored. The reconstituted ISC rallied to the Bolsheviks, characterizing the July Days as a "class struggle" in the streets of Petrograd, denouncing Kerenskii as "the symbol of the offensive waged against the will of the class-conscious proletariat," and urging international solidarity to counteract the revolution's temporary "defeat."[39] With its most important affiliates engaged in the effort to achieve a negotiated peace through the Stockholm conference project, the ISC sliding to the left, the Zimmerwald Left uncompromisingly rejectionist, and the Russian revolution reeling toward a new crisis, the Zimmerwald movement had lost all coherence and sense of purpose.

The movement received a temporary reprieve due to the collapse of the Stockholm conference project during September. Though it was the refusal of the allied governments to grant travel permits to would-be delegates that finally sealed the project's fate, the failure was a bitter blow to the ISB, which even at the eleventh hour could not assemble socialist representatives of the belligerent powers around a common table. Lenin's cynical dismissal of the undertaking had not been far off the mark. On 2 September the ISC issued a postmortem, concluding that "only the Zimmerwaldist course" could lead to peace and announcing that a third general conference would be held beginning 5 September as planned.[40] Despite the need for hasty last-minute arrangements, the conference was able to begin on schedule. The Zimmerwald movement once again demonstrated its capacity to act where the ISB could not, but it had yet to resolve the problem of determining what the "Zimmerwaldist course" actually was. The third general conference was to be the movement's last hurrah.

The Zimmerwald Left in Stockholm

The hesitancy of the moderate opposition faced with the problems posed by the Russian revolution contrasted sharply with the resolution of Lenin and the revolutionary forces aligned with him. From the first days of the war Lenin looked forward to the moment when its accumulated ravages would enable revolutionaries "to rouse the people and thereby to hasten the abolition of capitalist class rule." During 1917 the scenario of the Stuttgart resolution played itself out. The failed initiative of the Soviet and the dogged determination of the Provisional Government to persevere in the war effort, coupled with the enthusiasm created by the fall of the monarchy, created a revolutionary conjuncture that the Bolsheviks moved to exploit. The story of the October revolution has been told many times and need not be repeated here. More to the point are the international dimensions of Bolshevik strategy during the March-October period. Though its character changed as a result of the dislocation provoked by the revolution, the Zimmerwald Left remained the primary channel through which the Bolsheviks' international policies were articulated. From its new base in Stockholm the Left's informal executive continued to agitate for revolutionary priorities within the Zimmerwald movement and defended an interpretation of events in Russia consistent with the premises of Lenin's visionary internationalism.

The challenge to the Provisional Government enunciated in the April Theses was accompanied by an equally strong appeal for a break with Zimmerwald and the creation, on the basis of the Left, of "a new International, an International opposed to the *social chauvinists* and the 'center.'"[41] The demand was of course not new. Had the consequences of the February revolution made its realization more likely? In mid-April Lenin composed a brochure entitled "Problems of the Proletariat in Our Revolution," in which he repeated the argument that "tendencies" were making a break with the Zimmerwald majority inevitable.[42] Lenin's list of candidates for the new International, although long, was not particularly impressive. In addition to the "Liebknecht group" in Germany it named the Bremen Left Radicals, the Loriot wing of the CRRI, Guilbeaux's *Demain* group in Geneva, "parts" of the BSP and ILP, the left wing of the Socialist party of America, the U.S. Socialist Labor party, the Scandinavian left socialists, the Bulgarian Narrows, the PSI-left, the SDKPiL-Regional Presidium, and the Swiss and Austrian left radicals. Evaluated objectively, this was a motley group of factions that hardly provided a foundation for the kind of organization that Lenin envisioned. Many of the groups named were only marginally associated with the Zimmerwald Left, and the absence of larger, intact antiwar parties such as the PSI and USPD was telling.

Lenin's willful insistence upon an independent course could not disguise the Left's chronic weakness, its lack of an effective organization and organic ties to the mass movement. Nonetheless, the Russian revolution was creating new realities, and from the moment of Lenin's arrival at the Finland Station, the call for a third International took on a note of urgency that had been absent in the past. Enunciated simultaneously, the demands for a reckoning with the Provisional Government and a break with Zimmerwald were complementary dimensions of a revolutionary strategy informed by the ideal of world revolution. An article in the Bolshevik *Pravda* on 22(9) May drew the requisite conclusion: "We in Russia can contribute to the growth of the world revolution," it stated, "only by accomplishing *a transfer of power to the Soviets of Workers' and Soldiers' Deputies.*"[43]

The friction generated by Lenin's aggressive demands within the Bolshevik organization came to a head at the Seventh Party Conference in Petrograd on 7–12 May (24–29 April). Lenin's opening address clearly established his priorities. The party was assembled, he noted, in the midst of what was "not only a Russian, but also a mounting international revolution." Although the "duty to begin" had fallen to the Russian proletariat, their movement constituted "only a part of the world, revolutionary proletarian movement. . . . Only from this point of view can we resolve our own problems."[44] Lenin's revolutionary strategy in 1917 was developed in light of these convictions; the primacy of internationalism demanded that the Bolsheviks make use of the opportunity that had been provided them by attempting a revolutionary seizure of power, thereby pointing the way toward the creation of a new International.

Lenin's audacity was by no means universally shared. On the second day of deliberations it was agreed to refuse collaboration with the "diplomatic farce" being staged by the Dutch-Scandinavian committee, but a wide range of opinions were expressed concerning how categorical the rejection should be. One day later a more serious dispute erupted between Lenin and Piatakov over the old sore point of national self-determination, though in the end Lenin's position carried comfortably. When the conference turned to the problem of the International in its concluding session, however, Lenin found himself entirely isolated in demanding that the Bolsheviks sever their ties to Zimmerwald unilaterally. Opposition to a break with the movement was led, perhaps surprisingly, by Zinoviev, who read a resolution proposing that: "Our party should remain within the Zimmerwald bloc, posing for itself the task of defending there the tactics of the Zimmerwald Left, and moving rapidly toward the founding of a third International." Zinoviev and his supporters acknowledged the bankruptcy of the moderate opposition but insisted that ties be maintained in order "to attract away from Zimmerwald those groups that might be inclined to join with us." In the end Lenin stood alone. He was the only delegate to vote against Zinoviev's contention that "a definitive split with the Zimmerwaldists can only be undertaken *together* with our like-minded supporters within Zimmerwald," for which the time was "too soon."[45]

Lenin pursued the issue despite his defeat, turning back to the Zimmerwald Left group in the hope of splitting the movement from within. On 13 April, on the way from Zürich to Petrograd, Lenin and his entourage stopped briefly in Stockholm, where they consulted with Swedish left socialists and arranged for the establishment of an Agency of the Central Committee Abroad (ZPTSK) including Radek, Jakób Hanecki (Firstenberg), Vatslav Vorovskii, and Nikolai Semashko as collaborators.[46] Thereafter, the ZPTSK became the most important interface between the Bolshevik leadership in Petrograd and the international socialist movement. The agency also assumed the status of an executive bureau for the Zimmerwald Left, asserting the right to speak for the Left tendency and issuing proclamations in its name. Technically, the ZPTSK was a Bolshevik party organ. In a memoir Shliapnikov speaks of it "assuming the activities of the *former* Zimmerwald Left [my emphasis]."[47] In practice the distinction was not so easy to maintain. The Left had always been informally organized, and during the summer of 1917 the ZPTSK was the only executive forum it could claim.

The ZPTSK represented the interests of the Bolsheviks in a number of ways. Its first purpose was to provide a reliable channel for communication between the Central Committee in Petrograd and the outside world. Vorovskii and Hanecki traveled repeatedly between Stockholm and Petrograd during May and June and presided over a steady flow of correspondence and information. Dispatches were sent through Helsingfors (Helsinki) via courier, and up until July, aided by the prevailing confusion, the Bolsheviks were even able to make use of the official diplomatic pouch.[48] Equally important, the ZPTSK provided an outlet for agitational literature, published in German and aimed at an international audience. On 3 June the ZPTSK began to issue a weekly, mimeographed newssheet entitled *Russische Korrespondenz "Prawda"* (Russian Correspondence "Pravda") intended as an information source for the foreign press and consisting of translations from the Bolshevik press in Petrograd as well as documents, resolutions, and commentary. A more substantial journal was inaugurated on 15 September entitled *Bote der Russischen Revolution* (Herald of the Russian Revolution), eleven numbers of which were published through November.[49]

By providing Bolshevism with a voice within the international socialist community, the ZPTSK also served as a mechanism for challenging the right of the Menshevik-dominated Soviet to speak in the name of the Russian revolution. In June the Soviet set up a Foreign Affairs Committee in Stockholm. Its semiweekly newsletter, published in German, was constrained to devote much of its limited space to polemical attacks upon Bolshevik international policies, with the ZPTSK as a prime target.[50] A particular point of resentment was the ISC's announced intention to convene a third Zimmerwaldist conference independent of the Stockholm project. According to the Soviet Foreign Affairs Committee, "participation in such a conference, which will only bring together minority factions, creates the danger of dividing us from the majorities that continue to have a critical mass of the proletariat behind them, and thus potentially damages the cause of struggle for peace."[51] In a verbal duel with Tsereteli during the All-Russian Soviet Congress on 16(3) June, Zinoviev denounced the Soviet position as identical to that of Grimm and the Zimmerwald center, a disguised form of class collaboration bound to lead to ruin.[52] The battle for control of the revolution, in full swing in Petrograd, was spilling over into the international socialist movement as well.

Under Radek's tutelage the ZPTSK became a tribune for intransigent revolutionary internationalism and a voice for the Zimmerwald Left among the various socialist organizations represented in Stockholm. Though limited to a handful of collaborators the agency was a beehive of activity. In April its members were invited to attend the founding congress of the Swedish Left Socialist party and in

August were officially represented at the Stockholm congress of the Youth International. Quasi-conspiratorial links were maintained with left factions Europe-wide, and regular consultations organized with the left wings of visiting delegations.[53] Particularly close ties were established with the Bremen Left Radicals, a group that assumed heightened importance for the Left after Borchardt's International Socialists of Germany, never a very substantial organization at any rate, disintegrated in the wake of a personal scandal.[54] The German left radicals chafed at the constraints imposed by alliance with the Spartacus League. On 28 June, citing the "impotence" of the USPD and "inertia" of Spartacus, they announced the creation of an action committee tasked to prepare for the founding of an independent left radical party.[55] The spirit was willing, but in view of their continuing isolation Knief and his supporters refrained from taking the decisive step.

The Bremen left's dilemma was identical to that felt by the Zimmerwald Left group in Stockholm. On 11 July Lenin wrote to Radek: "I completely agree with you, that Zimmerwald has become a hindrance, that it is necessary to break with it. . . . It is necessary to hasten with all our strength a convocation of the lefts. . . . If we can organize an international convocation of the lefts quickly, it is even possible that a third International might be founded."[56] Throughout the summer Lenin pestered Radek with admonitions to act "immediately" to bring about a left conference. Radek and his collaborators hardly needed convincing, but the means to strike out independently were not yet at their disposal.

For the time being the ZPTSK continued to speak for a left bloc located within the Zimmerwald movement and concentrated its energies upon opposing collaboration with the Stockholm peace conference project. During the consultation between the Soviet delegation and the ISC on 3–4 July, Radek stated categorically that the Bolsheviks would withdraw from Zimmerwald unilaterally should the movement support participation.[57] The rejectionist posture garnered at least some support; the Spartacus League and Trotsky's small *Mezhraionka* group backed the Bolsheviks on the issue, and the Dutch Tribunists and Bulgarian Narrows published a joint statement in *Pravda* during May that labeled participation a "stab in the back" to committed internationalists such as Liebknecht.[58]

At the 13 July session of the ISC Radek and Kollontai presented a petition demanding that Zimmerwald affiliates "boycott" the Dutch-Scandinavian committee. On the following day the ZPTSK published an open letter inviting supporters of the Left to a consultative meeting on 5 August. "Due to the participation of the right wing of Zimmerwald in the social patriot conference [the proposed Stockholm peace conference]," the letter declaimed, "the Zimmerwald organization stands before a split. It is time to assemble the power of the revolutionary social democracy."[59] One week later the Zimmerwald Left issued a statement endorsed by the ZPTSK, the Swedish Left Socialists, the SDKPiL-Regional Presidium, and the Bulgarian Narrows, that described mass actions as the only realistic "peace program," and urged left factions to send delegates to Stockholm to discuss "the possible unification of all revolutionary social democratic elements."[60] For the moment, however, plans to engineer a schism remained no more than talk. Up to July the call for a break from Zimmerwald was still opposed by a majority within the Bolshevik organization and was regarded with trepidation by a substantial portion of the international left. Though some preparatory work was accomplished, the barriers to a conference of the left organized outside the framework of Zimmerwald were too great to be overcome.

The July Days and the subsequent suppression of Bolshevism made plans to convoke an international conference of the revolutionary left irrelevant. From hiding in Finland Lenin continued to urge independent action, but he could offer no solution for the practical problems blocking the way. As the Bolsheviks gradually emerged from the underground during August and September, preparations for a seizure of power had moved onto the agenda. The Zimmerwald Left played a significant role in the third general Zimmerwaldist conference in Stockholm on 5–9 September. Thereafter, the question of relations with the Zimmerwald bloc lost a good deal of its vitality.

Radek later accepted responsibility for the failure of a break with Zimmerwald to materialize during the summer of 1917, claiming that despite Lenin's council he held to the conviction that conditions were unripe. Until recently, Soviet historians have tended to blame the "opportunism" and "treachery" of Radek, Zinoviev, and Kamenev for thwarting Lenin's will.[61] In retrospect, however, Radek appears to have been entirely correct. Even had a conference of the left been assembled in Stockholm, its unrepresentative character would have left it devoid of significance. Lenin himself commented on several occasions during the period that a "substantial" third International could not come into being without a victorious socialist revolution and an end to the war. Once in power the Bolsheviks would require more than a year to organize a founding congress for the Third International. During the hectic summer and autumn of 1917 the pressure of time, political uncertainties, and the Zimmerwald Left's manifest weaknesses simply made the effort unfeasible. The front line of the world revolution was at any rate moving outside the confines of Zimmerwald. Mass action was the order of the day, a priority reflected in the zPTSK's agitational literature. "The new international of struggle will not be born in conference halls," it wrote with premonition on 19 August, "but amidst the gunsmoke of civil war."[62]

State and Revolution

To avoid arrest during the ban placed upon Bolshevism in July, Lenin left Petrograd and went into hiding in neighboring Finnish Karelia. Here, during August and September, he composed what would become the culmination of the theoretical reevaluation begun with the Theses on the War in September 1914. *State and Revolution* is one of Lenin's most stimulating works but also one of the most problematic.[63] Its stated intention is to offer a contribution to the "struggle against opportunistic prejudices concerning the state," which had come to a logical culmination in the "unheard of shame" of the policy of 4 August. The theoretical issues at stake were relatively abstract, but they served as a point of departure for an exploration of political issues with burning contemporary relevance.

Lenin's first purpose in *State and Revolution* is to explain the Second International's surrender to nationalism, which he attributes directly to its conception of the state as an impartial arbiter standing above society, a neutral institution that the working class could come to control democratically. While noting that the role of the state as "broker" is acknowledged by Marx, Lenin insists that this aspect of the state's activities does not represent its essence. Reconciliation between classes might occasionally become a tactical goal, but the bourgeois state could not be neutral. It was primarily an instrument of class domination, structured to coerce and dominate the masses. The proletarian revolution would not "win over" its predatory mechanisms, but rather destroy them, and proceed to construct a radical alternative.

State and Revolution develops two related themes in support of these conclusions. The first is summarized by the phrase "dictatorship of the proletariat," which Lenin uses to characterize the exercise of state power by a revolutionary authority during the phase of transition to socialism. The second, more novel theme takes up Engels' concept of the "withering of the state" and seeks to specify the forms that it will assume as the revolutionary process goes forward. The themes are illustrated with copious references to Marx's studies of the French revolution of 1848 and the Paris Commune. But another analogy repeatedly intrudes upon Lenin's theoretical analysis and lends it a particular immediacy: the Russian revolution then in progress in nearby Petrograd.

Lenin disposes of the perception of the state as impartial arbiter with a concise definition derived from Engels: "The state is a product and manifestation of the *irreconcilability* of class antagonisms . . . an organ of class *hegemony*, an organ for the *oppression* of one class by another." Emerging historically as a result of the need to impose civic order, centralized state power remains essentially coercive. Its typical institutions—a centralized administrative bureaucracy and organized armed forces (police and military)—defend the vested interests of a privileged ruling class and confront the masses as an alien, impersonal force. The coercive essence of the state, Lenin insists, is independent of the political forms through which it operates. Some of the most striking passages in *State and Revolution* are devoted to an exposé of the "omnipotence of wealth" in the bourgeois republic, scathingly described as "the best possible political shell for capitalism." In the age of imperialism the "swindle" of bourgeois parliamentarianism only served to disguise a polity that systematically excluded the masses from a decisive role in political life. During the First World War the bourgeois state system was rapidly evolving toward mature monopoly state capitalism. The state apparatus had become "extraordinarily strengthened," the ultimate bastion of the monopoly bourgeoisie, intolerant and authoritarian beneath its occasionally democratic facade. The revisionists' hope to conquer this modern Leviathan from within by means of a democratic challenge was vain, a "petty-bourgeois utopia inextricably related to the concept of the state standing above classes," which "has in practice led to the betrayal of the interests of the laboring classes."

As an alternative, Lenin poses the revolutionary dismantlement, or "smashing," of the bourgeois state. "All prior revolutions have perfected the state mechanism," he writes, "whereas it must be broken, smashed. This is the chief and fundamental conclusion concerning the state in Marxism." Clearly, the destruction of the bourgeois state implied a need for revolutionary violence, with the armed uprising as its archetypal form. Once in power a revolutionary regime would likewise need to be defended until the threat of counterrevolution became less acute. The exercise of force against the proletariat's class enemies is the essential function of the dictatorship of the proletariat, "the organization of the vanguard of the oppressed class as the ruling class for the purpose of suppressing the oppressors." The agent of the process was the vanguard party, whose task was precisely to take up the reins of power and use it to forge the trail toward a new social order. A victorious revolutionary party would need state power, "the centralized organization of force and organized violence," in order to break the back of resistance and preside over the construction of a socialist economy. An unavoidable prerequisite for the achievement of the dictatorship of the proletariat was therefore the "elimination and destruction" of the existing bourgeois state apparatus.

These conclusions culminate the polemic with revisionism that Lenin had been pursuing since the 1890s. Any attempt to build socialism by means of gradual democratic reform, he implies, was doomed to failure. Democratic forms would quickly disappear at the moment when real, far-reaching structural change moved onto the political agenda. Revolutionary socialism was therefore not a quixotic adventure, but the only realistic alternative, and the dictatorship of the proletariat was the key to its success. With proletarian hegemony firmly in place the fetters of the past could be unbound and a socialist society constructed without the need for compromise with (and surrender to) bourgeois institutions and ethics.

A later generation of Marxists, building upon the work of Antonio Gramsci, has argued that in *State and Revolution* Lenin places too much emphasis upon force as the key to bourgeois hegemony and upon the armed uprising (or "war of movement" in Gramsci's terminology) as the means to overcome it. In fact, it is countered, bourgeois hegemony rests as much upon complex sociopsychological mechanisms rooted in civil society as it does upon coercive institutions. The bourgeois state is an "integral" state, combining persuasion with coercion in order to maintain domination. The war of movement and tactic of direct assault were not unavoidable; bourgeois hegemony could also be challenged by a "war of position" waged around the themes of democratization and structural reform. Lenin was not insensitive to the problem, though in the autumn of 1917 his emphasis was naturally placed upon insurrectionary means. His main point was that only after the entire apparatus of bourgeois hegemony was dismantled could truly democratic institutions take form. Lenin builds his rejection of revisionism and Kautsky's "strategy of attrition" upon an antiliberal thesis with which Gramsci was in complete accord: the undemocratic essence of the bourgeois state in the age of imperialism.[64] The dictatorship of the proletariat is designed to effect the transition to a "new kind" of state power, capable of realizing democracy in fact as well as in form.

At the same time that he argues the necessity of the dictatorship of the proletariat, Lenin attempts to look beyond it to the "withering of the state" and the disappearance of the need for coercive force as an instrument of social control. A victorious revolution, he suggests, can lead almost immediately to a considerable expansion of popular democratic participation. First, by eliminating hereditary privilege the socialist revolution will sweep away the single largest barrier to real civic equality. The socialization of the means of production will create space for democracy unimaginable in the context of class society. Second, arguing dialectically, Lenin insists that the prerequisites for a democratization of the administrative function have already been perfected within bourgeois society itself. In the process of refining the instrumentalities of class rule, the bourgeois state reduced the business of administration to simple, mechanical tasks that "any educated worker" can master. Under the dictatorship of the proletariat, the permanent state bureaucracy could rapidly be dismantled. Third, once the bourgeois counterrevolution was defeated, the proletariat "organized as the state" would no longer be so absolutely reliant upon intimidating force as an instrument of control. The dictatorship of the proletariat was "a transitional state and no longer a state in the proper sense of the term." Its reliance upon a special mechanism for repression would be conditioned by the fact that the defeat of counterrevolution was a "comparatively easy" task. Moreover, it would be "compatible with the extension of democracy to such an overwhelming majority of the population that the need for a *special mechanism* of suppression will begin to disappear."

For Lenin the goal toward which the dictatorship of the proletariat presses is "extended democracy." Indeed, what Lucio Colletti calls the "profound democratic inspiration" of *State and Revolution* is the key to unlocking its conclusions.[65] Lenin uses Marx's evaluation of the Paris Commune to illustrate what constructing socialism under the aegis of the proletariat might entail; the involvement of the masses in the work of state administration on all levels, replacement of the police and standing army by a popular militia, limitation of wages for all bureaucratic posts to the level of "the average wage of a competent worker," etc. These are examples chosen haphazardly that do not combine to form a "blueprint" for political development, but the larger point is sufficiently clear. "To develop democracy *completely*," Lenin concludes, "is one of the constituent tasks of the struggle for social revolution."

The most original dimension of Lenin's analysis, and the one most directly related to the work of the Zimmerwald Left, is his insistence that the socialist revolution can only unfold as a global process. In *State and Revolution* extended democracy becomes the concrete form that the "withering of the state" will assume during the epoch of transition from capitalism to socialism. Lenin praises Engels' choice of terms; at issue was not an event but a trend toward greater degrees of popular initiative and control. Just as democracy cannot be created within institutions designed to reinforce bourgeois hegemony, so it cannot develop within an international system built upon the principle of sovereignty and the struggle of all against all. Socialist democracy must be extended beyond the bourgeois state and can only be realized in the context of the world revolution. Lenin's image of extended democracy is therefore impregnated with internationalism. Much more than tactical squabbles over attrition or frontal assault, it is the goal of a new kind of transitional state power, and the vision of a transformed international system, that constitutes a fundamental line of demarcation between the Second and Third Internationals.

Lenin attempts to combine the "smashing" of the bourgeois state and "extended democracy" into a dialectically related whole. In many ways, however, his two lines of analysis are conflictual. The desire to avoid the fate of the Commune by eliminating the repressive apparatus of the former ruling class is juxtaposed uncomfortably with the goal of moving rapidly to realize the ideal of voluntary association. Lenin parallels the "Commune state" that Marx saw emerging from the Paris experiment, the Commune as "the form at last discovered" within which the emancipation of labor could be realized, with the Soviet system in revolutionary Russia. Unfortunately, the problem of reconciling participatory democracy with the real-life demands of intractable class and national rivalry is insufficiently addressed.

Lenin's case for extended democracy rests upon at least three conceptual errors. Firstly, he overestimates the ease with which the proletariat can assume administrative functions in a complex modern state. The consequences of the misperception are considerable, for without the capacity to democratize civic administration a major pillar of Lenin's "new type" of state power falls away. Secondly, Lenin is contradictory in describing the kind of coercive force appropriate to the dictatorship of the proletariat. In his writings of the period the terms "armed people," "popular militia," and "organized armed force" are used interchangeably. How they are presumed to differ from a "special machinery of repression" is in no way specified, and in general the problem of counterrevolution seems to be understated. Thirdly, Lenin's theoretical perspective fails to make allowance for a socialist revolution triumphing in a single state and confronting the threat of an extended encirclement by imperialist rivals—an eventuality that he himself considered likely.

The Russian revolution, Lenin notes in the preface to the first edition of *State and Revolution*, "may only be understood as one of the links in a chain of proletarian socialist revolutions called into being by the imperialist war." This assumption rests upon a conceptual leap, from crisis of imperialism to the imminence of world revolution, not necessarily justified by the balance of forces. The ability of a victorious revolution at least to begin to phase out elements of coercion is critical to a scenario for extended democracy, but in a world system characterized by unequal development and international anarchy an equally likely outcome would clearly be the exaggerated reliance upon coercion of an isolated and beleaguered revolutionary authority lacking other means of self-defense. With the concept of the dictatorship of the proletariat *State and Revolu-*

tion provides a formula for the starkly centralized and repressive "party state" to emerge as the mailed fist of *la révolution en danger*. The outline of mechanisms for extending democracy is considerably less realistic. Should a socialist revolution in a single state remain isolated for any length of time, the vanguard function assigned to the party would inevitably threaten to become institutionalized. Herein lay the essence of Luxemburg's later critique of the October revolution. The dictatorship of the proletariat, she wrote, must be the work of a class, not its self-appointed representative.[66]

State and Revolution reinforces the strategic priorities that Lenin sought to impress upon the Zimmerwald Left. Its characterization of the bourgeois state fully justifies the controversial notion of "defeatism." The International's inability to challenge the premises of defensism in 1914 rested upon a refusal to reject bourgeois hegemony, a surrender to liberalism. The war exposed the repressive and undemocratic essence of the modern imperialist hegemon. It discredited the "fraud" of reformism and made revolutionary alternatives essential. The sufferings that it occasioned made it possible to contemplate overthrowing the established order by storm and actually constructing the dictatorship of the proletariat. With the world revolution in course, and a revolutionary third International as its avatar, the road toward the creation of an authentically international society could begin to be charted at last. In *State and Revolution* the internationalist vision with which Lenin sought to counter the collapse of 4 August 1914 comes to fruition.

There remained the need to put theory into practice, and in a ringing conclusion Lenin signals his determination to make the attempt. The fatal flaw of revisionism, he repeats, was its readiness to accept the institutions of the bourgeois state as sufficient theaters for political action, "to keep everything within the bounds of the bourgeois democratic republic." "But we will break with the opportunists; and the entire class-conscious proletariat will be with us in the fight—not to 'shift the relation of forces' but *to overthrow the bourgeoisie, to destroy* bourgeois parliamentarianism, to achieve a democratic republic on the model of the Commune or a republic of soviets of workers' and peasants' deputies, to achieve the revolutionary dictatorship of the proletariat." With these words Lenin summarized the Zimmerwald Left's call to arms. The test of his program's viability was now to follow.

The Third Zimmerwaldist Conference

Before the Bolsheviks could begin their revolutionary experiment, the final act of the Zimmerwald movement remained to be played out. The third Zimmerwaldist conference, which convened in Stockholm on 5–9 September, had little in the way of concrete tasks to accomplish. It was perceived by its organizers as a kind of vindication for the socialist antiwar movement in view of the failing aspirations of the Dutch-Scandinavian committee. In an account of the conference published in *Demain*, Balabanov emphasized the contrast between the frustrated efforts of the centrist opposition and the Zimmerwaldists' capacity for action. Zimmerwald, she boasted, had "saved the honor and future of the International" by proving that "there does exist during these years of war a collective International that has not abdicated its principles, its traditions, its honor and duty."[67]

There is no doubt that the Stockholm meeting possessed some importance as a symbol of perseverance. It did not lead to any significant progress for the Zimmerwald movement. The friction between partisans of the Left and center, what Carl Landauer refers to as the "curse" of Zimmerwald, continued to block consensus.[68] The impending collapse of the Stockholm peace conference project (it was formally "postponed" by the Dutch-Scandinavian committee on 15 September) left the movement's moderate wing at a loss for options, while the Left grew larger and less cooperative. In an atmosphere of hostility and mutual defiance, little could be done to develop the movement in new, more positive directions.

On the eve of the conference Radek published an article in *Jugend-Internationale* that signaled the Left's intentions. Zimmerwald, he wrote, had now to resolve the duality between "active and passive" internationalism that it had carried within itself since its origins. What must be determined was whether the Left could "capture" the movement or would be forced to generate a schism:

The [third] Zimmerwaldist conference will have to decide whether Zimmerwald may serve as the cornerstone for a third International, which will be an International of deeds, or whether it will prove to have been merely a transitional shelter for war-weary opportunists . . . Zimmerwald as a bloc of revolutionary internationalist social democrats with wavering elements now faces liquidation . . . the time has come to choose.[69]

It was a choice that the Zimmerwald majority refused to make. The conference's preliminary agenda limited discussion to issues that had for all purposes already been resolved, such as the Stockholm conference project, the "Grimm affair," and the catchall of "proletarian action for peace." The single theme of overweening relevance, the Russian revolution, was not scheduled to be debated, probably because it was obvious that any attempt to achieve a common position would lead directly to a split. Though the Zimmerwald movement could still assemble, there was little else it could do. Its affiliates lacked a sufficient sense of common purpose, and events in Russia were shifting the focus of antiwar action away from rhetorical gestures.

The Stockholm conference was organized in haste and became procedurally chaotic, with delegations constantly arriving and departing in the midst of discussions. The absence of British, French, and Italian delegations diluted the weight of the center, but the Zimmerwald Left group, though large and vociferous, remained in the minority.[70] Many delegates supported the Left's positions on individual issues while refusing to associate with it as a tendency. The large number of Russian participants also left a mark upon the deliberations, despite the efforts of chairperson Carl Lindhagen to keep the issue of the revolution off the agenda.

After a few introductory remarks from Balabanov, the embarrassing Grimm affair was disposed of with a minimum of fanfare by unanimously approving the findings of an ISC-appointed investigatory committee that condemned Grimm's "indiscretion." The matter of relating to the Dutch-Scandinavian committee's Stockholm peace conference project proved more controversial even though it was essentially a moot point. A proposal from the Zimmerwald Left submitted by Radek, Höglund, Balabanov, Yrjö Sirola, and Duncker categorically rejected any collaboration with the Dutch-Scandinavian or Soviet peace committees.[71] In response Aksel'rod and Mark Makadziub (Panin) for the Menshevik Organization Committee announced that their party had mandated them to participate only on the condition that cooperation with the Stockholm project be approved. Makadziub subsequently relinquished his mandate in protest against the criticism to which the peace conference project was subjected. The discussion of peace action likewise raked over familiar coals, with polarization between Left and center patent. Radek made use of the occasion to read a resolution for the Zimmerwald Left group that described the division of the social democratic movement as a "universal fact," called upon revolutionaries to work for the world revolution by opposing a "capitalist compromise peace," and exhorted the masses to bring their struggle for peace into the streets.[72]

Uncertainty as to what might emerge from the boiling revolutionary cauldron of Petrograd made the delegates wary, and the Left was visibly buoyed by the dramatic revival of Bolshevism since the July Days. Radek profited from the atmosphere of crisis, assuming the role of gadfly and agitating for radical priorities in the most brash and uncompromising manner. On 9 September a drafting commission, a majority of whose members were close to the Zimmerwald Left, was charged with composing a manifesto.[73] It drew up a vigorous appeal, denouncing the "swindle" of a capitalist-sponsored negotiated peace and urging the international proletariat to follow the Russian example. In a daring gesture, originally proposed by the moderate Ledebour, the manifesto specified the "general international mass strike" as a potential means of struggle and even began to draw up guidelines for its coordination. Though these measures might have carried more weight in August 1914, the implied determination to pass from words to deeds was very real. Aksel'rod responded with a firm refusal to sign the text (which became the first Zimmerwaldist document not accorded unanimous approval) and launched into an attack upon Bolshevik tactics in Russia. Vatslav Vorovskii of the Bolshevik Central Committee used the opportunity to demand a formal discussion of the Russian problem, but his request was promptly turned down. The conference, and the movement that it represented, had already reached the limits of its tolerance.

During the latter stages of the Stockholm debates the Zimmerwald Left group was virtually dictating policy. The shift to the left was less dramatic than it seemed, however. The unrepresentative character of the assembly and the lack of consensual goals worked to dampen its impact. Moreover, detailed accounts of the sessions were deliberately kept out of the public eye. In view of the possibility of reprisals against signatories, it was resolved to delay publication of the manifesto until a more auspicious moment. The German Independents, who together with the Mensheviks constituted the bastion of the center at Stockholm, particularly opposed its release. The party was already engaged in litigation concerning the role played by its agitators in the North Sea naval mutinies and feared that the manifesto could become the pretext for a crackdown. The ZPTSK strongly resisted the decision and sought to pressure the ISC into reversing it; Balabanov speaks of being badgered by "daily, even hourly" petitions via telephone and post. On 28 September Louise Zietz of the USPD visited Stockholm to reiterate her party's opposition to publication, and in a formal session, over Radek's protest, the ISC agreed to withhold the text at least until November.[74] At this point Radek, who had long since lost any concern for the prerogatives of the Zimmerwald movement, simply "leaked" several copies to the socialist press. The cavalier action indicated the extent to which cooperation with Zimmerwald had become a pure convenience for the Left, to be dispensed with when circumstances required.

In an evaluation of the third Zimmerwaldist conference published in *Bote der russischen Revolution* on 13 October, the ZPTSK interpreted the results as a triumph for the Left. "That which the Zimmerwald Left has struggled for at the earlier conferences," the Left's executive proposed, had "now become the general orientation." The results represented yet another "step forward" and justified the Left's continued representation within the Zimmerwald bloc.[75] From hiding in Finland Lenin voiced his disagreement and continued to demand an "immediate" break. In September he began to draft an article to defend his views publicly.[76] The article was never completed, for the entire issue was rapidly becoming irrelevant. On the eve of the October revolution the "conference politics" that Zimmerwald embodied was entirely too narrow. The decision to prepare an armed insurrection in Petrograd, finalized at an extraordinary session of the Bolshevik Central Committee on 23(10) October, represented a step in a new direction.

Internationalism by the Deed

Rivalry between socialist factions in Stockholm during 1917 was carried on in the shadow of the Russian revolution. The peace conference project of the Dutch-Scandinavian and Soviet committees, and the insurrectionary line defended by Lenin, though designed in part as responses to the crisis of the Provisional Government, also corresponded to alternative strategies for the international movement. Options posed at Zimmerwald and Kiental as abstract points of theory had now become the poles of a choice that brooked no delay. Implicit in the debate were radically different images of the events in Russia and their international implications. Was the revolution primarily Russian in nature, an expression of contradictions peculiar to the rickety edifice of czarism, or could it serve as a model for other peoples similarly caught up in an endless war? Were bourgeois-democratic or socialist goals the order of the day? In their efforts to bring the war to an end should socialist leaders seek to adapt to the mechanisms of classical diplomacy and statecraft or to defy and transcend them? In attempting to resolve these questions, the competing wings of the Zimmerwald bloc moved toward contrasting fates.

In the final number of its international bulletin, which appeared in Stockholm on 17 November, the former Soviet Committee for Foreign Affairs published a lengthy, despairing analysis that, quite appropriately, reacted to the "ruin" of the revolution with an elegy for the Stockholm peace conference.[77] From the outset, the committee argued, the continuation of the war represented the single greatest threat to the stabilization of democratic institutions in Russia. An international socialist conference supported by the mass parties of the left, with the charismatic force of the revolution behind it, might well have become the prelude to a cease-fire. With a negotiated peace on the horizon a large step would have been taken toward securing Russia's place in a more stable postwar world order, both as a member of the community of democratic states and as a force within a revitalized socialist International. If linked to an effective process of domestic reform, the future of the revolution would have been assured. In the words of the Menshevik Iulii Veinberg, the Stockholm peace conference project and the Constituent Assembly were "the two goals most filled with promise for Russian democracy."[78] The Stockholm project's failure, for the Mensheviks and all partisans of a peace strategy, represented an immense tragedy for Russia and the world.

Lenin and the Bolsheviks were not to be moved by teary laments for what might have been. The entire weight of the analysis developed by the Zimmerwald Left stood in contrast to the Menshevik scenario. Bourgeois democracy was neither a desirable nor a realistic goal for the Russian revolution, which was not national in essence, but rather the reflection of a larger crisis of imperialism. The bourgeois state system that had given birth to the war lay at the source of the problem, the Left's spokespersons insisted, and it was only by acting on behalf of the world revolution that solutions could begin to be devised.

In a series of brilliant, biting commentaries that surpassed even his own high standards for vituperative political journalism, Radek again carried the Left's message to the international community in the weeks between the third Zimmerwaldist conference and the October revolution. Correctly appraising the Stockholm project as "the symbol of the foreign policy of the majority leadership of the Soviet," he absolutely rejected the conventional diplomatic assumptions upon which it rested. The capitalist world order was "a corpse that the working class must eliminate if it does not want to perish itself" and the Russian revolution "only a part of the great process of transformation that will lead to the liquidation of war."[79] The tone had become apocalyptic, a reflection of the heady prospects that now appeared within reach. It was the responsibility of the Russian proletariat, Radek argued, to initiate the world revolution by seizing state power. "We are deeply convinced," he explained, "that a transformation in Russia will inspire a transformation in all belligerent nations. The rupture of the Russian revolution with capital will turn the international solidarity of the proletariat into a reality." An attempt to establish the dictatorship of the proletariat in backward Russia was justifiable if the revolution was perceived in its international context, and as always Radek located the key to success in Germany: "If the German working class would follow the example of the Russians, there would be no more war."[80] The Soviet Committee for Foreign Affairs perceptively mocked these "one-sided, monstrously exaggerated, and historically ungrounded hopes . . . for the impact of our revolution upon the German proletariat," but its own peace initiatives had not provided a viable alternative.[81]

The October revolution, consummated on 7–8 November (25–26 October), placed the Bolsheviks in a position to begin their experiment with a new kind of international politics. Determined to internationalize the struggle that the Russian proletariat had begun, and confident in their prospects, they came to power with the intention to challenge rather than accommodate to a world order judged destructive and unjust. Ultimately, the justification for the October revolution rested squarely upon the visionary internationalism of the Zimmerwald Left. The seizure of power was an act of internationalism by the deed, a call to arms that would inaugurate the world revolution, initiate the transition to socialism, and in so doing "destroy the very seed of war itself."

In Stockholm on 8 November Radek defended the Bolsheviks' action before an extraordinary session of the ISC, and read the text of the "Decree on Peace" promulgated by the Soviet as the first official act of the new revolutionary government. In a joint statement the ISC and ZPTSK declared that "the workers and soldiers have chased out . . . the [Provisional] Government just as they chased out the czar. Their first word is *peace*," thus linking the October revolution to the heritage of Zimmerwald.[82] The road to peace was to prove to be a difficult one, but for the time being boundless optimism held sway. During the second week of November, in a series of international appeals, the ISC claimed that the Russian proletariat had taken up arms with "a belief in the international proletariat" and called upon the workers of Europe to follow their example.[83] The power of revolutionary internationalism had been vividly demonstrated, and factions linked to the Zimmerwald Left took up the call Europe-wide.[84] For a brief moment it seemed that the flames of war had ignited *l'éruption de la fin*, and that *la lutte finale* of which the Second International so often sang had at last begun.

7

The Origins of Communist
Internationalism

We could be joyous, infinitely wealthy
children upon our infinitely bountiful
earth, but have become creatures of
money, greedy for success, pitiful, impoverished scoundrels, reduced to
state-sanctioned murderers. War has
only made the real war more evident.

—Leonhard Frank, *Der Mensch ist gut*

WITH the Bolsheviks heirs to state power the Zimmerwald movement lost whatever relevance it had managed to retain. After the disbanding of the ZPTSK, and in view of its own isolation, the Soviet regime was required to pursue its international policies unilaterally. Lenin and his comrades hoped to secure Soviet power in Russia while simultaneously encouraging the revolutionary process elsewhere. These goals were not perceived to be inevitably contradictory, but by assuming power within the confines of a sovereign state the Bolsheviks had clearly placed themselves in an anomalous position. Russia was still at war, and the revolution's survival depended upon its ability to disengage from the fighting. The Russian Republic demonstrated its contempt for the conventions of bourgeois diplomacy by announcing the confiscation without indemnification of foreign property, publishing and condemning the czar's secret treaties, and releasing a steady stream of inflammatory agitational statements. Despite a confident belief in the imminence of revolution in Europe, however, the matter of dealing with the German armies poised along the Soviet frontier brooked no delay. From the outset Soviet foreign policy was torn between the conflicting demands of internationalist conviction and national responsibility.

The dilemma was already expressed in the text of the Soviet's "Decree on Peace." Compared with the fiery proclamations of the Zimmerwald Left, it struck a surprisingly diplomatic tone, calling for a "just and democratic" peace without annexations or contributions—pages torn from the book of the moderate opposition. Predictably, the decree's appeal for a general settlement went unanswered, leaving the Bolsheviks no choice but to confront the unpalatable step of a separate peace with the Central Powers. Although treatying with Imperial Germany was perceived by some as a "betrayal" of a hypothetical German revolution, it could be defended as an unavoidable necessity imposed upon the revolution by isolation and weakness. "National" survival was at any rate not an issue. For the Bolsheviks the referent object for political choice had become the world system. By defending the victorious revolution with the means at their disposal, including maneuver and concession, the world revolutionary process would also be furthered.

While the young Soviet regime struggled to stabilize its institutions, the final act of the war was played out on the western front. In the spring of 1918 victory still seemed to be within reach of the Central Powers. The collapse of the Russian Imperial Army freed German troops for reassignment to the west, where Hindenberg and Ludendorff were preparing what they hoped would be a decisive offensive. Utilizing novel assault tactics, the Germans struck on 21 March at the point of intersection between the British and French sectors. The most impressive breakthroughs of the entire war followed, culminating with the fall of Château-Thierry on 1 June, less than one hundred kilometers from Paris. By the second week of June, however, a front was reestablished, with the American expeditionary corp under General George Pershing stepping into the breach. The German offensive recommenced on 15 June but failed to make progress. When the allies counterattacked several days later, the second battle of the Marne was won. Germany's last-ditch effort had fallen just short.

On 8 August, described by Ludendorff as the "black day of the German army," the morale of the Kaiser's soldiery began to crack, occasioning a general retreat. Economically exhausted despite its military exploits, and without any prospect for redressment, Berlin had no choice but to sue for peace. A general armistice was signed on 11 November, accompanied by the Kaiser's abdication and the creation of a democratic successor regime dominated by the defensist wing of the SPD. As revolutionaries such as Lenin and Luxemburg consistently predicted would be the case, the war had been fought to the utter exhaustion and collapse of the weaker protagonist. During 1919 the treaty of Versailles, vindictive and punitive rather than reconciliatory, transformed a humiliated Germany into a permanent opponent to the European status quo. The Great War and its aftermath had indeed merely set the stage for new and more terrible confrontations.

The contest for mastery in Europe was also a world war. Over sixty-five million men were mobilized to fight its battles, including millions of Indians, Indochinese, Africans, North Americans, Australians, and New Zealanders. More than eight and one-half million soldiers perished. The ghastly images of the western front would remain as an enduring symbol for the spiritual bankruptcy of Western civilization. The political effects of the carnage were no less dramatic. Europe's international stature was seriously eroded, and the disintegration of colonial empires given a tremendous impetus. In 1914 France was the only nonmonarchist great power to take to the field. By 1918, true to Engels' prediction, crowns were "rolling in the street." A contest that began to avenge the assassination of the crown prince to a medieval dynasty concluded with socialist revolution and Soviet power in the largest country on earth. The communist alternative was not the result of a putsch; it had matured in the midst of a major crisis of international order.

At their seventh party congress in March 1918 the Bolsheviks renamed themselves the Russian Communist party and called on left groups worldwide to follow their example. The choice of nomenclature, which intentionally evoked the sources of Marxism, was intended to symbolize the creation of an alternative to the compromised social democratic heritage of the Second International. Gradually, an international communist movement came into being, rallied around the platform of the Zimmerwald Left and the principle of allegiance to the October revolution. Small organizations affiliated with Lenin's position and capable of leading the fight for an autonomous communist left were already on hand, but the process of disaggregation within national parties was complex and would require years to resolve itself. Meanwhile, although in postwar Europe revolutionary stirrings were visceral, nowhere did they translate into a conjuncture allowing the left to seize and hold power. When the founding congress of the Third Communist International (Comintern) was held in Moscow during March 1919, it was an unrepresentative affair speaking for a movement in its infancy. All the same, the gesture was decisive. The Soviet Republic and the international communist movement, described by Charles Rappoport as the bourgeoisie's "punishment for the great crime of the war," would henceforward cast long shadows upon the internal and external affairs of states.[1] Viewed in retrospect, they appear to have been the war's most significant and enduring legacies.

Though the evolution of Soviet foreign policy and the tragic history of the Comintern lie beyond the scope of the present study, it is important to note that in both cases the legitimacy of communism as a radical alternative was rooted in the experiences of the war years and the challenge first articulated by the Zimmerwald Left. The premises of the Soviet approach to international relations were not learned from scratch once the Bolsheviks achieved state power. They rested upon the platform developed by the Left in the context of the Zimmerwaldist opposition. The international communist movement was never a simple expression of solidarity with the October revolution. It possessed its own conceptual identity and international infrastructure, grown up in reaction to the war crisis and the policy of 4 August. While the responsibilities of governance after October 1917 demanded that a certain kind of pragmatism be respected, Lenin never failed to justify his actions as head of state in terms of a larger internationalist perspective. Soviet power and the Comintern were not ends in themselves. They were intended as steps toward the creation of a new international society.

Revolution and Realpolitik

The ISC maintained a modest institutional identity in Stockholm for nearly a year following the October revolution. The committee continued to attract an occasional new affiliate and issued editions of the *ISK Nachrichtendienst* at irregular intervals through September 1918.[2] More substantial initiatives were now beyond its power. By supporting the Bolshevik seizure of power the ISC cut itself off from the majority of Zimmerwald affiliates, who reacted critically to Lenin's "adventurism." The uneasy relationship between center and left upon which the Zimmerwald bloc had rested was now irretrievably shattered.

Two themes dominated the ISC's agitational literature during the final months of its existence. In the best Zimmerwaldist tradition the international proletariat was exhorted to follow the Russian example by rising up to demand peace, with the October revolution characterized as the beginning of a new stage in the international class struggle.[3] "The Russian revolution," proclaimed an ISC manifesto on 1 May 1918, was "an appeal to the masses of the entire world, to the labor parties of all nations, compelling them to impose an end to the war and realize by mass antiwar actions the resolutions of the congresses of the Socialist International."[4] The ISC likewise strove to defend the Bolsheviks' actions before the international community. The peace negotiations commenced with Germany in

December 1917 were described as "a struggle between two world-views, two social classes, and not at all between two antagonistic nations," and the concessions forced upon the Soviets defended as unavoidable.[5] By the time that its final manifesto was issued in September, the ISC had come to equate the cause of peace and socialism with the survival of the Soviet state, said to represent "the general interests of the proletariat of all nations."[6] These hortatory pronouncements revealed an emotional predilection beginning to make itself felt on the international left, but they expressed hope more than tangible expectation. With almost all its ties to affiliated organizations broken, the last remaining Zimmerwald forum could do little more than to urge on the revolution from the sidelines. After the October revolution the ISC was reduced to the isolated voice of a divided movement that events were transcending.

The cause of the Zimmerwald Left was more effectively represented by the Bolsheviks in their attempts to achieve a "people's peace" and to craft a new kind of international policy for Soviet Russia. Speaking before the Congress of Soviets on 8 November (26 October), at the culmination of the Bolshevik seizure of power, a Trotsky now fully converted to Leninism made clear where it was that the revolution looked for its salvation. Though it was impossible to ignore the official representatives of the hostile powers, he regretted, the Bolsheviks had no illusions concerning the prospects of peace negotiations. "We place all our hopes," Trotsky intoned, "upon the revolution igniting the European revolution. If the rising of the peoples of Europe does not crush imperialism, we will be crushed . . . this is certain."[7]

Even allowing for some rhetorical exaggeration, Trotsky's conclusion accurately reflected one of the most important premises upon which the decision to take power rested. The Russian revolution's capacity to inspire the proletariat of industrial Europe was presumed to be the key to its survival. Evaluating prospects in late November, Radek noted that the organized left in Europe remained too weak to serve as a catalyst to revolt but expressed confidence in the energy of the masses, upon which "everything will depend."[8] Such faith in spontaneous mass action, deeply rooted in the left radical tradition, was now to be put to a trial by fire.

No amount of exhortation could put off the issue of war and peace. The Bolsheviks came to power pledged to end the war, and without an army they possessed scant leeway for making good their promise. After the Soviet's Decree on Peace failed to elicit a response, the Bolsheviks reluctantly turned to the German high command with the offer of an armistice. Hardened German officers such as Ludendorff received the initial proposal with some skepticism, but once the Soviet regime's readiness to make concessions was discerned, peace talks were scheduled to open in December at the Polish fortress city of Brest-Litovsk.[9]

The search for peace demanded a "deal with the devil" in the person of German militarism. With their proposal for a general peace in abeyance, however, it is difficult to see what other options the Bolsheviks had. Repeated Soviet appeals to the Entente powers urging them to join the negotiations remained unanswered, and revolution in Europe was evidently not yet on the agenda. Negotiations proceeded slowly, as the Soviet representatives stalled in order to ward off the need for concessions, but on 15 December an armistice went into effect along the entire length of the eastern front. Though it was certainly not the Bolsheviks' first choice, the stage for a separate peace was now set.

By the dawning of the new year it was clear that a strategy of "buying time" had its limits. During the second week of January a reinforced Soviet delegation with Trotsky at its head arrived at Brest-Litovsk in order to represent the Soviet position with greater authority. Though the People's Commissar for Foreign Affairs proved adept as a tribune and in verbal repartee with his counterparts, it was painfully obvious that his position rested on sand. On 18 January the Germans abruptly presented an ultimatum, threatening to resume hostilities lest significant territorial concessions were not agreed to. The Bolsheviks were now confronted with a choice between capitulation to superior force or suicidal resistance. Horrified at the prospect of so abject a surrender, a significant portion of the Central Committee, led by Bukharin, adopted a "left communist" position urging the abandonment of negotiations and preparations for a revolutionary war against German imperialism.[10] Bukharin's plea for resistance à outrance, based upon a literal reading of the theses of the Zimmerwald Left, suited the emotional preference of many Bolsheviks uncomfortable with the exercise of power and garnered considerable support.

In his wartime writings Lenin had also endorsed the concept of revolutionary war in defense of socialism. Under the circumstances, however, he was convinced that it was not a realistic option. On 19 January he presented to the Central Committee his "Theses on the Question of the Immediate Conclusion of a Separate and Annexationist Peace," in which the acceptance of the German ultimatum was justified in view of the retarded pace of the European revolution. Though the "final victory" of socialism rested upon the ability of the revolution to expand into developed Europe, Lenin argued, "it would be a mistake to construct a tactic for the socialist government of Russia on the attempt to determine whether the European, and especially the German revolution, will or will not break out in the next six months."[11] The survival of the Russian revolution was important to prospects for socialism elsewhere, and its leaders confronted a choice that would spell the difference between victory and defeat. International revolution was the goal, but tactics "for the socialist government of Russia" demanded a degree of flexibility. The Bolsheviks were not abandoning principle or surrendering to realpolitik, Lenin insisted. With the red flag flying over Moscow the political context was transformed. The first responsibility of any revolutionary regime was to ensure its own survival. If that demanded a temporary bargain with one or another imperialist bloc, there was no choice but to "crawl in the mud" and submit.

With the Central Committee split down the middle between the partisans of Bukharin and Lenin, it remained for Trotsky to present a stopgap alternative to the stark options of revolutionary war or annexationist peace. He suggested continued stalling backed up, if the bluff was called, by a "unilateral" declaration of peace. The proposal was bizarre but not without its merits. With preparations for the offensive on the western front well-advanced, there were powerful forces in Berlin determined to avoid further operations in the east if at all possible. In response to a new German ultimatum on 10 February, Trotsky announced dramatically that Russia was leaving the war without a negotiated agreement. Unfortunately, his "no war, no peace" solution quickly proved to be a lost wager. Once they recovered their composure, the German authorities declared that the war would be resumed and on 16 February issued even more severe conditions for a cease-fire. Staring disaster in the face, Lenin was now able to force his party to agree to accept the German demands.

In the treaty of Brest-Litovsk, signed on 3 March 1918, the Bolsheviks surrendered an immense swath of territories including over a third of the population of the former czarist empire.[12] The experience was harsh, but its role as a lesson for Bolshevik "utopians" in the dog-eat-dog world of international politics has been greatly exaggerated. Soviet leaders accepted the treaty reluctantly and under extreme duress. They entertained no illusions concerning the tender mercies of their imperialist rivals and emerged with their commitment to world revolution unshaken. To an important extent their very willingness to sign the outrageous accord, which dismantled the physical base of their state's power, revealed an underlying scorn for the norms of diplomacy and a confident identification with revolutionary alternatives.

The Bolsheviks did their best to encourage the decisive intervention of the European proletariat upon which they had staked their fortune. With the zptsk disbanded after November 1917, agitation on behalf of the world revolution began to be channeled through a variety of official Soviet organs, including a hodgepodge of transitory committees and working groups designed to facilitate international contacts. On 24 January the Central Committee organized an international conference of revolutionary organizations represented in Petrograd in order to discuss the issue of a new International, but its representative character was very limited. The assembly appointed a coordinating bureau, and a follow-up session was held on 14 March, giving rise to a so-called "Federation of Foreign Communist Groups of the Central Committee of the rsdrp (Bolshevik)."[13] Though undertaken in good faith, such attempts to coordinate the international left consistently ran aground upon the isolation imposed upon the Soviet republic. Without the Zimmerwald forum as an interface, the Bolsheviks lacked extensive contacts with the representatives of other socialist organizations. Unable to provide concrete assistance to revolutionary movements abroad, and with limited agitational means, they were forced to rely upon their revolution's inspirational appeal.

Hopes for a European revolution were concentrated, as always, in Germany. There was some ground for optimism, for by the autumn of 1918 the prospect of defeat served to create a real revolutionary conjuncture. On 7 October, belatedly attempting to distance themselves from the moderate opposition, the Spartacus League and the Bremen Left Radicals held a joint conference and criticized the

USPD's lack of resolution.[14] The collapse of the monarchy one month later briefly opened the door to the most extravagant prospects. During the final week of October an amnestied Liebknecht was carried through the streets of Berlin on the shoulders of soldiers decorated with iron crosses. Speaking from the balcony of Schloss Berlin on 9 November, he proclaimed "the free, socialist republic of Germany" and called on German workers "to complete the world revolution."[15]

On New Years Day 1919 the Spartacists and their left radical allies announced the creation of a German Communist party (KPD). Lenin responded joyfully that "now the *foundation* for a truly proletarian, truly international, truly revolutionary IIIrd International, the *Communist International*, has become a *fact*."[16] Before the newly founded organization could begin to establish itself, however, it was caught up in a tragedy. Later in January a poorly conceived and uncoordinated uprising in Berlin ended in the suppression of the left and the brutal murders of Liebknecht and Luxemburg, the most respected leaders of the international movement after Lenin himself. "Order" had prevailed due to a tacit agreement worked out between the SPD-right and the German military. On 10 November, fresh from participating in the formation of a "revolutionary" government, SPD leader Friedrich Ebert accepted an offer made via telephone by General Wilhelm Groener offering the military's support for a transitional democratic regime in exchange for "a common front against Bolshevism."[17] The decision to opt for accommodation with the established order in opposition to the left, an apotheosis of the betrayal of 4 August 1914, would weigh heavily upon the future of Germany and Europe. For the immediate future it pushed prospects for an authentic German revolution into the realm of the Greek calends. Though during 1919 Soviet republics were briefly declared in Braunschweig, Bavaria, and Hungary, in no case were they able to stabilize their authority. The European revolution, it was becoming obvious, was to be a more problematic affair than originally hoped.

The Communist International was finally hurried into being without support from the European revolution and virtually without preliminary planning in order to head off a plan to revive the Second International. The collapse of the Stockholm peace conference project in 1917 did not bring an end to efforts to coordinate the social democratic movement internationally. Third and fourth Inter-Allied Socialist Conferences were held in London during February and September 1918, and an informal dialogue with socialist representatives of the Central Powers was initiated. Though the familiar problems of mutual distrust and official obstruction insured that no substantial international action would result, a base of informal interactions among feuding organizations was established. It was obvious that upon the conclusion of the war it would be only a matter of time before an attempt was made to rebuild the Socialist International.

Immediately following Germany's capitulation, the executive committee of the French CGT issued a manifesto requesting a convocation of the Second International. The proposal was taken up by the "Joint Committee on International Affairs" that had been appointed by the fourth Inter-Allied Conference and seconded by Huysmans in the name of the ISB.[18] Even with the fighting at an end finding common ground among the alienated remnants of the prewar movement proved difficult. Though invitations to a general conference without preconditions were issued to all ISB affiliates, the POB continued to refuse joint work with the Germans, while a good portion of the former left opposition (the Bolsheviks, Spartacus League/KPD, PSI, SPS, Bulgarian Narrows, and Social Democratic parties of Serbia and Romania) declined to participate alongside the "social patriots." In spite of such resistance, on 3 February 1919 a general conference was convened in Bern, assembling the defensist wing of the movement together with several important leaders of the moderate opposition, including Longuet, Haase, MacDonald, and Friedrich Adler. Reconciliation was the word of the day, and despite important differences of opinion, the Bern conference represented a first step toward the rebirth of the prewar International.

The Bolsheviks responded to word of the impending Bern conference with a hurried effort to preempt it. On 25 December *Pravda* ran the text of a statement, previously radiogrammed to the West, that denounced the project, refused Soviet participation, and called upon revolutionary Marxists "to assemble around the already intact structure of the International that has nothing in common with the open social imperialists or those wavering elements which provide them with assistance."[19] Grigorii Chicherin, soon to replace Trotsky as Commissar for Foreign Affairs, was put in charge of organizing a founding congress for the third International, and he turned to the task with characteristic diligence. Lenin advised that invitations be issued to all socialist organizations "that have broken with their social patriots" and mentioned either his own project program for the Russian Communist party or Luxemburg's pamphlet "What Does the Spartacus League Want?" as possible platforms.[20] The goal was to attract the broadest possible participation, and affiliation with the Zimmerwald movement was not made a criterion for attendance. The text of an appeal for revolutionary socialists to gather in Moscow to found a third International was published in *Pravda* on 24 January 1919 and mailed to thirty-nine communist and left radical organizations representing a cross-section of the international left.

The Communist International was brought into being at a congress in the Moscow Kremlin on 2–6 March 1919. In many ways the moment chosen for the event was inauspicious. Russia was torn by anarchic fighting, with the worst battles of a full-scale civil war still to come. Military contingents large and small representing no fewer than fourteen sovereign states were pouring across Russia's undefended borders, and in some cases openly abetting the counterrevolutionary white armies. With the prospects of Soviet power so uncertain the creation of an international organization pledged to world revolution was an act of almost desperate defiance.

The composition of the delegations also left much to be desired. The KPD, so often invoked as the "key" to a viable revolutionary International, had scarcely regrouped after being decimated during the Berlin uprising. Its surviving leaders had yet to discuss the Bolshevik initiative, and the KPD representative in Moscow, Hugo Eberlin, possessed no fixed instructions from his parent organization. Hastily organized and poorly attended due to its venue in virtually inaccessible Moscow, the Comintern was created by a small and unrepresentative group of revolutionary activists, with the Soviet comrades far outweighing their foreign guests. Nonetheless, the impression of weakness was deceptive. The Bolsheviks would go on to win their civil war, and the international movement that the Comintern aspired to lead was waxing.

Anxious to establish a claim to the mantle of Marxist orthodoxy, the Moscow congress asserted a direct link to the revolutionary wing of the classical social democracy through the intermediary of the Zimmerwald movement. Speaking for the ISC, Balabanov emphasized the service that Zimmerwald had rendered as a forum for anti-war action. At the same time she took pains to distinguish the movement from the Comintern, describing it as "a temporary organization, bearing an essentially defensive character against the imperialist war."[21] A resolution introduced by Fritz Platten and signed by the Zimmerwaldists Lenin, Radek, Rakovski, and Zinoviev announced the movement's formal merger with the Comintern, but also downplayed its significance. Zimmerwald was described as having been meaningful "at a time when it was important to unite all elements of the proletariat against the imperialist murders." Its impact was unfortunately dampened by the presence of "centrists, pacifists, and wavering elements" alongside the representatives of the revolutionary left. The end of the war and the new horizons opened up by the Russian revolution had now brought the alliance of convenience to an end: "The Zimmerwald union has outlived itself. All that was truly revolutionary in the Zimmerwald union has passed over to and joined with the Communist International."[22]

Zimmerwald would not be forgiven its domination by the center. According to an interpretation that has become standard in communist historiography, the movement was important merely as the passive vehicle that allowed revolutionary Marxists to maintain an international presence during the war years.[23] Indeed, it is ironic to note that despite their divergent premises, both Western and Soviet accounts have tended to agree in deemphasizing Zimmerwald's independent accomplishments. In the first instance the movement's antiwar efforts are judged to have been compromised by politically marginal extremists. In the second instance the revolutionary impulse of the Left is perceived as having been hemmed in and frustrated by the obstructionism of the moderate majority. In both cases the movement is reduced to the status of what Radek called a "transitional shelter," a kind of alpine way station where internationalists took refuge while waiting for the storms of war to subside.

Attempts to understate the significance of Zimmerwald are generally insensitive to the extent to which the experience of the war conditioned the political environment that emerged after 1918. The European social democratic movement, born in the wake of the French revolution, rallied around the theoretical premises of Marx and Engels, and assembled as an international force under the banner of the Second International, had by 1914 arrived at the end of a road. The underlying source of its eventual schism was the clash between reformists and revolutionaries revealed during the revisionist controversy at the turn of the century, but the war crisis was the catalyst that made differences irreconcilable. The fourth of August 1914 was a moment of catharsis that destroyed the artificial unity imposed by the prewar centrist consensus. Thereafter, the movement's rival wings were forced to come to terms with their disagreements and grope their way toward new patterns of interaction. The sense of treason engendered in the left by the sudden abandonment of the movement's antiwar program, the surprisingly strong attachment to the national community that welled up on the socialist right, and the images of horror emerging from the fronts all combined to reinforce political rivalries and lend them an emotional intensity that would not soon be overcome. Lenin was among the first to draw the conclusion that the "betrayal" of 4 August 1914 made it imperative for the revolutionary left to go its own way. It was in reacting against the International's collapse, the triumph of nationalism on its right wing, and the tragic consequences of the war that he refined the principles upon which the world communist movement would subsequently rest.

Though the Brest-Litovsk negotiations revealed that Lenin was capable of lucid political realism, he was never a proponent of realpolitik, understood as an all-embracing approach to the practice of international relations based upon the immutability of national sovereignty. Between 1914 and 1918 Lenin and his associates constructed a revolutionary theory of world politics that was distinct above all for the emphasis that it placed upon visionary internationalism. Their conclusions were not only expressed abstractly; they were realized by the initiatives of the Zimmerwald Left. Due in good measure to the Left's interventions, the Zimmerwald movement became much more than a "temporary and defensive" alliance. It was the crucible within which the great schism of the socialist labor movement was brought to fruition and the communist alternative forged.

The Brother of the War

The Comintern's founding congress, poorly attended and procedurally chaotic, represented little more than a symbolic gesture. When the second world congress met in Moscow from 7 July to 8 August 1920, the international environment was considerably altered. The European revolution had not arrived, but the new "Red Army of Workers and Peasants" had succeeded in vanquishing its major rivals.

Led by the brilliant twenty-seven-year-old front commander Mikhail Tukhachevskii, its advance guard was marching on Warsaw with the goal of bringing a "revolution from without" to Poland and linking up with communist forces in Germany.[24] The conference hall in the Kremlin was adorned by a large map, upon which the daily progress of Soviet armies was indicated. Though the Polish campaign would end in defeat, the second congress was temporarily buoyed by a mood of optimism. Its most important initiative, approval of the famous twenty-one "Conditions for Admission into the Communist International," reflected militant self-assurance. The conditions were a *profession de foi* that defined the movement's character for a generation to come.[25]

It is striking to note how closely the twenty-one conditions correspond to the platform of the Zimmerwald Left. Consistent with Lenin's long-standing conviction, revisionism is described as the root cause of social democracy's collapse, and the rejection of a reformist road to socialism is set in place as the Third International's keystone. Institutional safeguards are defined to guarantee that opportunism will not once again corrupt the movement from within, including acknowledgment of the dictatorship of the proletariat as a "principle line of demarcation" from opportunism, the expulsion from communist organizations of "centrists," and an organizational break with reformist trade unions. The strictest administrative centralism is imposed upon affiliated communist parties, which are obligated to follow directives issued by the Comintern's executive committee without question. On the assumption that the pursuit of structural change will ultimately lead to a confrontation with the repressive apparatus of the bourgeois state, the maintenance of an underground organization is made mandatory. In a personal triumph for Lenin, support for the unity of national liberation struggles in the colonial world with the proletarian labor movement within the advanced industrial states becomes a point of reference for the communist left. A final, draconian condition directs that affiliates who refuse to accept the conditions in their entirety must be automatically expelled. The Third International defined by the twenty-one conditions would be uncompromisingly revolutionary, rigorously centralized, and committed to a global definition of the revolutionary process, an institutional embodiment of Lenin's conception of communist internationalism.

The Zimmerwald Left's bequest to the international communist movement was considerable. Well prior to the creation of the Comintern, the international left was able to achieve a degree of self-sufficiency based upon affiliation with Lenin's Left tendency. The ideological premises developed by Lenin and his supporters in the course of their battles with both the "social chauvinists" and the moderate opposition founded the communist alternative upon a rigorous and compelling theory of world politics. The twenty-one conditions were a loyal rendering of organizational attributes for the international movement such as the Left had come to define them. Not least, the communist movement could draw legitimacy from the heritage of the Left's resistance to the imperialist war, crowned by the victory of the October revolution.

Like any other mass-based social movement, twentieth-century communism has moved away from its original defining principles, sometimes transcending, sometimes abandoning, and sometimes betraying them. These principles nonetheless retain a certain importance. The commitments that animated the international communist movement at its origin provide a standard against which to measure its achievements and failures. They help to account for the movement's ability to maintain an autonomous political identity in a dramatically changed international environment. They reveal the sources of some of the contradictions that have plagued international communism in the effort to realize its own promise, and for some they remain a font of inspiration. By way of conclusion some of the ways in which the legacy of the Zimmerwald Left contributed to shaping these commitments may be explored.

Organizational Filiation

The growth of left radical factions and splinter groups aligned with the Zimmerwald Left tendency into independent communist parties was a complicated process that did not proceed uniformly.[26] Those former leftists such as Gustave Hervé or Paul Lensch who transformed themselves into social patriots after 4 August 1914 found counterparts in defensists such as Marcel Cachin or radical pacifists such as Jules Humbert-Droz, who converted to communism after October 1917. The many poets and humanists associated with the Zimmerwald Left, including Gorter, Höglund, Nerman, and Roland-Holst, did not fare well in the unforgiving world of communist politics, and the left radical fringe, denounced by Lenin during 1920 for its "infantile leftism," soon found itself hounded from the movement.[27]

There was nonetheless a discernible organizational filiation between left groups associated with the Zimmerwald Left and the communist parties that grew up between 1917 and 1921. In most cases these groups constituted the militant core around which the communist-oriented left assembled, bringing with them a set of priorities formed during the war years that would mark the movement indelibly. The Austrian left radicals, whose ties with the party center were already effectively broken following the January strike of 1918, formed the Communist party of Austria in November 1918. In Germany the Spartacus League and the left radical movement launched the KPD on 1 January 1919. The French CRRI issued several short-lived newspapers (including *La Plèbe* and the *Journal du Peuple*) in the name of the Zimmerwald Left during 1918. In May 1919 it renamed itself the *"Comité de la Troisième Internationale"* and became a force urging the SFIO and CGT toward communism.[28] The Communist party of Great Britain was created in August 1920 by a merger between the BSP, the Socialist Labour party, and Sylvia Pankhurst's "Dreadnought" women's federation, with the BSP playing the dominant role. At the PSI's September 1918 party congress the revolutionary intransigent tendency commanded a clear majority: "In fact," comments Luigi Ambrosoli, "Italy's communist party had already been born."[29] For independent parties already oriented toward the Left such as the Swedish Left Socialists, the Bulgarian Narrows, the SDKPiL, the SDP, and the Serbian Socialist party, the transition to communism was more straightforward. Inspired by the Bolshevik example, and encouraged by association with a dynamic international movement, the left factions of the war years were in a position to begin to construct mass organizations.

The World Revolution

The concept of the world revolution emerged from Lenin's theory of imperialism. According to the Bolshevik leader, by transforming capitalism into a world system and internationalizing the class struggle, capitalist imperialism created the objective preconditions for the achievement of socialism on a global scale. The First World War, Lenin argued, exposed the contradictions rending the capitalist world system and initiated an era of revolutionary confrontations. Though Kautsky, in *The Road to Power*, also spoke of the "entire world" as the future battleground for the "liberation struggles of laboring and exploited humanity," his observation did not lead forward to any significant revision of social democratic tactics.[30] Encouraged by the war crisis, the Zimmerwald Left insisted upon specifying the consequences. Confrontation with imperialism demanded a break with reformism, a rejection of the bourgeois state as an adequate context for building socialism, and the creation of a new International that would defend internationalism "by the deed." The attempt to realize the internationalist implications of Marxist theory during an historical conjuncture where socialism had become both possible and necessary was the alpha and omega of the communist left.

Lenin repeatedly described the world revolution as a complex process extending over "an epoch." He was nonetheless convinced that the Russian revolution would soon be followed by similar upheavals within the developed industrial states of Western Europe, permitting socialist relations of production rapidly to be imposed upon a significant portion of the world economy. Lenin's optimistic faith in the imminence of revolution in Europe, as Neil Harding notes perceptively, was "bound up with his indictment of the savagery and butchery of the First World War."[31] In reacting against the war's horror Lenin and his comrades leaped to the conclusion that such violations were bound to extract an equivalent price. The phrase "world revolution" accurately expressed the magnitude of the task that the war placed on the agenda—globally coordinated mass struggle against imperialism. Only an engagement of such magnitude could offer a real alternative to a continuing disintegration of international society. The immense, moralistic fervor with which the Left's theorists contemplated the "*Götterdämmerung* of the bourgeois order" that they believed the war to have begun was an integral dimension of their theoretical outlook. The Russian revolution was a ray of light in the darkness, and its universal implications were immediately seized upon and exaggerated. The German revolutionary shop steward Emil Barth expressed a widespread conviction when he described it as "merely a stride in the mighty progress of the world revolution, which is itself the twin brother of the war."[32]

In his brochure *The World Revolution*, completed in July 1918 and dedicated to Lenin, Herman Gorter sought to make the implications of the concept explicit. By realizing Soviet power, he suggests, the Russian revolution provided a model for dismantling the bourgeois state. In order for a restructuring of the international system to begin, the revolution must now be extended into the heartland of industrial Europe, where the prerequisites for an "authentic" socialism were in place. The need to defend the achievements of the Russian revolution was obvious, but the dilemmas which it confronted could only be resolved by reaching beyond the boundaries of the backward czarist empire.[33] Taking further the analysis that he began during 1915 in *Imperialism, the World War, and Social Democracy*, Gorter concludes that the world revolution will emerge both as a consequence of and antidote to imperialism's inability to master the unified world economy that is its own creation. Gorter is in some ways Lenin's best intellectual disciple, and his perceptions were shared by the entire revolutionary left. "Our necessity," wrote Luxemburg in *The Crisis of Social Democracy*, "will assume its rightful function from the moment when the contrasting necessity of bourgeois class domination ceases to be the instrument of historical progress and becomes an obstacle and danger to further social development. The present world war has revealed precisely this point."[34] Here, in a nutshell, was the justification for the communist alternative.

The problem was that the "necessity" of imperialism was not quite so exhausted as the war crisis seemed to reveal. The First World War unleashed a period of revolutionary turmoil, but it was also, in the words of Immanuel Wallerstein, "the stage of the *consolidation* of the industrial capitalist world economy."[35] The emergent American colossus, in particular, added an element of stability to a system that would prove far more adaptable than originally assumed. In effect, Lenin was only partly correct. At the Finland Station in April 1917, when describing the Russian revolution as the first blow of "the socialist revolution on a global scale," it was still possible for him to consider the arrival of the European revolution as imminent.[36] By the time of the Brest-Litovsk debate such hopeful expectations had to be abandoned. History, it seemed, had posed the task but not yet provided the means for its accomplishment.

The consequence of the "temporary restabilization" of world capitalism following the war was "socialism in one country," a contradiction in terms according to Marx, for whom a socialism worthy of the name could only emerge as the result of the cooperative efforts of the world's leading nations. It was possible to argue that, even without spreading into Europe, Soviet power in Russia could contribute to the world revolutionary process by posing a permanent challenge to the hegemony of imperialism and providing support and encouragement to the forces of movement. It remained the case that confined to Russia the revolution could not hope to advance beyond a "socialism of poverty" sharing little in common with Marx's vision. The role of the USSR as a "base" for the world revolution has been an important source of legitimization for Soviet power, but it has also led to self-defeating contradictions. The failure of the revolution to expand almost immediately forced the Bolsheviks away from internationalist priorities and toward their own, pragmatic variant of revolutionary defensism. After Lenin's death the contradictions of socialism in one country would undermine many of the revolution's most cherished principles and lead directly toward the monstrous distortions of Stalinism.

War, Peace, and Revolution

Lenin acknowledged that by mobilizing the masses and revealing to them the venality of the established order, war created unique opportunities for the partisans of revolutionary change.[37] He never regarded war as a necessary or desirable prerequisite for social revolution, which could arrive as a consequence of war, but also in any number of other ways. War was defined by the theorists of the Zimmerwald Left as a product of contradictions rooted in the injustices of class society. In the long term, therefore, preventive antiwar strategies reliant upon conflict management were futile. War would only disappear when the world revolution had created the prerequisites for communism. "Peace," cried Luxemburg passionately in her keynote address to the founding congress of the KPD, "means the world revolution of the proletariat."[38]

The Left's hostility toward the peace strategy of the Zimmerwald majority made clear how deeply impregnated its analysis was with old-fashioned Guesdist fundamentalism. In the summer of 1915 Radek already sought to relativize the issue of peace by subsuming it within the larger context of social transformation:

> We are entering a period of struggle for the dictatorship of the proletariat with the overcoming of capitalism as the goal. At issue is not the act of a proletarian uprising, but an epoch of

victories and defeats leading up to the day of final triumph. Our peace action is the first step that leads the way toward this epoch, and only when regarded from this point of view do the contradictions that would otherwise seem to frustrate it disappear.[39]

Though the gesture of peace action was considered necessary, the potential of such action actually to affect the priorities of the belligerent powers was evaluated pessimistically. The point was to act in the spirit of the 1907 Stuttgart resolution and make use of the crisis provoked by the war in order to encourage revolution. Regarded in isolation, the demand for peace represented just one more revisionist illusion. The Bolsheviks carried these convictions with them to power, and they passed into the communist tradition intact. Peace was considered a function of social justice, incompatible with the aggressive essence of capitalist imperialism.

The literature of the Zimmerwald Left contains a powerful image of peace as the product of social harmony, and some Soviet scholars have accused "bourgeois historiography" of intentionally downplaying Leninism's antiwar aspects by overemphasizing the polemics launched against pacifism during the special circumstances of 1914–1918.[40] The critique seems to miss the point that Lenin's primary intention was precisely to define ways in which peace could become something more than a pious wish by restoring the movement's commitment to the militant pursuit of maximalist goals. A preventive antiwar strategy designed to ward off clashes via moral example or diplomatic refinements had failed in 1914, he argued, and would fail again in the future. Revolutionary Marxists must grasp that it was only by defeating imperialism and its corresponding system of international relations that the cycle of interstate conflict could be broken and war as an institution eliminated. Lenin's attacks against radical pacifism were unrelenting and expressed nothing but scorn for disarmament as a goal in itself. The terror unleashed at the fronts had given revolutionaries a lesson in the role of force and encouraged the assumption that violent confrontations were inevitable in the pursuit of social change.

The armed defense of the revolution, the creation of a centralized and hierarchical Red Army, and the short-lived doctrine of the "revolution from without" were all entirely compatible with the theses of the Zimmerwald Left. The establishment of a Soviet national security policy beginning in 1918 did not represent an abandonment of principles, but rather their consistent application under changed circumstances. Reliance upon "organized armed force," justified by Lenin theoretically and sanctioned by the experience of civil war and foreign intervention, was correctly regarded as necessary if the revolution was to survive. In rejecting a naive faith in spontaneous popular initiative and diplomatic good will, however, the Bolsheviks often moved to another extreme. The civil war contributed to a brutalization of Soviet power and created the potential for what Stalin himself later referred to as "red militarism."[41] International communism was built upon the conviction, enunciated by Gerrard Winstanley centuries before and by Leonhard Frank in his passionate antiwar novel *Man Is Good* during 1918, that war was only the ultimate expression of man's inhumanity to man. Peace has been a constant theme in the movement's agitation, and the current program of the Communist party of the Soviet Union continues to describe the elimination of war as the "historic task of socialism."[42] Attempts to pursue this goal with military means, and within the logic of a military system, have nonetheless led to cruel dilemmas that in the age of nuclear weaponry have occasionally taken on aggravated form.

The National Question

Lenin's position on the national question, contested within the Zimmerwald Left but absorbed whole into the program of the Comintern, proved to be a source of real dynamism for the communist left. By aligning the movement with the cause of national liberation, Lenin tapped into one of the motive forces of contemporary history. Important political actors in the colonial world, inspired by the call for national self-assertion, impressed by the Bolshevik example, and contemplating the European metropolises weakened by war, were poised to accept the kind of direction that association with the international communist movement could provide. The young Vietnamese revolutionary Ho Chi Minh, upon reading Lenin's theses on the national question, claimed to have been "moved to tears."[43] Bukharin, Lenin's nemesis during the war, was by the mid-1920s posing the Bolshevik revolution as a model for socialist-oriented development in transitional societies. In his immensely influential *Foundations of Leninism*, published after Lenin's death in 1924,

Stalin identified "the contradiction between the handful of ruling, 'civilized' nations and the hundreds of millions of colonial and dependent peoples of the world" as one of the three basic contradictions of imperialism.[44] Within the Soviet Union the "right" of national communities to self-determination remained a dead letter. Externally, it became a fundamental line of orientation.

The First World War greatly accelerated the transformation of a formerly Eurocentric world order. Russia's revolution occurred in a developing nation with an advanced industrial sector but also a primitive rural economy still weighed down by traces of feudalism, on the periphery of the world centers of industrial capitalism. The Bolsheviks seemed to provide a positive example for movements committed to socialism but operating outside the European mainstream. Even the Second International's left Marxist wing located the battle for socialism exclusively within the advanced industrial states. Lenin's position on the national question reflected his perception of the interdependence of the capitalist world system in the age of imperialism, and the need for a global strategy to oppose it. It anticipated a shift in the center of gravity within the world revolutionary process, away from the relatively prosperous industrial metropolises and toward the "weak links" where the contradictions of unequal and imbalanced development were felt most directly. The emphasis was subtle, and Lenin never abandoned the conviction, an inheritance of classical Marxism, that the industrial proletariat of Europe and North America held the key to the socialist future. All the same, by arguing the existence of an organic link between proletarian class struggle and anti-imperialist national movements, he provided international communism with a "third-worldist" orientation that has been the source of some of its greatest triumphs.

Determinism and Voluntarism

The theorists of the Zimmerwald Left held the original sin of socialist defensism to be Bernstein's revisionist elevation of the "movement" above the "goal." Overidentification with the social democratic minimum program, they believed, paved the way toward the collapse of 4 August 1914. Preoccupation with the "possible" had become a fetter that left the movement unprepared to confront discontinuity and crisis.

Marxism defined a delicate balance between determinism and voluntarism, between the impersonal forces working to shape history and the role of human will as a factor capable of promoting change. The leading theorists of the Second International—the Kautskys, Plekhanovs, Guesdes, and Labriolas, whose intellectual formation was tied up with the effort to disengage Marxism from anarchism— leaned toward a preference for "objective preconditions" that allowed for the conscious intervention of the human will only under carefully defined circumstances. The result was often a cloying caution that tended to reinforce an emphasis upon evolutionary change. The war crisis made it imperative to reassert a balance by reviving aspects of Marxism that had become neglected, including dialectical rather than normative interpretations of social phenomena, the priority of changing the world, and the final goal of communism. For the Zimmerwald Left it was axiomatic that after 4 August 1914 the Marxism of the Second International would have to be "purged of opportunism" and restored as a living guide to action, a philosophy of praxis.

A neglected key to Lenin's perception of the problem is his *Philosophical Notebooks*, a series of commentaries on Aristotle, Hegel, Feuerbach, and Plekhanov composed between September 1914 and May 1915.[45] In these preliminary studies Lenin strives to demonstrate that mechanistic determinism rests upon false premises, distorts the essence of Marxism, and thwarts revolutionary initiative. As an alternative, he poses a dialectical materialist approach whose leitmotif is the unity of theory and practice. After August 1914 the willingness to urge mass actions against the war even at the risk of isolation, to march against the current, became Lenin's litmus test for revolutionary Marxists. The will to force the issue of radical change, confident that engagement could move mountains, set the Zimmerwald Left apart from its social democratic rivals.

The Third International was intended to represent what Pannekoek called a "Marxism of the deed," a slogan that after the October revolution became widely popular.[46] The young Antonio Gramsci announced his conversion to Bolshevism in November 1917 with a famous article entitled "The Revolution Against *Capital*," by contrasting Lenin's "revolutionary will" with the dogmatic fatalism of the Second International. The Bolsheviks, he claimed, were not "Marxists" in that they have not compiled on the basis of the work of the master an artificial doctrine of dogmatic and indisputable affirmations. They live the thought of Marx, that which can never die, which is the continuation of Italian and German idealist thought, and which in Marx was contaminated by positivistic and naturalistic incrustations. And this thought poses always, as the major historical factor, not raw economic facts, but rather man, rather the society of man.[47]

Whatever one chooses to make of Gramsci's references to the Crocean and Hegelian strains in Marxism, his remarks make explicit another attribute of the original communist credo. The Third International was to be an act of the spirit, inspired by a faith in humankind's ability consciously to transform its social environment.

Not surprisingly, the first generation of communist activists was predominantly youthful, radicalized by the war, and inspired by the image of a world healed and remade, the image of communist society.[48] Arno Mayer, comparing Lenin and Woodrow Wilson as purveyors of alternative models for international society in the period of disillusionment that followed the peace of Versailles, emphasizes the "hopeful and utopian quality" of the former's "ultimate objective of the classless society in a warless world."[49] For A. J. P. Taylor, Leninism represented "a new morality, in which sovereign states would cease to exist," that after the October revolution "took on practical form."[50] After the degradation of the trenches many found in communism's millenarian vision a cause at last worth fighting for.

The idealism expressed in the Zimmerwald Left's Promethean challenge to the "proud tower" of a civilization built upon violence and exploitation would not survive the onset of Stalinism. The Soviet state, which adopted *The Internationale* as its national hymn in 1917, would abandon it after 1941 in favor of a more traditional anthem that praised Stalin by name. Almost all of Lenin's closest associates during the war were annihilated physically, and often morally as well, during the terror of the 1930s.[51] Their efforts are no less significant for that reason. The cloud-storming enthusiasm born with the international communist movement, the confidence in people's ability to make their own history, has left its traces despite failures and betrayals.

The Third International

During the First World War the need for an international socialist organization was still considered to be self-evident. The "revival" of the International after the fighting ceased was a consensual goal, shared by all strains of socialist opinion. Lenin's position was distinguished by his invocation of a "new type" of International, structured to oppose revisionism and class collaboration. The creation of a third International implied a settling of accounts with opportunism and the ouster of its representatives from the proletarian movement for liberation. It meant the creation of a radical alternative, guided by a consistently revolutionary theory of international relations, codified by Lenin during the war and justly described by Robert Gilpin as the first complete "Marxist theory of international political change in the capitalist era."[52]

Lenin's determination to begin anew was conditioned by his disgust for the treason of the Second International. Radek repeatedly emphasized, and with some justification, that it was not the Left which made a schism inevitable, but rather the extremism of the social democratic right. His former left Marxist comrade Paul Lensch was arguing by 1917 that capitalism had already accomplished the world revolution and that social democratic organizations should limit themselves to "positive cooperation" with the established order.[53] At the international socialist conference in Bern during February 1919 Hjalmar Branting referred to Wilson as a "pioneer of the international policy of the working class."[54] Such conceptions laid the groundwork for an unabashedly reformist social democracy, whose horizons for change were limited to schemes for international arbitration and an extension of the welfare state.

For the Zimmerwald Left it was indisputable that under the influence of revisionism the social democratic movement had abandoned the revolutionary masses and sold its soul to the bourgeois state. Henceforward there would be only one party of labor, the communist party, committed to radical transformations that would place real power in the hands of the dispossessed. The indictment of reformist social democracy as a pillar of bourgeois hegemony, of "social fascism" promulgated by the Comintern's sixth world congress during 1928, was not an aberration, but a perception rooted in the essence of the communist challenge. Partisans of reconciliation on the left have repeatedly been frustrated by the fact that, after 1917, communism and social democracy were not merely alternative routes toward the same destination, but fundamentally different approaches to the problems of social change and historical development. The emotional legacy of the war and its aftermath, where communists and social democrats confronted one another from opposite sides of the barricades, reinforced what had become irreconcilable premises and priorities.

Although communism rested its prospects upon revolutionary mass action, Lenin's strategy revealed a characteristic lack of confidence in the masses "left to themselves" with their "trade union consciousness." His skepticism was reinforced by the wave of nationalism that carried away the European proletariat during 1914. Part of the reason why the International proved incapable of generating antiwar action was its lack of discipline, its inability to lead. These were the evils that Lenin sought to purge from the Russian movement after the turn of the century with the organizational postulates of *What Is To Be Done?* The masses made history, but not automatically; in order to channel spontaneous revolutionary energy into an effective direction, an ideologically rigorous organization was required. Georg Lukács would later assert that the "leading role" assigned to the organizational factor was the most important distinguishing feature of Leninism, particularly vis-à-vis the Luxemburgist wing of the revolutionary left.[55] The third International was to be a centralized, fighting organization capable of controlling and disciplining its affiliates. As the tactical coordinator of the world revolution, it would not merely oversee the movement, it would command it. Here was Lenin's concept of the vanguard party writ large, what Gramsci was later to call the "embodied will" of the revolutionary international proletariat.[56]

The consequences of the Second International's exaggerated federalism were readily apparent, but the dangers of Lenin's alternative should have been no less so. The combination of the Bolshevik triumph with the failure of revolution in the West elevated the Soviet experience to the status of a universal model and encouraged the imposition of tactics corresponding to Soviet priorities. Within a decade "Bolshevization" was the Comintern's leading slogan, with the recalcitrant subject to administrative reprisals and expulsion.

The Zimmerwald Left's emphasis upon "betrayal," by allowing the Bolsheviks to leap over the critical question of why European workers remained passive in an "objectively revolutionary situation," proved counterproductive. Structural differences between East and West Europe were not adequately explored, the Russian revolution's distinctively national traits ignored, and an homogeneous political line imposed by fiat upon a diverse international movement. Forbidden the option of expressing itself as "a multitude of lines, tendencies, movements, and parties," international communism moved rapidly toward self-effacement in the shadow of Soviet power.[57] In the long run "socialism in one country" was incompatible with the type of organization that Lenin and the Left heralded at Zimmerwald during 1915. The disbanding of the Comintern during 1943 was as clear a reflection of Stalin's abandonment of Leninist priorities as could be desired, but it was a belated gesture. The spirit had left the Comintern long before its formal interment.

A Summary

The collapse of the Second International in August 1914 exposed the limitations of the conception of internationalism that it had absorbed and adapted from the theoretical postulates of Marx and Engels. As a loose federation of national parties, the International provided its affiliates with little more than a consultative forum. Its leading parties were preoccupied with the problem of advancing social justice within states by increasing the political leverage of the organized proletariat and with encouraging accommodation between states by championing positive international cooperation. The maximalist goal of transforming the international system, though acknowledged theoretically, was irrelevant to their real concerns. Despite its oft-expressed commitment to oppose war, the International was incapable of responding as an institution during the July Crisis that led to the First World War. On 4 August 1914 its most prestigious affiliates rallied to the premises of defensism. Thereafter, the International fell into quiescence, unable to sponsor unified antiwar actions or to enforce a consensual point of view. Its passivity, by any standard, was a considerable abrogation of responsibility.

The Zimmerwald movement arose as a protest against the International's lack of initiative. Though unified around the need demonstrably to oppose the war, its affiliates were divided from the outset between partisans of moderate and radical priorities. The Zimmerwald majority, led by Robert Grimm, adopted a peace strategy that emphasized the need for antiwar action as a means to revive the movement's traditional commitments to class struggle and internationalism. Under Grimm's guidance Zimmerwald attacked the policy of 4 August but refused to contemplate an abandonment of the Second International. Its goal was to win back and restore the movement rather than to lead it in new directions. In contrast, the Zimmerwald Left based its critique upon the assumption that in view of the apostasy of the "social chauvinists," reconciliation was impossible. Defensism was judged to be only the most glaring example of the corrosive effects of opportunism, which must now be exposed and burnt out root and branch. The Left's call for the creation of a third International summarized a determination to recast the socialist labor movement in a consistently revolutionary mold.

Although it remained relatively unstructured, the Zimmerwald Left succeeded in establishing itself as an acknowledged international political tendency. Critical accounts that emphasize the Left's marginality, pointing to its lack of organic contacts with the mass movement, or characterizing its international initiatives as "a kind of diplomacy carried on between different labor organizations," are not entirely unfair.[58] Too often, however, such conclusions rest upon a refusal to accord any legitimacy whatsoever to revolutionary politics, when the whole point of the Left was to reassert the vitality of a revolutionary tradition. Evaluated in their own terms, the Left's efforts bore considerable fruit. Between 1914 and 1917 a body of analysis was developed that subsequently provided the international communist movement with a solid ideological foundation. The radical factions aligned with the Left became the seeds from which communist mass parties would spring after 1919. Not least, the perceptions that social democracy had reached a dead end, that an independent revolutionary left was necessary, and that the Zimmerwald Left was its logical standard-bearer were reinforced. The communist left's rejection of reformism was the product of a deep disillusionment, "conceived in the terror of 1915, in the din of autumn offensives . . . the daughter of the war."[59] The Zimmerwald Left's program was elevated in stature by the October revolution and institutionalized with the creation of the Comintern. Consistent with the scenario sketched by Lenin in 1914, the war did conclude by sparking a social revolution, splitting the labor movement, and giving birth to a political alternative that has become an important force in twentieth-century world affairs.

Communist internationalism was conceived as a radical alternative to a capitalist world system presumed to be responsible for an unprecedented paroxysm of violence and destruction. It was grounded upon the theory of capitalist imperialism and the assumption that the European war had given rise to an open-ended crisis, an era of world revolution. In order to exploit the crisis, to realize the unity of the proletariat as an international class "without a Fatherland," and to transform socialism from a dream into a reality, an international vanguard was required, capable of imposing a uniform strategy upon the spontaneous mass movement. It was global in its aspirations, reaching beyond the citadels of industrial capitalism to embrace struggles for national liberation and social justice worldwide, struggles that would soon call hundreds of millions of people onto the stage of history. It was ultimately both visionary and utopian, with a militant self-assurance reinforced by the glimpses of Armageddon unveiled on the battlefields of the war. The world revolution was the key to untangling the contradictions that bedeviled the Second International in its efforts to combine internationalism with a commitment to work through the political mechanisms of the bourgeois state. By exposing revisionist illusions, creating the dictatorship of the proletariat, extending participatory democracy and self-management, and spreading proletarian hegemony over a larger and larger domain, it would eventually create a context within which what Engels referred to as the "withering" of the state could become a living, historical process.

The Comintern's image of internationalism was itself flawed. Self-assurance could all too readily become intolerance, encouraging a dogmatic insensitivity to alternative perspectives. The crisis of imperialism was not so far advanced as the Left's theorists supposed, and their confidence in the imminence of revolution in Europe proved overly optimistic. There is no doubt that Lenin's accomplishments during the war years were monumental and that the October revolution did permanently alter the terms of world politics. By successfully launching their revolutionary challenge in the midst of the Great War, with its horrifying scenes of mutual annihilation, the

Bolsheviks gave birth to a political myth that lies at the foundation of the communist alternative and continues to exert an appeal. Contrary to expectations, however, the "final conflict" was not on the verge of being won. Indeed, it had only just begun.

In crafting a strategy for the world revolution, Lenin and his supporters were overly sanguine, exaggerating the inspirational appeal and universal relevance of the Russian revolutionary experience. In defining revisionism as the root of all political evil, they overemphasized institutional means to combat its influence. In exhorting the downtrodden masses of the colonial world to rise up against imperialism, they leaped over the torturously difficult problem of socialist construction in the context of severe underdevelopment. The October revolution, which insured the dominance of Lenin's priorities by bringing him to power, also created challenging new problems. Isolated and besieged in their revolutionary fortress, the Bolsheviks were left with no choice other than to attempt to coexist with a capitalist world system that had evidently not yet exhausted its potential. Inevitably co-opted by the imperatives of survival, the *Staatspolitik* that the Bolsheviks had set out to transcend would return in new forms to haunt them and the international communist movement.

Postscript

Communism and Social
Democracy: The
Enduring Challenge

THREE-quarters of a century after first being articulated, what relevance, if any, does Lenin's image of communist internationalism still possess? Voices do not lack to argue that the entire political tradition founded by Lenin has been overtaken, that the rivalry between communists and social democrats born during the First World War no longer bears any relevance to contemporary problems, and that eventually, if the socialist left does not want entirely to be effaced, it must seek to overcome its antiquated internal divisions. The target of such criticism is seldom the ideal of socialism itself. At stake is the continued viability of the international communist movement in the forms that it has assumed since the October revolution.

The problem of world order posed by the theorists of the Zimmerwald Left between 1914 and 1918 is tragically far from being resolved. In the decades since 1945 over twenty-five million people have died as a result of wars both large and small. The imposing nuclear arsenals of the "superpowers" have only aggravated the security dilemma, given rise to an open-ended arms race, and contributed to a militarization of international politics as a whole. At the time of this writing the technologically advanced postindustrial societies count over thirty million unemployed, while the gap between rich and poor on a global scale grows ever wider. Torn by violence, fatally divided between haves and have-nots, unable to maintain balanced growth, the contemporary international system bears much more resemblance to that portrayed by Lenin than many would care to admit.

If Lenin's critique of capitalism's insufficiencies has in some ways been borne out, his hopes for the communist alternative have been substantially disappointed. Regimes dedicated to the principles of communism now rule a third of the world's people, but the communist state system is mired in crisis, struggling to overcome its Stalinist past and caught up in an unprecedented reform process that is calling many of its most basic assumptions into question. Meanwhile, international communism as a movement of political contestation has become virtually moribund. Almost everywhere that they exist in the world communist parties find themselves on the defensive, in gradual or precipitous decline, unable to inspire the young or rally around themselves a significant portion of left-wing opinion. The handful of communist organizations that continue to play a significant role do not alter the fact that international communism in the manner that Lenin sought to define it, as a militant movement with a unifying ideology and inspirational sense of mission, has nearly ceased to exist.

Recent years have seen several significant attempts to restore to the communist tradition at least some of its lost vitality. One of the most discussed has been the so-called Eurocommunist initiative, launched with great fanfare during the 1970s, subsequently run aground, but far from having exhausted its potential. Even more dramatic, and with potentially larger consequences, are the reform programs being implemented in the People's Republic of China (PRC) and the Soviet Union. Although these initiatives concern respectively the international communist opposition and the communist party states, they are closely related. Both have in common the attempt to revive the communist movement by reconciling it with assumptions once considered to be the preserve of social democracy, including the acknowledgment of a democratic road toward socialism, a repudiation of Stalinism, acceptance of the market mechanism and an important private sector as prerequisites for economic progress, and the rejection of universal models for social change. Though it is not clear where these various experiments will lead, enough has already been accomplished to raise the question whether, in undertaking them, international communism is not also progressively abandoning many of the traits that once lent it historical individuality. A good deal of Lenin's energy during the First World War was devoted to differentiating the nascent communist left from the "bankrupt" social democracy of the Second International. As the communist movement begins to draw closer to social democracy once again, what will remain of its own autonomous character?

Viewed historically, Eurocommunism may be considered as an attempt by Western European communist parties to assert an identity distinct from that of the USSR. Its origins lie in the immediate post-Stalin period, as Western parties sought to use the leeway provided by a reform-oriented leadership in Moscow in order to achieve a greater degree of autonomy. The 1960s saw several acts of defiance to Moscow's habit of dictating priorities, a challenge given theoretical substance in the writings of the Italian Communist party (PCI) leader Palmiro Togliatti. The Soviet military suppression of the Czechoslovakian "Prague Spring" reform movement during 1968 had the effect of drawing battle lines between two divergent conceptions of communism: the dogmatic neo-Stalinism of Leonid Brezhnev's USSR and a reformist course calling for significant liberalization, albeit within the confines of the party-state model.

The lessons of the Prague Spring were drawn most consistently in Western Europe. In 1972 a "Union of the Left" joined the French socialist and communist parties in an electoral alliance based upon a common program that was essentially reformist in inspiration. The failure of the traditionalist Portuguese Communist party to benefit from the collapse of the dictatorship of Marcello Caetano after April 1974 further encouraged the search for new directions. Beginning in 1975 the diverse strands of a critique that had been long in the making began to be assembled. In a series of conferences, publications, and public interventions—culminating with the "Madrid Summit" of March 1977 which brought together Georges Marchais, Enrico Berlinguer, and Santiago Carillo of the French, Italian, and Spanish communist parties—the term "Eurocommunism" was coined as the emblem of a political alternative geared to the needs of parties operating within modern, parliamentary industrial states.

Though never formally codified, the foundations of the Eurocommunist position may be summarized in four points: (1) a critique of existing communist systems, which are no longer regarded as models or ideal types; (2) a break with "Leninism," understood as a rigorous set of ground rules for political practice, and particularly the concept of the dictatorship of the proletariat; (3) the sanctioning of a peaceful, democratic transition to socialism; and (4) an insistence upon complete autonomy for individual, national communist parties. These points rest upon the assumption that the Soviet Union may no longer claim to be the "natural leader" of communist parties operating in very different social and historical environments. Taken together, they represent a substantial challenge to the entire theory and practice of international communism since Lenin, with extremely far-reaching implications.

No sooner were the principles of Eurocommunism enunciated than the informal coalition created in order to defend them began to fall apart. Internal rivalry within the Spanish party, abetted by a sabotage campaign sponsored by the Soviet Union, split the movement and alienated a good part of its popular support. In France, once it became apparent that the Union of the Left was working to the advantage of François Mitterand's socialists, the communist party shifted backward toward a more traditionalist posture. The numerous smaller parties associated with the Eurocommunist position usually remained loyal, but by the end of the 1970s the only major Western party still in the fold was Enrico Berlinguer's PCI. The inflated hopes of the mid-1970s now gave way to a phase during which the Italian party took on the role of Eurocommunism's *cavalier seul*.

The PCI's special status is explained in part by its unique historical experience. Long years of resistance to fascism waged from the underground, systematic exclusion from a role in national government during the postwar period, and the distinguished theoretical contributions of its historical leaders Gramsci and Togliatti all sensitized the party to the special importance of maintaining a solid mass base. The success of the PCI's populism, which made it the world's largest communist party out of power at a time when most other communist organizations experienced an erosion of support, encouraged further evolution in the same direction. By the late 1970s the party's inflection toward social democracy seemed to be irreversible. Undeterred by the disappointing results of an "historic compromise" with the Italian Christian Democracy, the PCI launched campaigns on behalf of a "New Internationalism" freed from Moscow's sponsorship, declared itself to be a part of a "Euroleft" encompassing the entire gamut of communist and noncommunist progressive forces, and built its domestic strategy upon a "democratic alternative" reliant upon cooperation with the social democrats.

The PCI defended its initiatives as the beginning of a third phase in the historical struggle for socialism. According to this categorization, the first phase was that characterized by the creation and development of the socialist parties grouped around the Second International. The second phase was that launched by the October revolution and dominated by the thought and example of Lenin. Writing in the PCI's central organ *L'Unità* (Unity) on 30 December 1981, in the wake of the outlawing of the Solidarity movement and the imposition of martial law in Poland, the party's directorate concluded that the second phase "has now exhausted its motive force in the same way that the phase . . . of the Second International was exhausted." Given the terms of comparison, this was a very dramatic conclusion indeed. By the mid-1980s the PCI's declared intention had become to create a rapprochement between the communist and social democratic movements and to reunite the socialist left. The mutations that were transforming the character of world capitalism and the exhaustion of the Soviet model, it was argued, made traditional political alternatives increasingly irrelevant.

With these conclusions the Eurocommunist initiative seemed to have been brought to fruition. If the PCI hoped that the new course would further solidify its mass base, however, it was to be sadly disappointed. The party's greatest electoral feat arrived during the European parliamentary elections of 17 June 1984, when, riding the wave of emotion that followed the sudden death of Enrico Berlinguer, the PCI briefly became Italy's leading party with 33 percent of the vote. Subsequently, the party's electoral base has disintegrated dramatically, with most of the defections moving directly to the socialist party of Bettino Craxi. By blurring the distinction between the communist and social democratic alternatives, it appears that the PCI may have played into the hands of its rivals. At present the Italian party is a divided and troubled organization. If its right wing, the *"miglioristi"* (improvers), continues to press for an opening toward the center, a reviving left wing insists that too much has already been given up. It is possible that the PCI's drift toward social democracy has reached its limit and that a correction to the left will eventually move onto the agenda. Regardless of how the party evolves, one must conclude that the most consistent attempt to date to realize the premises of Eurocommunism has led to a very ambiguous outcome. If adjusting to contemporary realities means that communists must become social democrats in all but name, it is difficult to see where their movement's future lies.

A more cautious and perhaps more convincing attempt to draw a line of demarcation between communism and social democracy in Europe has resulted from consultations between the West German SPD and the East German Socialist Unity party (SED). In August 1987, after lengthy deliberation, special commissions appointed by the two rival organizations released a joint statement which carefully described their points of accord and disaccord. Although shared priorities and areas for cooperation are duly outlined, an important emphasis is placed upon enduring differences. From the social democratic perspective communism remains inherently prone to political repression, economic inefficiency, and cultural rigidity. For the communists social democracy is no more capable now than ever before of offering a real alternative to the crying injustices and dangerous instability of capitalist imperialism. The theoretical divergencies between the two currents, often expressed in much the same form in which they emerged after 1914, remain virtually intact.

With the respective positions of the two commissions clearly staked out, the joint statement goes on to sketch a foundation for pragmatic cooperation. Despite their differences, it is asserted, communism and social democracy are required to coexist. Although competition will continue, it must be conducted uniquely via convincing positive examples. Only in a climate of trust and détente can either party hope to fulfill its best aspirations and contribute to resolving the essential problems of our time, described as the quest for disarmament, the fight against hunger and underdevelopment, and the ecological crisis. The joint statement's emphasis upon the problems of European security and coexistence is partly a function of its "inter-German" character, but its larger implications are not difficult to detect. Although the communist and the social democratic alternatives confront problems of adjustment, both are amenable to reform. Each of the major subdivisions of the twentieth-century labor movement can play a positive role in building a more humane future without surrendering its distinctive identity.

The SED is probably correct to insist that the communist movement has no choice other than to seek to build upon its own traditions. At present the problem has become to determine in what it is that these traditions actually consist. The verities of Stalinism and Mao-Zedong-thought have been substantially dismantled, and the reforms in progress in the USSR and the PRC are changing the face of world communism in dramatic and unexpected ways. While the Chinese reforms arrived first in time and to date have proceeded the furthest, the most significant of these efforts, commensurate with the USSR's more dynamic role in world affairs, is the process of restructuring associated with the name of Mikhail Gorbachev. The Gorbachev leadership, in its fifth year in office, has already presided over a period of impressive innovation: a top-to-bottom revamping of the Soviet economy, a sweeping transformation of political institutions undertaken in the name of democratization, a no-holds-barred assault upon the Stalinist past, and a long list of new initiatives in the realm of international affairs. The implications of these changes for the international communist movement have been little discussed, yet they are potentially quite substantial.

One of the most pointed commentaries to emerge to date from the Gorbachev team concerning the present state of the international communist movement is that made just prior to his retirement by central committee secretary for international affairs Anatoli Dobrynin on the occasion of the thirtieth anniversary of the journal *Problems of Peace and Socialism* on 12 April 1988 in Prague. As the semiofficial voice of the pro-Soviet wing of the movement, the journal has consistently represented the kind of dogmatic and inflexible positions that are now more and more often coming under attack. Dobrynin's choice of forum may therefore be interpreted as an admonition to the movement to begin to heal itself from within.

In his remarks Dobrynin lists three problems standing in the way of progress for the international communist movement. Firstly, he suggests, the movement has failed to adjust to the changing nature of its social base and to the more complex circumstances under which the struggle for socialism must proceed worldwide. Two examples are offered: the altered profile of the working class within the advanced industrial states and the fact that third world countries are being constrained to develop within the confines of the capitalist world economy. Merely to refer to these problems signifies a break with the prevailing orthodoxy of the Brezhnev years, though the least that one can say is that they will not be easy to resolve. Secondly, Dobrynin acknowledges that the attractiveness of the socialist alternative has declined, a fact that he attributes to the inability of the socialist states to provide convincing demonstrations of democratization and effective solutions for the problems of economic development. Finally, the decline of international cooperation between communist parties is lamented. The principle of autonomy for national parties being inviolable, what is required is not the creation of a new international center in the image of the Comintern, but rather more "positive interaction" on all levels within the context of the movement as presently structured.

The solutions to these problems lie within the broad reform direction designated by the terms *glasnost* (openness) and *perestroika* (rebuilding). The international communist movement is urged to overcome its inherited divisions, particularly the Sino-Soviet rift. It is asked to provide a more honest and critical evaluation of its own past and to recast its strategic assumptions on the basis of a realistic appraisal of contemporary situations. Most importantly, a long-term effort designed to transform the communist party states into more open and dynamic systems capable of exerting a real international appeal must take priority over revolutionary adventurism. The communist movement, Dobrynin insists, must abandon claims to possess a monopoly of historical understanding, reground itself upon universal, humanistic values, and commit itself to an intensified dialogue with social democracy on behalf of shared, progressive goals. Although no reference is made to a "third phase," the implication that international communism stands before a series of fundamental redefinitions is unmistakable.

As is the case with Gorbachev's entire program, these redefinitions are justified as a return to the unsullied sources of Leninism. What is Leninist about them in fact? The communism of the "twenty-one conditions" is clearly not what is being proposed. Stalin's violations are rejected en masse, and yet care is also taken not to collapse the movement back into categories associated with reformist social democracy. What is offered for the moment is a series of guidelines that aim at restoring some of the movement's original élan by drawing upon Lenin's legacy selectively, in order to address problems that the leader of the Zimmerwald Left could scarcely have foreseen. The goal is a communist reformation that will rescue the kernel of the original doctrine by jettisoning deadwood and ruthlessly exposing failures and abuses.

An international communist movement reorganized according to these guidelines would be polycentric, open to a variety of organizational forms and political strategies, and committed to realizing the principles of socialist democracy. It would nonetheless rest upon a series of premises that clearly distinguish the communist and social democratic branches of the international left. As Dobrynin's successor as central committee secretary Vadim Medvedev puts it in a January 1988 edition of the Communist party journal *Kommunist*: "In the development of the international workers' movement, in essence, conditions are making possible a gradual shift toward dialogue and cooperation between communism and social democracy in the context of the preservation of the independence and uniqueness of each of these political tendencies." Communism continues to be defined in terms derived from Lenin's *Imperialism the Highest Stage of Capitalism* as a conscious and creatively evolving alternative to a capitalist world system in permanent crisis. Its foundations include allegiance to the ideal of internationalism as it is manifested in today's interdependent world, to include the principle of peaceful coexistence between states with different social systems, and respect for the positive accomplishments of the communist party states. Dobrynin describes a chastened movement whose immediate horizons are considerably lower than those envisioned by the Zimmerwald Left. His guidelines express skepticism about the prospects for catastrophic crisis within the advanced industrial states, downplay the potential for radical transformations to occur in the underdeveloped world, and make the future importantly dependent upon the ability of communist regimes in power to perform more efficiently and present themselves more attractively. The prescription is very different from that offered by Lenin during the First World War, but the spirit of Leninism, combining an inspired vision of the socialist future with a harshly realistic estimation of current possibilities, is not entirely absent.

Nothing is easier than to define these goals, and nothing will be more difficult than to achieve them. Resentment against the bullying domination exerted by the Soviet Union over the international communist movement for so long is strongly felt and makes suspect almost any initiative stemming from Moscow. The bitterness engendered by the forced Sovietization of Central and Eastern Europe during the Cold War has left deep traces and, tied up as it is with the Soviet security dilemma, represents a major barrier to reform. Sino-Soviet rivalry has many dimensions, and though an eventual normalization of relations is likely, a legacy of mistrust is certain to remain. The weight of conservative and neo-Stalinist opinion within ruling circles in the communist world is substantial and will not be overcome without strenuous efforts. Still, the Gorbachevians seem to have taken the bull by the horns. By acknowledging their movement's insufficiencies they have at least opened the door to an attempt at redressment.

The legacy of the Zimmerwald Left, from which a part of the movement's legitimacy continues to derive, will have its role to play in any attempted revival. Lenin's insistence upon the need for a centralized, revolutionary International is obviously outdated. His strictures concerning the problems of war and peace have in important ways been invalidated by the new strategic realities of the nuclear age. His formula for the dictatorship of the proletariat has been abused in practice to the point where it is completely irredeemable. It remains the case nonetheless that an international communist movement without some foundation in the premises of Leninism, as the Eurocommunists may discover to their chagrin, becomes too insubstantial to perpetuate itself. What has survived and proved most worthy in the Leninist tradition are precisely its less tangible dimensions, the priority accorded to the "utopian" ideals of visionary internationalism and of socialism itself as ethical norms, sources of motivation, and standards for political conduct. These are perhaps the only values that can rescue the communist movement from the exaggerated cynicism, the record of repression, and the concessions to national egotism that threaten to destroy it.

It is certain that the coming years will see an intensified dialogue between the communist and the social democratic left. It is quite unlikely that the dialogue will proceed as far as the PCI has tried to take it. Communism and social democracy continue to represent significantly different historical experiences and to rest upon contrasting premises. Nor is it only matters of principle that are at stake; communist and social democratic organizations are also competing bureaucracies with their own vested self-interests. To date efforts by communist parties to draw closer to their social democratic rivals have led to very mixed results, sufficient to encourage caution. The crisis of international communism is quite real, but the movement retains certain sources of strength. These include the relative stability of the leading communist regimes, the absence of firmly based rivals on the left, the chronic instability of the capitalist world system, and the failure of social democracy to generate its own convincing reformist alternative. On the eve of the twenty-first century, the specter of communism continues to haunt world politics. No combination of forces is likely to make it disappear.

Notes

Preface

1   Recent Western studies include Agnes Blänsdorf, *Die Zweite Internationale und der Krieg: Die Diskussion über die internationale Zusammenarbeit der sozialistischen Parteien 1914–17* (Stuttgart, 1979); Martin Grass, *Friedensaktivität und Neutralität: Die skandinavische Sozialdemokratie und die neutrale Zusammenarbeit im Krieg, August 1914 bis Februar 1917* (Bonn/Bad Godesburg, 1975); and David Kirby, *War, Peace and Revolution: International Socialism at the Crossroads 1914–1918* (New York, 1986).

An interesting Soviet historiographical perspective is provided in a review of literature concerning the Zimmerwald movement by N. I. Kondarantsev and G. G. Kuranov, "Novye materialy o tsimmerval'dskom dvizhenii," *Novaia i noveishaia istoriia* 4 (1969): 128–40. Kondarantsev and Kuranov criticize the collection of documents selected from the Grimm Archive by Horst Lademacher (*Die Zimmerwalder Bewegung: Protokolle und Korrespondenz*, 2 vols. [The Hague, 1967]) for intentionally suppressing material relevant to the Zimmerwald Left—an unfounded accusation but revealing of a set of priorities.

1   Marxism, War, and the International

1   *Protokoll des Internationalen Arbeiter-Kongresses zu Paris, 1889* (Nürnberg, 1890), p. 2.
2   K. Kautsky, "Der Stuttgarter Kongress," *Die Neue Zeit*, vol. 2, 1906–1907, pp. 724, 730.
3   Romain Rolland, *Journal des années de guerre, 1914–1919* (Paris, 1952), pp. 32–33.
4   Leonard Hamilton, ed., *Gerrard Winstanley: Selections from His Works* (London, 1944), pp. 117–18.
5   Ibid., pp. 170–71.
6   Phillipe Buonarroti, *Conspiration pour l'égalité dite de Babeuf*, vol. 1 (Brussels, 1828), pp. 238, 247–49.
7   Karl Marx and Friedrich Engels, *Werke*, vol. 4 (Berlin, 1959), p. 479.
8   Ibid., p. 473.

9   Ibid., vol. 23, p. 779.
10 Saul K. Padover, ed., *The Karl Marx Library* (New York, 1973), vol. 3, *On the First International*, pp. 11–12.
11 Marx and Engels, *Werke*, vol. 17, p. 539.
12 Ibid., vol. 4, p. 466.
13 Ibid., p. 472.
14 Padover, *On the First International*, p. 261.
15 Ibid.
16 Marx and Engels, *Werke*, vol. 19, p. 228. Compare with the famous passage from Engels' *Anti-Dühring* (ibid., vol. 20, p. 262):

> The first act, by means of which the state steps forward as a true representative of the entire society—the expropriation of the means of production in the name of society—is also its last independent act as a state. State interference in social relations, in one area after another, will become superfluous and gradually disappear. The government of persons is replaced by the administration of things and the management of the productive process. The state will not be "abolished," *it withers away.*

17 See Pekka Suvanto, *Marx und Engels zum Problem des gewaltsamen Konflikts* (Helsinki, 1985).
18 Marx and Engels, *Werke*, vol. 17, pp. 538–49, and Padover, *On the First International*, pp. 30–31. Some social democrats sought to avoid the term "militia," which was considered to reflect the priorities of the reform-oriented International League for Peace and Freedom, created in Geneva in 1867. The terms "people's army" or "armed people" were usually preferred. Walter Wittwer, *Streit um Schicksalsfragen: Die deutsche Sozialdemokratie zu Krieg und Vaterlandsverteidigung, 1907–1914* (Berlin, 1964), pp. 13–15.
19 Marx and Engels, *Werke*, vol. 17, pp. 613–25.
20 Ibid., p. 5.
21 *Protokoll des Internationalen Arbeiter-Kongresses zu Paris, 1889*, p. 120.
22 Jean Longuet, *Le mouvement socialiste international: Encyclopédie socialiste, syndicale et coopérative de l'Internationale ouvrière*, vol. 5 (Paris, 1913), p. 72.
23 Peter Gay, *The Dilemma of Democratic Socialism: Eduard Bernstein's Challenge to Marx* (New York, 1952), and Thomas Meyer, *Bernsteins konstruktives Sozialismus: Eduard Bernsteins Beitrag zur Theorie des Sozialismus* (Berlin, 1977) offer occasionally contrasting interpretations of Bernstein's theoretical contributions. *The Prerequisites for Socialism and the Tasks of Social Democracy* has been translated as Eduard Bernstein, *Evolutionary Socialism* (New York, 1963).
24 The right/center/left distinctions are useful as categories so long as they are understood to characterize political tendencies not rigidly demarcated and organized factions. For descriptions see Merle Fainsod, *International Socialism and the World War* (Cambridge, Mass., 1935), pp. 19–31; Karl-Heinz Klär, *Der Zusammenbruch der zweiten Internationale* (Frankfurt am Main, 1981), pp. 49–60; and chapters 2–4 of Leszek Kolakowski, *Main Currents of Marxism: Its Rise, Growth, and Dissolution*, vol. 2 (Oxford, 1978), pp. 31–114.
25 Dmitur Blagoev, "Oportunizm ili Sotsializm," in *Izbrani proizvedeniia*, vol. 2 (Sofia, 1951), pp. 39–62, describes the schism from the perspective of the Narrows. See also Dmitur Blagoev, "Die sozialistische Arbeiterbewegung in Bulgarian," *Die Neue Zeit*, vol. 1, 1909–1910, pp. 563–71, and William Vettes, "The 1903 Schism of the Bulgarian Social Democracy and the Second International," *The American Slavic and East European Review*, December 1960, pp. 521–30.

26 Jerry Holzer, "Devant la guerre et déchiré. Le mouvement ouvrier polonais," *Le mouvement social* 49 (October–December 1964): 107–18. The PPS-L's first program is given in Georg W. Strobel, *Quellen zur Geschichte des Kommunismus in Polen 1878–1918: Programme und Statuten* (Cologne, 1968), pp. 253–58.

27 Described by Henrietta Roland-Holst, "Parteiverhältnisse und Parteikämpfe in Holland," *Die Neue Zeit*, vol. 2, 1909–1910, pp. 796–806, and "Die Spaltung in der holländischen Sozialdemokratie," ibid., pp. 964–71.

28 Gaetano Arfé, *Storia del socialismo italiano (1892–1926)* (Turin, 1965), pp. 136–62.

29 Quoted in Wilhelm Schröder, ed., *Handbuch der Sozialdemokratischen Parteitage* (Munich, 1910), p. 522.

30 Rosa Luxemburg, *Gesammelte Werke* (hereinafter cited as GW), vol. 1 (Berlin, 1982), pp. 367–466.

31 Karl Kautsky, "Zwischen Baden und Luxemburg," *Die Neue Zeit*, vol. 2, 1909–1910, pp. 724–30.

32 The severity of Lenin's wartime polemics against him have left Kautsky an oft-maligned figure. For balanced reinterpretations of his political strategy prior to and during the war, see Massimo Salvadori, *Kautsky e la rivoluzione socialista, 1880–1938* (Milan, 1976), pp. 167–208, and Gary P. Steenson, *Karl Kautsky, 1854–1938: Marxism in the Classical Years* (Pittsburgh, 1978), pp. 181–228.

33 For investigations of the love/hate relationship between center and left in the prewar SPD, see Detlef Lehnert, *Reform und Revolution in den Strategiediskussion der klassischen Sozialdemokratie: Zur Geschichte der deutschen Arbeiterbewegung von den Ursprüngen bis zum Ausbruch des 1. Weltkrieges* (Bonn/Bad Godesburg, 1977); Gary P. Steenson, *"Not One Man! Not One Penny!" German Social Democracy, 1863–1914* (Pittsburgh, 1981); and Carl Schorske, *German Social Democracy, 1905–1917: The Development of the Great Schism* (Cambridge, Mass., 1955).

34 The best discussion of the problem, particularly as concerns the French movement, remains Milorad M. Drachkovitch, *Les socialistes français et allemands et le problème de la guerre, 1870–1914* (Geneva, 1953). See also Wolfram Wette, *Kriegstheorien deutscher Sozialisten—Marx, Engels, Lassalle, Bernstein, Luxemburg. Ein Beitrag zur Friedensforschung* (Stuttgart, 1971).

35 Cited in Jules Humbert-Droz, *L'origine de l'Internationale communiste: De Zimmerwald à Moscou* (Neuchâtel, 1968), p. 29.

36 *Rapport du Congrès international ouvrier tenu à Bruxelles* (Brussels, 1893), pp. 65–72, and *Protokoll des internationalen Arbeiterkongresses in der Tonhalle Zürich* (Zürich, 1894), pp. 20–28.

37 *Compte-rendu analytique du VIIe Congrès international, tenu à Stuttgart du 16 au 24 août 1907* (Brussels, 1908).

38 Ibid., pp. 421–424, and Olga Hess Gankin and H. H. Fisher, eds., *The Bolsheviks and the World War: The Origins of the Third International* (Stanford, 1940), pp. 57–59.

39 *Compte-rendu analytique du VIIIe Congrès socialiste international, tenu à Copenhague, du 28 août au 3 septembre 1910* (Gent, 1911), pp. 471–75. The Copenhagen congress also officially designated Eugène Pottiers' "The Internationale" as the movement's anthem.

40 *Compte-rendu analytique du Congrès socialiste international extraordinaire tenu à Bâle* (Brussels, 1912).

41 See the discussion in Markku Hyrkkänen, *Sozialistische Kolonialpolitik: Eduard*

Bernsteins Stellung zur Kolonialpolitik und zum Imperialismus 1882–1914: Ein Beitrag zur Geschichte des Revisionismus (Helsinki, 1986).

42 Karl Kautsky, *Patriotismus und Sozialdemokratie* (Leipzig, 1907), pp. 3, 23–24.

43 Karl Kautsky, "Der erste Mai und der Kampf gegen den Militarismus," *Die Neue Zeit*, vol. 2, 1911–1912, pp. 170–74.

44 Cited in Eduard David, *Die Sozialdemokratie im Weltkrieg* (Berlin, 1919), pp. 32–33. At the SPD's 1907 Essen congress Bebel also remarked that in the event of war he himself, "old lad" that he was, would consent to shoulder a rifle. According to Karl Retzlaw, *Spartakus: Aufstieg und Niedergang: Erinnerungen eines Parteiarbeiters* (Frankfurt am Main, 1972), p. 29, the remark was constantly cited by German workers during the war and did "inestimable damage" by providing an "alibi" for defensism.

45 See the discussion in Jean Jaurès, *L'armée nouvelle* (Paris, 1915), pp. 435–64, and Gian Mario Bravo, "Patria e internazionalismo in Jean Jaurès," *Critica Marxista* 4 (1986): 77–90.

46 Luxemburg, GW, vol. 5, pp. 391–92.

47 Ibid., vol. 2, pp. 525–29, and vol. 3, p. 25.

48 V. I. Lenin, *Polnoe sobranie sochinenii* (hereinafter cited as PSS), vol. 17 (Moscow, 1961), pp. 186–96.

49 Karl Radek, "Der deutsche Imperialismus und die Arbeiterklasse," in *In der Reihen der deutschen Revolution, 1909–1919* (Munich, 1921), p. 153. See also Karl Radek, "Zu unserem Kampfe gegen den Imperialismus," *Die Neue Zeit*, vol. 2, 1911–1912, pp. 194–99, and "Wege und Mittle im Kampfe gegen den Imperialismus," *Bremer Bürgerzeitung*, 14 September 1912.

50 The most detailed accounts of Lenin's activities within the prewar International remain those produced by Soviet historians during the 1920s. See D. Baevskii, "Bol'sheviki v bor'be za III Internatsional," *Istorik marksist* 2 (1929): 12–48, and S. Bantke, "V. I. Lenin i Bol'shevizm na mezhdunarodnoi arene v dovoennyi period," *Proletarskaia revoliutsiia* 2/3 (85/86) (1929): 3–57. For a somewhat different perspective placing more weight upon the war as a catalyst for Lenin's views, see K. Pol, "Bol'sheviki i dovoennyi II Internatsional," *Proletarskaia revoliutsiia* 2/3 (109/110) (1931).

51 Participants included Guesde and Charles Rappoport of France, Louis de Brouckere of Belgium, A. Braun of Austria, Lenin, Plekhanov, Zinoviev, and David Riazanov of Russia, Pablo Iglesias of Spain, and Julian Marchlewski of Poland. See G. Zinov'ev, "Komintern i Tov. Lenin," *Pravda*, 6 March 1924; Bantke, "V. I. Lenin i Bol'shevizm na mezhdunarodnoi arene," p. 34; and *Lenin v bor'be za revoliutsionnyi Internatsional* (Moscow, 1970), p. 179. Lenin's notes for the pamphlet "The European War and European Socialism," prepared during the first months of the war (Lenin, PSS, vol. 26, pp. 8–11), included references to the meeting. *Leninskii sbornik*, vol. 14 (Moscow, 1930), pp. 19, 22.

52 Luxemburg, GW, vol. 1/2, pp. 422–46. In his tract *The Way to Power*, much admired by Lenin, Kautsky also explicitly rejected a "revolution-making" role for the party. Karl Kautsky, *Der Weg zur Macht* (Berlin, 1909), p. 44.

53 Georges Haupt, ed., *Correspondance entre Lénine et Camille Huysmans, 1905–1914* (Paris, 1963), pp. 136–40.

54 Angelica Balabanoff, *Erinnerungen und Erlebnisse* (Berlin, 1927), p. 55. Humbert-Droz, *L'origine de l'Internationale communiste*, pp. 43–44, contains the text of the statements released at Brussels, which are remarkable for their irresolution.

55 The complete text of Haase's speech is given in Susanne Miller, *Burgfrieden und*

Klassenkampf: Die deutsche Sozialdemokratie im Ersten Weltkrieg (Düsseldorf, 1974), pp. 62–63.
56 Konrad Hänisch, *Die deutsche Sozialdemokratie in und nach dem Weltkriege* (Berlin, 1919), pp. 110–11.
57 Wilhelm Kolb, *Die Sozialdemokratie am Scheidewege: Ein Beitrag zum Thema, Neuorientierung der deutschen Politik* (Karlsruhe, 1915), pp. 26, 51.
58 Phillip Scheidemann, *Der Zusammenbruch* (Berlin, 1921), p. 2.
59 David Kirby, *War, Peace and Revolution: International Socialism at the Crossroads 1914–1918* (New York, 1986), p. 31.
60 Cited in Karl Grunberg, ed., *Internatsional i mirovaia voina* (Petrograd, 1919), p. 212.
61 Humbert-Droz, *L'origine de l'Internationale communiste*, p. 52.
62 Zino Zini, *La tragedia del proletariato in Italia: Diario, 1914–1926* (Milan, 1973), pp. 72–73.

2 Against the Current

1 Grunberg, *Internatsional i mirovaia voina*, p. 314. Aleksandr Shliapnikov, observing events from the Bolshevik underground in Saint Petersburg, had the same impression. See Alexander Shlyapnikov, *On the Eve of 1917* (London, 1982), pp. 16–17. Aleksandr Kerenskii later claimed that the Menshevik Duma fraction refused to support war credits on 8 August (26 July) because it believed that the SPD had opposed them. Alexander Kerensky, *Crucifixion of Liberty* (New York, 1934), p. 237.
2 *Pis'ma P. B. Aksel'roda i Iu. O. Martova, 1901–1916* (The Hague, 1967), p. 299.
3 Discussed in Agnes Blänsdorf, *Die Zweite Internationale und der Krieg: Die Diskussion über die internationale Zusammenarbeit der sozialistischen Parteien 1914–1917* (Stuttgart, 1979), pp. 90–109, and Georges Haupt, *Le Congrès manqué: L'Internationale à la veille de la première guerre mondiale* (Paris, 1965).
4 Cited in Pierre Miquel, *La grande guerre* (Paris, 1983), p. 139.
5 W. Lenin and G. Sinowjew, *Gegen den Ström: Aufsätze aus den Jahren 1914–1916* (Hamburg, 1921).
6 Described in Shlyapnikov, *On the Eve*, pp. 9–30. See also "Vo vremia imperialisticheskoi voiny," *Krasnaia letopis'* 1 (10) (1924): 86; D. Baevskii, "Partiia v gody imperialisticheskoi voiny," in M. N. Pokrovskii, ed., *Ocherki po istorii Oktiabrskoi revoliutsii*, vol. 1 (Moscow, 1927), pp. 350–51; and Horst Lademacher, ed., *Die Zimmerwalder Bewegung: Protokolle und Korrespondenz*, vol. 2 (hereinafter cited as Lademacher 2) (The Hague, 1967), pp. 258–64. Antiwar slogans including "war on war" became a part of Bolshevik agitation already during the July strikes. *Listovki peterburgskikh bol'shevikov, 1902–1917*, vol. 2 (Moscow, 1939), p. 114.
7 S. V. Tiutiukin, *Voina, mir, revoliutsiia: Ideinaia bor'ba v rabochem dvizhenii Rossii 1914–1917 gg.* (Moscow, 1972), pp. 25–26, counts seventy antiwar leaflets issued during the first four months of war. The Stockholm Arbetarrörelsens Arkiv (hereinafter cited as AAA), section *Sovjetunionen*, holds a small collection of such leaflets, one of which, dated November 1914 and issued by the RSDRP "N-Group," is entitled "Down with the War" and makes a strong internationalist appeal. See also A. Badaev, *Bol'sheviki v gosudarstvennoi dume: Bol'shevistskaia fraktsiia v IV gosudarstvennoi dume i revoliutsionnoe dvizhenie v Peterburge* (Moscow, 1939), pp. 345–47; Grunberg, *Internatsional i mirovaia voina*, pp. 254–58; and Baevskii, "Partiia v gody imperialisticheskoi voiny," p. 345.

8 The votes for defensism were justified in the name of the "defense of the French revolution." See Alfred Rosmer, *Le mouvement ouvrier pendant la guerre: De l'union sacrée à Zimmerwald* (hereinafter cited as Rosmer 1) (Paris, 1936), pp. 466–69; Bertram Wolfe, "War Comes to Russia in Exile," *The Russian Review* 20 (October 1961): 297; Alfred Erich Senn, *The Russian Revolution in Switzerland, 1914–1917* (Madison, 1971), pp. 17–18; I. P. Khoniavko, "V podpol'e i v emigratsii (1911–1917 gg.)," *Proletarskaia revoliutsiia* 4(16) (1923): 168; and for a memoir G. Belen'kii, "Parizhskaia sektsiia i voina 1914 g.," *Pravda*, 13 August 1924.

9 Ia. Ganetskii, "Arest V. I. Lenina v Avstrii v 1914 g.," *Leninskii sbornik*, vol. 2, pp. 171–87, and "Wie Victor Adler Lenin rettete," *Arbeiter-Zeitung*, 21 January 1949.

10 Lenin, PSS, vol. 49, p. 7. During their sojourn in Bern, Lenin and Krupskaia resided at four separate addresses in the city's Länggasse quarter, an indication that they never intended to establish a permanent residence.

11 In a postwar memoir Radek described his conversion to Bolshevism during the war as a process stimulated by "daily intercourse with Lenin" in Bern. Karl Radek, "Avtobiografiia," *Entsiklopedicheskii slovar'*, 7th ed., vol. 41, part 2 (Moscow: Russkii bibliograficheskii Institut Granat, 1928), p. 157. This account was written at a time when deference to Lenin's "genius" was mandatory and is unquestionably exaggerated. For a more analytical account of Radek's motives, see Warren Lerner, *Karl Radek: The Last Internationalist* (Stanford, 1970), pp. 38–39.

12 Lenin, PSS, vol. 25, pp. 450–51.

13 Ibid., vol. 26, pp. 1–7. Present at the meeting were Inessa Armand, Krupskaia, Fedor Samoilov, Vladimir Kasparov, Grigorii Shklovskii, Georgii Safarov, Kornblium (apparently the pseudonym of a collaborator at Shklovskii's chemical laboratory in Bern), and others. Accounts are provided in F. N. Samoilov, *Po sledam minuvshego* (Moscow, 1934), p. 357; M. L. Goberman, "V. I. Lenin i Bernskaia sektsiia bol'shevikov," in *Partiia bol'shevikov v gody mirovoi imperialisticheskoi voiny: Dokumenty i materialy* (Moscow, 1963), pp. 298–304; Willi Gautschi, *Lenin als Emigrant in der Schweiz* (Zürich, 1973), pp. 103–4; and V. A. Lavrin, *Bol'shevistskaia partiia v nachale pervoi mirovoi imperialisticheskoi voiny (1914–1915 gg.)* (Moscow, 1972), pp. 23–24.

14 *Lenin v bor'be za revoliutsionnyi internatsional* (Moscow, 1970), pp. 178–80.

15 Copies of the Theses on the War were carried to Petrograd by Samoilov. See Samoilov, *Po sledam minuvshego*, p. 263; Badaev, *Bol'sheviki v gosudarstvennoi dume*, pp. 363–65; and V. A. Karpinskii, "Vladimir Il'ich Lenin za granitsei v 1914–1917 gg.," in *Zapiski Instituta Lenina*, vol. 2 (Moscow, 1927), pp. 83–84. The text of "The War and Russian Social Democracy" is in Lenin, PSS, vol. 26, pp. 13–23.

16 Soviet historians have had some difficulty attempting to justify the harsh slogan. Note the elaborate rationalization in Tiutiukin, *Voina, mir, revoliutsiia*, pp. 127–56. For evidence of dissent see Baevskii, "Partiia v gody voiny," pp. 378–79; M. Filiia, "Iz davnikh vstrech," *Pravda*, 25 August 1927; *Leninskii sbornik*, vol. 11, pp. 255–57; A. Shliapnikov, "Sotsial-demokratiia i voina 1914–1917," *Proletarskaia revoliutsiia* 3(15) (1923): 181; and M. Syromiatnikova, "Bernskaia konferentsiia zagranichnykh organizatsii R.S.D.R.P. v 1915 g.," in "Bernskaia konferentsiia 1915 g.," *Proletarskaia revoliutsiia* 5(40) (1925): 151. Lavrin, *Bol'shevistskaia partiia*, p. 51, attempts to downplay the extent of resistance to Lenin's line.

17 G. V. Plekhanov, *Voprosy voiny i sotsializma* (Petrograd, 1917), p. 26, and *Mysl'*, 13 January 1915.

18 [Iurii] Martov, "Mir," *Golos*, 3 October 1914; Iu. Martov, "Mifologiia poslednei

voiny," *Golos*, 8 October 1914; and Iu. Martov, "Protiv metafiziki i idealizma," *Nashe Slovo*, 21–24 August 1915.

19 Neil Harding, *Lenin's Political Thought*, vol. 2 (London, 1981), p. 17.

20 Lenin, PSS, vol. 49, p. 324.

21 Ibid., pp. 15, 24–26.

22 The assertion that Lenin took perverse pleasure in viewing the carnage of the war is commonly made but of questionable accuracy. Certainly the Bolshevik leader was aware of the revolutionary possibilities inherent in the war, but to speak of "sardonic satisfaction" as does Albert S. Lindemann, *The "Red Years": European Socialism versus Bolshevism* (Berkeley, 1974), pp. 18–19, seems unwarranted. Lenin made the necessary distinction in an interview with a Polish journalist in April 1914: "No, I don't want war. . . . I don't desire for millions of proletarians to be forced to destroy one another to pay for the insanity of capitalism. To objectively foresee war, to attempt in the event of such a misfortune to make use of it in the best manner possible—this is one thing. To want war and to work for it—this is something completely different." Cited in *Vladimir Il'ich Lenin: Biografiia* 2d ed. (Moscow, 1963), p. 213.

23 Baevskii, "Partiia v gody imperialisticheskoi voiny," pp. 383–84, and "Vo vremia imperialisticheskoi voiny," p. 88. For the texts see "Vo vremia imperialisticheskoi voiny," pp. 102–8; Badaev, *Bol'sheviki v gosudarstvennoi dume*, pp. 353–71; *Listovki peterburgskikh bol'shevikov*, pp. 119–21; and *Sbornik dokumentov mestnykh bol'shevistikh organizatsii: Bol'sheviki v gody imperialisticheskoi voiny, 1914–Fevral' 1917* (Moscow, 1939), pp. 1–13. The text of Vandervelde's letter is given in Emile Vandervelde, *Souvenirs d'un militant socialiste* (Paris, 1939), pp. 185–86.

24 Tiutiukin, *Voina, mir, revoliutsiia*, p. 42, and *Listovki peterburgskikh bol'shevikov*, p. 126.

25 Lavrin, *Bol'shevistskaia partiia*, pp. 56–57, 97–101. Badaev, *Bol'sheviki v gosudarstvennoi dume*, pp. 373–412, provides an insider's account of the trial. On the witness stand Kamenev claimed that his personal opinion did not correspond to the Bolshevik party line. His comportment earned harsh criticism from Lenin. Lenin, PSS, vol. 49, p. 68.

26 Four numbers of *Proletarskii Golos* were issued during the war. They are reprinted in their entirety in "Vo vremia imperialisticheskoi voiny," pp. 133–66. See also Lenin, PSS, vol. 49, p. 117, and G. Zinov'ev, "Kak Vandervel'de s kniazem kudashevym 'obratyvali' obshchestvennoe mnenia russkikh sotsialistov," in G. Zinov'ev, *Sochineniia*, vol. 5 (Moscow, 1924), pp. 87–97.

27 Lenin urged Shliapnikov not to attend the Copenhagen conference, which he labeled "an intrigue . . . of the German general staff." *Leninskii sbornik*, vol. 2, p. 215. For the text of Shliapnikov's statement, see Shlyapnikov, *On the Eve*, pp. 42–44. Litvinov's prepared statement is given in "Bernskaia konferentsiia," p. 148, and an account of his stormy appearance can be found in Rosmer 1, p. 402.

28 Oliver Radkey, *The Agrarian Foes of Bolshevism* (New York, 1958), pp. 91–93.

29 L. M. Shalaginova, "Esery-internatsionalisty v gody pervoi mirovoi voiny," in *Pervaia mirovaia voina* (Moscow, 1968), pp. 324–28, and Tiutiukin, *Voina, mir, revoliutsiia*, pp. 66–76.

30 His position is summarized in G. V. Plekhanov, *O voine: Otvet tovarishchu Z. P.* (Paris, 1914).

31 See A. N. Potresov, *"Internatsionalizm" i kozmopolitanizm* (Petrograd, 1916), and V. B. Stankevich, *Vospominaniia, 1914–1919* (Berlin, 1920), pp. 19–20.

32 P. B. Axelrod, "Russland und der Krieg," *Berner Tagwacht*, 26–27 October 1914;

"P. B. Aksel'rod ob Internatsional i voina," *Golos*, 22–23 December 1914; and P. B. Axelrod, *Die Krise und die Aufgaben der internationale Sozialdemokratie* (Zürich, 1915).

33 *Golos'* first number appeared on 1 September 1914. It was banned by the French government on 16 January 1915 but immediately revived under the new title *Nashe Slovo*. Alfred Erich Senn, "The Politics of *Golos* and *Nashe Slovo*," *International Review of Social History* 17(1972): 675–704, and Isaac Deutscher, *The Prophet Armed: Trotsky, 1879–1921* (Oxford, 1954), pp. 215–24.

34 Lenin, PSS, vol. 49, pp. 60–63; *Nashe Slovo*, 6 March 1915; and Abraham Ascher, *Pavel Axelrod and the Development of Menshevism* (Cambridge, Mass., 1972), pp. 312–14.

35 The declaration was published in full in the *Berner Tagwacht*, 27 February 1915, and in abbreviated form in *Nashe Slovo*, 27 February 1915. See also *Leninskii sbornik*, vol. 17, pp. 199–200.

36 *Pis'ma Aksel'roda i Martova*, pp. 303, 305, 307.

37 Horst Lademacher, ed., *Die Zimmerwalder Bewegung: Protokolle und Korrespondenz*, vol. 1 (hereinafter cited as Lademacher 1) (The Hague, 1967), pp. 13–19, 73.

38 Lenin, PSS, vol. 26, p. 31, and vol. 49, p. 20.

39 *International Instituut voor Sociale Geschiedenis* (hereinafter cited as IISG), Collection Axelrod, A.40.

40 Lenin, PSS, vol. 49, p. 64.

41 *Sotsial-Demokrat* was published in Geneva in a tirage of 1500. Altogether twenty-six numbers were issued at irregular intervals during the war. V. Volosevich, *Bol'shevizm v gody mirovoi voiny* (Leningrad, n.d.), p. 122.

42 Lenin's motives are outlined by Krupskaia in a letter to Ol'ga Ravich dated 10 January 1915. *Leninskii sbornik*, vol. 2, pp. 134–37.

43 Participants included Shklovskii (Bern section); Ravich (Geneva section); M. I. Movshovich and Ilin [a pseudonym] (Lausanne section); M. M. Kharitonov (Zürich section); Grigorii Belen'kii (Paris section); Nikolai Bukharin, Nikolai Krylenko, Elena Rozmirovich, and Aleksandr Troianovskii (Baugy-en-Clarens section); and Lenin, Zinoviev, Krupskaia, Zlata Lilina, Vladimir Kasparov, and Kornblium representing the Central Committee, the staff of *Sotsial-Demokrat*, and the party's women's bureau. Georgii Piatakov and Evgeniia Bosh arrived late (after an escape from Siberian exile and an around-the-world journey) and cooperated with the Baugy-en-Clarens group. See Alfred Erich Senn, "The Bolshevik Conference in Bern, 1915," *The Slavic Review* 25(1966): 676–78; "Bernskaia konferentsiia," pp. 134–93; and Gankin and Fisher, pp. 173–91. A particularly detailed account is provided by A. P. Iakushina, *Zagranichnye organizatsii RSDRP (1905–1917 gg.)* (Moscow, 1967), pp. 81–131.

44 "Bernskaia konferentsiia," pp. 159–60.

45 The Montpellier and Toulouse sections were not represented at Bern, but they forwarded the texts of their project resolutions. Ibid., pp. 167–74.

46 Bukharin supported the slogan and attempted to link it to the theme of civil war, envisioning a unity built upon proletarian solidarity expressed "from below." On his interventions see Stephen F. Cohen, *Bukharin and the Bolshevik Revolution: A Political Biography, 1888–1938* (New York, 1973), pp. 31–34, and D. Baevskii, "Bor'ba Lenina protiv Bukharinskikh 'shatanii mysli'," *Proletarskaia revoliutsiia* 1(96) (1930): 44.

47 Armand's remark is cited in "Bernskaia konferentsiia," p. 165.

48 Gautschi, *Lenin*, p. 119.

49 J. P. Nettl, *Rosa Luxemburg*, vol. 1 (Oxford, 1966), p. 40.

50 Lenin, PSS, vol. 49, p. 13.

51 Grunberg, *Internatsional i mirovaia voina*, pp. 254–58, gives the text of their statement. See also Ivan Avakumovic, *History of the Communist Party of Yugoslavia*, vol. 1 (Aberdeen, 1964), pp. 13–16; M. A. Birman, "V. I. Lenin i bor'ba revoliutsionnykh sotsial-demokratov balkanskikh stran protiv imperialisticheskoi voiny v 1914–1915 gg.," *Sovetskoe slavianovedenie* 2(1965): 8–9; and T. Katzlerowitsch, "Bericht aus Serbien," *Internationale Sozialistische Kommission zu Bern: Bulletin* (hereinafter cited as ISK Bulletin), no. 4, 22 April 1916, pp. 12–14.

52 Augustin Deak, "Le parti social-démocrate de Roumanie durant les premières deux années de la première guerre mondiale," in N. Todorov and E. Safarov, eds., *Actes du premier Congrès international des études balkaniques et sud-est européenes*, vol. 4 (Sofia, 1969), pp. 613–20.

53 George B. Leon, *The Greek Socialist Movement and the First World War: The Road to Unity* (New York, 1976), pp. 19–33.

54 Blagoev, *Izbrani proizvedeniia*, vol. 2, pp. 656–97.

55 The resolutions of the congress are given in *Bulgarskata Kommunisticheska Partiia v rezoliutsii i resheniia na kongresite, konferentsite, i plenumite TsK, 1891–1918*, vol. 1 (Sofia, 1957), pp. 321–22. See also Khristo Kabakchiev and R. K. Karakolov, "Bolgaria v pervoi mirovoi imperialisticheskoi voiny," *Istorik marksist* 89(1941): 58–72; L. Panaiotov, *Barbata na BRSDP (t.s.) protiv zavoevatelnata i avantiuristichna politika na bulgarskata burzhuaziia v period na voinite (1912–1918)* (Sofia, 1956), p. 57; and accounts by party secretary G. Kyrkov in Lademacher 2, pp. 24–27 and "Die bulgarische Sozialdemokratie und der Krieg," *Berner Tagwacht*, 18 March 1915.

56 Vasil Kolarov, *Izbrani proizvedeniia* (Sofia, 1954), p. 257. Delegates to the Balkan conference included Blagoev, Kyrkov, Kolarov, and Georgii Dmitrov for the Narrows; Sideris for the Saloniki Federation; and Rakovski of Romania. See Rakovski's description in Lademacher 2, p. 86. A Serbian delegation was unable to attend but telegrammed support. The text of their message is given in *Srpski socijalistički pokret za vreme prvog svetskograta* (Belgrad, 1958), pp. 365–66. See also M. A. Birman, "Bor'ba levykh sotsial-demokratov balkanskikh stran protiv imperialisticheskoi voiny v 1914–1915 gg. i obrazovanie balkanskikh rabochei sotsial-demokraticheskoi federatsii (iiul' 1915 g.)," in *Actes*, pp. 608–9.

57 Yves Collart, *Le parti suisse et l'Internationale 1914–1915: De l'union nationale à Zimmerwald* (Geneva, 1969), pp. 202–3, and A. Manfred, "Tsimmerval'dskoe dvizhenie v shveitsarskoi sotsial-demokratii," *Proletarskaia revoliutsiia* 7(90) (1929): 15–20.

58 David A. Shannon, *The Socialist Party of America: A History* (New York, 1955), pp. 82–90, and Alexander Trachtenberg, ed., *The American Socialists and the War: A Documentary History of the Attitude of the Socialist Party toward War and Militarism since the Outbreak of the Great War* (New York, 1917).

59 Gerald Meaker, *The Revolutionary Left in Spain, 1914–1923* (Stanford, 1974), pp. 23–28, downplays the weight of the Spanish left. "Few of the minoritarians," he writes, "accepted, or perhaps even knew of, "Lenin's 'Left-Zimmerwald' position" (p. 25). Carlos Forcadell, *Parlamentarismo y bolchevización: El movimiento obrero español, 1914–1918* (Barcelona, 1978), pp. 103–12, provides a strikingly different appraisal with greater emphasis upon the sophistication of the left opposition. See also Klär, *Der Zusammenbruch*, pp. 130–31.

60 Martin Grass, *Friedensaktivität und Neutralität: Die skandinavische Sozial-*

demokratie und die neutrale Zusammenarbeit im Krieg, August 1914 bis Februar 1917 (Bonn/Bad Godesburg, 1975), p. 12.

61 Fainsod, *International Socialism*, p. 74, and Knut Bekstrem, "K voprosu o vozniknovenii kommunisticheskoi partii Shvetsii," *Voprosy istorii KPSS* 6(1959): 94. For Höglund's position see his interventions at the youth league conference in *AAA: Socialdemokratiska Ungdomsförbundet*, File A1-1, and his articles "Socialdemokratin och regeringsmakten," *Stormklockan*, 10 October 1914, and "Regeringssocialismen och militarismen," *Stormklockan*, 14 November 1914.

62 Lenin kept informed concerning Höglund's activities via Shliapnikov and Kollontai. In October 1914 he described him to Shliapnikov as "only a naive, sentimental antimilitarist; we must say to such people, either the slogan civil war, or remain with the opportunists and social chauvinists." Lenin, PSS, vol. 49, p. 22. Lenin met Höglund during the International's 1910 Copenhagen congress.

63 Cited in Ia. G. Temkin, *Lenin i mezhdunarodnaia sotsial-demokratiia 1914–1917* (Moscow, 1968), p. 158. See also A. Gansen, "Nekotorye momenty sovremennogo rabochego dvizheniia v Norvegii," *Sbornik Sotsial-Demokrata* 2(December 1916): 44.

64 A. J. Koejemans, *David Wijnkoop: Een mens in de strijd voor het socialisme* (Amsterdam, 1967), pp. 124–28, and the statement of position "Demobilisatie!" *De Tribune*, 26–27 and 31 December 1914.

65 Herman Gorter, *Het imperialisme, de wereldoorlog en de sociaal-demokratie* (Amsterdam, 1915), pp. 75, 84, 116. See also the excellent summary in Herman de Liagre Böhl, *Herman Gorter: Zijn politieke aktiviteiten van 1909 tot 1920 in de opkomende kommunistische beweging in nederland* (Nijmegen, 1973), pp. 119–29.

66 In the first German edition of *Imperialism, the World War, and Social Democracy*, also published in the spring of 1915, Gorter added a passage emphasizing the weakness of the opposition outside of Germany and reiterating criticisms of the "radicals." Herman Gorter, *Der Imperialismus, der Weltkrieg, und die Sozialdemokratie* (Munich, 1915), pp. 74–89.

67 Lenin, PSS, vol. 49, p. 69. Lenin read the Dutch text with the aid of a dictionary and claimed 40 percent comprehension. Ibid., pp. 74–75.

68 William English Walling, ed., *The Socialists and the War* (New York, 1915), pp. 156–160, and Stephen Richards Graubard, *British Labour and the Russian Revolution, 1917–1924* (Cambridge, Mass., 1956), pp. 12–13.

69 Francis Carsten, *War Against War: British and German Radical Movements in the First World War* (London, 1982), p. 271, and Marvin Swartz, *The Union of Democratic Control in British Politics During the First World War* (Oxford, 1971), pp. 42–48. Many ILP members were active in pacifist circles. See Keith Robbins, *The Abolition of War: The "Peace Movement" in Britain 1914–1919* (Cardiff, 1976), pp. 77–78.

70 The "Internationalists" developed their position in a series of articles published in the BSP central organ *Justice* on 14 September, 1 October, 12 November, and 3 December 1914. See also Walter Kendall, *The Revolutionary Movement in Britain: The Origins of British Communism* (London, 1969), pp. 84–95, and Siegfried Bünger, *Die sozialistische Antikriegsbewegung in Grossbritanien 1914 bis 1917* (Berlin, 1967), p. 26.

71 Cited in Temkin, *Lenin*, p. 125.

72 Described in W. Gallacher, *Revolt on the Clyde* (London, 1936), and John Broom, *John Maclean* (Luanhead, 1973).

73 Maurice Labi, *La grande division des travailleurs: Première scission de la C.G.T.*

(1914–1921) (Paris, 1964), and V. M. Dalin, "Vseobshchaia Konfederatsiia Truda v nachale pervoi imperialisticheskoi voiny," *Franzuskii ezhegodnik 1964* (Moscow, 1964), pp. 227–35.

74   The text of Monatte's letter is given in Rosmer 1, pp. 177–80. On the growth of the opposition see Christian Gras, *Alfred Rosmer (1877–1964) et le mouvement révolutionnaire international* (Paris, 1971), pp. 98–135; Annie Kriegel, *Aux origines du communisme français 1914–1920: Contribution à l'histoire du mouvement ouvrier français*, vol. 1 (Paris, 1964), pp. 77–82; Robert Wohl, *French Communism in the Making 1914–1924* (Stanford, 1966), pp. 58–62; and Heinrich Grossheim, *Sozialisten in der Verantwortung: Die französischen Sozialisten und Gewerkschafter im ersten Weltkrieg 1914–17* (Bonn, 1978), pp. 104–29.

75   Rosmer 1, pp. 250–58, and Jean Maitron and Colette Chambelland, eds., *Syndicalisme révolutionnaire et communisme: Les archives de Pierre Monatte 1914–1924* (Paris, 1968), pp. 92–95.

76   Text in Rosmer 1, pp. 351–54.

77   Ibid., pp. 292–296, 300–305.

78   Maitron and Chambelland, *Syndicalisme révolutionnaire*, p. 139.

79   See the statement of position coauthored by Filippo Turati, Camillo Prampolini, and Benito Mussolini in *Avanti!* 21 September 1914, and Luigi Ambrosoli, *Né aderire né sabotare, 1915–1918* (Milan, 1961), pp. 325–27.

80   Mussolini announced his conversion to interventionism on 18 October in *Avanti!* Ambrosoli, *Né aderire né sabotare*, p. 51, argues that the Mussolini affair reinforced the PSI's antiwar position. See also Angelica Balabanoff, "Die angebliche Spaltung in der italienischen Partei," *Berner Tagwacht*, 21 December 1914.

81   Resolutions condemned the defensist orientation of the SPD majority, heaped praise upon Liebknecht, and criticized the ISB for inactivity. The party's position was reiterated by the directorate on 17–18 June in its first session following Italy's declaration of war. Alberto Malatesta, *I socialisti italiani durante la guerra* (Milan, 1926), pp. 73–75, 228–29; Ambrosoli, *Né aderire né sabotare*, pp. 343–45; and Leo Valiani, "Il partito socialista italiano nel periodo della neutralità, 1914–1915," in *Annali* (Milan, 1962): 260–386.

82   Friedrich Adler's first reactions to the war crisis appear in Friedrich Adler, *Die Erneuerung der Internationale* (Vienna, 1918), pp. 3–7. See also Hans Hautmann, *Die Anfänge der Linksradikalen Bewegung und der Kommunistischen Partei Deutschösterreichs 1916–1919* (Vienna, 1970), pp. 3–5, and F. Adler, "Die Internationale der Tat," *Der Kampf* 4(April 1915): 145–47. Opposition in the non-Germanic regions of the empire is described in Grunberg, *Internatsional i mirovaia voina*, pp. 475–79; Z. Sholle, *Rabochee dvizhenie v cheshskikh zemliakh vo vremia mirovoi imperialisticheskoi voiny 1914–1918 gg.* (Moscow, 1955), pp. 32–33; and D. Nemes, "Die Ungarländische Sozialdemokratische Partei und der erste Weltkrieg," *Acta historica* 20(1974): 23–54.

83   In 1914 five separate social democratic organizations existed in Russian Poland alone, with other organizations active in Austrian and German Poland. In Austrian Poland the Polish Social Democratic party of Galicia and Silesia was closely associated with the Austrian German movement and dominantly reformist. In the German provinces a weak Polish Socialist party emphasized the demand for national autonomy. In Russian Poland the Social Democracy of the Kingdom of Poland and Lithuania (SDKPiL) divided in 1911 into a SDKPiL-Main Presidium based around a leadership in exile (Luxemburg, Leo Jogiches, Julian Marchlewski) and a SDKPiL-Regional Presidium (sometimes referred to as the Warsaw Committee) that favored closer alignment with Bolshevism. Both groups supported the left

radical critique within the Second International. The sDKPiL had originally split away from the Polish Socialist party (PPS) in the 1890s. Subsequently, the PPS in Russian Poland fractured into three parts: the revolutionary PPS-Left (PPS-L), a PPS-Revolutionary Faction led by Józef Pilsudski and archly nationalistic, and a PPS-Opposition. On the eve of the war four Polish parties were represented in the ISB: the sDKPiL-Main Presidium, the PPS-L, the PPS-Revolutionary Faction, and the Polish Social Democratic party of Galicia and Silesia. See Marian K. Dziewanowski, "World War I and the Marxist Movement of Poland," *The American Slavic and East European Review* 12 (1953): 72–92; Holzer, "Devant la guerre," pp. 107–18; and Feliks Tych, "La participation des partis ouvriers polonais au mouvement de Zimmerwald," *Annali* (Milan, 1961): 90–125.

84 Grunberg, *Internatsional i mirovaia voina*, pp. 138–44; Strobel, *Quellen*, p. 304; and G. Kamenskii, *Iz istorii bor'by pol'skogo proletariata (1914–1918)* (Moscow/Leningrad, 1926), p. 27. The editors of *Gazeta Robotnitsa* included Bronislaw Stein, Mieczyslaw Bronski, Henryk Stein, and Radek.

85 Otto Braun, "Tätigkeitsbericht der lettischen Sozialdemokratie," *ISK Bulletin*, no. 3, 29 February 1916, pp. 11–13; the Bund's statement of position "Tsentral'nyi Komitet Bunda o voine," *Informatsionnyi listok' zagranichnoi organizatsii Bunda* 7(January 1915): 1–6, and their manifesto "Ko vsemu tsivilizovannomu miru," in *AAA: Sovjetunionen*, no. 996; and V. Levinskii, "Ukraina i voina," *Sotsial-Demokrat*, 12 February 1915.

86 Zinov'ev, *Sochineniia*, vol. 5, pp. 83–85. Lenin commented similarly in November 1914: "In Germany a *left* is beginning to stir; *if* a split occurs, *then* perhaps the International will be saved from putrification." Lenin, PSS, vol. 49, p. 27.

87 A. Kollontai, "Avtobiograficheskii ocherk," *Proletarskaia revoliutsiia* 3(1921): 291.

88 Victor Adler, *Briefwechsel mit August Bebel und Karl Kautsky* (Vienna, 1954), p. 630.

89 Karl Liebknecht, *Gesammelte Reden und Schriften*, vol. 8 (Berlin, 1958), pp. 25, 63–64, 78–94, 103–10; "Die deutsche Partei und der Krieg," *Berner Tagwacht*, 30 October 1914; and Helmut Trotnow, *Karl Liebknecht: Eine politische Biographie* (Cologne, 1980), pp. 73–95.

90 Jürgen Kuczynski, *Der Ausbruch des ersten Weltkrieges und die deutsche Sozialdemokratie: Chronik und Analyse* (Berlin, 1957), pp. 100–115, and Carsten, *War Against War*, pp. 18–19. The Berlin group included Luxemburg, Mehring, Ernst Meyer, Julian Marchlewski, and Wilhelm Pieck. Konrad Hänisch, no friend of the opposition, attests to its steady growth after October 1914. Hänisch, *Die deutsche Sozialdemokratie*, p. 44.

91 Heinrich Laufenberg and Fritz Wolffheim, *Imperialismus und Demokratie: Ein Wort zum Weltkrieg* (Hamburg, 1914), pp. 1, 33–36, 44–48.

92 Heinrich Ströbel, "Aus dem Parlamenten. Der Riss in der preussischen Landtags-Fraktion," *Die Internationale* 1(1915): 53–61, and Parabellum [Karl Radek], "Zwei Parteien," *Berner Tagwacht*, 5 March 1915.

93 Luxemburg, GW, vol. 4, pp. 20–32.

94 Miller, *Burgfrieden und Klassenkampf*, pp. 106–12.

95 "Das Zentrum der Partei," *Lichtstrahlen* (July 1915): 257–60.

96 Karl Radek, "Kopf hoch! Trotz alledem!" *Berner Tagwacht*, 1 May 1915, and particularly Parabellum [Karl Radek], "Sozialdemokratie oder nationale Arbeiterpartei?" *Berner Tagwacht*, 2 March 1915.

97 Kirby, *War, Peace and Revolution*, p. 64.

3 The Zimmerwald Movement

1   Karl Kautsky, "Die Internationale und der Krieg," *Die Neue Zeit*, vol. 1, 1914–1915, p. 248.
2   A protocol is provided in Lademacher 1, pp. 5–27. See also Lademacher 2, pp. 3–7; Blänsdorf, *Die Zweite Internationale*, pp. 77–90; Humbert-Droz, *L'origine de l'Internationale communiste*, pp. 93–96; and Collart, *Le parti suisse et l'Internationale*, pp. 87–138.
3   Blänsdorf, *Die Zweite Internationale*, pp. 109–33, and Grass, *Friedensaktivität und Neutralität*, pp. 107–38. After several protests from the SPS invitations to the Copenhagen conference were extended to the SPS, the PSI, and the Socialist party of America. The SPS refused to participate in any capacity. The PSI delegated Morgari as an "observer," but in the end he did not arrive in Copenhagen. See Collart, *Le parti suisse et l'Internationale*, p. 166, and *Schweizerisches Sozialarkhiv* (hereinafter cited as SSA); "Protokol der Sitzungen der Geschäftsleitung und des Parteivorstandes," 2 October and 13 November 1914.
4   "Für den Kampf um den Frieden," in Clara Zetkin, *Ausgewählte Reden und Schriften*, vol. 1 (Berlin, 1957), p. 481.
5   The text of Armand's appeal is in "O mezhdunarodnoi zhenskoi sotsialisticheskoi konferentsii v 1915 g.," *Istoricheskii arkhiv* 3(1960): 109. See also Ol'ga Ravich, "Mezhdunarodnaia zhenskaia sotsialisticheskaia konferentsiia 1915 g.," *Proletarskaia revoliutsiia* 10(1925): 165, and "Iz istorii bor'by bol'shevikov za proletarskii internatsionalizm v mezhdunarodnom zhenskom sotsialisticheskom dvizhenii, 1915 g.," *Novaia i noveishaia istoriia* 4(1959): 109.
6   In Zetkin, *Ausgewählte Reden*, vol. 1, pp. 635–38. See also "O mezhdunarodnoi zhenskoi sotsialisticheskoi konferentsii," pp. 110–12.
7   Cited in D. Baevskii, "Bor'ba za III Internatsionala do Tsimmerval'd," *Proletarskaia revoliutsiia* 4(1934): 28.
8   The available protocols make no reference to the last names of delegates. The seven German participants included Zetkin, Bertha Thalheimer, and Käthe Duncker. Krupskaia, Armand, Lilina, Ol'ga Ravich, and Elena Rozmirovich represented the Bolsheviks, Angelica Balabanov and Irina Izolskaia the Mensheviks, and Anna Kamenska the SDKPIL-Regional Presidium. Saumoneau was present for the French Women's Action Committee for Peace; Anny Morf and Agnes Robmann for Switzerland; and Marian Phillips, Mary Longman, and Ada Salter for the ILP and the British International Women's Council. Letters of support arrived from Kollontai in Norway, Theresa Schlesinger in Austria, and a Belgian women's league. The following account of the conference is based upon summaries in Ravich, "Mezhdunarodnaia zhenskaia sotsialisticheskaia konferentsiia," pp. 169–70; Zetkin's description in *Dokumente und Materialen zur Geschichte der deutschen Arbeiterbewegung*, vol. 2 (Berlin, 1958), pp. 119–24; "Internationale sozialistische Frauenkonferenz in Bern. Offizieller Verhandlungsbericht," *Beilag zur Berner Tagwacht*, 3 April 1915; I. Izolskaia, "Internatsionalnaia zhenskaia sotsialisticheskaia konferentsiia," *Nashe Slovo*, 13 April 1915; and Temkin, *Lenin*, pp. 128–33. Temkin draws on the official protocol, which is kept in the Soviet Central Party Archive in Moscow.
9   Cited in Ravich, "Mezhdunarodnaia zhenskaia sotsialisticheskaia konferentsiia," pp. 171–73.
10 Zetkin, *Ausgewählte Reden*, vol. 1, pp. 668–71.
11 Saumoneau's organization in Paris rejected the text of her resolution as overly

conservative. It was eventually withdrawn in deference to Zetkin. See Gankin and Fisher, *Bolsheviks and the World War*, p. 291; Samuil S. Bantke, "Lenin i tsimmerval'dskoe dvizhenie vo Frantsii," *Proletarskaia revoliutsiia* 3(1934): 118; S. S. Bantke, *Bor'ba za sozdanie kommunisticheskoi partii vo Frantsii* (Moscow, 1936), p. 43; and Rosmer 1, pp. 306–7.

12 Lenin, PSS, vol. 26, pp. 206–8.

13 Balabanoff, *Erinnerungen und Erlebnisse*, p. 101; *Leninskii sbornik*, vol. 30, p. 245; and Temkin, *Lenin*, p. 132.

14 *Dokumente und Materialen der deutschen Arbeiterbewegung*, vol. 2, p. 121.

15 Gankin and Fisher, *Bolsheviks and the World War*, pp. 299–300.

16 Ibid., pp. 300–301.

17 A. Balabanov, *Iz lichnykh vospominanii tsimmerval'dtsa* (Moscow/Leningrad, 1925), p. 48. See also her extremely positive contemporary account, A. Balabanoff, "Die Internationale Frauenkonferenz zu Bern," *Lichtstrahlen* (April 1915): 191–93. Carsten, *War Against War*, p. 36, cites evidence of the wide distribution of the women's conference manifesto in Germany.

18 V. Miuntsenberg, *S Libknekhtom i Leninym: Piatnadtsat' let v proletarskom iunosheskom dvizhenii* (Moscow, 1930), pp. 92–93; Babette Gross, *Willi Münzenberg: A Political Biography* (East Lansing, 1974), pp. 44–48; Arnold Reisberg, *Lenin und die Zimmerwalder Bewegung* (Berlin, 1966), pp. 147–48; and Lademacher 2, pp. 287–88. Danneberg wrote to Münzenberg to explain that it was his inability to communicate with national sections rather than political conviction that led him to oppose a conference. Cited in Richard Schüller, A. Kurolla, and R. Chitaro·v, *Geschichte der Kommunistischen Jugend-Internationale*, vol. 1 (Berlin, 1929), p. 79. Both Danneberg and Münzenberg were victims of Nazi terror in 1942.

19 Delegations included Friedrich Notz, Georg Dietrich, and Stirner [Sturm] (Germany); Grimm, Platten, Münzenberg, and Hans Vogel (Switzerland); Armand and G. I. Safarov [Egorov] (RSDRP-Bolsheviks); Ansgar Olaussen (Norway); Christiansen (Denmark); Bernd Luteraan (the Netherlands); S. Minev (Bulgaria); Amadeo Catanesi (Italy); and Bronislaw Stein [Dabrowski] (Poland). Balabanov also took an active part in the proceedings. No members of the current International Youth Bureau (Danneberg of Austria, Höglund of Sweden, Hendrik de Man of Belgium, Emanuel Skatula of Bohemia, and Helge Krogh of Norway) took part. The following description is based upon accounts in V. Miuntsenberg, *Shtutgartskaia i Bernskaia konferentsii sotsialisticheskogo molodezhi* (Khar'kov, 1929), pp. 31–36; Lademacher 2, p. 73; Temkin, *Lenin*, pp. 133–36; and Eugène Olaussen, "Ungdomsinternationalens konferens," *Stormklockan*, 24 April 1915.

20 Text in "Internationale sozialistische Jugendkonferenz in Bern. Offizieller Verhandlungsbericht," *Berner Tagwacht*, 17 April 1915.

21 Procedural demands included the request for a voting mandate for Stein from the SDKPiL-Regional Presidium and the granting of two voting mandates for each country represented. The text of the Bolshevik project resolution has been lost. According to a report in the *Berner Tagwacht* on 17 April, it was supported by Armand, Safarov, Stein, and Luteraan. Balabanoff, *Erinnerungen und Erlebnisse*, p. 102, describes Lenin's role as the architect of Bolshevik strategy from behind the scene.

22 Text of the motion in Gankin and Fisher, *Bolsheviks and the World War*, pp. 307–8. Höglund later emphasized that antimilitarism and the campaign for general and complete disarmament represented the youth movement's most fundamen-

tal commitments. Z. Höglund, "Ungdomsinternationalen mot kriget," *Storm-klockan* (undated special edition, 1915).

23 Cited in Temkin, *Lenin*, p. 135.

24 Edwin Hörnle, "Die Internationale ist tot! Es lebe die Internationale!" *Jugend-Internationale* 1(1915): 5. Gross, *Münzenberg*, pp. 46–51, describes efforts to implement the conference's decisions. The Italian delegate to the new youth bureau Amadeo Catanesi was killed in action during 1915 and replaced by Isaaco Schweide. See the memorium in *Jugend-Internationale* 1(1915): 2.

25 Renato Allio, "Morgari e l'internazionale socialista durante la grande guerra," *Bolletino storico bibliografico subalpino* 73(1975): 554–59, 568–73.

26 Gautschi, *Lenin*, p. 114, and Christian Voight, *Robert Grimm: Kämpfer, Arbeiter-führer, Parlamentarier. Eine politische Biografie* (Bern, 1980), pp. 113–17. The correspondence is held in the private archive of Frau Jenny Grimm-Kuhn in Bern.

27 Robert Grimm, "Klassenkampf und Nation," *Neues Leben* 1(January 1915): 1–11, and "Wir müssen wagen!" *Neues Leben* 3(March 1915): 65–70.

28 Voight, *Robert Grimm*, pp. 120–21. Collart, *Le parti suisse et l'Internationale*, p. 213, comes to a similar conclusion.

29 *SSA*: "Sitzungen der Geschäftsleitung," 2 October 1914 and 13 November 1914; Collart, *Le parti suisse et l'Internationale*, pp. 150–51; and Humbert-Droz, *L'origine de l'Internationale communiste*, pp. 100–101.

30 *SSA*: "Sitzungen der Geschäftsleitung," 22 January 1915.

31 Ibid., 18 and 22 February 1915, and Lademacher 2, pp. 22–23.

32 Lademacher 2, pp. 29–31.

33 Lademacher 2, pp. 36–37, and Blänsdorf, *Die Zweite Internationale*, pp. 205–6.

34 *SSA*: "Sitzungen des Parteivorstandes," 28 March 1915. The vote at the session divided sixteen/ten.

35 Ibid., "Sitzungen der Geschäftsleitung," 22 April 1915. The text of the invitation is given in Lademacher 2, pp. 49–50, and the text of Greulich's manifesto in Collart, *Le parti suisse et l'Internationale*, pp. 293–95.

36 Ambrosoli, *Né aderire né sabotare*, pp. 74–75; Rosmer 1, pp. 368–71; and Valiani, "Il Partito Socialista Italiana," pp. 300–303. A substantial delegation from the SFIO was present at the meeting, including Albert Thomas, Edouard Vaillant, Pierre Renaudel, Jules Guesde, Marcel Sembat, and Gustave Hervé.

37 Lademacher 2, pp. 61–62, 80–81.

38 The Romanian party's acceptance was delivered to Grimm by Rakovski. Ibid., p. 33. The Bulgarian Narrow's response may be consulted in the SPS party archives. Signed by Kyrkov, it provides a lengthy elaboration of the party's position on the war issue.

39 Cited from Martov and Stanislaw Lapinski, "La vie de l'Internationale," *La Sentinelle*, 3 March 1915. Martov's letter to Grimm in Lademacher 2, pp. 50–54, provides a lengthy description of his encounter with Morgari in Paris. See also *Pis'ma Aksel'roda i Martova*, p. 332, and Israel Getzler, *Martov: A Political Biography of a Russian Social Democrat* (Cambridge, 1967), pp. 144–45.

40 "Rebuilding the International," *The Labour Leader*, 12 August 1915.

41 Malatesta, *I socialisti italiani*, pp. 228–29, 233, and the statement by Constantino Lazzari, "Nell' Internazionale," *L'Avanguardia*, 8 July 1915.

42 *SSA*: "Sitzungen des Parteivorstandes," 22 May 1915.

43 Lademacher 2, pp. 83–84.

44 Ibid., p. 65.

45 *Pis'ma Aksel'roda i Martova*, p. 332.

46 Gautschi, *Lenin*, pp. 132–40; Temkin, *Lenin*, p. 173; and Reisberg, *Lenin*, p. 154.

47 Lenin, PSS, vol. 49, pp. 80–82.
48 The delegates were Grimm (Switzerland), Morgari (Italy), Zinoviev (RSDRP-Bolshevik), Aksel'rod (RSDRP-Menshevik), Balabanov (Italy), Adolf Warszawski [Warski] (SDKPiL-Main Presidium), and Walecki (PPS-L). Radek was not able to attend as he was not delegated by an ISB affiliate. The following account of the session is based upon the protocol in Lademacher 1, pp. 29–42.
49 "Otvet delegata TsK-RSDRP o predvaritel'nom soveshchanii sostaiavshemsia 11 iiulia 1915 g., po voprosu o sozyve mezhdunarodnoi konferentsii," Leninskii sbornik, vol. 5, pp. 463–65.
50 Maitron and Chambelland, Syndicalisme révolutionnaire, pp. 136–81; Rosmer 1, p. 372; and Lademacher 1, pp. 95–96. An Italian police file in Archivio Centrale dello Stato (hereinafter cited as ACS), Ministero dell' interno, busta 71/143/14-1 describes Morgari's voyages in the weeks prior to Zimmerwald. He is claimed to have arrived in London on 30 August and remained until 4 September, proceeding on to Paris, the Netherlands, and Bern. Contacts named include Frederick Jowett, Phillip Snowden, and MacDonald of the ILP, Thomas Kennedy of the BSP, Merrheim, Monatte, and Trotsky in Paris, and "a number of Germans" in the Netherlands.
51 Lenin, PSS, vol. 26, pp. 209–65, 307–50.
52 Lenin's intellectual encounter with Clausewitz is described in Werner Hahlweg, "Lenin und Clausewitz: Ein Beitrag zur politischen Ideengeschichte des 20. Jahrhunderts," Archiv für Kulturgeschichte, vol. 36 (Munich/Cologne, 1954), pp. 20–59, 357–387; Gautschi, Lenin, pp. 123–32; and N. N. Avovtsov, V. I. Lenin i sovetskaia voennaia nauka (Moscow, 1981), pp. 10–45. See also Lenin's notebooks on Clausewitz in Leninskii sbornik, vol. 12, pp. 387–452.
53 Lenin, PSS, vol. 26, p. 311.
54 Ibid., pp. 311, 341–42.
55 Ibid., p. 340, and [Anton] Pannekoek, "Imperializm i zadachi proletariata," Kommunist 1/2(1915): 70–77, including Lenin's editorial comment.
56 Lenin, PSS, vol. 49, pp. 94–95, 124–25, 127, 130, 136–37, and Gankin and Fisher, Bolsheviks and the World War, pp. 315–20. Lenin also circulated the text of a project resolution for the left. Lenin, PSS, vol. 26, pp. 282–85, and Leninskii sbornik, vol. 14, pp. 166–72.
57 Lademacher 2, pp. 89–90, 94–96. The Bolsheviks' letter mentions the Tribunists, the Bulgarian Narrows, the Swedish and Norwegian Youth Leagues, the Lichtstrahlen group, the SDKPiL-Regional Presidium, and the Lettish Social Democratic party as candidates for invitations.
58 Lenin, PSS, vol. 49, pp. 95, 116, 117.
59 Kolarov, Izbrani proizvedeniia, p. 257.
60 See Wijnkoop's letter to Lenin in Pis'ma V. I. Lenina iz-za rubezha (Moscow, 1966), pp. 45–47; A. S. Leeuw, "De S.D.P. en Zimmerwald," De Communist, 3 March 1931, pp. 80–91; and de Liagre Böhl, Herman Gorter, p. 135.
61 Lenin, PSS, vol. 49, p. 83.
62 Ibid., pp. 116–17.
63 Cited from an unpublished manuscript in the Soviet Central Party Archives in Temkin, Lenin, pp. 193–95.
64 Cited in ibid., pp. 198–99.
65 In the end the criterion of ISB affiliation was not applied. Delegations included Lenin and Zinoviev (RSDRP-Bolshevik); Aksel'rod and Martov (RSDRP-Menshevik); Mark Natanson [Bobrov] and Viktor Chernov (SR-Internationalist Wing);

Trotsky (*Nashe Slovo* group); P. L. Girs [Lemanski] (Bund); Jan Berzin (Lettish Social Democracy); Bertha Thalheimer and Ernst Meyer (International Group); Borchardt (International Socialists of Germany); Georg Ledebour, Adolf Hoffmann, Ewald Vogtherr, Minna Reinhart, Heinrich Berges, Gustav Lachenmaier, and Jozef Herzfeld (SPD-Opposition); Merrheim and Albert Bourderon (CGT and SFIO-Opposition); Lazzari, Morgari, Serrati, Giuseppe Modigliani, and Balabanov (PSI); Grimm, Charles Naine, Carl Moor, and Platten (SPS-Opposition); Höglund and Ture Nerman (Swedish and Norwegian Youth Leagues); Rakovski (Romanian Social Democracy); Roland-Holst (SDAP-Opposition); Kolarov (Bulgarian Narrows); Radek (SDKPiL-Regional Presidium); Adolf Warszawski [Warski] (SDKPiL-Main Presidium); and Pavel Lewinson [Stanislaw Lapinski] (PPS-L). Münzenberg was refused a mandate on behalf of the new Youth International.

66 Leon Trotsky, *My Life: An Attempt at an Autobiography* (New York, 1930), p. 249.

67 V. Kolarov, "Vospominanii o Tsimmerval'de," *Pravda*, 6 September 1925. Though a part of the original *Beau Séjour* remains standing, the guest house where Lenin resided was torn down in 1971. Its site is occupied by the village post office. Despite several attempts, local resistance has prevented any monument to the conference from being constructed in Zimmerwald.

68 See Ture Nerman, "20 Jahre Zimmerwald," *Berner Tagwacht*, 5 September 1935. According to Nerman (whose recollections are sometimes faulty), Lenin met arriving delegations on the train platform and led them straight to a nearby inn for conversations that also included Zinoviev, Radek, Berzin, and Platten. See also Merrheim's account of having received such treatment cited in Bantke, "Lenin i tsimmerval'dskoe dvizhenie," p. 123.

69 Lenin, PSS, vol. 27, p. 487, and Temkin, *Lenin*, p. 200. The three Polish Zimmerwaldist groups also caucused in Bern and agreed in principle upon united action—a commitment that was not always honored. Tych, "La participation des partis ouvrière polonais," pp. 205–6.

70 Described in Ia. G. Temkin, *Tsimmerval'd-Kintal'* (Moscow, 1962), p. 48; Reisberg, *Lenin*, pp. 160–67; and D. Baevskii, "Lenin i tsimmerval'dskaia levaia," *Bor'ba klassov* 3(1934): 38. Personal recollections are provided by Ture Nerman, *Allt var rött: Minne och redovisning* (Stockholm, 1950), pp. 167–68, and Zeth Höglund, *Minnen i fackelsken*, vol. 2, *Från Branting till Lenin, 1912–1916* (Stockholm, 1953), p. 179.

71 Opening reports are summarized in G. Shklovskii, "Tsimmerval'd," *Proletarskaia revoliutsiia* 9(44) (1925): 73–106. The following account of the conference and all citations are drawn from the official protocol in Lademacher 1, pp. 43–180.

72 Morgari was attacked upon his return to Italy for his obstructionist comportment. A letter from Arturo Vella on 8 April 1916 typifies reactions, scolding that "this time [referring to the upcoming Kiental conference] *you must* (and really *must*) speak out and represent our internationalists and Zimmerwaldists." *ACS: Collection Morgari*, busta 11, f. 25, sotto. 1–3.

73 Lademacher 1, pp. 124, 166–69.

74 Ibid., pp. 153–54. The statement was signed by Lenin, Zinoviev, Berzin, Radek, Höglund, and Nerman. Borchardt and Platten, who were not formally empowered as delegates, refrained from signing in order to guard the document's official character.

75 Hostile reactions immediately seized upon the creation of the ISC as a move toward a schism. In Sweden, for example, the mainstream socialist press de-

nounced Zimmerwald as a gathering of "anarchist elements." Branting wrote to Stauning that its intention was to found a new International "where all national viewpoints will be reduced to a meaningless nothing." Cited in Grass, *Friedensaktivität und Neutralität*, p. 211.

76 Balabanoff, *Erinnerungen und Erlebnisse*, p. 112. The Zimmerwald conference also approved a statement of sympathy for the victims of the war and a joint Franco-German declaration of solidarity. The latter text was considered by some to be the conference's most important accomplishment. Trotsky, who was a member of the drafting commission, later described the atmosphere during deliberations as cool and the results as universally disappointing. Maitron and Chambelland, *Syndicalisme révolutionnaire*, p. 203.

77 "Die Taktik des Schweigens," *Berner Tagwacht*, 28 September 1915, and *ISK Bulletin*, no. 2, 27 December 1915, p. 1. A German military intelligence report of 17 November lamented the manifesto's appearance among the soldiery. Cited in Erich Otto Volkmann, *Der Marxismus und das deutsche Heer im Weltkriege* (Berlin, 1925), p. 278.

78 Malatesta, *I socialisti italiani*, pp. 86–87.

79 *Nashe Slovo*, 19 October 1915.

80 Robert Grimm, "Die internationale Konferenz," *Berner Tagwacht*, 20 September 1915.

81 Humbert-Droz, *L'origine de l'Internationale communiste*, p. 100. See also Wohl, *French Communism*, p. 63.

82 Blänsdorf, *Die Zweite Internationale*, p. 217. A similar conclusion is drawn by Viktor Chernov, *Pered burei: Vospominaniia* (New York, 1953), pp. 308–9. Kirby, *War, Peace and Revolution*, p. 235, calls the movement "a moral critique of the failing of social democracy," a formulation that seems at least partially misleading. Dietrich Geyer's characterization of Zimmerwald as "radical democratic pacifism" is certainly well off the mark. Dietrich Geyer, *Die russische Revolution: Historische Probleme und Perspektiven* (Stuttgart, 1968), p. 51.

83 The citations are from Fainsod, *International Socialism*, p. 89, and Julius Braunthal, *Geschichte der Internationale*, vol. 2 (Hannover, 1963), pp. 60–61. Similar judgments are offered by Voight, *Robert Grimm*, pp. 128–29, and Gautschi, *Lenin*, p. 152.

84 Kollontai and Shliapnikov discussed Lenin's project resolution for the left with Höglund, Nerman, and other Swedish leftists in Stockholm during August. Persistent disagreements, particularly over the disarmament issue, led the Scandinavians to prepare their own project resolution rather than endorsing Lenin's text. Höglund, *Minnen i fackelsken*, vol. 2, p. 178.

85 Blagoev, "Internatsionalut i voinata," in *Izbrani proizvedeniia*, vol. 2, pp. 677–83; Gorter, *Het imperialisme*; Liebknecht's "theses" in Gilbert Badia, "L'attitude de la gauche social-démocrate allemande dans les premiers mois de la guerre," *Le mouvement social* 49 (October/December 1964): 103–4; Leo Trotzki, *Der Krieg und die Internationale* (Zürich, 1914); and A. Pannekoek, "Der Zusammenbruch der Internationale," *Berner Tagwacht*, 20, 21, and 22 October 1914.

86 *ACS: Ministero dell' interno*, 70.146.6.

87 Lademacher 2, pp. 246–47.

88 "Ein unveröffentlichter Brief Rosa Luxemburgs," *Die Rote Fahne*, 15 January 1929, and Walter Bartel, *Die Linken in der deutschen Sozialdemokratie im Kampf gegen Militarismus und Krieg* (Berlin, 1958), p. 257.

89 Luxemburg, GW, vol. 4, pp. 168–69.

90 *Nashe Slovo*, 24 and 25 November 1915.

4 The Zimmerwald Left

1 Nerman, "20 Jahre Zimmerwald," provides the most detailed account. He notes that the Swedish and Norwegian Youth Leagues also offered the Left financial support.

2 Gautschi, *Lenin*, p. 154.

3 N. K. Krupskaia, *Reminiscences of Lenin* (Moscow, 1959), p. 311.

4 Lenin, PSS, vol. 27, pp. 37–43, 45. Zinoviev's conclusions, "Pervaia mezhdunarodnaia konferentsiia," in Zinov'ev, *Sochineniia*, vol. 5, pp. 218–25, were nearly identical.

5 Arnold Struthahn [Karl Radek], "Die internationale sozialistische Konferenz," *Neues Leben* (September 1915): 262, and K. Radek, "Der erste Schritt," *Lichtstrahlen* (October 1915): 3–5.

6 See his letter to Radek in Lenin, PSS, vol. 49, pp. 145–46, and Temkin, *Lenin*, p. 250.

7 *ISK Bulletin*, no. 1, 21 September 1915. Grimm elaborated upon the point in "Die internationale Konferenz," *Berner Tagwacht*, 2 October 1915.

8 Lenin, PSS, vol. 49, pp. 145–46, 512.

9 Ibid., p. 163. Lenin's letter reached Kollontai in North America, where she was conducting a lecture tour. See G. D. Petrov, "A. M. Kollontai v gody pervoi mirovoi voiny," *Istoriia SSSR* 3(1968): 92–94, and Barbara Evans Clements, *Bolshevik Feminist: The Life of Aleksandra Kollontai* (Bloomington, 1979), pp. 94–97. Kollontai was outside of Europe from September 1915 to March 1916.

10 *Internationale Flugblätter*, no. 1 (November 1915), p. 1.

11 *Nashe Slovo*, 7 January 1916.

12 Harding, *Lenin's Political Thought*, vol. 1, pp. 176–81, and John R. Ehrenberg, "Making the Turn: The Political Roots of Lenin's Theory of the Party Press," *Studies in Soviet Thought* 21(1980): 119–39.

13 Lademacher 2, p. 165.

14 Henriettë Roland-Holst, "Verhältnisse und Voraussichten in der Holländischen Arbeiterbewegung," *IISG: Collection Grimm*, H-28, a report sent to Grimm during 1915, provides a detailed account of the origins of the RSV. Documentation is given in *De Internationale: Orgaan van het Revolutionnair Socialistisch Verbond* 1/2(May–June 1915), the first number of the RSV's central organ. See also R[oland] H[olst], "De Roem van Zimmerwald," *De Internationale* 7(November 1915): 113–20, and H. Roland-Holst, "De Internationale Socialistische Konferentie van Zimmerwald," *De Nieuwe Tijd* 10(1915): 590–99.

15 Lademacher 2, p. 136, and H. Roland-Holst, "Der Kampf um Zimmerwald im Holland," *Der Vorbote* 1(January 1916): 64–68.

16 See his letter to Willem van Ravestejn cited in Koejemans, *Wijnkoop*, p. 131, and D. J. Wijnkoop, "De geest van Zimmerwald," *De Nieuwe Tijd* 1(1916): 61. Wijnkoop's position on Zimmerwald is developed at some length in D. J. Wijnkoop, "De internationale Konferentie," *De Tribune*, 25 September 1915, and "Zimmerwald," *De Tribune*, 2 October 1915. Wijnkoop wrote out German translations of these articles for Grimm. Texts in *IISG: Collection Grimm*, H-10.

17 A[nton] P[annekoek], "Nog eens Zimmerwald," *De Tribune*, 5 January 1916. See also Anton Pannekoek, *Herinneringen* (Amsterdam, 1982), p. 41. The controversy was a luxury for a small organization dominated by radical intellectuals. Roland-Holst and SDP member H. W. J. Sannes estimated SDP membership at around five hundred in 1915. See Lademacher 2, pp. 136–38, and H. W. J. Sannes, "Zimmerwald en de S.D.P.," *De Nieuwe Tijd* 12(1915): 704. According to *De Tribune*, 11

June 1918, membership more than doubled during the war. SDAP membership was about 25,000. See also de Liagre-Böhl, *Gorter*, p. 143, and G. G. Bauman, "Niderlandskaia burzhuaznaia i sotsial-reformistskaia istoriografiia o Tribunistakh," *Voprosy istorii* 6(1978): 58–72.

18 See Roland-Holst's justification for the merger in R[oland] H[olst], "Links', . . . Richt U!" *De Internationale* 10(February 1916): 202–4.

19 Lademacher 2, pp. 101–3. On the division within the SDP concerning the Entente see de Liagre Böhl, *Gorter*, pp. 131–52.

20 Lademacher 2, pp. 186–89, 201–8. Pannekoek expressed regret about the inability to include Luxemburg and Liebknecht. He lamented the need to work through Roland-Holst but described her support as essential. See his manuscript, "Internationale Arbeiderspolitiek," in *IISG: Collection van Ravestejn*.

21 Lademacher 2, pp. 214–15, 223–29.

22 Ibid., pp. 314–15.

23 L. J. van Rossum, "Ein unveröffentlichter Brief Trotskij's von Anfang 1916," *International Review of Social History* 2(1969): 255.

24 Ibid., p. 257.

25 Lademacher 2, pp. 159–60, 413–14, 497.

26 Outlined in Peretz Merhav, "Klassenkampf und Nationale Frage zur Zeit der II. Internationale," *Annali* (Milan, 1976): 165–87.

27 I. V. Stalin, *Sochineniia*, vol. 2 (Moscow, 1946), p. 296.

28 See his "Natsional'nyi vopros v nashoi programme," Lenin, PSS, vol. 7, pp. 233–42. The Bolshevik position on the national question is usefully summarized in E. H. Carr, *The Bolshevik Revolution 1917–1923*, vol. 1 (London, 1950), pp. 549–66.

29 Discussed in Arduino Agnelli, *Questione nazionale e socialismo: Contributo allo studio del pensiero di K. Renner e O. Bauer* (Bologna, 1969), and Arduino Agnelli, "Socialismo e problema della nazionalità in Otto Bauer," *Annali* (Milan, 1973): 364–86. See also Otto Bauer, *Die Nationalitätenfrage und die Sozialdemokratie* (Vienna, 1907).

30 Luxemburg's writings on the national question in Polish and German are collected in Horace B. Davis, ed., *The National Question: Selected Writings by Rosa Luxemburg* (New York, 1976). See also Michael Lowy, "Rosa Luxemburg et la question nationale," *Partisans* (May–August 1971): 65–67, and Nettl, *Rosa Luxemburg*, vol. 2, pp. 842–62.

31 D. Baevskii, "Partiia v gody voiny," pp. 445, 516–19; "Iz materialov Instituta Marksa-Engelsa-Lenina," *Bol'shevik* 22(1932): 76–96; and Cohen, *Bukharin*, pp. 36–43.

32 Text in Davis, *The National Question*, pp. 302–20. The theses were written by Radek, Hanecki, Bronislaw Stein, and Mieczyslaw Bronski. They were published in *Gazeta Robotnicza* 6(October 1916) and *Der Vorbote* 2(April 1916). They were rejected at the Zimmerwald conference, and in deference to Morgari a reference to self-determination as an "unshakable foundation" for interstate relations was written into the Zimmerwald manifesto. Rosmer explains the circumstances in a letter to Monatte in Maitron and Chambelland, *Syndicalisme révolutionnaire*, p. 201.

33 Parabellum [Karl Radek], "Annexionen und Sozialdemokratie," *Berner Tagwacht*, 28 and 29 October 1915, and Lenin, PSS, vol. 27, pp. 61–68.

34 K. Radek, "Das Selbstbestimmungsrecht der Völker," *Lichtstrahlen* (December 1915): 50–52.

35 The guidelines were distributed as a leaflet with the title "Leitsätze über die Aufgaben der internationalen Sozialdemokratie," and were attached as an appen-

dix to Luxemburg's *The Crisis of Social Democracy.* Luxemburg, GW, vol. 4, pp. 43–47. According to Ernst Meyer, "Zur Entstehungsgeschichte der Junius-Thesen," *Unter dem Banner des Marxismus* 2(1925–1926): 416–32, several points led to friction between Luxemburg and Liebknecht. Participants at the 1 January meeting included Liebknecht, Mehring, Ernst Meyer, Käthe Duncker, Bertha Thalheimer, Rühle, Georg Schumann, and Paul Lindau. Johann Knief was also present as an observer. Gilbert Badia, *Le Spartakisme* (Paris, 1967), pp. 81–84.

36 Luxemburg, GW, vol. 4, pp. 136, 162.

37 Lenin, PSS, vol. 27, pp. 61–68, 252–66, and vol. 30, pp. 1–58.

38 Ibid., pp. 257, 261.

39 Cited in Demetrio Boersner, *The Bolsheviks and the National and Colonial Question (1917–1918)* (Geneva, 1957), p. 55.

40 Lenin, PSS, vol. 30, p. 112.

41 See *V. I. Lenin: Biograficheskaia khronika,* vol. 3 (Moscow, 1972), p. 433; Temkin, *Lenin,* pp. 260–61; and Lenin, PSS, vol. 29, pp. 177–78.

42 K. Radek, "Grundsätzliche und taktische Streitfragen der deutschen Opposition," *Der Vorbote* 1(January 1916): 28–42.

43 Described in *Lenin: Biograficheskaia khronika,* vol. 3, p. 437, and Temkin, *Lenin,* p. 263.

44 Lademacher 2, pp. 495–99, and Lenin, PSS, vol. 29, pp. 189–92.

45 Significantly, the first number of *Sbornik Sotsial-Demokrata* contained two major statements by Lenin on the national question. Lenin, PSS, vol. 30, pp. 1–58.

46 Senn, *The Russian Revolution in Switzerland,* pp. 127–28, calls the Lenin-Radek feud "a natural clash of independent personalities working toward the same end." Lerner, *Radek,* pp. 44–47, more accurately focuses on the theoretical foundations of their differences. To date most Soviet accounts, in the worst Stalinist manner, portray Radek as a traitor working to sabotage the Left. See Temkin, *Lenin,* pp. 259–65, and for a more balanced view, Tiutiukin, *Voina, mir, revoliutsiia,* p. 233.

47 Lenin, PSS, vol. 29, pp. 181–82. Lenin announced that in the future he would only communicate with Radek via Zinoviev.

48 Ibid., pp. 192–96, 229–33, 331. The tone of Lenin's commentary is abusive to an extreme, labeling Radek a "fool" and a "scoundrel," with "kasha between his ears."

49 Miller, *Burgfrieden und Klassenkampf,* pp. 117–33. Haase was not the first oppositionist to be expelled. Liebknecht had met the same fate on 12 January 1916, and two days later Rühle resigned as a gesture of solidarity.

50 Liebknecht, *Gesammelte Reden,* vol. 7, p. 448, and Julian Borchardt, "Warum ich nicht mit der Opposition gehe," *Lichtstrahlen* (January 1916): 73–80. See also Luxemburg's comment, "Die Lehre des 24. März," Luxemburg, GW, vol. 4, pp. 181–86.

51 Lademacher 1, pp. 452–55.

52 *Spartakusbriefe* (Berlin, 1958), pp. 134–35, 141, and Bartel, *Die Linken,* p. 296.

53 Lenin, PSS, vol. 30, p. 2, and, for Luxemburg's text, Luxemburg, GW, vol. 4, pp. 49–164. All citations are drawn from the German text.

54 Erhard Lucas, *Die Sozialdemokratie in Bremen während des Ersten Weltkrieges* (Bremen, 1969), pp. 58–65; Carsten, *War Against War,* pp. 160–61; and Badia, *Le Spartakisme,* p. 219. Background on the split in Bremen is provided by Karl-Ernest Moring, *Die Sozialdemokratische Partei in Bremen 1880–1914: Reformismus und Radikalismus in der Sozialdemokratischen Partei Bremens* (Hannover, 1968).

55 See Friedrich Adler's manifesto "The Internationalists of Austria to the Interna-

tionalists of all Nations," in Leopold Hornik, "Die Zimmerwalder Linke und die Linksradikalen in Oesterreich," *Weg und Ziel* (January 1965): 657. For the proceedings of the national conference, marked by a father/son clash between Victor and Friedrich Adler, see Rudolf Neck, ed., *Arbeiterschaft und Staat im Ersten Weltkrieg 1914–1918*, vol. 1 (Vienna, 1964), pp. 50–66. The opposition was weakly represented. Only sixteen of one hundred fifty votes were cast for Friedrich Adler's motions condemning the war and greeting the Zimmerwald action. Their texts are given in the *ISK Bulletin*, no. 4, 22 April 1916, p. 7, and no. 6, 6 January 1917, p. 8.

56   F. Koritschoner, "Iz istorii internatsionalistskogo dvizheniia v Avstrii," *Proletarskaia revoliutsiia* 2/3(97/98) (1939): 91. Friedrich Adler chaired the association. It counted approximately forty members in October 1916. Neck, *Arbeiterschaft und Staat*, vol. 1, p. 140.

57   Hautmann, *Die Anfänge der Linksradikalen Bewegung*, pp. 5–6, and Peter Kulemann, *Am Beispiel des Austromarxismus: Sozialdemokratische Arbeiterbewegung in Oesterreich von Hainfeld bis zur Dollfuss Diktator* (Hamburg, 1979), pp. 197–200.

58   Kriegel, *Aux origines*, vol. 1, pp. 120–22, and *ISK Bulletin*, no. 4, 22 April 1916, p. 14. On 6 November the SFIO formally condemned the Zimmerwald action. See the text in *Pendant la guerre: Le parti socialiste, la guerre et la paix* (Paris, 1918), pp. 128–29. See also Longuet's intervention at the conference of the Federation of the Seine during December in Alfred Rosmer, *Le mouvement ouvrier pendant la première guerre de Zimmerwald à la révolution russe* (hereinafter cited as Rosmer 2) (Paris, 1959), pp. 46–47.

59   Bourderon's resolution condemning the *union sacrée* was not supported by the Longuetist center and was voted down by a count of 2736 to 76. Text in Rosmer 2, pp. 46–55. The text of the majority resolution is given in *Pendant la guerre*, pp. 129–35.

60   Rosmer 2, pp. 137–43. The gesture was less appreciated by partisans of the Zimmerwald Left, who regarded Longuet's minoritaires as nothing more than a watered-down version of the SPD center. See Radek's letter in *Le Populaire*, 12–25 February 1916.

61   Cited from the CRRI's first official document, the broadsheet *Aux organisations socialistes et syndicales à leur militants* (January 1916). The origins of the CRRI are described in Rosmer 1, pp. 417–19.

62   Annie Kriegel, "Lénine et le mouvement zimmerwaldien français," in *Le pain et les roses* (Paris, 1968), pp. 145–49; Wohl, *French Communism*, pp. 76–78; and Grossheim, *Sozialisten in der Verantwortung*, pp. 129–33.

63   On the Saint Nazaire group see Temkin, *Lenin*, p. 300, and Rosmer 1, p. 463. Rosmer indicates that he never heard of Stal' until meeting her in Moscow during 1920. Ibid., p. 457. Stal's description of the Action Committee's work, provided in a letter to Krupskaia cited by Temkin, *Lenin*, p. 314, indicates that it consisted mostly of agitation at the base. See also her articles "Sous le voile de l'union sacrée," *La Sentinelle*, 23–24 September and 4 October 1914, concluding with the call "to transform the war between peoples into a civil war . . . a war for socialism."

64   Lenin, PSS, vol. 49, p. 169.

65   Cited in Branko Lazitch, *Lénine et la IIIe Internationale* (Paris, 1951), p. 70. The future leader of the Zimmerwald Left tendency in France, Fernand Loriot of the Teachers' Federation, composed a tract for the CRRI in April 1916 that raised the call for revolution. It has been hailed by one Stalinist historian as "the first real

leftist tract" to emerge from the French opposition. J. Rocher, *Lénine et le mouvement zimmerwaldien en France* (Paris, 1934), p. 71. Inconveniently, the tract makes no mention of Lenin or the Left and was written with the assistance of Trotsky. See Rosmer 2, p. 145.

66 See the account of the party's activities prepared as a report for Grimm by ILP secretary Francis Johnson in Lademacher 2, pp. 472–74, and Carsten, *War Against War*, pp. 55–56, 170–71, 201. ILP membership topped 40,000 during the war, with the largest increases coming in Scotland.

67 Maclean's comments on Zimmerwald, originally published in *The Vanguard*, are collected in Nan Milton, ed., *John Maclean: In the Rapids of Revolution* (London, 1978), pp. 91–93. They make no mention of the Zimmerwald Left and are harshly agitational in tone.

68 Kendall, *The Revolutionary Movement in Britain*, pp. 97–99, and the letter to Grimm from Tom Quelch of the BSP in Lademacher 2, pp. 332–34.

69 Cited in N. E. Korolev, *Lenin i mezhdunarodnoe rabochee dvizhenie 1914–1918* (Moscow, 1968), p. 105.

70 See the situation reports in *ISK Bulletin*, no. 3, 29 February 1916, p. 11, and no. 4, 22 April 1916, pp. 12–14; Forcadell, *Parlamentarismo y bolchevización*, pp. 103–36; and Sheridan Johns, "The Birth of the Communist Party of South Africa," *International Journal of African Historical Studies* 3(1976): 371–400.

71 Manfred, "Tsimmerval'dskoe dvizhenie v shveitsarskoi sotsial-demokratii," p. 26, and A. E. Ivanov, "Frits Platten," *Voprosy istorii* 6(1983): 84–85. Three contrasting motions were presented at Aarau: a condemnation of Zimmerwald submitted by the party's right wing, an endorsement submitted by Grimm, and a motion from the left stating conditional support but also urging "revolutionary action by the working class." The texts are available in *SSA: Zimmerwalder Konferenz*, document 2. The left's motion, sponsored by Ernst Graber and Charles Naine of the Neuchâtel section, was eventually withdrawn in deference to Grimm, whose position carried by 330 to 51. The SPS managing committee voted on 7 and 15 October by eight to two to reject Zimmerwald. Aarau thus revealed considerably greater militance among the party's rank and file.

72 *ACS: Collection Morgari*, busta 12, fasc. 24, sotto. 1.

73 Höglund's accounts make no mention whatsoever of the Left. Z. Höglund, "Internationalens återförening," *Stormklockan*, 25 September 1915, and "De internationella socialisternas konferens," *Stormklockan*, 2 October 1915. Nerman described right, center, and left factions within the movement and characterized the latter as "Lenin's group." Ture Nerman, "I Zimmerwald," *Stormklockan*, 8 and 15 January 1916.

74 *ISK Bulletin*, no. 4, 22 April 1916, pp. 18–20.

75 *SSA: Internationale Sozialistische Kommission zu Bern*, "Sitzungsprotokolle," 10 September 1915.

76 Lademacher 1, pp. 183–89.

77 Ibid., pp. 191–94. Affiliations arrived steadily through 1916. At its height on the eve of the Russian revolution, the movement counted the following members: (1) PSI; (2) SPS; (3) BSP; (4) ILP; (5) Social Democratic party of Romania; (6) RSDRP-Central Committee (Bolshevik); (7) RSDRP-Organization Committee (Menshevik); (8) SR-International Group; (9) Jewish Workers' Bund; (10) SDKPiL-Regional Presidium; (11) SDKPiL-Main Presidium; (12) PPS-L; (13) Social Democratic party of Bulgaria-Narrows; (14) Socialist party of Portugal; (15) Socialist Workers Federation of Saloniki; (16) Socialist Youth League of Sweden; (17) Socialist Youth League of Norway; (18) Socialist Labor party of America; (19) Socialist party of

America; (20) Socialist party of America-German Section; (21) Social Democratic party of Latvia; (22) Socialist Youth League of Denmark; (23) Socialist Youth of Madrid; (24) International Socialist League of South Africa; (25) CGL; (26) Bulgarian Federation of Trade Unions; (27) SPD-Section Böckingen (Württemburg); (28) Social Democratic party of Bulgaria-Broads.

A complete fiscal record for the Zimmerwald movement is preserved in the *IISG: Collection Grimm*, Section K; "Geschäftlich." Contributions were the most important source of funding. George David Herron, an erratic American resident in Geneva, was a significant private donor. Henri Guilbeaux, a member of the Zimmerwald Left, eventually protested to Grimm that Herron's subvention could come to compromise the movement politically. Lademacher 2, pp. 687–88.

78 At the ISC session of 18 December 1915, Grimm was formally charged with pursuing contacts with the centrist opposition in Germany and France. *SSA: Internationale Sozialistische Kommission*, "Sitzungsprotokolle," 18 December 1915.

79 Camille Huysmans, *The Policy of the International* (London, 1916), p. 12, and Grass, *Friedensaktivität und Neutralität*, p. 227.

80 *SSA: Internationale Sozialistische Kommission*, "Sitzungsprotokolle," 18 December 1915, and Lademacher 2, pp. 358–60.

81 Ibid., pp. 407–10.

82 See ibid., p. 180, for Zinoviev's first communication with Grimm concerning the report. The final text appears in *ISK Bulletin*, no. 2, 27 November 1915, pp. 7–8.

83 Lademacher 2, pp. 189–90, 192–93, 212–13.

84 Lenin, PSS, vol. 49, pp. 167–68.

85 Lademacher 2, pp. 176, 217–19, 250. Sergei Nechaev was a nineteenth-century Russian revolutionary conspirator whose name had become synonymous with unprincipled manipulation.

86 Lademacher 2, pp. 296–97. Borchardt's letter was dated 15 November and addressed to Grimm care of Radek. Radek appears to have distorted its content, mentioning only his own name and not those of Lenin and Zinoviev as the recipient of Borchardt's mandate. He also added an endorsement from Knief.

87 *SSA: Internationale Sozialistische Kommission*, "Sitzungsprotokolle," 2 February 1916.

88 Participants included Grimm, Naine, Balabanov, and Morgari (ISC); Elia Musatti, Serrati, Modigliani (PSI); Rinaldo Rigola (CGL); Mark Natanson [Bobrov] (SRS); Zinoviev, Lenin (RSDRP-Central Committee); Martov (RSDRP-Organizational Committee); Radek (SDKPiL-Regional Presidium); Warszawski [Warski] (SDKPiL-Main Presidium); Lapinski (PPS-L); Bertha Thalheimer (SPD-Württemberg Section); Gustav Laukant (SPD-Berlin and Niederrhein Sections); Kolarov (Bulgarian Narrows); Rakovski (Social Democratic party of Romania); Olaussen (Socialist Youth League of Norway); Edmondo Peluso (Socialist party of Portugal); Münzenberg (Youth International); Platten (SPS). The following account of the enlarged committee sessions is based upon the official protocol in Lademacher 1, pp. 195–262.

89 Ibid., pp. 254–59. Zinoviev later wrote that: "*Everyone* on the commission opposed Grimm's draft, except Grimm and our representative [Zinoviev himself]. In spite of that, Grimm's draft was used as the basis for the appeal, as there was no other draft ready." Cited in G. Shklovskii, "Tsimmerval'd," *Proletarskaia revoliutsiia* 9(44) (1925): 95.

90 Cited in Temkin, *Lenin*, p. 92.

91 Text in Shklovskii, "Tsimmerval'd," pp. 94–98.

92 Zinov'ev, *Sochineniia*, vol. 5, pp. 251–56.
93 Retzlaw, *Spartakus*, p. 52.
94 Lenin, PSS, vol. 30, p. 51.
95 Michael Voslensky, *Nomenklatura: Les privilégiés en URSS* (Paris, 1980), p. 68.

5 Zimmerwald Left and Zimmerwald Center

1 Trotsky, *My Life*, p. 234.
2 *ISK Bulletin*, no. 3, 29 February 1916, p. 1. The official invitations were issued in the form of a circular letter (ibid., pp. 2–3).
3 Lademacher 1, p. 261.
4 *ISK Bulletin*, no. 3, 29 February 1916, pp. 4–8.
5 G. Sinowjew, "Weiteres über den Bürgerkrieg," in *Gegen den Ström*, pp. 321–27, and Lenin, PSS, vol. 27, pp. 267–74. See also the report published in the *ISK Bulletin*, no. 4, 22 April 1916, pp. 2–4. Lenin spoke in Zürich on 17 and 21 February on the themes "Two Internationals" and "The Conditions for Peace." He repeated the latter address on 1 March in Geneva. Temkin, *Lenin*, pp. 374–75, provides summaries.
6 Lenin, PSS, vol. 49, pp. 215–16, 219.
7 The proposals presented to Grimm concerning voting mandates reflected the priorities of both moderate and radical wings. Hoffmann and Ledebour petitioned to deny a mandate to the Spartacus League; the Bolsheviks protested against representation for the Menshevik Organization Committee; and the *Nashe Slovo* group, the Zürich-based *Eintracht* League, and the Youth International requested independent mandates. *Eintracht*'s request was accompanied by a set of theses that announced its allegiance to the Zimmerwald Left. Lademacher 2, pp. 452–56, 521–24, 527–30.
8 Ibid., pp. 450–51.
9 A useful summary of the "center's" position at the Kiental conference is provided in the position paper prepared for the conference by the Menshevik Organization Committee. *Kriegs- und Friedensprobleme der Arbeiter Klasse: Entwurf eines Manifestes vorgelegt der Zweiten Zimmerwalder Konferenz* (Zürich, 1916), particularly pp. 6–7, 17. In essence the terms of Martov's peace strategy are reposed here.
10 The following account is based upon the official protocol in Lademacher 1, pp. 263–390. Participants included Adolf Hoffmann, Hermann Fleisner, Georg Hermann, Anna Schubert (German Working Group); Bertha Thalheimer, Ernst Meyer (Spartacus League); Paul Frölich (Bremen Left Radicals); Lenin, Zinoviev, Armand (RSDRP-Central Committee); Aksel'rod, Martov (RSDRP-Organization Committee); Mark Natanson, Vlasov [a pseudonym], Maksimilian Savel'ev (SR-Internationalist); Radek, Bronski, Stein (SDKPiL-Regional Presidium); Warszawski (SDKPiL-Main Presidium); Lapinski (PPS-L); Pierre Brizon (SFIO-Federation of Allier and CRRI); Alexandre Blanc, Jean-Pierre Raffin-Dugens (SFIO-Federations of Vaucluse and Isère); Henri Guilbeaux (*La Vie Ouvrière* group); Serrati, Lazzari, Modigliani, Enrico Dugoni, Camillo Prampolini, Elia Musatti (PSI); Platten, Nobs, Robmann, Graber (SPS); Kaclerović (Serbian Social Democratic party); Edmondo Peluso (Portuguese Socialist party); Münzenberg (Youth International); and Grimm, Balabanov, Naine, Morgari (ISC). Emily Hobhouse of the British ILP was present as an observer without a mandate from her organization. Greulich of the SPS was denied a mandate after a protest from the PSI concerning certain potentially embarrassing financial improprieties with which he had been involved.

274 Notes

11 E. Peluso, "Notes et impressions d'un délégué," *Demain* (May 1916): 343. The Hotel Bären is still in place. The owner possesses the registry for the Kiental conference with the names of delegates listed in Grimm's handwriting. Contrary to Peluso's impression, by contemporary standards the dining room is not spacious, but intimate.

12 The motion was signed by Lenin, Zinoviev, Armand, Radek, Bronski, Stein, Natanson, Vlasov, Savel'ev, Frölich, Münzenberg, Guilbeaux, Serrati, Peluso, Platten, Nobs, Robmann, Graber, and Kaclerović. Lademacher 1, pp. 307–8.

13 The members of the commission for the peace question were Meyer, Grimm, Martov, Graber, Hoffmann, Modigliani, Radek, Brizon, and Natanson. The commission on the ISB was made up of Schubert, Lenin, Naine, Thalheimer, Aksel'rod, Lazzari, and Warszawski. Lademacher 1, p. 345.

14 Described in Balabanov, *Erinnerungen und Erlebnisse*, p. 131. Gautschi, *Lenin*, p. 202, citing an interview with Nobs conducted decades after the event in question, has Grimm exclaiming "We will not allow ourselves to be intimidated by a minority!" Nobs recalls that "steering through Lenin's obstructions" was Grimm's primary task at Kiental. Ernst Nobs, "Lenin und die Schweizer Sozialdemokratie," *Rote Revue* 3(March 1954): 59.

15 The vote on the six project resolutions broke down as follows: drafting commission majority resolution, 10; drafting commission minority resolution, 12; Hoffmann's resolution, 2; Lapinski's resolution, 15; Serrati's resolution, 10; Zinoviev's resolution, 19. Lademacher 1, p. 374.

16 Angelica Balabanoff, *My Life as a Rebel* (New York, 1938), p. 141. The sun did rise over the Alps on the morning of 1 May 1916. According to Platten the weather during the Kiental sessions was "always lovely." Cited in Markus Mattmüller, *Leonhard Ragaz und der religiöse Sozialismus*, vol. 1 (Zürich, 1968), p. 181.

17 Lademacher 1, pp. 403–7.

18 *Spartakusbriefe*, p. 179. Liebknecht's leaflet "Auf zur Maifeier!" in Liebknecht, *Gesammelte Reden*, vol. 8, pp. 613–16, written for the 1916 May Day demonstration, also contains a critique of "conference politics."

19 Lenin, PSS, vol. 49, pp. 221–23.

20 Zinov'ev, *Sochineniia*, vol. 5, pp. 258–73. The evaluation by M. Bronski, "Die 2. Internationale Sozialistische Konferenz," *Jugend-Internationale* 4(January 1917): 3–4, is similarly ambivalent.

21 Participants included Hoffmann, Schubert, Meyer, Thalheimer (Germany); Natanson, Martov, Zinoviev (Russia); Radek, Warszawski, Lapinski (Poland); Brizon (France); Kaclerović (Serbia); Modigliani (Italy); and Robmann (Switzerland). The protocol is given in Lademacher 1, pp. 391–402.

22 Ibid., pp. 429–30.

23 Lenin, PSS, vol. 27, pp. 299–426. All citations are from the Russian text. See also D. Baevskii, "Kak leninskii 'Imperializm' uvidel svet," *Proletarskaia revoliutsiia* 1(1928): 31–37.

24 Lenin, PSS, vol. 26, pp. 29–30. E. G. Vasilevskii, *Razvitie vzgladov V. I. Lenina na imperializm (1893–1917 gg.)* (Moscow, 1969) provides a detailed and informative survey of the development of Lenin's conception of imperialism.

25 Lenin, PSS, vol. 28.

26 J. P. Hobson, *Imperialism: A Study* (London, 1902); Rudolf Hilferding, *Das Finanzkapital: Eine Studie über die jüngste Entwicklung des Kapitalismus* (Vienna, 1910); Luxemburg, GW, vol. 5; and Nikolai Bukharin, *Imperialism and World Economy* (New York, 1973). Bukharin's work originally appeared as "Mirovoe khoziaistvo i imperializm," *Kommunist* 1/2(1915): 4–49. K. Radek, "Die

Triebkräfte des Imperialismus," *Neues Leben* 3(March 1915): 70–79, summarizes left radical interpretations of imperialism from the point of view of the wartime left. See also Brynjolf J. Horde, "Socialistic Theories of Imperialism Prior to the Great War," *Journal of Political Economy* 5(October 1928): 569–91.

27 Allen Oakley, *Marx's Critique of Political Economy: Intellectual Sources and Evolution*, vol. 2 (London, 1985), pp. 207–77, and Ernest Mandel, *Marxist Economic Theory*, vol. 2 (New York, 1962), pp. 441–84.

28 K. Kautsky, "Nochmals unsere Illusionen: Eine Entgegnung," *Die Neue Zeit*, vol. 2, 1914/1915, pp. 230–41, 264–75.

29 Robert Grimm, "Von Zimmerwald bis Kiental," *Neues Leben* 5(May 1916): 129–37. On the Hague conference see Blänsdorf, *Die Zweite Internationale*, pp. 307–29, and Grass, *Friedensaktivität und Neutralität*, pp. 225–42.

30 Carsten, *War Against War*, p. 149. For accounts of the unrest in Germany see ibid., pp. 74–79; *Dokumente und Materialen der deutschen Arbeiterbewegung*, vol. 1, pp. 373–79; and "Situationsbericht aus Deutschland," *ISK Bulletin*, no. 6, 6 January 1917, pp. 3–6. Liebknecht's arrest is described by Paul Frölich, *Rosa Luxemburg: Her Life and Work* (London, 1940), p. 253. A report of 2 March 1916 from the German war ministry emphasizes the "growing effect" of revolutionary agitation. Volkmann, *Der Marxismus und das deutsche Heer*, pp. 279–82.

31 Lenin, PSS, vol. 27, pp. 294–95.

32 Edwyn Bevan, *German Social Democracy During the War* (London, 1918), p. 132.

33 Miller, *Burgfrieden und Klassenkampf*, pp. 133–43, and *Dokumente und Materialen der deutschen Arbeiterbewegung*, vol. 1, pp. 455–80.

34 "Einheit oder Spaltung der Partei?" in Radek, *In den Reihen der deutschen Revolution*, p. 337, and [Karl Radek], "An der Schwelle des dritten Kriegsjahres," *Die Arbeiterpolitik*, 5 August 1916. The latter article, like most of Radek's contributions to the *Arbeiterpolitik*, was published anonymously. According to Lerner, *Radek*, p. 50, "some issues of *Arbeiterpolitik* carry more writing by Radek than all the other contributors combined."

35 "Einheit oder Spaltung der Partei?" in Radek, *In den Reihen der deutschen Revolution*, p. 418.

36 Text in Eugen Prager, *Geschichte der U.S.P.D.: Entstehung und Entwicklung der Unabhängigen Sozialdemokratischen Partei Deutschlands* (Berlin, 1921), p. 128. Prior to the conference representatives of the Spartacus League, the Bremen Left Radicals, and the International Socialists of Germany met to discuss the creation of a left radical party, a step that the Spartacists vetoed. Heinz Wohlgemuth, *Die Entstehung der Kommunistischen Partei Deutschlands* (Berlin, 1968), p. 196.

37 Histories of the USPD by Robert F. Wheeler, *USPD und Internationale: Sozialistischer Internationalismus in der Zeit der Revolution* (Berlin, 1975), and David Morgan, *The Socialist Left and the German Revolution: A History of the German Independent Social Democratic Party, 1917–1922* (Ithaca, 1975) concur in emphasizing the organization's lack of coherence and long-term direction. Peter Lösche, *Der Bolschewismus im Urteil der deutschen Sozialdemokratie 1903–1920* (Berlin, 1967), p. 75, calls it a "hodge-podge." In addition to the Spartacists the USPD contained a radical left wing close to the Zimmerwald Left. See the statement by Heckert of Chemnitz (Karl-Marx-Stadt) at Gotha in Prager, *Geschichte der U.S.P.D.*, pp. 148–51, and Wolfgang Berg and Hermann Gram, eds., *Die revolutionäre Illusion: Zur Geschichte des linken Flügels der USPD: Erinnerungen von Curt Geyer* (Stuttgart, 1976).

38 See their joint statement in Emil Eichhorn, ed., *Protokoll über die Verhandlungen*

des Gründungsparteitag der U.S.P.D., vom 6. bis 8. April 1917 in Gotha (Berlin, 1921), pp. 26–28.

39 Jogiches' statement is cited in *Illustrierte Geschichte der deutschen Revolution* (Berlin, 1929), p. 147. The Bremen Left Radicals' response is contained in "Das Kompromis von Gotha," *Die Arbeiterpolitik*, 14 and 21 April 1917.

40 Hautmann, *Die Anfänge der linksradikalen Bewegung*, p. 7.

41 Hornik, "Die Zimmerwalder Linke und die Linksradikalen," p. 662. The center's motion received twenty-four votes. A left radical motion—which denounced the war as a product of imperialism, demanded the rejection of war credits, and backed the right to self-determination—could not be officially presented due to the lack of an accredited delegate willing to serve as sponsor.

42 Lenin, PSS, vol. 49, pp. 311–14. Radek offered a similar evaluation. K. Radek, "F. Adler und sein Tat," *Jugend-Internationale* 6(1916): 9–11, and "Die Tragödie des 21. Oktober," in *In den Reihen der deutschen Revolution*, pp. 397–401.

43 Hautmann, *Die Anfänge der linksradikalen Bewegung*, pp. 13–14, and F. Korit-schoner, "Iz zhizni avstriiskoi sotsial-demokratii," *Sbornik Sotsial-Demokrata* 2(December 1916): 44–45. In May 1917 a small conference of left radical leaders (thirty-two delegates were present) in Sankt Egyden (near Klagenfurt) approved the Kiental manifesto as the movement's "platform." Hornik, "Die Zimmer-walder Linke und die Linksradikalen," pp. 664–65.

44 Rosmer 2, pp. 186–91.

45 Cited in Bantke, "Lenin i tsimmerval'dskoe dvizhenie vo Frantsii," p. 113.

46 Described in Wohl, *French Communism*, pp. 76–87, and Kriegel, *Aux origines*, p. 138. Annie Kriegel, "Sur les rapports de Lénine avec le mouvement zimmerwaldien français," *Cahiers du monde russe et soviétique* 2(April–June 1962): 305, estimates that approximately one hundred militants were active members of the CRRI during 1916.

47 Rosmer 2, pp. 209–13.

48 During January 1917 a petition began to circulate among Zimmerwald affiliates calling for support for Wilson. Lademacher 2, p. 671. Loriot traveled to Switzerland during April to consult with Lenin prior to his departure for Russia.

49 Bekstrem, "K voprosu o vozniknovenie K. P. Shvetsii," pp. 97–98; Lars Björlin, "Vänstersocialism—kommunism 1916–1924," *Meddelande från Arbetarrörelsens Arkiv och Bibliotek* 24/25 (1982/1983): 6–12; and Höglund's comment "I vänstersocialismens tecken," *Stormklockan*, 19 May 1917. See also J. P. Mousson-Lestang, "Le parti social-démocrate suédois et le problème de la défense nationale (1914–1917)," *Revue historique* 90(1974): 373–408.

50 AAA: *Socialdemokratiska Ungdomsförbundet*, vol. 30, Kollontai to Ström, 18 February 1917, and Lenin, PSS, vol. 49, pp. 393–94.

51 BSP, *Sixth Annual Conference, Salford, 8–9 April* (London, 1917), pp. 43–45; Kendall, *The Revolutionary Movement in Britain*, p. 171; and Carsten, *War Against War*, pp. 105–7. The United Socialist Council was originally formed in 1913.

52 Malatesta, *I socialisti italiani*, pp. 117–18, and Ambrosoli, *Né aderire né sabotare*, pp. 157–58.

53 Paolo Spriano, *Storia del Partito comunista italiano*, vol. 1 (Turin, 1967), pp. 7–8, and Helmut König, *Lenin und der italienische Sozialismus 1915–1921: Ein Beitrag zur Gründungsgeschichte der Kommunistischen Internationale* (Tübingen, 1967), pp. 20–21. According to Spriano, the revolutionary intransigent current involved approximately 100 party sections.

54 The dynamism of the Left tendency and its inevitable growth toward the status of

a "movement" is emphasized by Karl Radek, "Zusammenbruch und Auferstehung der Internationale: Polemische Randglossen," *Neues Leben* 5(May 1916):
152–56, and H. Gorter, "Tegen het Pseudo-Marxisme," *De Nieuwe Tijd* 21(1916):
3–18, 66–69, 184–85.

55 Cited in Tiutiukin, *Voina, mir, i revoliutsiia*, p. 31.

56 Lenin's letter to Kharitonov of November 1915 in Lenin, PSS, vol. 49, pp. 165–66,
describes his first approaches to the Zürich left. On the Zürich left radical group,
an outgrowth of the Eintracht League, see M. Bronski, "Uchastie Lenina v shveitsarskom rabochem dvizhenii," *Proletarskaia revoliutsiia* 4(1924): 37; Hans-
Ulrich Jost, *Linksradikalismus in der deutschen Schweiz 1914–1918* (Bern,
1973), pp. 67–70; and Gautschi, *Lenin*, pp. 193–95. Regular participants included
Münzenberg, Platten, Bronski, Schweide, Giulio Mimiola, Nobs, Kharitonov,
Anny Morf, Willy Trostel, and Max Barthel. The group was nicknamed the
"Kegelklub" (bowling club).

57 SSA: "Sitzung des Parteivorstandes," 7 April 1916.

58 On the Aarau conference see Manfred, "Tsimmerval'dskoe dvizhenie v shveitsarskoi sotsial-demokratii," pp. 33–34, and Collart, *Le parti suisse et l'Internationale*, pp. 51–71. A powerful example of pacifist agitation within the SPS,
provided by a young Christian socialist about to evolve into a militant Leninist, is
Jules Humbert-Droz, *Guerre à la guerre: A bas l'armée* (La Chaux-de-Fonds,
1916). The pamphlet is the text of a speech delivered by Humbert-Droz in court
prior to his sentencing for refusal to enter military service.

59 The texts of the majority and minority theses, with Lenin's original marginal
notations, are given in *Leninskii sbornik*, vol. 17, pp. 42–54, and in the *Berner
Tagwacht*, 14 July and 16 August 1916. See also Robert Grimm, "Die Militärfrage," *Neues Leben* (July–August 1916): 193–222, and Robert Grimm, *Ab
Traktandum mit der Militärfrage* (Bern, 1917).

60 See Grimm, *Ab Traktandum*, p. 19, and Voight, *Robert Grimm*, p. 134.

61 A summary of the SPS-left's position is provided by Ernst Nobs, "Neuere Ent-
wicklungstendenzen in Militärwesen; Ein Beitrag zur Diskussion der Militärfrage," *Neues Leben* 6(June 1916): 170–181. Radek wrote to Nobs and Platten on
30 July asking them *not* to break entirely with Grimm, thus placing himself at
odds with Lenin on the issue. Lademacher 2, pp. 594–97.

62 SSA: "Sitzungen der Geschäftsleitung und des Parteivorstandes," 14 July and 5
August 1916.

63 In letters to Armand of 4 and 7 November, Lenin describes the meeting in some
detail. Lenin, PSS, vol. 49, pp. 318–19, 322–23.

64 *Protokoll über die Verhandlungen des Parteitages vom 4. und 5. November 1916,
abgehalten im Gesellschaftshaus "z. Kaufleuten" in Zürich* (Zürich, 1917), pp.
77–78. Lenin also briefly addressed the congress on behalf of the RSDRP. Lenin,
PSS, vol. 30, pp. 180–83.

65 For diverse examples of support for the slogan disarmament within factions close
to the Zimmerwald Left, see Implacabilis, "Antimilitarism," *Jugend-Internationale* 2(December 1915): 6–7; Eugen Olaussen, "Der Antimilitarismus in der
norwegischen Sozialdemokratie," *Jugend-Internationale* 3(March 1916): 8–10;
Henriette Roland-Holst, "Miliz oder Abrüstung?" *Neues Leben* 10/11(Octo-
ber/November 1915) and 12(December 1915): 324–31, 365–73; Robbins, *The
Abolition of War*, pp. 77–78; and Carsten, *War Against War*, pp. 66–70. The slogan
was also a source of conflict for the Tribunists. The SDP's sixth party congress in
Utrecht during 1915 debated the issue at length before approving a resolution

written by Gorter with strongly antimilitaristic, but not pacifistic, conclusions. See de Liagre Böhl, *Gorter*, p. 142.

66 They include "The Military Program of the Proletarian Revolution," written in September 1916 and subsequently published in somewhat altered form in *Sbornik Sotsial-Demokrata*; "The Tasks of the Zimmerwald Left in the Swiss Social Democratic Party," written in October and circulated as a brochure in French and German; "Theses on the Attitude of the Swiss Social Democratic Party toward War"; "A Principled Approach to the Military Question"; and others. Lenin, PSS, vol. 30, pp. 131–43, 151–62, 196–222.

67 Ibid., p. 133.

68 Ibid., pp. 152, 157.

69 Tiutiukin, *Voina, mir̃, i revoliutsiia*, pp. 280–87.

70 Arnold Struthahn [Karl Radek], "Nach dem Parteitage der Schweizer Sozialdemokratie," *Die Arbeiterpolitik*, 2 December 1916. In letters to Nobs and Platten written late in 1916, Radek claimed that the debate over the military question had completely altered his opinion of Grimm, who, he now believed, "must be struggled against." *IISG: Collection Nobs*, Radek to Nobs and Platten, n.d.

71 See the contrasting sets of project theses prepared by Lenin and Platten in Lenin, PSS, vol. 30, pp. 380–81, and *Leninskii sbornik*, vol. 17, pp. 54–64.

72 *SSA*: "Sitzungen der Geschäftsleitung und des Parteivorstandes," 26 December 1916 and 7 January 1917. The following citations are taken from the official protocols. A session of the managing committee on 6 January also opted for postponement by a narrow seven-five margin. For Grimm's justification for his position, see his letters to Nobs, Platten, and Radek in Lademacher 2, pp. 673–76.

73 See particularly his "Open Letter to the I.S.C. in Bern," in Lenin, PSS, vol. 30, pp. 286–95.

74 Ibid., vol. 49, pp. 357–58.

75 Münzenberg's recollection of the session mentions Lenin, Zinoviev, Radek, Krupskaia, Platten, Mimiola, Paul Levi, and a "member of the Swiss executive" as attendees. Gankin and Fisher, *Bolsheviks and the World War*, p. 538. Levi, Rosa Luxemburg's lawyer prior to the war and a future leader of the German Communist party, was a member of the Spartacus League. Gautschi, *Lenin*, p. 229, demonstrates that the session took place on 15 January. In many sources it is erroneously placed in early February.

76 Lenin, PSS, vol. 49, p. 383.

77 *SSA: Zimmerwald*, Schweizerische Gruppe der Zimmerwalder Linke, *Gegen die Lüge*; Gautschi, *Lenin*, pp. 230–33; and Lenin, PSS, vol. 30, p. 362. The Left resolution, signed by Affolter, Graber, Naine, Nobs, and Shmidt, was published in the Zürich social democratic newspaper *Volksrecht* on 9 January 1917. It was defeated by a vote of 189 to 32.

78 A protocol of the session is available in *SSA: Internationale Sozialistische Kommission zu Bern*, "Sitzungsprotokolle," 22 August 1916. See also Grimm's correspondence concerning the session and the text of invitations in Lademacher 1, pp. 433–34, and Lademacher 2, pp. 589, 594, 598.

79 *SSA: Internationale Sozialistische Kommission zu Bern*, "Sitzungsprotokolle," 12 December 1916.

80 Lademacher 1, pp. 435–38.

81 Lademacher 2, pp. 637–41.

82 Ibid., p. 641. Radek concludes that he speaks "for himself" but "is certain" that the Left organization stands behind him.

83 *SSA: Internationale Sozialistische Kommission zu Bern*, "Privat Besprechung

zwischen der ISK und von in der Schweiz anwesenden Genossen von einigen Zimmerwald angeschlossenen Parteien," Olten, 1 February 1917. See also the unofficial (and extremely cynical) account in Lademacher 2, pp. 682–84. Attendees included Grimm, Balabanov (ISC); Martov, Zinoviev, Natanson, and "a Bundist" (Russia); Radek (Poland); Levi (Germany); Peluso (Portugal); Guilbeaux (France); and Münzenberg (Youth International). Lenin gloated over the results, which he perceived as a blow to Grimm. Lenin, PSS, vol. 49, p. 379.

84 Ibid., pp. 340, 384, and vol. 30, p. 328. The Bolshevik organization was also weakened by late 1916, with *Sotsial-Demokrat* reduced to a tirage of three hundred copies. *Leninskii sbornik*, vol. 38, pp. 113, 170, and *Voprosy istorii KPSS* 4(1975): 8. In December 1916 the Petrograd party section began to call for cooperation with the Menshevik Central Initiative Group, the *Mezhraionka* (Interregional Group) (a small group seeking to bridge the gap between Bolsheviks and Mensheviks eventually to include Trotsky as a member), and the left SRs. See their statement "K voprosu o sovmestnykh vystupleniiakh," *Proletarskii Golos* 4(18 December 1916): 1.

85 Described in Fritz Platten, *Die Reise Lenins durch Deutschland im plombierten Wagen* (Berlin, 1924), and Michael Pearson, *The Sealed Train* (New York, 1975).

86 Lenin, PSS, vol. 31, p. 2.

87 *IISG: Collection Pannekoek*, no. 149. Cited from a manuscript written in 1952 as a tribute to Herman Gorter.

88 Karl Radek, "Zusammenbruch und Auferstehung der Internationale: Polemische Randglossen," *Neues Leben* 7/8(July/August 1916): 238–46.

89 Ibid., pp. 245–46.

6 Petrograd and Stockholm

The epitaph in blank verse which begins this chapter is inscribed on the monument to the victims of the February revolution on the Field of Mars in Leningrad.

1 According to reports from the high command, which may well have been distorted in an attempt to blame the breakdown in morale upon sedition, CRRI propaganda was instrumental in undermining discipline. Miquel, *La grande guerre*, p. 411. The interpretation is challenged by Guy Pedroncini, *Les mutineries de 1917* (Paris, 1967), who attempts to distinguish between "political" motivation and general war-weariness. See also Paul Painlevé, *Comment j'ai nommé Foch et Pétain* (Paris, 1924), pp. 165–75.

2 In Britain over a million workers struck during 1917, with more than six million labor days lost. In France the number of strikes more than doubled from 1916 to 1917, with over two million labor days lost. M. M. Karliner, *Rabochee dvizhenie v Anglii v gody pervoi mirovoi voiny 1914–1918* (Moscow, 1961), and Labi, *La grande division des travailleurs*, p. 77. On the Turin uprising see John Cammett, *Antonio Gramsci and the Origins of Italian Communism* (Stanford, 1967), pp. 47–55, and Paolo Spriano, *Torino operaia nella grande guerra* (Turin, 1960).

3 These events are described in Volkmann, *Der Marxismus und das deutsche Heer*, pp. 165–66, 176–82; Willi Gautschi, *Der Landesstreik 1918 (Einsiedeln, 1968)*; Forcadell, *Parlamentarismo y Bolchevización*; Sigurd Klockare, *Svenska revolutionen 1917–1918* (Halmstad, 1967), pp. 31–84; and Kulemann, *Am Beispiel des Austromarxismus*, pp. 200–205.

4 Bünger, *Die sozialistische Antikriegsbewegung*, pp. 159–63, and Graubard, *British Labour and the Russian Revolution*, pp. 36–37.

5 Max Weber, *Wahlrecht und Demokratie in Deutschland* (Berlin, 1918), p. 44.

6 See Kirby, *War, Peace and Revolution*, p. 151, and the entire discussion on pp. 130–51.

7 The key intermediary was Alexander Helphand (Parvus). See Winfried B. Scharlau and Zbynek A. Zeman, *Freibeuter der Revolution: Parvus-Helphand, eine politische Biographie* (Cologne, 1964), pp. 260–261, and P. G. Chesnais, *Parvus et le parti danois* (Paris, 1918). According to Fritz Fischer, *Germany's Aims in the First World War* (London, 1977), p. 150, the German Foreign Ministry elected to "put all its money on the Bolsheviks" as early as November 1915.

8 Luxemburg, GW, vol. 4, pp. 242–45; A. Pannekoek, "Rusland, Duitsland, Amerika," *De Nieuwe Tijd* (March 1917): 229–32; and "Die Revolution in Russland," *Die Arbeiterpolitik*, 24 March 1917.

9 Robert Paul Browder and Alexander F. Kerensky, eds., *The Russian Provisional Government 1917: Documents*, vol. 1 (Stanford, 1961), pp. 157–58. Miliukov's commitment to the Entente is rationalized and interpreted in P. N. Miliukov, *Pochemu i zachem my voiuem?* (Petrograd, 1917); P. N. Miliukov, *Istoriia vtoroi russkoi revoliutsii* (Sofia, 1921), pp. 61–70; and Thomas Riha, *A Russian European: Paul Miliukov in Russian Politics* (South Bend, 1969), pp. 281–94.

10 Frank Alfred Golder, ed., *Documents of Russian History 1914–1917* (New York, 1927), pp. 325–26, and N. N. Sukhanov, *Zapiski o revoliutsii*, vol. 2 (Berlin, 1922), pp. 144–49. Sukhanov was the principle author.

11 Ziva Galila y Garcia, "The Origins of Revolutionary Defensism: I. G. Tsereteli and the 'Siberian Zimmerwaldists'," *The Slavic Review* 3(1982): 454–76; Rex A. Wade, "Irakli Tsereteli and Siberian Zimmerwaldism," *Journal of Modern History* 4(1967): 425–31; and W. H. Roobol, *Tsereteli—A Democrat in the Russian Revolution: A Political Biography* (The Hague, 1976), pp. 66–182. See also Tsereteli's defense of his policy before the Petrograd Soviet in *Izvestiia Petrogradskogo Soveta*, 21 March 1917, pp. 2–3.

12 Golder, *Documents of Russian History*, pp. 329–31.

13 M. N. Pokrovskii and I. A. Iakovlev, eds., *1917 god v dokumentakh i materialakh*, vol. 4 (Moscow, 1927), pp. 39–40, and Browder and Kerensky, *The Russian Provisional Government*, vol. 2, pp. 1082–85.

14 *Listovki peterburgskikh bol'shevikov 1902–1917*, vol. 2 (Leningrad, 1957), pp. 251–52.

15 Cited in Aleksandr G. Shliapnikov, *Semnadtsatyi god*, vol. 2 (Moscow, 1931), pp. 183–84.

16 Lenin, PSS, vol. 31, pp. 113–14. See also his "Letters From Afar," ibid., p. 53.

17 Cited in Rex A. Wade, *The Russian Search for Peace February–October 1917* (Stanford, 1969), p. 32.

18 Browder and Kerensky, *The Russian Provisional Government*, vol. 2, p. 1098.

19 General discussions of the Provisional Government's foreign policy are provided by Dietrich Geyer, "Die russischen Räte und die Friedensfrage im Frühjahr und Sommer 1917," *Vierteljahrshefte für Zeitgeschichte* (Stuttgart, 1957), pp. 220–40; L. P. Morris, "The Russians, the Allies, the War, February–July 1917," *The Slavonic and East European Review* 118(1972): 29–48; Wade, *The Russian Search for Peace*; Jürgen Stillig, *Die russische Februarrevolution 1917 und die sozialistische Friedenspolitik* (Cologne, 1977); and A. V. Ignat'ev, *Vneshniaia politika vremennogo pravitel'stva* (Moscow, 1974).

20 The allied socialist parties originally declined to participate in a general conference, while the SPD was supportive. The members of the Dutch-Scandinavian committee were Branting, Gustav Möller, Ernst Söderberg (Sweden); Stauning (Denmark); Jakob Vidnes (Norway); and Troelstra, Huysmans, Hendrik van Kol,

Florentius Wibaut, and Johan Albarda (The Netherlands). See Gankin and Fisher,
pp. 590–93. Kirby, *War, Peace and Revolution*, p. 89, cites a remark by Stauning
specifying the committee's intention to "head off" the Zimmerwald movement.

21 Pokrovskii and Iakovlev, *1917 god*, vol. 4, pp. 95–97, and vol. 1, p. 101.

22 Ibid., vol. 1, pp. 127–28, and vol. 2, pp. 428–34; Golder, *Documents of Russian
History*, pp. 340–43; and Shliapnikov, *Semnadtsatyi god*, vol. 4, pp. 34–35. The
Mensheviks divided over the issue, and at a party conference on 20–24(7–11)
May, a "Menshevik-Internationalist" faction led by Martov split away. Martov
urged an ultimatum to the allies demanding a common peace platform and if need
be a "separate war" waged by Russia alone.

23 The convoluted negotiations are described in Fainsod, *International Socialism*,
pp. 163–190; Hildamarie Meynell, "The Stockholm Conference of 1917," *International Review of Social History* 1/2 (1960): 1–25, 200–225; Kirby, *War, Peace
and Revolution*, pp. 95–129, 152–87; and S. A. Mogilevskii, "Taktika mezhdunarodnogo opportunizma v voprosakh voiny i mira (fevral'–oktiabr' 1917 g.),"
Voprosy istorii 12(1963): 103–14.

24 Lenin, PSS, vol. 31, p. 367.

25 Edmund Wilson, *To the Finland Station: A Study in the Writing and Acting of
History* (New York, 1940).

26 The session is described by Balabanoff, *Erinnerungen und Erlebnisse*, pp. 135–37.
The ISC had already met with representatives of the Russian Zimmerwaldist
organizations in Bern on 19–20 February, during the crisis leading up to the fall of
the czar, in a session marked by a sharp clash between Zinoviev and Martov. *SSA:
Internationale Sozialistische Kommission*, "Konferenz zwischen der ISK und den
Vertretern der russischen Revolution." In a letter to Morgari written on 15 May
Grimm called the transfer of the ISC to Stockholm "indispensable if we want to
accomplish anything." *ACS: Collection Morgari*, busta 14, fasc. 30, sotto. 1–3.

27 Angelica Balabanoff, *Die Zimmerwalder Bewegung, 1914–1919* (Leipzig, 1928),
pp. 57–58.

28 *ACS: Collection Morgari*, busta 14, fasc. 30, sotto. 14. At Grimm's urging Morgari
made a yeoman effort to arrive in Stockholm but, as a representative of an allied
power, could not arrange for a naval booking. He wrote to Grimm on 16 June
announcing that he was abandoning the effort and delegated Balabanov to represent the PSI in Stockholm. Ibid., busta 31, fasc. 31, sotto. 3.

29 Cited from a letter addressed to the ISC in *AAA: Internationella Socialistiska
Kommissionen*, no. 10.

30 Their activities are described in Balabanoff, *Erinnerungen und Erlebnisse*, pp.
153–54. Grimm was clearly anxious to reach the Russian capital. On 26 April, at
the last session of the SPS managing committee that he attended prior to departing, he announced that he would enter Russia "on 19 May" in order to help
facilitate the return of political émigrés. *SSA:* "Sitzung der Geschäftsleitung," 26
April 1917. In the Swiss socialist press on 21 April he announced his imminent
departure "for Russia" as a representative of the "Central Committee for Russian
Political Refugees in Switzerland." "Grimm n'est pas à Stockholm," *La Sentinelle*, 21 April 1917.

31 Accounts are provided by Balabanoff, *Erinnerungen und Erlebnisse*, pp. 148–50,
and Balabanoff, *Die Zimmerwalder Bewegung*, pp. 58–59. In addition to Grimm
and Balabanov those present included Kamenev, Lenin, Zinoviev (RSDRP-Central
Committee); Rafail Abramovich (Bund); Natanson (SRS); Lapinski (SDKPiL-Main
Presidium); Martov, Mikhail Lurie (Larin), Grigorii Bienstok, Martynov (RSDRP-Organization Committee and Menshevik-Internationalist); Rakovski (Social

Democratic party of Romania); and Riasanov, Mikhail Uritskii, and Trotsky (*Mezhraionka*). The *Mezhraionka* organization, which counted approximately 150 members, merged with the Bolsheviks during August.

32 Balabanoff, *Die Zimmerwalder Bewegung*, pp. 59–60.

33 The entire "Grimm affair" is thoroughly documented in Lademacher 1, pp. 573–644. Aksel'rod was particularly active on Grimm's behalf, while ISC member Naine led a campaign calling for his expulsion. During the late summer of 1917, after a bout with illness, Grimm composed the pamphlet *Zimmerwald-Kiental* (Bern, 1917), which, with its eloquent evocation of the goal of peace, serves as a kind of testament for his stewardship of the Zimmerwald movement.

34 *ACS: Collection Morgari*, busta 14, fasc. 30, sotto. 1–3.

35 The activities of the ISC in Stockholm during the remainder of 1917 are sometimes difficult to document. Balabanov's memoirs are the basic source, but they must be used judiciously. The memoirs of Ture Nerman, *Allt var rött*, and Zeth Höglund, *Minnen i fackelsken*, vol. 3, *Revolutionernas år 1917–1921* (Stockholm, 1963), discuss the period but scarcely mention the ISC. The committee maintained a small office at Regeringsgatan 67. The unpublished memoir of Wilhelm Dittmann describes a meeting between USPD delegates and the ISC conducted in the office on 31 July, which according to Dittmann was dominated by Balabanov. Balabanov characterized her position at the moment as closest to that of the Menshevik-Internationalists, but added with characteristic bathos that "my heart is pulling me toward the Bolsheviks." *IISG*: Dittmann-Kotowski, *Erinnerungen*, pp. 804–6.

36 Balabanoff, *Die Zimmerwalder Bewegung*, pp. 66–68. In attendance were Balabanov (ISC); Rosanov, Goldenberg, Gurevich (Petrograd Soviet); Kyrkov (Bulgarian Narrows); Yrjö Sirola (Finnish Social Democratic party); Kautsky, Haase, Zietz, Kohn (USPD); Olaussen (Norwegian Youth League); Otto Lang (SPS); Vorovskii, Radek, Hanecki (Bolshevik Agency of the Central Committee Abroad); and Boris Reinstein (U.S. Socialist Labor party).

37 Lademacher 1, pp. 442–43.

38 Iu. I. Vorobtsova, *Deiatel'nost' predstavitel'stva TsK RSDRP(b) v Stokgol'me (Aprel'–Noiabr' 1917 g.)* (Moscow, 1968), p. 130. A brief protocol of the session is available in *AAA: Internationella Socialistiska Kommissionen*, no. 3. The *ISK Nachrichtendienst*, no. 15, 22 July 1917, had tentatively proposed the scheduling of a third Zimmerwaldist conference for 10 August.

39 See "Die Retter der russischen Revolution," *ISK Nachrichtendienst*, no. 15, 22 July 1917, and the circular letter published in ibid., no. 20, 20 August 1917.

40 Balabanoff, *Die Zimmerwalder Bewegung*, pp. 86–89.

41 Lenin, PSS, vol. 31, p. 116.

42 Ibid., pp. 149–86.

43 "Revoliutsiia rastet vo vsem mir," *Pravda*, 9 May 1917.

44 Lenin, PSS, vol. 31, p. 341.

45 The account of the conference and all citations are taken from the official protocol, *Sed'maia ("Aprel'skaia") vserossiiskaia i petrogradskaia obshchegorodskaia konferentsiia RSDRP(b), Aprel' 1917* (Moscow, 1934). The clash between Lenin and Zinoviev was not incongruent. At issue was a tactical point, not a question of general orientation. What is more, Zinoviev was never entirely subservient to Lenin's views. Though a less incisive theorist, he maintained an independent perspective that was most clearly revealed later in the year with his attempt to oppose the decision to take power. See Myron W. Hedlin, "Zinoviev's Revolutionary Tactics in 1917," *The Slavic Review* 1(March 1975): 19–43.

46 The activities of the agency are described in Iu. I. Vorobtsova, "Zagranichnoe predstavitel'stvo TsK RSDRP(b) v 1917 g.," *Voprosy istorii KPSS* 6(1966): 30–38, and Vorobtsova, *Deiatel'nost' predstavitel'stva TsK.* Also of interest are the recollections of Ia. Ganetskii, *O Lenine* (Moscow, 1933), pp. 65–66, and V. V. Vorovskii, *Sochineniia*, vol. 3 (Moscow, 1933), pp. 358–63. N. E. Korolev, "V. I. Lenin i tsimmerval'dskoe ob"edinenie (Fevral'–Oktiabr' 1917 goda)," *Voprosy istorii KPSS* 2(1960): 139–55, cites a number of sources relevant to its activities from the Soviet Central Party Archive and the Central State Archive of the October Revolution. According to Vorobtsova its official archive has been lost.

47 A. Shliapnikov, "Fevral'skaia revoliutsiia i evropeiskie sotsialisty," *Krasnyi arkhiv* 16(1926): 32.

48 Vorobtsova, "Zagranichnoe predstavitel'stvo," pp. 32–33, and *Deiatel'nost' predstavitel'stva TsK*, pp. 17–18. For a humorous description of the use made of the diplomatic pouch, see I. Ganetskii, *V. V. Vorovskii: bibliograficheskii ocherk* (Moscow/Leningrad, 1925), pp. 51–52.

49 B. M. Volin, "Biulleteni bol'shevistskoi partii vykhodivshie v Stokgol'me v 1917 godu," *Voprosy istorii* 4(1955): 124–27.

50 The journal was entitled *Bulletin des Ausschusses für Angelegenheiten des ZK der Arbeiter- und Soldatendelegiertenräte* (Bulletin of the Committee for Foreign Affairs of the Central Committee of the Soviet of Workers' and Soldiers' Deputies) (hereinafter cited as *Bulletin des Ausschusses*). Thirty-one numbers were issued in Stockholm during 1917. Much of the material is translated from the Soviet organ *Izvestiia Petrogradskogo Soveta.*

51 *Bulletin des Ausschusses*, nos. 3 and 7, 5 and 15 July 1917.

52 Pokrovskii and Iakovlev, *1917 god*, vol. 4, pp. 50–60, and *Bulletin des Ausschusses*, no. 2, 30 June 1917.

53 Vorobtsova, *Deiatel'nost' predstavitel'stva TsK*, pp. 110–47.

54 The International Socialists of Germany disbanded after the embarrassing disclosure, in July 1917, that their leader Borchardt had been contributing articles under a pen name to a right wing, mildly pornographic Berlin tabloid. For a comment from the left see "Abtrünnig!" *Die Arbeiterpolitik*, 4 August 1917.

55 "An die linksradikalen Ortsgruppen und Genossen!" *Die Arbeiterpolitik*, 28 July 1917.

56 Lenin, PSS, vol. 49, p. 440. Lenin was not deterred by the prospect of temporary isolation. "Better a small fish than a large cockroach," he wrote to Radek. Ibid., pp. 443–44.

57 Balabanoff, *Die Zimmerwalder Bewegung*, p. 67.

58 See Bartel, *Die Linken in der deutschen Sozialdemokratie*, p. 475; de Liagre Böhl, *Gorter*, pp. 159–63; I. Samoilov, *S bolshevite v borba za nov Internatsional: Partiata na tesnite i tsimmervaldskoto obedidenie* (Sofia, 1964), pp. 153–80; and Lev Trotskii, *Programma mira; K Stokgol'mskoi konferentsii* (Petrograd, 1917). The Tribunist leadership divided over the Stockholm project, with Wijnkoop and van Ravestejn remaining open to collaboration while Gorter and Luteraan supported the Left in calling for an unconditional boycott. See the latter's typewritten manuscript "Internationale Arbeiderspolitiek," dated 25 October 1917, in *IISG: Collection van Ravestejn.*

59 "Die Offensive und die Stockholmer Friedenskonferenz," *Russische Korrespondenz "Prawda"*, 14 July 1917, pp. 1–5. On the ISC session see Balabanoff, *Die Zimmerwalder Bewegung*, pp. 74–75, and Shliapnikov, "Fevral'skaia revoliutsiia," p. 32.

284 Notes

60 Balabanoff, *Die Zimmerwalder Bewegung*, pp. 75–82. The statement was published in *Politiken* on 27 July and the German *Vorwärts* on 28 July.

61 Radek, "Avtobiografiia," p. 116; Vorobtsova, *Deiatel'nost' predstavitel'stva TsK*, pp. 125–27; and Temkin, *Lenin*, pp. 578–80.

62 *Russische Korrespondenz "Prawda"*, 19 August 1917.

63 Lenin, PSS, vol. 33, pp. 4–118. All citations in the discussion that follow are drawn from the Russian text.

64 For an interpretation of Gramsci's thought as an extension of Leninism, see Christine Buci-Glucksmann, *Gramsci et l'Etat* (Paris, 1975). F. M. Burlatskii, *Lenin, gosudarstvo, politika* (Moscow, 1970), pp. 121–22, suggests that the Russian word used by Lenin to denote "state" (*gosudarstvo*) does not primarily connote centralized authority, but rather "the entire political structure of society," a concept close to Gramsci's "organic state."

65 Lucio Colletti, *From Rousseau to Lenin: Studies in Ideology and Society* (New York, 1972), pp. 224–25.

66 Luxemburg, GW, vol. 4, pp. 332–65.

67 Angelica Balabanoff, "La IIIe Conférence de Zimmerwald," *Demain* (December 1917): 93–100. The same point is made in "Kring fredskonferenserna: Stockholm eller Zimmerwald?" *Stormklockan*, 8 September 1917.

68 Carl Landauer, *European Socialism: A History of Ideas and Movements*, vol. 1 (Berkeley, 1959), p. 612.

69 K. Radek, "Zimmerwald an der Scheidewege," *Jugend-Internationale* 9(September 1917): 2–4.

70 The following account is based upon the brief protocol in Lademacher 1, pp. 445–84; Balabanoff, *Die Zimmerwalder Bewegung*, pp. 90–107; and Nerman, *Allt var rött*, pp. 214–15. Delegations included Ledebour, Haase, Arthur Stadthagen, Duncker, Adolf Hofer, Robert Wengels (USPD); Aksel'rod, Makadziub (RSDRP-Organization Committee); Osip Ermanskii (Menshevik-Internationalists); Vorovskii (RSDRP-Central Committee); Radek, Hanecki (SDKPiL-Regional Presidium); Kharlakov, Popovich (Bulgarian Broads); Kyrkov, Kolarov (Bulgarian Narrows); Sirola (Finnish Social Democratic party); Alexander Constantinescu, Jon Frimu (Romanian Social Democratic party); Nobs, Rosa Bloch (SPS); James Eads How, Fritz Rozin (U.S. Socialist Propaganda League); Egede Nissen, Ernst Christian, Johannes Erwig (Norwegian Socialist Youth League); Oskar Samuelson, Ström, Carl Lindhagen, Jeory Lindström (Swedish Left Socialist party and Swedish Socialist Youth League); Therese Schlesinger, Luzzato (Austrian Social Democratic Labor party); and Balabanov, Carleson, Höglund, and Nerman (ISC). Motions presented on behalf of the Zimmerwald Left were supported by the Bolsheviks, the SDKPiL-Regional Presidium, the Scandinavian Left Socialists, the Bulgarian Narrows, the Austrian left radicals, the U.S. Socialist Propaganda League, and Duncker for the Spartacus League.

71 Balabanoff, *Die Zimmerwalder Bewegung*, pp. 93–95.

72 Gankin and Fisher, *Bolsheviks and the World War*, pp. 676–77. Duncker also submitted a peace program on behalf of the Spartacus League that once again challenged Lenin's position on the national question. Full text in Prager, *Geschichte der U.S.P.D.*, pp. 157–60.

73 The members of the committee were Haase, Ledebour, Ermanskii, Radek, Balabanov, Schlesinger, Höglund, and Duncker. Balabanoff, *Die Zimmerwalder Bewegung*, p. 97.

74 Ibid., p. 108, and Balabanov, *Iz lichnykh vospominanii*, p. 159.

75 "Die dritte Zimmerwalder Konferenz," *Bote der russischen Revolution*, no. 5, 13 October 1917, p. 9. This article was almost certainly written by Radek.
76 Korolev, "Lenin i tsimmerval'dskoe ob"edinenie," p. 155, and Vorobtsova, *Deiatel'nost' predstavitel'stva TsK*, pp. 137–38.
77 "Die Revolution in Gefahr," *Bulletin des Ausschusses*, no. 31, 17 November 1917, pp. 1–10.
78 J. Weinberg, "Die Imperialisten gegen Frieden und Sozialismus," ibid., no. 10, 27 July 1917.
79 K. Radek, "Nach Sechs Monaten," *Bote der russischen Revolution*, no. 1, 15 September 1917, and "Stockholm," ibid., pp. 6–12.
80 "Die dritte Zimmerwalder Konferenz," p. 8, and K. Radek, "Die Revolution und der Bruch mit der Bourgeoisie in Russland," *Bote der russischen Revolution*, no. 4, 6 October 1917, pp. 1–5. See also the identical conclusions in H. Gorter, "De taktiek der Russische maximalisten," *De Tribune*, 18 September 1917.
81 "Die Revolution in Gefahr," p. 8.
82 "An die Proletarier aller Länder!" *ISK Nachrichtendienst*, no. 28, 10 November 1917, and for the "Decree on Peace," *Dokumenty vneshnei politiki SSSR*, vol. 1 (Moscow, 1957), p. 12.
83 Texts in Balabanoff, *Die Zimmerwalder Bewegung*, pp. 113–15; *KPSS v bor'be za pobedy Velikoi Oktiabrskoi Sotsialisticheskoi revoliutsii: Sbornik dokumentov, 5 iulia-5 noiabria 1917 g.* (Moscow, 1937), pp. 69–72; and *Bote der russischen Revolution*, no. 9/10, 17 November 1917.
84 For examples, see "Der Sieg der Bolschewiks," *Die Arbeiterpolitik*, 17 November 1917 (the entire edition is printed on red paper); the statement issued by the PSI-revolutionary intransigent faction after a caucus in Florence on 18 November in König, *Lenin und der italienische Sozialismus*, pp. 22–23; and the manifesto "Pour l'Action," composed for the CRRI by Loriot during November in Rolland, *Journal*, p. 1185.

7 The Origins of Communist Internationalism

1 Cited from *L'Humanité*, 24 April 1919.
2 New affiliates included the Social Democratic party of Bosnia and Herzegovina and the Socialist Labor party of Denmark (created in April 1918 on the model of the Swedish Left Socialist party). Balabanov dominated the ISC in its post-October 1917 phase.
3 "Kommt das Befreiungslicht nur vom Osten?," *ISK Nachrichtendienst*, no. 29, 22 November 1917, pp. 1–3.
4 "Debout, pour la manifestation du premier mai," ibid., no. 39, 1 April–1 May 1918, p. 1.
5 "An die Zimmerwalder Parteien. An die Arbeiterklasse," ibid., no. 35, 6 February 1918, pp. 1–3.
6 "Appel de la Commission de Zimmerwald aux masses ouvrières de tous les pays," ibid., no. 44, 1 September 1918.
7 *Vtoroi vserossiiskii s"ezd sovetov* (Petrograd, 1917), pp. 24–25.
8 Karl Radek, "Die Friedensfrage und unsere Aufgabe," *Bote der russischen Revolution*, no. 11, 28 November 1917, p. 2.
9 Good accounts of the Brest-Litovsk negotiations are provided by John W. Wheeler-Bennett, *Brest-Litovsk: The Forgotten Peace, March 1918* (London, 1938), and Richard K. Debo, *Revolution and Survival: The Foreign Policy of Soviet Russia*

1917–18 (Toronto, 1979), pp. 45–169. There is a large Soviet literature, including A. O. Chubar'ian, *Brestskii mir* (Moscow, 1964).

10   The left communist tendency is analyzed by Robert Vincent Daniels, *The Conscience of the Revolution: Communist Opposition in Soviet Russia* (Cambridge, Mass., 1960), pp. 70–91; Leonard Schapiro, *The Origin of the Communist Autocracy: Political Opposition in the Soviet State: The First Phase, 1917–1922* (London, 1955), pp. 130–46; and Cohen, *Bukharin*, pp. 62–69.

11   Lenin, PSS, vol. 35, p. 245.

12   The text of the treaty is given in *Dokumenty vneshnei politiki SSSR*, vol. 1, pp. 119–205.

13   These meetings are reported in *Pravda*, 12 February and 17 March 1918. See also Reisberg, *Lenin und die Zimmerwalder Bewegung*, p. 262. The "Federation of Foreign Communist Groups" devoted most of its efforts to work among prisoners of war.

14   *Spartakusbriefe*, pp. 469–71.

15   Cited from Ruth Fischer, *Stalin und der deutsche Kommunismus: Der Uebergang zur Konterrevolution* (Frankfurt am Main, 1950), p. 60.

16   Lenin, PSS, vol. 37, p. 455.

17   Wilhelm Groener, *Lebenserinnerungen* (Göttingen, 1957), p. 467.

18   The proposal was dated 14 November 1918. Its origins are described in Fainsod, *International Socialism*, pp. 241–47.

19   Samuil S. Bantke, ed., *Bor'ba Bol'shevikov za sozdanie Kommunisticheskogo Internatsionala. Materialy i dokumenty 1914–1919 gg.* (Moscow, 1934), pp. 105–6.

20   Texts in Lenin, PSS, vol. 50, pp. 460–62, and Luxemburg, GW, vol. 4, pp. 440–49.

21   *Pervyi kongress Kominterna* (Moscow, 1933), p. 123.

22   Ibid., pp. 132–33.

23   The continuity of Lenin's struggle for a revolutionary International is the theme of Ia. G. Temkin and B. M. Tupolev, *Ot vtorogo k Tret'emu Internatsionalu* (Moscow, 1978), in some ways a summary of the best and worst in Soviet scholarship devoted to the Zimmerwald Left. See also the critical review by L. A. Slepov in *Voprosy istorii* 4(1979): 179–81.

24   Warren Lerner, "Attempting a Revolution from Without: Poland in 1920," in Thomas T. Hammond, ed., *The Anatomy of Communist Takeovers* (New Haven, 1975), pp. 94–106, and M. N. Tukhachevskii, *Voina klassov* (Moscow, 1921).

25   Text in Helmut Gruber, ed., *International Communism in the Age of Lenin: A Documentary History* (New York, 1972), pp. 241–46.

26   See James Hulse, *The Forming of the Communist International* (Stanford, 1964).

27   See his pamphlet "Left-Wing Communism: An Infantile Disorder," in Lenin, PSS, vol. 41, pp. 1–104.

28   At the congress of Orléans in September–October 1920, the CGT left opted to affiliate with the communist movement in remarking that it was "necessary to go to Moscow just as, in 1915, it was necessary to go to Zimmerwald." Cited in Labi, *La grande division des travailleurs*, p. 188.

29   Ambrosoli, *Né aderire né sabotare*, p. 302, and König, *Lenin und der italienische Sozialismus*, p. 23.

30   Kautsky, *Der Wer zur Macht*, p. 104.

31   Harding, *Lenin's Political Thought*, vol. 2, p. 237.

32   Emil Barth, *Aus der Werkstatt der deutschen Revolution* (Berlin, 1919), p. 8.

33   Herman Gorter, *Die Wereldrevolutie* (Amsterdam, 1918). See also the summary in de Liagre Böhl, *Gorter*, pp. 194–200.

34 Luxemburg, GW, vol. 4, p. 160.
35 Immanuel Wallerstein, *The Capitalist World System* (Cambridge, 1979), p. 30.
36 Lenin, PSS, vol. 31, p. 98.
37 Georges Haupt, "Guerre et révolution chez Lénine," *Revue française de science politique* 2(1971): 256–81.
38 Luxemburg, GW, vol. 4, p. 507.
39 Karl Radek, "Die internationale Friedensaktion des Proletariats," *Neues Leben* 7(July 1915): 247.
40 For example Z. P. Iukhimovich, "Marksistskaia kontseptsiia mira: traditsii i sovremennost'," *Voprosy istorii* 5(1986): 11–13. A good example of antiwar literature reflecting the priorities of the Zimmerwald Left is Aleksandra Kollontai, *Komu nuzhno voina?* (Munich, 1916).
41 The remark, attributed to Stalin by Marshall Sergei Biriuzov in his introduction to a republication of the collected works of Mikhail Tukhachevskii, may be apocryphal. M. N. Tukhachevskii, *Izbrannye proizvedeniia*, vol. 1 (Moscow, 1964), p. 12.
42 *Programma Kommunisticheskoi Partii Sovetskogo Soiuza: Novaia redaktsiia* (Moscow, 1986), pp. 20–21. See also O. Bykov, "Revoliutsionnaia teoriia izbavleniia chelovechestva ot voin," *Mirovaia ekonomika i mezhdunarodnye otnosheniia* 4(1983): 3–17.
43 Ho Chi Minh, *De la révolution 1920–1966* (Paris, 1968), p. 25.
44 Stalin, *Sochineniia*, vol. 28, p. 468.
45 V. I. Lenin, *Filosofskie tetradi* (Moscow, 1969).
46 Anton Pannekoek, "Marxismus als Tat," *Lichtstrahlen* (March 1915): 99–102.
47 Antonio Gramsci, *Scritti giovanili 1914–1918* (Turin, 1958), p. 150.
48 According to Milorad Drachkovitch and Branko Lazitch, *The Revolutionary Internationals, 1864–1943* (Stanford, 1966), p. 162, "the overwhelming majority of Comintern leaders in the period between 1919 and 1921 were under thirty years of age, and many of them under twenty-five."
49 Arno Mayer, *The Political Origins of the New Diplomacy, 1917–1918* (New Haven, 1959), p. 393.
50 A. J. P. Taylor, *The Struggle for Mastery in Europe* (Oxford, 1954), pp. xx–xxi.
51 Victor Serge, *Mémoires d'un révolutionnaire* (Paris, 1957), p. 225, recounts an attempt by Zinoviev to use the legacy of Zimmerwald to rally opposition to Stalin's tightening grip upon the machinery of the Comintern during 1927. "We'll recommence the Zimmerwald movement," he quotes Zinoviev as stating to a group of dissidents. "Do you remember, all Europe at war and this handful of internationalists gathered in a Swiss village—we're already stronger than we were then." Serge notes his astonishment at Zinoviev's *"simplisme."*
52 Robert Gilpin, *War and Change in World Politics* (Cambridge, 1981), p. 76.
53 Paul Lensch, *Drei Jahre Weltrevolution* (Berlin, 1917), pp. 8, 16. See also Robert Sigel, *Die Lensch-Cunow-Hänisch Gruppe: Eine Studie zum rechten Flügel der SPD im Ersten Weltkrieg* (Berlin, 1976).
54 *Official Bulletin of the International Labour and Socialist Conference, Berne, 3rd. February 1919*, vol. 1, nr. 1, p. 2.
55 Georg Lukacs, *History and Class Consciousness: Studies in Marxist Dialectics* (Cambridge, 1971), pp. 302–3.
56 See his famous essay "The Modern Prince" in Antonio Gramsci, *Selections From the Prison Notebooks* (New York, 1971), pp. 121–205.
57 Cited from the essay "Leninismo e socialdemocrazia," in Lucio Colletti, *Tra marxismo e no* (Bari, 1979), pp. 189–96.

58 Robert F. Wheeler, "Revolutionary Socialist Internationalism: Rank-and-File Reaction in the USPD," *International Review of Social History* 22 (1977): 329.
59 Cited from Raymond Lefebvre, *L'Internationale des Soviets* (1919) in Wohl, *French Communism*, pp. 145–46.

Selected Bibliography

There is an immense scholarly literature devoted to the general themes of international socialism and the First World War. Only works with some direct relevance to the present study are cited below. A number of works that are referenced on one occasion only in the text are not listed.

Archival Sources

Arbetarrörelsens Arkiv (AAA), Stockholm
   File Internationella Socialistiska Kommissionen
   File Socialdemokratiska Ungdomsförbundet
   Filé Sovjetunionen
   Collection Nerman

Archivio Centrale dello Stato (ACS), Rome
   Collection Morgari (Fondo "Mostra della rivoluzione fascista, Ia parte")
   File Ministero Interno, Divisione Generale della Pubblica Sicurezza, Divisione Affare Generali e Riservati (1914–1926)

Internationaal Instituut voor Sociale Geschiedenis (IISG), Amsterdam
   Collection Axelrod
   Collection Balabanov
   Collection Grimm
   Collection Roland-Holst
   Collection Nobs
   Wilhelm Dittmann-Kotowski, *Erinnerungen* (manuscript)

Labour Party Archive (LPA), London

Schweizerisches Sozialarchiv (SSA), Zürich
   Protokoll der Sitzungen der Geschäftsleitung und des Parteivorstandes, 1914–1916
   File Sozialismus: II. Internationale Zusammenbruch 1914; Zimmerwald 1915; Kiental 1916

Protocols, Document Collections, Reports

Balabanoff, Angelica. *Die Zimmerwalder Bewegung, 1914–1919*. Leipzig, 1928.
Bantke, Samuil S., ed. *Bor'ba Bol'shevikov za sozdanie Kommunisticheskogo Internatsionala. Materialy i dokumenty, 1914–1919 gg.* Moscow, 1934.
British Socialist Party. *Report of the Fifth Annual Conference, Salford, 23–24 April 1916.* London, 1916.
Browder, Robert Paul, and Kerensky, Alexander F., eds. *The Russian Provisional Government 1917: Documents.* 3 vols. Stanford, 1961.
Bulgarskata Kommunisticheska Partiia v rezoliutsii i resheniia na kongresite, konferentsite, i plenumite TsK, 1891–1918. Sofia, 1961.
Compte-rendu analytique du VIII Congrès socialiste international, tenu à Copenhague, du 28 août au 3 septembre 1910. Gent, 1911.
Compte-rendu analytique du VII Congrès socialiste international, tenu à Stuttgart du 16 au 24 août 1907. Brussels, 1908.
Dokumente und Materialen zur Geschichte der deutschen Arbeiterbewegung. Reihe 2: 1914–1945, Bd. 1: Juli 1914–Oktober 1917. Berlin, 1958.
Dokumenty vneshnei politiki SSSR. Vol. 1. Moscow, 1957.
Drahn, Ernst, and Leonhard, Susanne, eds. *Unterirdische Literatur im revolutionären Deutschland während des Weltkrieges.* Berlin, 1920.
Eichhorn, Emil, ed. *Protokoll über die Verhandlungen des Grundungsparteitages der USPD vom 6. bis 8. April 1917 in Gotha.* Berlin, 1921.
Gankin, Olga Hess, and Fisher, H. H., eds. *The Bolsheviks and the World War: The Origins of the Third International.* Stanford, 1940.
Gruber, Helmut, ed. *International Communism in the Era of Lenin: A Documentary History.* New York, 1972.
Grunberg, Karl, ed. *Internatsional i mirovaia voina.* Petrograd, 1919.
Haupt, Georges. *La deuxième Internationale, 1889–1914. Etude critique des sources, essai bibliographique.* Paris, 1964.
Humphrey, A. W., ed. *International Socialism and the War.* London, 1915.
Lademacher, Horst, ed. *Die Zimmerwalder Bewegung: Protokolle und Korrespondenz.* 2 vols. The Hague, 1967.
Leninskii sbornik. 35 vols. Moscow, 1930.
Listovki peterburgskikh bol'shevikov, 1902–1917. Vol. 2. Leningrad, 1957.
Maitron, Jean, and Chambelland, Colette, eds. *Syndicalisme révolutionnaire et communisme: Les archives de Pierre Monatte 1914–1924.* Paris, 1968.
Neck, Rudolf, ed. *Arbeiterschaft und Staat im Ersten Weltkrieg.* 2 vols. Vienna, 1968.
Partiia bol'shevikov v gody imperialisticheskoi voiny. Dokumenty i materialy. Moscow, 1963.
Pendant la guerre. Le parti socialiste, la guerre et la paix: Toutes les résolutions et tous les documents du parti socialiste, de juillet 1914 à fin 1917. Paris, 1918.
Pervyi kongress Kominterna. Moscow, 1933.
Pokrovskii, M. N., and Iakovlev, Ia. A., eds. *1917 god v dokumentakh i materialakh.* 10 vols. Moscow, 1925–1939.
Protokoll des Internationalen Arbeiter-Kongresses zu Paris, 1889. Nürnberg, 1890.
Protokoll des internationalen Arbeiterkongresses in der Tonhalle Zürich. Zürich, 1894.
Protokoll über die Verhandlungen des Parteitages vom 4. und 5. November 1916, abgehalten im Gesellschaftshaus "z. Kaufleuten" in Zürich. Zürich, 1917.
Rapport du Congrès international ouvrier socialiste tenu à Bruxelles. Brussels, 1883.

Riddel, John, ed. *Lenin's Struggle for a Revolutionary International. Documents, 1907–1916.* New York, 1984.
Sbornik dokumentov mestnykh bol'shevistikh organizatsii. Bol'sheviki v gody imperialisticheskoi voiny, 1914–Fevral' 1917. Moscow, 1939.
Sed'maia ("Aprel'skaia") vserossiiskaia i petrogradskaia obshchegorodskaia konferentsiia RSDRP (bol'shevikov), Aprel' 1917. Moscow, 1934.
Sed'moi ekstrennyi s"ezd RKP (b). Mart 1918 goda: Stenograficheskoi otchet. Moscow, 1962.
Shestoi s"ezd RSDRP (bol'shevikov), Avgust 1917 goda. Protokoly. Moscow, 1958.
Spartakusbriefe. Berlin, 1958.
Strobel, Georg W., ed. *Quellen zur Geschichte des Kommunismus in Polen 1878–1918: Programme und Statuten.* Cologne, 1968.
Trachtenberg, Alexander, ed. *The American Socialists and the War: A Documentary History of the Attitude of the Socialist Party towards War and Militarism since the Outbreak of the Great War.* New York, 1917.
Walling, William E., ed. *The Socialists and the War.* New York, 1915.

Periodicals

Die Arbeiterpolitik: Wochenschrift für wissenschaftlichen Sozialismus (Bremen)
L'Avanguardia (Milan)
Avanti! Giornale del partito socialista (Milan)
Berner Tagwacht: Offizielles Publikationsorgan der Sozialdemokratischen Partei der Schweiz (Bern)
Bote der russischen Revolution: Organ der ausländischen Vertretung der soc. dem. Arbeiterpartei Russlands (Bolschewiki) (Stockholm)
Bremer Bürgerzeitung: Organ für Interesse des Volkes (Bremen)
Bulletin des Ausschusses für auswärtige Angelegenheiten des ZK der Arbeiter und Soldatendelegiertenräte (Stockholm)
The Call: An Organ of International Socialism (London)
Demain: Pages et documents (Geneva)
Die Fackel (Petrograd)
Forward (Glasgow)
Die Gleichheit: Die Zeitschrift für die Interessen der Arbeiterinnen (Stuttgart)
Golos: Ezhednevnaia politicheskaia i obshchestvennaia gazeta (Paris)
L'Humanité: Journal socialiste (Paris)
Informatsionnyi listok' zagranichnoi organizatsii Bunda (Paris)
Die Internationale: Eine Monatschrift für Praxis und Theorie der Marxismus (no. 1, 1915) (Berlin)
Internationale Flugblätter (no. 1, 1915) (Zürich)
De Internationale: Orgaan van het Revolutionnair Socialistisch Verbond (Vereeniging) (Laren)
Internationale Sozialistische Kommission: Nachrichtendienst (Stockholm)
Internationale Sozialistische Kommission zu Bern: Bulletin (Bern)
Izvestiia zagranichnogo sekretariata organizatsionogo komiteta rossiiskoi sotsial-demokraticheskoi rabochei partii (Zürich)
Jugend-Internationale: Kampf und Propaganda Organ der internationalen Verbindung sozialistischer Jugend-organizationen (Zürich)
Justice: The Organ of the Social Democracy (London)
Kommunist (nos. 1/2, 1915) (Geneva)

Der Kampf: Sozialdemokratische Monatschrift (Vienna)
The Labour Leader: A Weekly Journal of Socialism, Trade Unionism and Politics (London)
Lichtstrahlen: Monatliche Bildungsorgan für denkende Arbeiter (Berlin)
Nashe Slovo: Obshchestvennaia i politicheskaia gazeta (Paris)
Die Neue Zeit: Wochenschrift der deutschen Sozialdemokratie (Stuttgart)
Neues Leben: Monatschrift für sozialistische Bildung (Bern)
De Nieuwe Tijd: Sociaaldemocratisch Maandschrift (Amsterdam)
Politiken (Stockholm)
Pravda: Organ Tsentral'nogo Komiteta Peterburgskogo Komiteta R.S.D.R.P. (1917) (Petrograd)
Proletarskii Golos: Organ peterburgskogo komiteta rossiiskoi S. D. rabochei partii (Petrograd)
Russische Korrespondenz "Prawda" (Stockholm)
Sbornik Sotsial-Demokrata (Geneva)
La Sentinelle: Quotidien socialiste (La Chaux-de-Fonds)
Sotsial-Demokrat: Tsentral'nyi organ rossiiskoi sotsial-demokraticheskoi rabochei partii (Geneva)
Stormklockan (Stockholm)
De Tribune: Soc. Dem. Orgaan (Amsterdam)
Der Völkerfriede/Mir Narodov (Petrograd)
Volksrecht: Sozialdemokratisches Tagblatt (Zürich)
Der Vorbote: Internationale Marxistische Rundschau (Bern)
Vorwärts: Berliner Volksblatt. Zentralorgan der Sozialdemokratischen Partei Deutschlands (Berlin)

Contemporary Texts, Correspondence, Memoirs

Adler, F. W. *Die Erneuerung der Internationale: Aufsätze aus der Kriegszeit (Oktober 1914 bis Oktober 1916)*. Vienna, 1918.
Adler, Victor. *Briefwechsel mit August Bebel und Karl Kautsky*. Vienna, 1954.
Axelrod, Paul. *Die Krise und die Aufgaben der internationalen Sozialdemokratie*. Zürich, 1915.
Badaev, A. *Bol'sheviki v gosudarstvennoi dume: Vospominaniia*. Moscow, 1939.
Balabanoff, Angelica. *Erinnerungen und Erlebnisse*. Berlin, 1927.
Balabanoff, Angelica. *My Life as a Rebel*. New York, 1938.
Barth, Emil. *Aus der Werkstatt der deutschen Revolution*. Berlin, 1919.
Bauer, Otto. *Die Nationalitätenfrage und die Sozialdemokratie*. Vienna, 1907.
Bernstein, Eduard. *Evolutionary Socialism*. New York, 1963.
Bernstein, Eduard. *Die Internationale, der Arbeiterklasse, und der europäische Krieg*. Tübingen, 1915.
Blagoev, Dmitur. *Izbrani proizvedeniia*. 2 vols. Sofia, 1951.
Boudin, Louis B. *Socialism and War*. New York, 1916.
Boulanger, Omer. *L'Internationale socialiste a vécu*. Paris, 1915.
Bourgin, Hubert. *Le parti contre la patrie: Histoire d'une sécession politique 1915–1917*. Paris, 1924.
Bukharin, Nikolai. *Imperialism and World Economy*. New York, 1973.
Chernov, V. M. *Pered burei: Vospominaniia*. New York, 1953.
David, Eduard. *Die Sozialdemokratie im Weltkrieg*. Berlin, 1919.
Frolich, Paul. *Rosa Luxemburg: Her Life and Work*. London, 1940.

Gorter, Herman. *Het imperialisme, de wereldoorlog en de sociaal-demokratie.* Amsterdam, 1915.

Gorter, Herman. *Die Wereldrevolutie.* Amsterdam, 1918.

Gramsci, Antonio. *Scritti giovanili 1914–1918.* Turin, 1958.

Greulich, Hermann. *Krieg und Internationale.* Zürich, 1915.

Grimm, Robert. *Ab Traktandum mit der Militärfrage?* Bern, 1917.

Grimm, Robert. *Zimmerwald und Kiental.* Bern, 1917.

Grumbach, Solomon. *Der Irrtum von Zimmerwald-Kiental.* Bern, 1916.

Guilbeaux, Henri. *Mon crime. Contre-attaque et offensive.* Geneva, 1918.

Guilbeaux, Henri. *Le mouvement socialiste et syndicaliste français pendant la guerre, 1914–1918.* Petrograd, 1919.

Guilbeaux, Henri. *Wladimir Iljitsh Lenin: Ein treues Bild seines Wesens.* Berlin, 1923.

Hänisch, Konrad. *Die deutsche Sozialdemokratie in und nach dem Weltkriege.* Berlin, 1919.

Haupt, Georges, ed. *Correspondance entre Lénine et Camille Huysmans, 1905–1914.* Paris, 1963.

Hilferding, Rudolf. *Das Finanzkapital: Eine Studie über die jüngste Entwicklung des Kapitalismus.* Vienna, 1910.

Hobson, J. P. *Imperialism: A Study.* London, 1902.

Höglund, Zeth. *Minnen i fackelsken.* Vol. 2: *Från Branting till Lenin, 1912–1916.* Vol. 3: *Revolutionernas år, 1917–1921.* Stockholm, 1953–1956.

Humbert-Droz, Jules. *Guerre à la guerre: A bas l'armée.* La Chaux-de-Fonds, 1916.

Humbert-Droz, Jules. *L'origine de l'Internationale communiste: De Zimmerwald à Moscou.* Neuchâtel, 1968.

Humbert-Droz, Jules. *Der Krieg und die Internationale: Die Konferenzen von Zimmerwald und Kiental.* Vienna, 1964.

Huysmans, Camille. *The Policy of the International.* London, 1916.

Jaurès, Jean. *L'armée nouvelle.* Paris, 1915.

Kautsky, Karl. *Die Internationale und der Krieg.* Berlin, 1915.

Kautsky, Karl. *Patriotismus und Sozialdemokratie.* Leipzig, 1907.

Kautsky, Karl. *Der Weg zur Macht.* Berlin, 1909.

von Kol, Henri H. *Der kommende Friede und die Sozialdemokratie.* Amsterdam, 1916.

Kolarov, Vasil. *Izbrani proizvedeniia.* Vol. 1. Sofia, 1954.

Kolb, Wilhelm. *Die Sozialdemokratie am Scheidewege: Ein Beitrag zum Thema, Neuorientierung der deutschen Politik.* Karlsruhe, 1915.

Kollontai, A. "Avtobiograficheskii ocherk." *Proletarskaia revoliutsiia* 3(1921): 261–302.

Kollontai, A. *Komu nuzhno voina?* Bern, 1916.

Kondrat'ev, K. "Vospominaniia o podpol'noi rabote peterburgskoi organizatsii RSDRP (b) v period 1914–1917 gg." *Krasnaia letopis'* 5(1923): 227–43 and 7(1923): 30–70.

Korichoner, F. "Iz istorii internatsionalistskogo dvizhenia v Avstrii." *Proletarskaia revoliutsiia* 2/3(97/98)(1930): 91–103.

Krupskaia, N. K. *Reminiscences of Lenin.* Moscow, 1959.

Laufenberg, Heinrich, and Wolffheim, Fritz. *Imperialismus und Demokratie: Ein Wort zum Weltkrieg.* Hamburg, 1914.

Lenin, V. I. *Polnoe sobranie sochinenii.* 55 vols. Moscow, 1958–1965.

Lenin, N., and Sinowjev, G. *Gegen den Strom: Aufsätze aus den Jahren 1914–1916.* Hamburg, 1921.

Lensch, Paul. *Die deutsche Sozialdemokratie und der Weltkrieg.* Berlin, 1915.

Lensch, Paul. *Drei Jahre Weltrevolution.* Berlin, 1917.

Liebknecht, Karl. *Gesammelte Reden und Schriften.* 9 vols. Berlin, 1958.

Luxemburg, Rosa. *Gesammelte Werke.* 5 vols. Berlin, 1983.

Martov, Iu. *Protiv voiny! Sbornik statei 1914–1916.* Moscow, 1917.

Martov, J., and Dan, F. *Geschichte der russischen Sozialdemokratie.* Berlin, 1926.

Marx, Karl, and Engels, Friedrich. *Werke.* 39 vols. Berlin, 1956–1959.

Maxc, Jean. *De Zimmerwald au bolchevisme ou le triomphe du marxisme pangermaniste: Essai sur les menées internationalistes pendant la guerre 1914–1920.* Paris, 1920.

Miliukov, P. N. *Istoriia vtoroi russkoi revoliutsii.* Sofia, 1921.

Miliukov, P. N. *Pochemu i zachem my voiuem?* Petrograd, 1917.

Milton, Nan, ed. *John Maclean: In the Rapids of Revolution. Essays, Articles, and Letters 1902–23.* London, 1978.

Miuntsenberg, V. *S Libknekhtom i Leninym: Piatnadtsat' let v proletarskom iunosheskom dvizhenii.* Moscow, 1930.

Münzenberg, W. *Die sozialistischen Jugend-Organization vor und während des Krieges.* Berlin, 1919.

Nerman, Ture, *Allt var rött: Minne och redovisning.* Stockholm, 1950.

Padover, Saul K., ed. *The Karl Marx Library.* Vol. 3. *On the First International.* New York, 1973.

Pis'ma P. B. Aksel'roda i Iu. O. Martova, 1901–1916. The Hague, 1967.

Platten, Fritz. *Die Reise Lenins durch Deutschland im plombierten Wagen.* Berlin, 1924.

Plekhanov, G. V. *O voine. Otvet tovarishchu Z. P.* Paris, 1914.

Postgate, R. W. *The International During the War.* London, 1918.

Potresov, A. N. *"Internatsionalizm" i kosmopolitanizm.* Petrograd, 1916.

Prager, Eugen. *Geschichte der U.S.P.D. Entstehung und Entwicklung der Unabhängigen Sozialdemokratischen Partei Deutschlands.* Berlin, 1921.

Racovski, Christian. *Das Wiedererwachen der Internationale: Rede gehalten am internationalen Massenmeeting vom 8. Februar im Volkshaus in Bern.* Bern, 1916.

Radek, Karl. *"Avtobiografiia." Entsiklopedicheskii slovar' "Granat".* 7th ed. Vol. 41, part 2. Moscow, 1928.

Radek, Karl. *In den Reihen der deutschen Revolution 1909–1919.* Munich, 1921.

Radek, Karl. *Vneshniaia politika sovetskoi rossii.* Moscow/Petrograd, 1923.

Ravich, Ol'ga. *"Mezhdunarodnaia zhenskaia sotsialisticheskaia konferentsiia 1915 g." Proletarskaia revoliutsiia* 10(45)(1925): 165–77.

Renner, Karl. *Oesterreichs Erneuerung.* Vienna, 1916.

Renner, Karl. *Marxismus, Krieg und Internationale: Kritische Studien über offene Probleme des wissenschaftlichen und des praktischen Sozialismus in und nach dem Weltkrieg.* Vienna, 1917.

Retzlaw, Karl. *Spartakus: Aufstieg und Niedergang: Erinnerungen eines Parteimitarbeiters.* Frankfurt am Main, 1972.

Rolland, Romain. *Journal des années de guerre 1914–1919.* Paris, 1952.

Rosmer, Alfred. *Le mouvement ouvrier pendant la guerre: De l'union sacrée à Zimmerwald.* Paris, 1936.

Rosmer, Alfred. *Le mouvement ouvrier pendant la première guerre mondiale: De Zimmerwald à la révolution russe.* Paris, 1959.

Samoilov, F. N. *Po sledam minuvshego.* Moscow, 1934.

Scheidemann, Phillip. *Memoiren eines Sozialdemokraten.* 2 vols. Berlin, 1928.

Scheidemann, Phillip. *Der Zusammenbruch.* Berlin, 1921.

Serrati, G. Menotti. *Dalla seconda alla terza Internazionale.* Milan, 1920.

Shklovskii, G. "Tsimmerval'd." *Proletarskaia revoliutsiia* 9(44)(1925): 73–106.
Shliapnikov, A. "Fevral'skaia revoliutsiia i evropeiskie sotsialisty." *Krasnyi arkhiv* 15(1926): 61–85 and 16(1926): 25–43.
Shliapnikov, A. "Sotsial-demokratiia i voina, 1914–1917." *Proletarskaia revoliutsiia* 3(15)(1923): 178–95.
Shliapnikov, Aleksandr G. *Semnadtsatyi god.* 4 vols. Moscow, 1923–1931.
Shlyapnikov, Alexander. *On the Eve of 1917.* London, 1982.
Sukhanov, N. N. *Zapiski o revoliutsii.* 7 vols. Berlin, 1922.
Trotsky, Leon. *My Life: An Attempt at an Autobiography.* New York, 1930.
Trotzki, Leo. *Der Krieg und die Internationale.* Zürich, 1914.
Tsereteli, Irakli G. *Vospominaniia o fevral'skoi revoliutsii.* 2 vols. Paris/The Hague, 1963.
Vandervelde, Emile. *Souvenirs d'un militant socialiste.* Paris, 1939.
Zetkin, Clara. *Ausgewählte Reden und Schriften.* Vol. 1. Berlin, 1957.
Zévaès, Alexandre. *La faillite de l'Internationale: Faits et documents.* Paris, 1917.
Zini, Zino. *La tragedia del proletariato in Italia: Diario, 1914–1926.* Milan, 1973.
Zinov'ev, G. *Sochineniia.* 15 vols. Moscow, 1920–1924.

Secondary Sources

Agnelli, Arduino. *Questione nazionale e socialismo: Contributo allo studio del pensiero di K. Renner e O. Bauer.* Bologna, 1969.
Agnelli, Arduino. "Socialismo e problema della nazionalità in Otto Bauer." *Annali* (Milan, 1973): 364–86.
Allio, Renata. "Morgari e l'internazionale socialista durante la grande guerra." *Bolletino storico bibliografico subalpino* 73(1975): 548–73.
Ambrosoli, Luigi. *Né aderire né sabotare, 1915–1918.* Milan, 1961.
Arfé, Gaetano. *Storico del socialismo Italiano (1892–1926).* Turin, 1965.
Ascher, Abraham. *Pavel Axelrod and the Development of Menshevism.* Cambridge, Mass., 1972.
Atsarkin, A. N., and Barulina, A. T. *Bor'ba bol'shevikov za osushchestvlenie leninskoi programy po voprosam voiny, mira, i revoliutsii, 1914–1917 gg.* Moscow, 1963.
Badia, Gilbert. "L'attitude de la gauche sociale-démocrate allemande dans les premiers mois de la guerre." *Le mouvement social* 49(1964): 81–105.
Badia, Gilbert. *Rosa Luxemburg: Journaliste, polémiste, révolutionnaire.* Paris, 1975.
Badia, Gilbert. *Le spartakisme: Les dernières années de Rosa Luxemburg et Karl Liebknecht, 1914–1917.* Paris, 1967.
Baevskii, D. "Bol'sheviki v bor'be za III Internatsional." *Istorik marksist* 11(1929): 12–48.
Baevskii, D. "Bol'sheviki v tsimmerval'de." *Proletarskaia revoliutsiia* 5(1935): 27–48.
Baevskii, D. "Bor'ba Lenina protiv bukharinskikh 'shatanii mysli'." *Proletarskaia revoliutsiia* 1(96) (1930): 18–46.
Baevskii, D. "Bor'ba za III Internatsional do tsimmerval'da." *Proletarskaia revoliutsiia* 4(1934): 12–36.
Baevskii, D. "Kak leninskii 'Imperializm' uvidel svet." *Proletarskaia revoliutsiia* 1(84)(1928): 31–37.
Baevskii, D. "Lenin i tsimmerval'dskaia levaia." *Bor'ba klassov* 3(1934): 33–47.
Bantke, S. S. *Bor'ba za sozdanie kommunisticheskoi partii vo Frantsii.* Moscow, 1936.
Bantke, S. "V. I. Lenin i tsimmerval'dskoe dvizhenie vo Frantsii." *Proletarskaia revoliutsiia* 3(1934): 113–47.

Bartell, Walter. *Die Linken in der deutschen Sozialdemokratie im Kampf gegen Militarismus und Krieg.* Berlin, 1958.

Bauer, Roland. *Die II. Internationale (1889–1914).* Berlin, 1958.

Bauman, G. G. "Niderlandskaia burzhuaznaia i sotsial-reformistskaia istoriografiia o Tribunistakh." *Voprosy istorii* 6(1978): 58–72.

Becker, Jean-Jacques. *Le carnet B: Les pouvoirs publics et l'antimilitarisme avant la guerre de 1914.* Paris, 1973.

Bekstrem, Knut. "K voprosy o vozniknovenii kommunisticheskoi partii Shvetsii." *Voprosy istorii KPSS* 6(1959): 91–102.

Berlau, Joseph A. *The German Social Democratic Party, 1914–1921.* New York, 1949.

"Bernskaia konferentsiia 1915 g." *Proletarskaia revoliutsiia* 5(40) (1925): 134–93.

Bevan, Edwyn. *German Social Democracy during the War.* London, 1918.

Birman, M. A. "V. I. Lenin i bor'ba revoliutsionnykh sotsial-demokratov balkanskikh stran protiv imperialisticheskoi voiny v 1914–1915 gg." *Sovetskoe slavianovedenie* 2(1965): 8–9.

Björlin, Lars. "Vänstersocialism—kommunism 1916–1924." *Meddelande från Arbetarrörelsens Arkiv och Bibliotek* 25/26(1982/1983): 6–12.

Blänsdorf, Agnes. *Die Zweite Internationale und der Krieg: Die Diskussion über die internationale Zusammenarbeit der sozialistischen Parteien 1914–1917.* Stuttgart, 1979.

Boll, Friedhelm. *Frieden ohne Revolution? Friedensstrategien der deutschen Sozialdemokratie vom Erfurt Programm bis zur Revolution 1918.* Bonn, 1980.

Braiovich, S. M. *Karl Kautskii: Evolutsiia ego vozzpenii.* Moscow, 1982.

Brand, Carl F. "British Labor and the International during the Great War." *The Journal of Modern History* 1(1936): 40–64.

Braunthal, Julius. *Geschichte der Internationale.* 2 vols. Hannover, 1961–1963.

Braunthal, Julius. *Victor und Friedrich Adler: Zwei Generationen Arbeiterbewegung.* Vienna, 1965.

Bravo, Gian Mario. "Patria e internazionalismo in Jean Jaurès." *Critica marxista* 4(1986): 77–90.

Bretscher, W., and Steinmann, E., eds. *Die sozialistische Bewegung in der Schweiz, 1848–1920.* Bern, 1923.

Bronskii, M. "Uchastie Lenina v shveitsarskom rabochem dvizhenii." *Proletarskaia revoliutsiia* 4(27)(1924): 30–39.

Broom, John. *John Maclean.* Luanhead, 1973.

Bünger, Siegfried. *Die sozialistische Antikriegsbewegung in Grossbritannien 1914 bis 1917.* Berlin, 1967.

Bykin, Ia. "V. I. Lenin v Sho-de-Fone, 10 Marta 1917 g." *Proletarskaia revoliutsiia* 1(96)(1930): 72–77.

Cammett, John W. *Antonio Gramsci and the Origins of Italian Communism.* Stanford, 1967.

Carr, Edward Hallett. *The Bolshevik Revolution 1917–1923.* 3 vols. New York, 1950–1953.

Carsten, Francis. *War Against War: British and German Radical Movements in the First World War* (London, 1982).

Challinor, Raymond. *The Origins of British Bolshevism.* London, 1977.

Chubarian, A. O. *Brestskii mir.* Moscow, 1964.

Clements, Barbara Evans. *Bolshevik Feminist: The Life of Aleksandra Kollontai.* Bloomington, 1979.

Cohen, Stephen F. *Bukharin and the Bolshevik Revolution: A Political Biography, 1888–1938.* New York, 1973.

Cole, G. D. H. *A History of Socialist Thought.* Vol. 4, pt. 1. *Communism and Social Democracy, 1914–1931.* London, 1958.

Collart, Yves. "La deuxième Internationale et la conférence de Zimmerwald." *Schweizerische Zeitschrift für Geschichte* 4(1965): 433–56.

Collart, Yves. *Le parti socialiste suisse et l'Internationale, 1914–1915: De l'union nationale à Zimmerwald.* Geneva, 1969.

Colletti, Lucio. *From Rousseau to Lenin: Studies in Ideology and Society.* New York, 1972.

Colletti, Lucio. *Tra marxismo e non.* Bari, 1979.

Conte, Francis. *Christian Rakovski (1873–1941): Essai de biographie politique.* 2 vols. Paris, 1975.

Cortesi, Luigi. *Le origini del PCI: Il PSI dalla guerra di Libia alla scissione di Livorno.* Bari, 1972.

Craver, Earlene J. *The Crisis of Italian Socialism and the Origins of the Italian Communist Party, 1912–1921.* Ann Arbor, 1972.

Debo, Richard K. *Revolution and Survival: The Foreign Policy of Soviet Russia, 1917–1918.* Toronto, 1979.

DeFelice, Franco. *Serrati, Bordiga, Gramsci.* Bari, 1971.

Deutscher, Isaac. *The Prophet Armed: Trotsky, 1879–1921.* Oxford, 1954.

Dogliani, Patrizia. *La "Scuola delle reclute:" L'Internazionale giovanile socialista della fine dell' ottocento alla prima guerra mondiale.* Turin, 1983.

Drachkovitch, Milorad M., and Lazitch, Branko, eds. *The Revolutionary Internationals, 1864–1943.* Stanford, 1966.

Dziewanowski, Marian K. *The Communist Party of Poland: An Outline of History.* Cambridge, Mass., 1959.

Egger, Heinz. *Die Entstehung der Kommunistischen Partei und des Kommunistischen Jugendverbandes der Schweiz.* Zürich, 1952.

van der Esch, Patricia. *La deuxième Internationale 1889–1923.* Paris, 1957.

Fainsod, Merle. *International Socialism and the World War.* Cambridge, Mass., 1935.

Ferro, Marc. *The Great War, 1914–1918.* London, 1973.

Fischer, Louis. *The Life of Lenin.* New York, 1964.

Forcadel, Carlos. *Parlamentarismo y Bolchevización: El movimiento obrero español, 1914–1918.* Barcelona, 1978.

Frossard, L. O. *De Jaurès à Lénine.* Paris, 1930.

Futrell, Michael. *Northern Underground: Episodes of Russian Revolutionary Transport and Communications through Scandinavia and Finland, 1863–1917.* New York, 1963.

Gautschi, Willi. *Lenin als Emigrant in der Schweiz.* Zürich, 1973.

Gay, Peter. *The Dilemma of Democratic Socialism: Eduard Bernstein's Challenge to Marx.* New York, 1952.

Getzler, Israel. *Martov: A Political Biography of a Russian Social Democrat.* Cambridge, 1967.

Gosiorovskii, M. *Istoriia slovatskogo rabochego dvizheniia 1848–1918 gg.* Moscow, 1955.

Gras, Christian. *Alfred Rosmer (1877–1964) et le mouvement révolutionnaire international.* Paris, 1971.

Grass, Martin. *Friedensaktivität und Neutralität: Die skandinavische Sozialdemokratie und die neutrale Zusammenarbeit im Krieg, August 1914 bis Februar 1917.* Bonn/Bad Godesburg, 1975.

Graubard, Stephen Richards. *British Labour and the Russian Revolution, 1917–1924.* Cambridge, Mass., 1956.

Bibliography

Gross, Babette. *Willi Münzenberg: A Political Biography*. East Lansing, 1974.
Grossheim, Heinrich. *Sozialisten in der Verantwortung: Die französischen Sozialisten und Gewerkschafter im ersten Weltkrieg 1914–17*. Bonn, 1978.
Harding, Neil. *Lenin's Political Thought*. 2 vols. London, 1981.
Haupt, Georges. *Le Congrès manqué: L'Internationale à la veille de la première guerre mondiale*. Paris, 1965.
Haupt, Georges. "Guerre et révolution chez Lénine." *Revue française de science politique* 2(1971): 256–81.
Haupt, Georges. *Socialism and the Great War: The Collapse of the Second International*. Oxford, 1972.
Hautmann, Hans. *Die Anfänge der linksradikalen Bewegung und der kommunistischen Partei Deutschösterreichs 1916–1919*. Vienna, 1970.
Hedlin, Myron W. "Zinoviev's Revolutionary Tactics in 1917." *The Slavic Review* 1(1975): 19–43.
Högger, Rudolf Martin. *Charles Naine, 1874–1926: Eine politische Biographie*. Zürich, 1966.
Holzer, Jerry. "Devant la guerre et déchiré. Le mouvement ouvrier polonais." *Le mouvement social* 49(1964): 107–18.
Hölzle, Erwin. *Lenin 1917. Die Geburt der Revolution aus dem Kriege*. Munich, 1957.
Hornik, Leopold. "Die Zimmerwalder Linke und die Linksradikalen in Oesterreich." *Weg und Ziel* (January 1953): 655–68.
Huber, Wolfgang, and Schwerdtfeger, Johannes, eds. *Frieden, Gewalt, Sozialismus: Studien zur Geschichte der sozialistischen Arbeiterbewegung*. Stuttgart, 1976.
Hulse, James W. *The Forming of the Communist International*. Stanford, 1964.
Hyrkkänen, Markku. *Sozialistische Kolonialpolitik: Eduard Bernsteins Stellung zur Kolonialpolitik und zum Imperialismus: Ein Beitrag zur Geschichte des Revisionismus*. Helsinki, 1986.
Iakushina, A. P. *Zagranichnye organizatsii RSDRP (1905–1917 gg.)* Moscow, 1967.
Ignat'ev, A. V. *Vneshniaia politika vremennogo pravitel'stva*. Moscow, 1974.
Istoriia vtorogo Internatsionala. 2 vols. Moscow, 1966.
Iuzefovich, I. S. *Osnovanie Kommunisticheskogo Internatsionala*. Moscow, 1940.
"Iz arkhivov Karla Libknekhta i Klary Tsetkina." *Bol'shevik* 13/14 (1934): 104–7.
"Iz materialov Instituta Marksa-Engelsa-Lenina." *Bol'shevik* 22(1932): 76–96.
"Iz perepiski russkogo biuro TsK s zagranitsei v gody voiny, (1915–1916)." *Proletarskaia revoliutsiia* 102/103(1930): 177–95.
Joll, James. *The Second International*. London, 1955.
Jost, Hans-Ulrich. *Linksradikalismus in der deutschen Schweiz 1914–1918*. Bern, 1973.
Kamenskii, G. *Iz istorii bor'by pol'skogo proletariata (1914–1918)*. Moscow/Leningrad, 1926.
Karliner, M. M. *Rabochee dvizhenie v Anglii v gody pervoi mirovoi voiny (1914–1918)*. Moscow, 1961.
Kendall, Walter. *The Revolutionary Movement in Britain: The Origins of British Communism*. London, 1969.
Khoniavko, I. P. "V podpol'e i v emigratsii (1911–1917 gg.)." *Proletarskaia revoliutsiia* 4(16)(1923): 159–75.
Kirby, David. *War, Peace and Revolution: International Socialism at the Crossroads 1914–1918*. New York, 1986.
Kirova, K. E. "Iz istorii tsimmerval'dskogo dvizheniia v Italii (1915–1916 gg.)" *Novaia i noveishaia istoriia* 3(1958): 84–106.
Kirova, K. E. *Revoliutsionnoe dvizhenie v Italii v 1914–1917*. Moscow, 1962.

Kirova, K. E. *Russkaia revoliutsiia i Italiia: Mart–Oktiabr' 1917 g.* Moscow, 1968.

Klär, Karl-Heinz. *Der Zusammenbruch der zweiten Internationale.* Frankfurt am Main, 1981.

Koejemans, A. J. *David Wijnkoop: Een mens in de strijd voor het socialisme.* Amsterdam, 1967.

Kolakowski, Leszek. *Main Currents of Marxism: Its Rise, Growth, and Dissolution.* 3 vols. Oxford, 1978.

König, Helmut. *Lenin und der italienische Sozialismus 1915–1921: Ein Beitrag zur Gründungsgeschichte der Kommunistischen Internationale.* Tübingen, 1967.

Korolev, N. E. "Bol'sheviki na tsimmerval'dskoi konferentsii." *Voprosy istorii KPSS* 9(1965): 14–28.

Korolev, N. E. *Lenin i mezhdunarodnoe rabochee dvizhenie, 1914–1918.* Moscow, 1968.

Korolev, N. E. "V. I. Lenin i tsimmerval'dskoe ob"edinenie (Fevral'–Oktiabr' 1917 goda)." *Voprosy istorii KPSS* 2(1960): 139–55.

Kozenko, B. D. *Rabochee dvizhenie v SShA v gody pervoi mirovoi voiny.* Saratov, 1965.

Kriegel, Annie. *Les Internationales ouvrières (1864–1943).* Paris, 1964.

Kriegel, Annie. *Aux origines du communisme français 1914–1920: Contribution à l'histoire du mouvement ouvrier français.* 2 vols. Paris, 1964.

Kuczynski, Jürgen. *Der Ausbruch des ersten Weltkrieges und die deutsche Sozialdemokratie: Chronik und Analyse.* Berlin, 1957.

Kulemann, Peter. *Am Beispiel des Austromarxismus: Sozialdemokratische Arbeiterbewegung in Oesterreich von Hainfeld bis zur Dollfuss Diktatur.* Hamburg, 1979.

Labi, Maurice. *La grande division des travailleurs: Première scission de la C.G.T. (1914–1921).* Paris, 1964.

Landauer, Carl. *European Socialism: A History of Ideas and Movements.* Vol. 1. Berkeley, 1959.

Lange, Alfred. "W. I. Lenins Kampf gegen die sozialchauvinistische und zentristische Verschleierung des Wesens des ersten Weltkrieges." *Wissenschaftliche Zeitschrift der Humboldt-Universität zu Berlin: Gesellschaftswissenschaftliche Reihe* 1(1984): 83–86.

Lavrin, V. A. *Bol'shevistskaia partiia v nachale pervoi mirovoi voiny 1914–15 gg.* Moscow, 1972.

Lazitch, Branko. *Lénine et la IIIe Internationale.* Paris, 1951.

Leder, V. "Natsional'nyi vopros v pol'skoi i russkoi sotsial-demokratsii." *Proletarskaia revoliutsiia* 2/3(61/62)(1927): 148–208.

Lehnert, Detlef. *Reform und Revolution in den Strategiediskussion der klassischen Sozialdemokratie: Zur Geschichte der deutschen Arbeiterbewegung von den Ursprüngen bis zum Ausbruch des 1. Weltkrieges.* Bonn/Bad Godesburg, 1977.

Lenin v bor'be za revoliutsionnyi Internatsional. Moscow, 1970.

Lenz, Josef. *Die II. Internationale und ihr Erbe (1889–1929).* Hamburg/Berlin, 1930.

Lenzner, W. "Die deutschen Linksradikalen und der Bolschewismus." *Die Kommunistische Internationale* 11(1928): 604–12 and 12(1928): 650–58.

Leon, George B. *The Greek Socialist Movement and the First World War: The Road to Unity.* Boulder, 1976.

Lerner, Warren. *Karl Radek: The Last Internationalist.* Stanford, 1970.

Leser, Norbert. *Zwischen Reformismus und Bolschewismus: Der Austromarxismus als Theorie und Praxis.* Vienna, 1968.

de Liagre-Böhl, Herman. *Herman Gorter: Zijn politieke aktiviteiten van 1909 tot 1920 in de opkomende kommunistische beweging in nederland.* Nijmegen, 1973.

Lichtheim, George. *Marxism: An Historical and Critical Study.* New York, 1961.

Livorsi, Franco. *Amadeo Bordiga: Il pensiero e l'azione politica 1912–1970.* Rome, 1976.

Lösche, Peter. *Der Bolschewismus im Urteil der deutschen Sozialdemokratie 1903–1920.* Berlin, 1967.

Louis, Peter. *La crise du socialisme mondial: De la IIe à la IIIe Internationale.* Paris, 1921.

Lowenthal, Richard. "The Bolshevization of the Spartakus League." *St. Anthony's Papers,* no. 9. London, 1960.

Löwy, Adolf. "La teoria dell' imperialismo in Bucharin." *Annali* (Milan, 1973): 887–98.

Lucas, Erhard. *Die Sozialdemokratie in Bremen während des Ersten Weltkrieges.* Bremen, 1969.

Maehl, William. "The Role of Russia in German Socialist Policy, 1914–1918." *International Review of Social History* 4(1959): 177–98.

Malatesta, Alberto. *I socialisti italiani durante la guerra.* Milan, 1926.

Manfred, A. "Tsimmerval'dskoe dvizhenie v shveitsarskoi sotsial-demokratii." *Proletarskaia revoliutsiia* 7(90)(1929): 15–47.

Mattick, Paul. "La prospettiva della rivoluzione mondiale di Anton Pannekoek." *Annali* (Milan, 1973): 344–63.

Mayer, Arno J. *The Political Origins of the New Diplomacy, 1917–1918.* New Haven, 1959.

Meaker, Gerald. *The Revolutionary Left in Spain, 1914–1923.* Stanford, 1974.

Melograni, Piero. *Il mito della rivoluzione mondiale: Lenin tra ideologia e ragio di stato 1917–1920.* Bari, 1985.

Merhav, Peretz. "Klassenkampf und nationale Frage zur Zeit der II. Internationale." *Annali* (Milan, 1976): 165–87.

Meyer, Ernst. "Zur Entstehungsgeschichte der Junius-Thesen." *Unter dem Banner des Marxismus* 1(1925/1926): 416–32.

Meyer, Thomas. *Bernsteins konstruktives Sozialismus: Eduard Bernsteins Beitrag zur Theorie des Sozialismus.* Berlin, 1977.

Meynell, Hildamarie. "The Stockholm Conference of 1917." *International Review of Social History* 1(1960): 1–25 and 2(1960): 200–25.

Mishark, John W. *The Road to Revolution: German Marxism and World War I, 1914–1919.* Detroit, 1967.

Morgan, David. *The Socialist Left and the German Revolution: A History of the German Independent Social Democratic Party, 1917–1922.* Ithaca, 1975.

Moring, Karl-Ernest. *Die Sozialdemokratische Partei in Bremen 1880–1914: Reformismus und Radikalismus in der Sozialdemokratischen Partei Bremens.* Hannover, 1968.

Morris, L. P. "The Russians, the Allies, and the War, February–July 1917." *The Slavonic and East European Review* 118(1972): 29–48.

Murashova, S. I., ed. *Partiia bol'shevikov v gody pervoi mirovoi voiny: Sverzhenie monarkhii v Rossii.* Moscow, 1963.

Nemes, D. "Die Ungarländische Sozialdemokratische Partei und der erste Weltkrieg." *Acta Historica* 20(1974): 23–53.

Nettl, J. P. *Rosa Luxemburg.* 2 vols. London, 1966.

Nikol'nikov, G. L. *Vydaiushchaia pobeda leninskoi strategii i taktiki: Brestskii mir ot zakliucheniia do razryva.* Moscow, 1968.

Nollau, Günther. *International Communism and World Revolution.* New York, 1961.

"O mezhdunarodnoi zhenskoi sotsialisticheskoi konferentsii v 1915 g." *Istoricheskii arkhiv* 3(1960): 106–25.

Oznobishin, D. V. *Ot Brest do Iureva: Iz istorii vneshnei politiki Sovetskoï vlasti 1917–1920 gg.* Moscow, 1966.

Page, Stanley W. *Lenin and World Revolution.* New York, 1959.

Palme-Dutt, R. *The Internationale.* London, 1964.

Paris, R. "La première expérience politique de Gramsci (1914–1915)." *Le mouvement social* 42(1963): 31–58.

Pedroncini, Guy. *Les mutineries de 1917.* Paris, 1967.

Petrov, G. D. "A. M. Kollontai v gody pervoi mirovoi voiny." *Istoriia SSSR* 3(1968): 83–97.

Petrov, G. D. "A. M. Kollontai nakanune i v gody pervoi mirovoi voiny." *Novaia i noveishaia istoriia* 1(1969): 67–81.

Pianzola, Maurice. *Lénine en Suisse.* Geneva, 1952.

Pokrovskii, Mikhail Nikolaevich, ed. *Ocherki po istorii oktiabrskoi revoliutsii.* Vol. 1. Moscow, 1927.

Postgate, R. W. *The Workers' Internationale.* London, 1921.

Přemysl, Janýr. "Die österreichische Sozialdemokratie und der erste Weltkrieg." *Die Zukunft* 15/16(1974): 25–29.

"Il PSI e la grande guerra." *Rivista storica del socialismo* 10(1970).

Rabinowitch, Alexander. *The Bolsheviks Come to Power: The Revolution of 1917 in Petrograd.* New York, 1976.

Rabinowitch, Alexander. *Prelude to Revolution: The Petrograd Bolsheviks and the July 1917 Uprising.* Bloomington, 1968.

Ratz, Ursula. *Georg Ledebour, 1850–1947. Weg und Wirken eines sozialistischen Politikers.* Berlin, 1969.

Rebérioux, Madelaine. "Le socialisme et la première guerre mondiale (1914–1918)," in Droz, J., et al. *Histoire générale du socialisme.* Vol. 2. *De 1875 à 1918.* Paris, 1974. Pp. 585–641.

Reisberg, Arnold. *Lenin und die Zimmerwalder Bewegung.* Berlin, 1966.

Robbins, Keith. *The Abolition of War: The 'Peace Movement' in Britain 1914–1919.* Cardiff, 1976.

Rocher, J. *Lénine et le mouvement zimmerwaldien en France.* Paris, 1934.

Roobol, W. H. *Tsereteli—A Democrat in the Russian Revolution: A Political Biography.* The Hague, 1976.

Rothschild, Joseph. *The Communist Party of Bulgaria: Origins and Development 1883–1936.* New York, 1959.

Salvadori, Massimo. *Kautsky e la rivoluzione socialista, 1880–1938.* Milan, 1976.

Samuilov, I. *S bolshevikite v borbe za nov Internatsional: Partiiata na tesnite sotsialisti i tsimmervaldskoto obedinenie.* Sofia, 1965.

Scharlau, Winfried, and Zeman, Zbynek A. *Freibeuter der Revolution: Parvus-Helphand, eine politische Biographie.* Cologne, 1964.

Schorske, Carl E. *German Social Democracy, 1905–1917: The Development of the Great Schism.* Cambridge, Mass., 1955.

Schüller, Richard. *Geschichte der Kommunistischen Jugend-Internationale.* Vol. 1. Berlin, 1931.

Schulze, Siegfried. "Karl Liebknecht und die revolutionnäre Arbeiterjugendbewegung in den Jahren des ersten Weltkrieges." *Beiträge zur Geschichte der Arbeiterbewegung* 1(1972): 20–34.

Seiranian, B. S. *Bor'ba bol'shevikov protiv voenno-promyshlennykh komitetov.* Erevan, 1961.

Senn, Alfred Erich. "The Bolshevik Conference in Bern, 1915." *The Slavic Review* 25(1966): 676–78.

Senn, Alfred Erich. "The Politics of *Golos* and *Nashe Slovo*." *International Review of Social History* 3(1972): 675–704.

Senn, Alfred Erich. *The Russian Revolution in Switzerland, 1914–1917*. Madison, 1971.

Shannon, David A. *The Socialist Party of America: A History*. New York, 1955.

Shklovskii, G. "Tsimmerval'd." *Proletarskaia revoliutsiia* 9(44)(1925): 73–106.

Sholle, Z. *Rabochee dvizhenie u cheshskikh zemliakh vo vremia mirovoi imperialisticheskoi voiny 1914–1918 gg.* Moscow, 1955.

Sigel, Robert. *Die Lensch-Cunow-Haenisch Gruppe: Eine Studie zum rechten Flügel der SPD im Ersten Weltkrieg*. Berlin, 1976.

von der Slice, Austin. *International Labor, Diplomacy and Peace 1914–1919*. Philadelphia, 1941.

Smirnova, A. D. "Iz istorii bor'by V. I. Lenina za splochenie levykh sotsial-demokratov v gody pervoi mirovoi voiny." *Voprosy istorii* 4(1959): 3–22.

Spriano, Paolo. *Storia del partito communista italiano*. Vol. 1. Turin, 1967.

Stansky, Peter, ed. *The Left and the War: The British Labour Party and World War I*. Oxford, 1969.

Steenson, Gary P. *Karl Kautsky, 1854–1938: Marxism in the Classical Years*. Pittsburgh, 1978.

Steenson, Gary P. *"Not One Man! Not One Penny!" German Social Democracy, 1863–1914*. Pittsburgh, 1981.

Steinberg, Hans-Josef. *Die Stellung der II. Internationale zu Krieg und Frieden*. Trier, 1972.

Stillig, Jürgen. *Die russische Februarrevolution 1917 und die sozialistische Friedenspolitik*. Cologne, 1977.

Suvanto, Pekka. *Marx und Engels zum Problem des gewaltsamen Konflikts*. Helsinki, 1985.

Swartz, Marvin. *The Union of Democratic Control in British Politics during the First World War*. Oxford, 1971.

Taylor, A. J. P. *The Struggle for Mastery in Europe 1848–1918*. Oxford, 1954.

Temkin, Ia. G. *Lenin i mezhdunarodnaia sotsial-demokratsiia 1914–1917*. Moscow, 1968.

Temkin, Ia. G. "Leninskaia kritika kautskianskoi pozitsii Trotskogo (1914–1917 gg.)" *Voprosy istorii KPSS* 7(1972).

Temkin, Ia. G. "Razoblachenie V. I. Leninym 'levogo' sektanstva v gody pervoi mirovoi voiny." *Voprosy istorii KPSS* 8(1964): 3–16.

Temkin, Ia. G. *Tsimmerval'd-Kintal'*. Moscow, 1967.

Temkin, Ia. G. "V. I. Lenin i obrazovanie tsimmerval'dskoi levoi." *Voprosy istorii KPSS* 8(1965): 15–26.

Temkin, Ia. G., and Tupelov, B. M. *Ot vtorogo k Tret'emu Internatsionalu*. Moscow, 1978.

Tiutiukin, S. V. *Voina, mir, revoliutsiia: Ideinaia bor'ba v rabochem dvizhenii Rossii 1914–1917 gg.* Moscow, 1972.

Trofimov, K. S. "Lenin i obrazovanie Kommunisticheskogo Internatsionala." *Voprosy istorii KPSS* 4(1957): 28–48.

Trotnow, Helmut. *Karl Liebknecht: Eine politische Biographie*. Cologne, 1980.

Tych, Feliks. "La participation des partis ouvriers polonais au mouvement de Zimmerwald." *Annali* (Milan, 1961): 90–125.

Valiani, Leo. "Il Partito Socialista Italiano nel periodo della neutralità, 1914–1915." *Annali* (Milan, 1962): 260–386.

Vasinkov, V. S. *Vneshniaia politika Vremennogo Pravitel'stva*. Moscow, 1966.

Vavilin, I. "Bol'sheviki i tsimmerval'd." *Krasnaia letopis'* 2(59) (1934): 10–23.

Voight, Christian. *Robert Grimm: Kämpfer, Arbeiterführer, Parlamentarier. Eine politische Biographie.* Bern, 1980.

Volin, B. M. "Biulleteni bol'shevistskoi partii, vykhodivshie v Stokgol'me v 1917 godu." *Voprosy istorii* 4(1955): 124–27.

Volkmann, Erich Otto. *Der Marxismus und das deutsche Heer im Weltkriege.* Berlin, 1925.

Volosevich, V. *Bol'shevizm v gody mirovoi voiny.* Leningrad, n.d.

Vorobtsova, Iu. I. *Deiatel'nost' predstavitel'stva TsK RSDRP (b) v Stokgol'me (Aprel'–Noiabr' 1917 g.).* Moscow, 1968.

Vorobtsova, Iu. I. "Zagranichnoe predstavitel'stvo TsK RSDRP (b) v 1917 g." *Voprosy istorii KPSS* 6(1966): 30–38.

"Vo vremia imperialisticheskoi voiny." *Krasnyi letopis'* 1(19)(1924): 86–200.

"Vozzranie zagranichnogo predstavitel'stva TsK RSDRP (b)." *Voprosy istorii KPSS* 3(1957): 159–64.

Wade, Rex A. "Irakli Tsereteli and Siberian Zimmerwaldism." *The Journal of Modern History* 4(1967): 425–31.

Wade, Rex A. *The Russian Search for Peace, February–October 1917.* Stanford, 1969.

Weinstein, James. *The Decline of Socialism in America, 1912–1925.* New York, 1967.

Wette, Wolfram. *Kriegstheorien deutscher Sozialisten—Marx, Engels, Lassalle, Kautsky, Bernstein, Luxemburg. Ein Beitrag zur Friedensforschung.* Stuttgart, 1971.

Wheeler, John W. *Brest-Litovsk: The Forgotten Peace, March 1918.* London, 1938.

Wheeler, Robert F. "Revolutionary Socialist Internationalism: Rank-and-File Reaction in the USPD." *International Review of Social History* 22(1977): 329–49.

Wheeler, Robert F. *USPD und Internationale: Sozialistischer Internationalismus in der Zeit der Revolution.* Frankfurt am Main, 1975.

White, Stephen. "The Soviets in Britain: The Leeds Convention of 1917." *International Review of Social History* 19(1974): 165–93.

Wildman, Allan K. *The End of the Russian Imperial Army: The Old Army and the Soldiers' Revolt (March–April 1917).* Princeton, 1980.

Winter, John M. *Socialism and the Challenge of War: Ideas and Politics in Britain, 1912–1918.* London, 1974.

Wohl, Robert. *French Communism in the Making 1914–1924.* Stanford, 1966.

Wohlgemuth, Heinz. *Burgkrieg, nicht Burgfrieden! Der Kampf Karl Liebknechts, Rosa Luxemburg und ihrer Anhänger um die Rettung der deutschen Nation 1914–1916.* Berlin, 1963.

Wohlgemuth, Heinz. *Die Entstehung der Kommunistischen Partei Deutschlands 1914 bis 1918.* Berlin, 1968.

Zagorsky, S. O. *State Control of Industry in Russia during the War.* New Haven, 1928.

INDEX

Defeatism, 36–37, 39, 43–44, 45, 94,
110, 114, 196
DeLeon, Daniel, 47, 51
Dictatorship of the proletariat, 159, 176,
191–96, 202, 220, 225, 240, 246
Dittmann, Wilhelm, 115
Dobrynin, Anatoli, 243–45
Duncker, Käthe, 69, 149, 198
Dutch-Scandinavian committee, 177–
78, 179, 182, 183, 185, 189, 197, 198,
200

Eberlin, Hugo, 217
Ebert, Friedrich, 215
Eintracht league, 47, 277 n. 56
Engels, Friedrich: on war and internationalism, 6–10, 110, 209; on withering of the state, 9, 18, 191, 194, 235,
250 n. 16; on "worker's aristocracy,"
146
Eurocommunism, 238–42, 246

Fairchild, Edwin, 51, 120–21, 154
Falkenhayn, Erich von, 133
Faure, Paul, 53
Federation of Foreign Communist
Groups of the Central Committee of
the RSDRP, 214
Ferri, Mario, 65
Feuerbach, Ludwig von, 229
Fineberg, Joe, 51
First International. *See* International
Workingman's Association
Foreign Bureau of the Bolshevik Central
Committee (ZPTSK), 186–90, 200, 203,
207, 214
Fraina, Louis, 104
Franco-Prussian war (1870–71), 44
Frank, Leonhard, 227
French army: mutinies in, 171–72
French Socialist party (SFIO): and com-
munism, 222; rise of opposition
within, 118–19, 135, 152–53, 155,
173; union of the left, 239–40; on war,
15, 22, 30, 52–55; and Zimmerwald,
80
Frölich, Paul, 136, 137, 141

Gallacher, Tom, 51
Gallipoli landings, 31, 32

Gautschi, Willi, 44, 99
General Confederation of Labor, French
(CGT), 52–53, 80, 119, 216, 222
General Confederation of Labor, Italian
(CGL), 53
German North Sea naval mutinies
(1917), 171, 200
German revolution (1918), 214–15
Gilpin, Robert, 231
Glasnost, 244
Goldman, Mikhail (Liber), 177
Gorbachev, Mikhail, 243–44, 246
Gorter, Herman, 49–50, 59, 93, 221,
223–24
Gotha conference (1917), 150–51
Graber, Ernst, 138, 156
Gramsci, Antonio, 192–93, 229–30,
232, 240
Grass, Martin, 48
Greek socialists, 46, 121
Greulich, Hermann, 65, 76, 158
Grimm, Robert: activities in Stockholm
and Petrograd, 179–81; direction of
Zimmerwald movement, 122–25,
234; "Grimm affair," 181–82, 198; at
Kiental conference, 135–37; on mili-
tary question, 156–61; relations with
Lenin, 100, 123–24, 160–61; on war
and internationalism, 73–76; and
Zimmerwald conference, 77–80, 85–
91
Groener, Wilhelm, 215
Guesde, Jules, 15, 23, 24, 82, 225, 229
Guilbeaux, Henri, 137, 138, 184

Haase, Hugo, 22, 29, 54, 79, 115, 149,
216
Hague conference of socialist neutrals
(1916), 142–43, 148
Hamburg left radicals, 55–56, 150
Hanecki, Jakób (Firstenberg), 186
Hänisch, Konrad, 22, 23
Hardie, Keir, 16, 40, 51
Harding, Neil, 37, 223
Haupt, Georges, 20
Heden, Erik, 121, 153
Hegel, Georg Friedrich, 229–30
Henke, Alfred, 118
Hervé, Gustave, 15, 23, 221
Herzfeld, Jozef, 115

About the Author

R. Craig Nation is an Associate Professor in the Johns Hopkins University School of Advanced International Studies, Bologna Center.

Library of Congress
Cataloging-in-Publication Data
Nation, R. Craig.
War on war : Lenin, the Zimmerwald
Left, and the origins of communist
internationalism/by R. Craig Nation.
p. cm.
Bibliography: p.
Includes index.
ISBN 0-8223-0944-0
1. Lenin, Vladimir Il'ich, 1870–1924.
2. Zimmerwald movement. 3. War and
socialism. 4. International Socialist
Congress—History. 5. Communist
International—History. I. Title.
HX313.8.L46N38 1989
324.1'7—dc20   89-35744

Related Titles from Haymarket Books

The Comintern

Duncan Hallas • This concise history of the Communist (Third) International, from its beginnings in 1919 as the center of world revolution through its degeneration at the hands of the Stalinist bureaucracy, draws lessons valid today to the work of rebuild a fighting Left. • ISBN 9781931859523

History of the Russian Revolution

Leon Trotsky • Regarded by many as among the most powerful works of history ever written, Trotsky's account of the events of 1917 reveals the October revolution's profoundly democratic, emancipatory character. Collected in a single, portable volume, with a thorough new index. • ISBN 9781931859455

The German Revolution

Pierre Broue • A magisterial, definitive account of the upheavals in Germany in the wake of the Russian Revolution. Broue meticulously reconstructs six decisive years, 1917–23, of social struggles in Germany, the defeat of which had profound consequences for the world. • ISBN 9781931859325

Lenin's Political Thought: Theory and Practice
in the Democratic and Socialist Revolutions

Neil Harding • Lost in most assessments of Lenin's legacy and leadership style is a critical appreciation of his theoretical contributions. Harding shows how Lenin's flexible and continuously changing theoretical, strategic, and tactical insights were firmly grounded in the emancipatory potential for working-class revolution in Russia and globally. • ISBN 9781931859899

Imperialism and War: Lenin's Imperialism and Bukharin's
Imperialism and World Economy

V.I. Lenin, Nikolai Bukharin, edited by Phil Gasper • With the eruption of American military power after 9/11, the concept of imperialism has reemerged in contemporary political debates. Here, collected in a single volume with annotation, are two foundational texts analyzing imperialism from a Marxist perspective. • ISBN 9781931859660 • Fall 2009

Lenin Rediscovered

Lars T. Lih • With this book, Lars T. Lih revolutionizes the conventional interpretation of V. I. Lenin's classic text, included here in an authoritative new translation. *What Is to Be Done?* has long been interpreted as evidence of Lenin's "elitist" attitude toward workers. Lih uses a wide range of previously unavailable contextual sources to fundamentally overturn this reading of history's most misunderstood revolutionary text. • ISBN 9781931859585

About Haymarket Books

Haymarket Books is a nonprofit, progressive book distributor and publisher, a project of the Center for Economic Research and Social Change. We believe that activists need to take ideas, history, and politics into the many struggles for social justice today. Learning the lessons of past victories, as well as defeats, can arm a new generation of fighters for a better world. As Karl Marx said, "The philosophers have merely interpreted the world; the point, however, is to change it."

We take inspiration and courage from our namesakes, the Haymarket Martyrs, who gave their lives fighting for a better world. Their 1886 struggle for the eight-hour day, which gave us May Day, the international workers' holiday, reminds workers around the world that ordinary people can organize and struggle for their own liberation. These struggles continue today across the globe—struggles against oppression, exploitation, hunger, and poverty.

It was August Spies, one of the Martyrs targeted for being an immigrant and an anarchist, who predicted the battles being fought to this day. "If you think that by hanging us you can stamp out the labor movement," Spies told the judge, "then hang us. Here you will tread upon a spark, but here, and there, and behind you, and in front of you, and everywhere, the flames will blaze up. It is a subterranean fire. You cannot put it out. The ground is on fire upon which you stand."

We could not succeed in our publishing efforts without the generous financial support of our readers. Many people contribute to our project through the Haymarket Sustainers program, where donors receive free books in return for their monetary support. If you would like to be a part of this program, please contact us at info@haymarketbooks.org.

Order these titles and more online at www.haymarketbooks.org or call 773-583-7884.